MYTHS AND MISUNDERSTANDINGS IN WHITE-COLLAR CRIME

Myths and Misunderstandings in White-Collar Crime uses real-world examples to explore the pathologies that hamper our ability to understand and redress white-collar crime. The book argues that misinterpretations about federal white-collar crime impede its lawmaking, enforcement, and discourse, leading it to be overcriminalized and under-enforced. Many of these pathologies can be traced to the federal code's failure to subdivide white-collar crimes by degrees of severity, and by the legislature's outsourcing of criminal lawmaking to other institutions. With deep knowledge of the federal code and theories of institutional design and behavioral psychology at her disposal, Miriam Baer offers a step-by-step framework for redressing these problems by paying greater attention to how we write, frame, and lay out our federal criminal code. A clearer, subdivided criminal code, she argues, paves the way for more informed and productive deliberation, and fewer myths and misunderstandings.

Miriam H. Baer is the Vice Dean and Centennial Professor of Law at Brooklyn Law School, where she has taught criminal law and procedure and white-collar crime for over a decade.

Myths and Misunderstandings in White-Collar Crime

MIRIAM H. BAER

Brooklyn Law School

CAMBRIDGE
UNIVERSITY PRESS

CAMBRIDGE
UNIVERSITY PRESS

Shaftesbury Road, Cambridge CB2 8EA, United Kingdom

One Liberty Plaza, 20th Floor, New York, NY 10006, USA

477 Williamstown Road, Port Melbourne, VIC 3207, Australia

314–321, 3rd Floor, Plot 3, Splendor Forum, Jasola District Centre, New Delhi – 110025, India

103 Penang Road, #05-06/07, Visioncrest Commercial, Singapore 238467

Cambridge University Press is part of Cambridge University Press & Assessment, a department of the University of Cambridge.

We share the University's mission to contribute to society through the pursuit of education, learning and research at the highest international levels of excellence.

www.cambridge.org
Information on this title: www.cambridge.org/9781009279802

DOI: 10.1017/9781009279758

© Miriam H. Baer 2023

First published 2023

A catalogue record for this publication is available from the British Library.

Library of Congress Cataloging-in-Publication Data
NAMES: Baer, Miriam H., author.
TITLE: Myths and misunderstandings in white-collar crime / Miriam H. Baer, Brooklyn Law School.
DESCRIPTION: First edition. | Cambridge, United Kingdom ; New York, NY : Cambridge University Press, 2023. | Includes bibliographical references and index.
IDENTIFIERS: LCCN 2022044110 (print) | LCCN 2022044111 (ebook) | ISBN 9781009279802 (hardback) | ISBN 9781009279796 (paperback) | ISBN 9781009279758 (epub)
SUBJECTS: LCSH: White collar crimes–Law and legislation–United States.
CLASSIFICATION: LCC KF9350 .B34 2023 (print) | LCC KF9350 (ebook) |
DDC 345.73/0268–dc23/eng/20230103
LC record available at https://lccn.loc.gov/2022044110
LC ebook record available at https://lccn.loc.gov/2022044111

ISBN 978-1-009-27980-2 Hardback
ISBN 978-1-009-27979-6 Paperback

Contents

Acknowledgments

More than twenty years ago, I was hired as a federal prosecutor and marveled at the enormous power and responsibility that accompanied the position. Although I was keenly aware of the discretion and responsibility that had been delegated to me, I was also cognizant of the ways in which the government often came up short in meeting its enforcement mission.

After I left the US Attorney's Office, I served as an assistant general counsel for compliance at a major American corporation. During that stint, I became intimately familiar with the challenges of serving multiple constituencies while also keeping abreast of major changes in law and enforcement policy. A few months after I entered the world of compliance, I found myself reading law review articles late at night. They focused on topics such as deterrence, corporate crime, and federal criminal law. Long before legal academia was my goal, I had immersed myself in the work of Bill Stuntz, Dan Richman, Kate Stith, Donald Langevoort, and Jennifer Arlen.

Seven months into my in-house tenure, I made the life-changing decision to seek a career in academia. It would be many more months before I became a lawyering professor at New York University (NYU) School of Law and another two years after that before I attained a tenure-track position at Brooklyn Law School. I remain indebted to the many people at NYU who taught me so much as a new academic, chief among them Rachel Barkow (my classmate in law school) and the late James Jacobs, whose mentorship, wisdom, and humor set many junior scholars like me on the right path.

In August 2008, just a few weeks before the collapse of Lehman Brothers, I began teaching at Brooklyn Law School. There, my colleague, Roberta Karmel, became my mentor and a valued friend. My earliest papers focused on corporate crime, organizational compliance, and deterrence theory. Later papers drew on theories of organizational theory, behavioral psychology, and law and economics. I remain immensely grateful to Brooklyn Law School, whose summer teaching and sabbatical stipends allowed me to research, write, and present my work in venues across the country.

I am thankful to the many colleagues who have been a great support throughout the years and to those who gave me wonderful feedback on this manuscript during a prepublication workshop: Sam Buell, Rick Bierschbach, Mihailis Diamantis, Brenner Fissell, Stuart Green, Todd Haugh, Adam Kolber, Julie O'Sullivan, Lauren Ouziel, Dan Richman, Alice Ristroph, Jessica Roth, and Kate Stith. I owe a debt of gratitude as well to Jennifer Arlen, Claire Hill, Zach Kaufman, Frank Pasquale, David Kwok, Jim Park, Andrew Lund, Darren Rosenblum, Todd Haugh, and Eugene Soltes, who separately read and commented on certain book chapters and offered very helpful research leads. My writing and thinking in this area has been vastly enhanced by conversations with friends and colleagues who teach and write about corporate and white-collar wrongdoing, among them: Donald Langevoort, Veronica Root Martinez, Elizabeth Pollman, Jim Fanto, Andrew Jennings, John Hasnas, Ellen Podgor, Joan Heminway, Greg Gilchrist, J.S. Nelson, Will Thomas, Karen Woody, and the late Peter Henning. Finally, I benefited from comments I received from participants in the Ostrom Workshop in November 2022 at Indiana University's Kelley School of Business, the ComplianceNet Annual Conference in Amsterdam in July 2022, Villanova University School of Law's 2022 faculty workshop, the National Business Law Scholars Conference in 2021, the SEALS annual meeting in 2021, and the Brooklyn Law School 2020 summer workshop.

I am grateful to the Edmond J. Safra Center for Ethics at Harvard University, whose scholars welcomed me as a visiting fellow for the 2021–22 school year and generously provided me with access to Harvard's library resources and a series of workshops while I was in the midst of my sabbatical. I learned a tremendous amount from the Safra Center's resident fellows and affiliated faculty, and their comments greatly improved two of the book's chapters.

It takes a village to publish a book, and my village was fortunate enough to include my law student and research assistant, Robin Berger, who kept the project on track and made sure my footnotes were coherent and in order. Samuel Coffin, Patrick Lin, and Timothy Snyder from Brooklyn Law School, as well as Jordan Dannenberg, a student I met while teaching a semester at Yale Law School, all contributed to the book's early research and writing.

This book's proposal was accepted for publication in the fall of 2019. Seven months later, I was teaching classes from my computer, scouring the Internet for surgical masks, and wiping down my groceries with alcohol wipes. I am accordingly thankful to Matt Gallaway and Cambridge University Press for their patience in the earlier stages of this project and their persistent editorial assistance in the latter stages.

Finally, I remain in awe of my family, whose love, humor, and support have enabled me to grow and thrive. My mother was my teacher long before I was old enough to enter first grade, and my late father instilled in me an appreciation for intellectual engagement and inquiry. Today, my husband, daughter, and son continue to teach me the great benefits of being able to keep calm and carry on, to laugh at myself, and to remain true to my principles. And when all else fails, my much beloved dog brings me back down to earth.

It is much easier to tear down a system than it is to fix it, much less live within it. This book is dedicated to the public and private servants who, despite many great challenges, often do their level-headed best to prevent, identify, and redress manifestations of white-collar crime. I hope they find this book's observations and proposals thought-provoking, illuminating, and useful. I also hope that they know that despite the many criticisms commentators rightfully bestow upon the criminal justice system, many of its observers remain just as grateful to the people who staff that system and strive to improve it in ways large and small. This book is for them.

Introduction[1]

In January 2013, Aaron Swartz, a brilliant computer programmer and activist, died by suicide. At the time, Swartz's prosecution for engaging in computer fraud – Swartz had reportedly broken into JSTOR, the digital academic library, and had made its content available to the public – was nearing trial in a Boston federal court.[2] In the wake of Swartz's death, critics vehemently blamed the prosecutors spearheading his case for charging him in a way that threatened to produce a potential jail sentence of thirty years' imprisonment. The United States Attorney contended that Swartz in fact realistically faced no such sentence; indeed, the jail term prosecutors sought in exchange for Swartz's guilty plea was a mere six months.[3] Amidst this back and forth, Swartz's case eventually receded into the background.

Nearly two years later, the Supreme Court heard arguments in the case of Yates v. United States.[4] John Yates, a commercial fisherman, was charged with obstructing justice by disposing of a portion of the grouper he had caught while out at sea. Federal law prohibits the concealment or destruction of a "tangible object" to

---

[1] This discussion is informed by work I have published over the past decade, including *Insuring Corporate Crime*, 83 IND. L. REV. (2008); *Linkage and the Deterrence of Corporate Fraud*, 94 VA. L. REV. 1295 (2008); *Governing Corporate Compliance*, 50 B.C. L. REV. 949 (2009); *Cooperation's Cost*, 88 WASH. U. L. REV. 963 (2011); *Too Vast to Succeed*, 114 MICH. L. REV. 1109 (2016); *Insider Trading's Legality Problem*, 127 YALE L.J. FORUM 129 (2017); *Reconceptualizing the Whistleblower's Dilemma*, 50 U.C. DAVIS L. REV. 2215 (2017); and *Sorting Out White-Collar Crime*, 97 TEX. L. REV. 225 (2019).

[2] For a helpful discussion of the legal issues underlying Swartz's computer fraud prosecution, see Orin Kerr, *The Criminal Charges against Aaron Swartz (Part I: The Law)*, VOLOKH CONSPIRACY (Jan. 14, 2013), http://volokh.com/2013/01/14/aaron-swartz-charges. To see JSTOR's factual recounting of events, see JSTOR evidence in United States v. Aaron Swartz, JSTOR (July 30, 3013), http://docs.jstor.org/summary.html.

[3] *See* Charles Arthur, *Aaron Swartz: US Attorney Says She Only Sought Six-Month Jail Term*, GUARDIAN (Jan. 17, 2013), www.theguardian.com/technology/2013/jan/17/aaron-swartz-attorney-defends-actions.

[4] 547 U.S. 528 (2015).

subvert a federal investigation.[5] Yates's case came about when a fisheries investigator boarded his ship and observed several pieces of grouper a few inches short of the size required by existing regulations. The investigator directed Yates to segregate the prohibited fish so that it could be weighed when the ship docked and Yates could be assessed an appropriate fine. When Yates's ship returned to port, however, the grouper in the ship's hold had magically grown in size. One of Yates's crewmen admitted that he had, at Yates's command, dumped the offending fish and replaced them with larger-size grouper. The obvious purpose in doing so was to avoid the fine.[6]

Yates's attorneys successfully persuaded the Supreme Court that undersized "fish" were not the "tangible objects" Congress had in mind when it criminalized the destruction of documents and other materials in anticipation of an investigation.[7] Besides the inevitable fish puns, what caught the attention of at least one Supreme Court justice was the length of sentence Yates might receive if convicted: "What kind of mad prosecutor would try to send this guy up for twenty years?" Justice Scalia reportedly inquired during oral argument.[8] Of course, Yates never realistically faced a twenty-year term. In fact, he received a sentence of just thirty days' imprisonment.[9] Nevertheless, the fact that Yates *could* have received such a sentence played a role in convincing a majority of the Court that Congress narrowly intended its statute to include documents or digital material when it adopted the term, "any tangible object."[10]

Finally, consider Bridget Anne Kelly, a New Jersey official who conspired with others to shut down part of the George Washington Bridge and cause some "traffic problems" in Fort Lee – all to punish Fort Lee's mayor for not endorsing Governor Chris Christie's reelection campaign.[11] Kelly held a relatively low-level position within Christie's office, but the evidence easily demonstrated her participation in

---

[5]   18 U.S.C. 1519.

[6]   Yates, 547 U.S. at 531.

[7]   *Id.* at 546. *See also* Debra Cassens Weiss, *Is a Fish a "Tangible Object"? Not in This Case, SCOTUS Rules in Parsing Post-Enron Law*, ABA J. (Feb. 25, 2015), www.abajournal.com/news/article/is_a_fish_a_tangible_object_scotus_rules_for_fisherman_prosecuted_for_under.

[8]   *Scales of Justice Meet Scales of Fish*, CBS NEWS, Nov. 6, 2014, www.cbsnews.com/news/scales-of-justice-meet-scales-of-fish-in-case-of-discarded-grouper. For further analysis, see Ellen S. Podgor, *"What Kind of a Mad Prosecutor" Brought Us This White Collar Case*, 41 VT. L. REV. 523 (2017).

[9]   Yates, 547 U.S. at 535.

[10] Justice Kagan's dissenting opinion criticized the plurality for allowing itself to be swayed by these concerns. Agreeing that Section 1519 was a "bad law – too broad and undifferentiated, with too-high maximum penalties," she nevertheless concluded that it was "an emblem of a deeper pathology in the federal criminal code" and that Congress was the only authority who could redress that pathology. "If judges disagree with Congress's choice, we are perfectly entitled to say so – in lectures, in law review articles, and even in dicta. But we are not entitled to replace the statute Congress enacted with an alternative of our own design." *Id.* at 570 (Kagan, J., dissenting).

[11] *See* Kelly v. United States, 140 S. Ct. 1565 (2020).

the bridge-closing scheme. After she was convicted on a mix of fraud and conspiracy counts in 2016, Kelly's attorneys blasted the government for stretching the law to cover low-level individuals like Kelly.[12] Kelly was sentenced to eighteen months in jail, but to hear her attorneys tell it, she was facing a term of least twenty years for playing a bit role in an ill-considered prank.[13] The Supreme Court eventually overturned her conviction because the property that was the supposed target of the offenders' scheme – moneys spent on a pretextual traffic control study – was too attenuated to serve as the basis of a mail or wire fraud prosecution.[14]

These examples underscore society's conflicting attitudes toward the body of law many of us have come to call "white-collar crime."[15] On one hand, an unmistakable overcriminalization theme pervades popular and academic discourse. We seem to make a federal case out of everything – from a local fisherman's decision to dump fish into the sea, to the prank one set of public officials decides to play on another.[16]

At the same time, there is just as strong an impression that white-collar crime, particularly *federal* white-collar crime, is underenforced.[17] Year in and year out, regardless of presidential administration, the federal government manages to over-look the most culpable players when it singles out businesspeople and politicians for prosecution. A few unlucky offenders find themselves at the end of the prosecutor's proverbial gun, but the rest appear to escape responsibility for their reckless behavior. How can that be so? This question is the focus of Chapter 1 of this book and prompts us to examine the multiple pathologies that cloud our understanding of white-collar crime.

Some contend that the odd juxtaposition of overcriminalization and underenforcement demonstrates nothing more than the instantiation of class difference and political power. Well-heeled corporate executives escape accountability for impos-ing massive costs on society while prosecutors celebrate convictions of bit players in tawdry conspiracy schemes. Government enforcement agencies punch down and suck up. From this perspective, the remedy seems remarkably simple: the govern-ment must commit itself to punishing the powerful more often, strengthening the

---

[12] *See* Kate Zernike, *Lawyers for Ex-Christie Aide Says She Was Made Scapegoat in Bridge Plot*, N.Y. TIMES (Oct. 19, 2016), www.nytimes.com/2016/10/20/nyregion/bridgegate-trial-bridget-anne-kelly.html.

[13] *See* Ryan Hutchins, *Baroni Sentenced to 2 Years in Prison for Role in Bridgegate Scandal; Kelly Gets 18 Months*, POLITICO (Mar. 29, 2017), www.politico.com/states/new-jersey/story/2017/03/baroni-sentenced-to-2-years-in-prison-for-his-role-in-bridgegate-scandal-110811.

[14] "The Government in this case needed to prove property fraud." Kelly v. United States, 140 S. Ct. 1565, 1571 (2020). "[P]roperty must play more than some bit part in a scheme: It must be an 'object of the fraud.'" *Id.* at 1573.

[15] For a fuller discussion of the debate over the term "white-collar crime," see Chapters 1 and 2.

[16] *See* Yates, 574 U.S. at 530; *see also* HARVEY Silverglate, THREE FELONIES A DAY: HOW THE FEDS TARGET THE INNOCENT (2011); MIKE CHASE, HOW TO BECOME A FEDERAL CRIMINAL: AN ILLUSTRATED HANDBOOK FOR THE ASPIRING OFFENDER (2019).

[17] *See, e.g.*, JESSE EISINGER, THE CHICKENSHIT CLUB: WHY THE JUSTICE DEPARTMENT FAILS TO PROSECUTE EXECUTIVES (2017).

penalties it imposes on corporate executives, and avoiding low-level prosecutions that do little more than prop up annual statistics.

This book draws a different set of conclusions. Class differences matter in white-collar crime, but they don't fully describe our government's enforcement efforts, much less explain white-collar crime's persistence. To our detriment, we have overlooked an alternative source of problems: our statutes and our legislature's unwillingness to meaningfully reform them. Our broken federal criminal code fuels alternative narratives of overcriminalization and underenforcement and leaves us bereft of the tools necessary to address related but distinct categories of economic wrongdoing. Regardless of how one views criminal law's mission, our white-collar statutes fail us as society. They undermine our criminal justice system's legitimacy and skew its signals. Rather than correcting or deterring wrongs, or generating healthy and prosocial norms, our white-collar penal statutes ultimately confuse and mislead.

A noxious mix of myths and misunderstandings has come to define federal white-collar practice, and as those myths and misunderstandings grow, they foreclose opportunities for intelligent discussion and meaningful reform. The middle section of this book surveys a series of pathologies. These pathologies have hampered our enforcement institutions' responses to economic and corporate wrongdoing. They have also obfuscated our understanding of what our enforcement institutions are trying to do and why they alternatively fail or overreach in spectacular fashion. As a result, our society often misunderstands the *laws* that purport to outlaw crimes of deception; the *sentences* and alternative punishments that the government imposes for violations of such laws; and the nature of *harms* caused by the various *offenders* who violate these laws. These misunderstandings explain why the government manages to look overly harsh and pathetically weak, all at the same time. They also suggest a very different set of remedies from those frequently touted on either side of our political divide.

ROADMAP

This book unfolds in three sections. The opening section (Chapter 1) surveys the competing claims that white-collar crime is "overcriminalized" and yet also "under-enforced." To some degree, this debate is reflective of our society's deeper anxieties about criminal law and its place in modern American culture. But white-collar crime's discourse operates independently of that larger debate. Politicians who identify as opponents of mass incarceration are just as inclined to label corporate industry executives "criminals" and support the enactment of strict liability laws that threaten corporate officers with jail.

Chapters 2–6 examine a series of pathologies that hamper our understanding of white-collar crime and its enforcement. Chapter 2 begins by examining the data the federal government collects and disseminates on federal prosecutions and convictions of "white-collar" offenses. For years, scholars have debated the meaning of the term "white-collar," which was itself coined by sociologist Edwin Sutherland in his 1939 address to the American Sociological Society. Legal theorists imagine a set of offenses in response to the term, while criminologists and sociologists associate the term with a certain group of offenders. As Chapter 2 explains, even a broad "offense-based" definition entails profound difficulties for enforcement institutions. A lack of uniform language and technical interoperability between the criminal justice system's various institutions all but ensures that the government's data collection will be unreliable and prone to misrepresentation.

Chapters 3 and 4 explore two distinct but related lawmaking pathologies. Chapter 3 focuses on the federal code's "flatness." Unlike state law statutes such as homicide or robbery, federal white-collar crime statutes generally do not subdivide core crimes according to their severity or wrongfulness. There is no such thing as first-degree fraud or second-degree fraud in the federal criminal code. Instead, the code distinguishes frauds by the mechanism the offender employs (e.g., the mails or interstate wires), or by the offender's victim (e.g., health care companies or banks). From a moral perspective, these labels are irrelevant and convey very little information about a fraud scheme's size or danger to others.

Chapter 4 examines a different phenomenon, that of the "underwritten" crime, or the statute that relies on prosecutors and the judiciary to give it meaning. I refer to this generally as a form of criminal outsourcing.

Many scholars are well acquainted with the legality principle, which requires penal laws to be the product of duly-elected legislatures. That principle is itself aspirational; criminal law casebooks are rife with examples of federal and state judges who "make" criminal law more often than legislatures. Such lawmaking is easily on display in the white-collar context. But, as Chapter 4 demonstrates, criminal law's "outsourcing" functions quite differently, depending on the circumstances. In some instances, the resulting "crime" (e.g., insider trading) is the product of multiple cross-checking institutions. In other instances, the legislature's cedes much of its "lawmaking" power to a single institution (such as corporate criminal liability).

The usual concern with outsourcing is that it devolves too much power in the hands of the prosecutor. As the insider trading example makes clear, that fear has not always been realized. Neither the Department of Justice (DOJ) nor the SEC can simply declare a morally wrongful market practice "insider trading"; they must instead rely on lower and appellate courts, and eventually the Supreme Court, to develop delineate insider trading's external boundaries.

Even if claims of prosecutorial power are overblown, there is still good reason to be concerned with criminal outsourcing, and it relates back to the discussion of flat laws in Chapter 3. When laws are "underwritten," prosecutors and judges must devote their energies to fleshing them out and to determining the boundaries between criminal and noncriminal conduct. The question of subdivision – of how to distinguish different variations within the same family of wrongdoing – falls by the wayside. Thus, if we want to fix the "flatness" discussed in Chapter 3, we must address Congress's tendency to outsource its criminal lawmaking duties, a pathology that forms the subject of Chapter 4.

Chapter 5 pivots from a discussion of lawmaking to a consideration of white-collar crime's enforcement. Using the 2008 Financial Crisis as its backdrop, Chapter 5 explores a familiar puzzle: Why is it that white-collar crime is so "broad" and yet often so difficult to prove? The answer lies in the recognition that white-collar crime often unfolds over two thresholds. The first is the line that separates innocence and liability, what one might call the *liability threshold*. The second is the line that separates viable from nonviable prosecutions, which is the *viability threshold*. The liability threshold is objective and transparent; we discover its boundaries by reading statutes and published judicial opinions. The viability threshold is opaque and more subjective. It reflects the government's collective determination of the evidence sufficient to follow a case through to its bitter end.

For many white-collar crimes, behavior easily crosses the liability threshold but falls short of the viability line, creating a temporal and conceptual gap. Within this gap, wrongdoers do their very best to avoid detection and convince prosecutors to forego prosecutions. The "gap" is thus a kind of corporate and financial purgatory, where pressures to hide one's wrongdoing increase, and where harms fester while they remain undiscovered. Many of the federal government's enforcement policies are best understood as an effort to mind this gap; that is, to use tools like corporate leniency and whistleblowing policies to gather just enough information to move a few cases over the viability line. The problem with these gap-minding strategies is that they never quite *remove* or *narrow* the space between liability and viability. Accordingly, they promote the belief that the government is merely spinning its wheels rather than making real progress in redressing white-collar crime.

Chapter 6, a chapter devoted to popular perception, identifies a series of myths and misunderstandings that are at the heart of white-collar crime's discourse. Reductive narratives about prosecutors, about the scope and nature of white-collar crime's harms, about its offenders, and about its offenses and sanctions crowd out more nuanced accounts of what has occurred and what continues to take place. Regrettably, the institutions that have the most to lose from these misunderstandings are poorly organized to recognize, much less rebut, them.

With these pathologies firmly in mind, Chapters 7 and 8 urge a series of reforms best characterized as code-design. Whereas the scholarship of institutional design queries how an institution's structure affects law's implementation, the study of code-design asks how the shape and form of a statutory code affects its content, its enforcement, and its public understanding. If code-design matters (and I argue that it does), its remedies for white-collar crime go much farther than urging Congress to rewrite a few statutes or the DOJ to focus more intently on the "real" bad guys. A code-design approach interrogates the labelling of white-collar statutes. It asks how they fit together, how they are defined, and how well they are subdivided to reflect proportionality and wrongfulness. Accordingly, the final two chapters of this book (Chapters 7 and 8) recommend a four-part agenda for reformers. For the sake of clarification, reformers should *unbundle* and *relabel* offenses that have been lodged under the same statutory umbrella. And for the sake of improving transparency and legitimacy, a good code should *consolidate* and *grade* statutes that define roughly the same conduct (fraud, bribery, and obstruction).

WHAT THIS BOOK DOES NOT DO

White-collar crime is a vast topic. Because my interest relates primarily to criminal prosecutions and federal criminal law, I generally do not take up pathologies in either the civil sector or in state criminal practice. Readers familiar with state and civil practice may nevertheless find that the problems described in Chapters 2–6 are generalizable to other contexts. Indeed, the remedial discussion in Chapters 7 and 8 has certainly been influenced by the vast literature on criminal code reform in the states. Moreover, although the complex relationship between federal and state enforcement agencies surely impacts the pathologies that are this book's focus, I nevertheless leave that examination for future research.[18]

Because so many scholars have already tackled white-collar crime's normative and philosophical underpinnings, I do not spend enormous amounts of time addressing whether a given instance of wrongdoing *should* be classified as a crime.[19] Nor do I delve into the finer doctrinal details of fraud, bribery, and obstruction statutes. Others have already performed this feat, and much of my own knowledge of white-collar criminal doctrine has been deeply enriched by their insights.[20]

By the same token, I write this book under the assumption that individuals who engage in crimes such as fraud, bribery, and obstructive misconduct do so for the

---

[18] For an overview of federal–state interactions in criminal law enforcement, see Anthony O'Rourke, *Parallel Enforcement and Agency Interdependence*, 77 MD. L. REV. 985 (2018); DANIEL C. RICHMAN, *The Changing Boundaries between Federal and Local Law Enforcement*, in 2 CRIMINAL JUSTICE 81, 91–96 (2000).

[19] For just a sampling, see, e.g., James Lindgren, *The Theory, History, and Practice of the Bribery-Extortion Distinction*, 141 U. PA. L. REV. 1695 (1993); STUART P. GREEN, LYING, CHEATING, AND STEALING: A MORAL THEORY OF WHITE COLLAR CRIME (2006); Samuel W. Buell, *What Is Securities Fraud?* 61 DUKE L.J. 511 (2011).

[20] I will not try to offer an exhaustive list, but those relatively new to this field would be greatly helped by reading: DANIEL C. RICHMAN, KATE STITH & WILLIAM J. STUNTZ, DEFINING FEDERAL CRIMES (2d ed. 2018) (cases and materials relating to federal criminal law and its interpretation, as well as fraud, bribery, and regulatory crimes); David Mills & Robert Weisberg, *Corrupting the Harm Requirement in White Collar Crime*, 60 STAN. L. REV. 1371 (2008) (helpful overview and critique of fraud, securities, and anticorruption law in the early 2000s); EDWARD J. BALLEISEN, FRAUD: AN AMERICAN HISTORY FROM BARNUM TO MADOFF (2017) (for an historical account of fraud's criminalization in the federal code and its enforcement).

usual mix of reasons first described by Donald Cressey's groundbreaking study of embezzlers: pressure, opportunity, and rationalizations, the dreaded "triangle" of factors that impels people to break the law and to usually do so in secret.[21] Criminologists have posited additional theories of white-collar criminality, but the opportunity-driven fraud triangle remains the explanation with the most purchase, both in regard to fraud cases and in respect to the corruption and obstruction cases that often overlap.

Finally, despite the temptation, this book does not directly spend much time examining Donald Trump, his malfeasance while in the White House, or his company's alleged crimes.[22] Although the Trump administration adopted a softer approach to corporate and white-collar crime, the pathologies that are the focus of this book easily predate Mr. Trump's presidential term and will extend far beyond it.[23] Moreover, Trump's politics and personality distract from the deeper, endemic problems that plague white-collar crime's institutions. Accordingly, I have made a deliberate decision not to focus on the obstructive behavior that served as the focus of the Mueller report, the extortionate behavior that triggered Trump's first impeachment, Trump's conduct in the wake of the 2020 presidential election, his alleged taking of classified documents following the close of his presidency, or the Trump Organization's alleged wrongdoing. Readers may find, however, the discussion in Chapter 5 particularly relevant to contemporary critiques of prosecutors who have failed, over the past several decades, to charge Trump and his contemporaries with violations of law. The story isn't always one of weak will or corrupt motives. Sometimes, our enforcement institutions fall into evidentiary ruts, searching for "badges" of wrongdoing that have made prior prosecutions victorious, even if those badges are nowhere to be found.

IS WHITE-COLLAR CRIME UNIQUE?

One might reasonably ask whether the problems described throughout Chapters 2–6 are truly unique. They are certainly the type one would expect to in any system built for preventing, identifying, and punishing crimes of deception. Deceptive

---

[21] "The fraud triangle is a three-pronged theory of why some individuals commit occupational fraud." Leandra Lederman, *The Fraud Triangle and Tax Evasion*, 106 Iowa L. Rev. 1153, 1156 (2021) (describing the concept's origins and evolution). Donald R. Cressey, Other People's Money: A Study in the Social Psychology of Embezzlement (1953).

[22] *See* Dan Mangan, *Trump Organization, Inaugural Committee Must Pay DC Attorney General $750k over Claims of Misspent Nonprofit Funds*, CNBC (May 3, 2022), www.cnbc.com/2022/05/03/trump-organization-presidential-inaugural-committee-settle-dc-lawsuit-.html.

[23] "[R]ecent statistics have demonstrated that penalties imposed in white collar cases have decreased during the Trump administration." Douglas K. Rosenbloom et al., *Hiding in Plain Sight: Obtaining Insurance Coverage in White-Collar Criminal Investigations*, 43 Champion 48, 49 (Apr. 2019).

crimes are at once protean and elusive. As a result, they create challenges for both lawmakers and enforcers, and create additional problems on the back end for data collection and public discourse. Preventing and punishing deceptive misconduct is hard work.

Still, some of the issues described here could easily be ascribed to *federal* criminal law generally, and not just crimes of deception. Excessive prosecutorial discretion, pervasive transparency gaps, and troubling legitimacy deficits are all issues that have long undermined the criminal justice system generally (including its federal variant), leading many to question the "justice" moniker and call for changes in federal prosecutorial practice. Accordingly, I make no definitive claim on the singularity of white-collar crime's issues. Some are white-collar-centric, whereas others may be reflective of broader and deeper infirmities. By the same token, although the solutions described in Chapters 7 and 8 have been designed to redress specific problems with federal criminal law's enforcement of white-collar crime, it is quite possible that one could apply those concepts to other areas of criminal law. If so, I see that as only good news.

DISPELLING MYTHS, IMPROVING INSTITUTIONS

The move to institute greater transparency in criminal proceedings has become a prominent focus of criminal justice reform and animates much of the latter third of this book. It should surprise no one that transparency in its broadest form poses challenges for white-collar crime's enforcement institutions. With only a few notable exceptions, the DOJ has traditionally resisted efforts to fully explain its decision-making, particularly decisions relating to its plea negotiations and charging decisions. One of the reasons for such resistance is that it fears that sunlight will undermine its effectiveness as an enforcer. Thus, reformers often call for "more transparency" and prosecutors often respond that they have provided as much transparency as they can.

One of the book's core insights is that clearer and better laws, including laws that feature better labelling and modest statutory gradation, can mitigate this stalemate. When there exist three or five degrees of the same fraud or bribery offense and the government chooses to charge a defendant with the least (or most) serious version of that charge, the charge itself conveys readily usable information. Moreover, in the aggregate, a series of charges allows us to learn just how serious last year's fraud "docket" was in relation to the docket that existed in the previous year. To be sure, gradation is no panacea for all that ails the criminal justice system, but it facilitates more accurate data collection and therefore a greater degree of transparency than currently exists.

Then again, if one believes federal prosecutors should act independently of public opinion and instead "do justice" according to professionally developed norms, then calls for transparency may simply be a fancy word for urging the DOJ to improve its public relations and poll numbers. Popularizing white-collar enforcement institutions is *not* the aim of this book. There exists a world of difference between crudely currying public favor and improving the public's understanding of white-collar crime's laws, institutions, and enforcement challenges.

Government prosecutors cannot do justice if the public they serve misunderstands their processes and distrusts their motives. Policymakers should register alarm when a pernicious and reductive narrative takes hold, insisting that prosecutors are interested in little more than churning cases and revolving into more prestigious jobs in the private sector. It behooves us to figure out *why* the public has such a negative view of white-collar criminal enforcement. If this perspective is erroneous or incomplete, we should identify the phenomena that produce it and make it so difficult to dislodge.

Answering these question leads not only to the dispelling of persistent myths, but also to the improvement of the institutions tasked with investigating and punishing white-collar crime.

Too Much or Too Little?

INTRODUCTION

On Friday, May 22, 2020, former Full House actress Lori Loughlin and her husband, Mossimo Giannulli, entered guilty pleas admitting to engaging in a multipronged bribery and fraud scheme, dubbed "Varsity Blues." The gist of the Varsity Blues scheme was that parents, with the help of a much sought-after college consultant, would bribe college coaches for highly coveted athletic admission spots on various sports teams, create fraudulent profiles falsely portraying their children's athletic prowess, and have professional test-takers take their ACT or SAT by securing special testing accommodations.[1]

According to the Varsity Blues complaint,[2] the scheme's key figure was the college consultant who had helped parents concoct laughably fraudulent histories of their offspring's athleticism, which were then accepted by college coaches in exchange for hundreds of thousands of dollars laundered through the consultant's fake charity. (In a stunning display of moxie, several of the parents claimed charitable tax deductions for their bribes.)[3]

Unbeknownst to the parents and coaches, their conversations were being recorded. Midway through the scheme, the admissions consultant became a government cooperator and taped numerous incriminating phone calls, excerpts of which were featured throughout the 200-page Varsity Blues complaint.[4] Almost immediately

---

[1] "Beginning in or about 2011, and continuing through the present, the defendants – principally individuals whose high-school aged children were applying to college – conspired with others to use bribery and other forms of fraud to facilitate their children's admission to colleges and universities in the District of Massachusetts and elsewhere, including Yale University, Stanford University, the University of Texas, the University of Southern California, and the University of California – Los Angeles, among others."

Affidavit in Support of Criminal Complaint at 3, United States v. Colburn, No. 1:19-cr-10080-NMG (D. Mass. Mar. 11, 2019).

[2] See id. at 3–4.

[3] See id. at 4, 145.

[4] See id. at 11, 60–61, 111–12.

following the criminal complaint's public release, the defendant-parents were showered with condemnation and shame; several were promptly fired from their high-level positions.[5] Coaches at several universities were also terminated from their jobs and eventually charged by prosecutors as coconspirators, prompting the Department of Education to open its own investigation. Several schools rescinded offers of admission. University athletic and admissions departments promised to review their internal practices to prevent debacles like this from ever happening again.[6]

Over fifty parents were charged in the government's first Operation Varsity Blues complaint. The United States Attorney in Boston described it as "the largest college admittance scheme ever charged by the Department of Justice [DOJ]."[7] This initial charging document alleged violations of mail fraud, honest services mail fraud (a form of bribery), and related crimes. Several of the university coaches and administrators who assisted in the scheme were charged in a separate document accusing them of racketeering and money laundering. Later indictments (charges placed before and approved by grand juries) charged several of the parents with money laundering and tax evasion.

The press releases and newspaper articles from this time breathlessly advise potential maximum sentences of twenty years' imprisonment (the maximum imprisonment for violations of the mail fraud and honest mail fraud statutes) or even more (assuming a judge decided to sentence an individual consecutively for each offense).[8] At least one of the charged parents hired an expensive consultant to advise on life in federal prisons.[9] Perhaps with these high numbers in mind, a few commentators wondered if criminal treatment was a mistake.[10]

---

[5] *See* Kate Gibson, *CEO Charged in College Scandal Says He Resigned, but Firm Says He Was Fired*, CBS News (Mar. 15, 2019), www.cbsnews.com/news/college-admissions-cheating-scandal-bill-mcglashan-tpg.

[6] *See* Elena Kadvany, *In Response to College-Admissions Scandal, Stanford to Prove Policies, Current Athletic Recruits*, Palo Alto Weekly (Mar. 21, 2019), https://paloaltoonline.com/news/2019/03/21/in-response-to-college-admissions-scandal-stanford-to-probe-policies-current-athletic-recruits; Kelly Meyerhofer, *UW-Madison Reviewed Admissions Policies in Wake of National Scandal and Made 2 Changes*, Wis. State J. (June 7, 2019), https://madison.com/wsj/news/local/education/university/uw-madison-reviewed-admissions-policies-in-wake-of-national-scandal-and-made-2-changes/article_493f74c9-9281-59bd-95d9-8fe142d62ffe.html.

[7] *Actress Felicity Huffman's Bond Set at $250K for Alleged College Admission Scheme*, WSB-TV (Atlanta) (Mar. 12, 2019), www.wsbtv.com/news/local/actresses-ceos-arrested-in-nationwide-college-admissions-cheating-scam/929684349.

[8] "All have been indicted for racketeering conspiracy and face up to 20 years in prison if convicted." Laurel J. Sweet, *First Wave of "Varsity Blues" Defendants Hits Federal Court Monday*, Bos. Herald (Mar. 24, 2019), www.bostonherald.com/2019/03/24/first-wave-of-varsity-blues-defendants-hits-federal-court-monday.

[9] *See* Peter Holley, *Parents Charged in the College Admissions Scandal Are Turning to This Convicted Felon for Advice on Life in Prison*, Wash. Post (Mar. 20, 2019), www.washingtonpost.com/technology/2019/03/20/meet-convicted-felon-helping-people-charged-college-admissions-scandal-prepare-prison.

[10] David Oscar Markus, *Felicity Huffman's 14 Day Sentence Is Unjust – Because It Is Too High*, The Hill (Sept. 14, 2019) ("It's important to keep things in perspective: Huffman didn't hurt anyone and it's not altogether clear that paying someone to take a test should even be a federal

When the defendants finally entered their guilty pleas, fears of long sentences were mostly allayed. To be sure, nearly all of the convicted Varsity Blues offenders were sentenced to some term of imprisonment, but the length of those terms reflected a mere fraction of the time observers had bandied about at the time of their arrests. Felicity Huffman was sentenced to just fourteen days in prison. Most received terms of a few months; a couple received more than a year.[11] Still, *none* of the Varsity Blues sentences came anywhere near the maximum term of twenty years' imprisonment that had been so eagerly (or critically) highlighted when the government first announced the case.

As the prosecution unfolded, a series of narratives emerged. One of those narratives stressed the criminal justice system's unequal kid-gloves treatment of wealthy offenders. A separate narrative heaped criticism on the government and its prosecutors. The case could have been pursued civilly or by issuing a public report, but prosecutors had decided to sensationalize and *criminalize* it.[12] Meanwhile, the government did little to address the college institutions themselves, whose claims of victimhood elicited more than one eye roll.

To anyone familiar with the college application process, the case highlighted a series of concerns: the need for better and more transparent college admission practices; for more meaningful reforms in how universities monitor their athletic departments; and for a standardized testing program less prone to manipulation. Whatever it is that Operation Varsity Blues accomplished, it did not – and probably could not – address these deeper structural concerns. It may have unearthed and brought attention to a problem, but except in the most superficial ways, it did very little to solve it.

Thus, Operation Varsity Blues ably highlights two competing critiques: first, that white-collar crime is overcriminalized, and second, that it is also underenforced. These critiques already pervade the criminal justice literature generally, although differences prevail.[13] *Outside* the white-collar context, we often say the government has criminalized far too much conduct, has punished offenders too severely, and has allowed the criminal justice system to eclipse nonpunitive approaches to

---

crime in the first place."); Ellen Podgor, *More Varsity Blues: Privilege and Perspective*, WHITE COLLAR CRIME BLOG (Sept. 24, 2019). ("Was there a better way to handle all of this? Yes. If prosecutors had proceeded on correcting this unethical conduct by exposure – a report – and sending a message to all that privilege in national testing will not be tolerated, then stopping this unethical conduct could have been accomplished. Using a broken criminal justice system to attempt to correct this process just ends up showing how broken the system really is.")

[11] Patricia Hurtado, *'Varsity Blues' Dad Gets Longest Sentence in Scandal Yet*, BLOOMBERG (Feb. 16, 2022), www.bloomberg.com/news/articles/2022-02-16/private-equity-investor-gets-longest-varsity-blues-sentence.

[12] *See* discussion *supra* at note 10.

[13] On society's overreliance on criminal law to fix social problems, see JONATHAN SIMON, GOVERNING THROUGH CRIME: HOW THE WAR ON CRIME TRANSFORMED AMERICAN DEMOCRACY AND CREATED A CULTURE OF FEAR (2007).

undesirable behavior.[14] *Inside* the white-collar context, the narrative is different. Underenforcement attracts far more attention, although cries of overcriminalization surface periodically as well, and when they do, they can feel just as intense. As a result, critics are equally confident that the government is doing too much and too little, all at the same time. These dueling narratives are the focus of this chapter.

1.1 THE THEORY OF UNDERENFORCEMENT

White-collar crime's underenforcement narrative divides into three branches: First, the government fails to *charge* criminal defendants as often as it should. Second, it fails to *reform* wrongdoers, particularly corporate entities. And third, even when the government charges an offender and secures a conviction, the system nevertheless fails to sufficiently *punish* individuals and entities, gifting them instead with outcomes that suggest that crime is just a price of doing business, and not a particularly steep one. I discuss each of these in greater detail in the following subsections.

1.1.1 *A Failure to Charge*

We often hear politicians of both parties asserting that corporate executives commit crimes with impunity. However strong this sentiment was before 2008, it became a shibboleth in the wake of the Financial Crisis. Why wasn't Dick Fuld, the CEO of the now-defunct Lehman Brothers, prosecuted for failing to disclose Lehman's precarious financial situation? Why didn't the government charge Angelo Mozzillo, the CEO of Countrywide Mortgage, with fraud charges relating to Countrywide's mortgage-lending practices? Why did Goldman Sachs, the architect of mortgage securities its own analysts bet against, squeak away with just a $500 million fine? Surely, it must be because the government *undercharges* white-collar wrongdoers and does so knowingly and deliberately.[15]

The view that the government deliberately undercharges corporate and white-collar offenders reflects deep-seated intuitions about prosecutors and their motives. A popular and somewhat sympathetic version is that white-collar crimes are, by their very nature, more difficult to prove than street crimes, and that federal prosecutors are pathologically risk-averse.[16] A second explanation portrays federal prosecutors as biased elites who implicitly fail to see the criminal side of economic misconduct

---

[14] On the different components of this critique and its implications for reform efforts, see Benjamin Levin, *The Consensus Myth in Criminal Justice Reform*, 117 MICH. L. REV. 259 (2018).

[15] *See* Gretchen Morgenson & Louise Story, *In Financial Crisis, No Prosecutions of Top Figures*, N.Y. TIMES (Apr. 14, 2011), www.nytimes.com/2011/04/14/business/14prosecute.html.

[16] JESSE EISINGER, THE CHICKENSHIT CLUB: WHY THE JUSTICE DEPARTMENT FAILS TO PROSECUTE EXECUTIVES (2017). A corollary of this claim is that the government lacks the resources to go to war with the company's attorneys; JOHN COFFEE, CORPORATE CRIME AND PUNISHMENT: THE CRISIS OF UNDERENFORCEMENT (2020).

because they identify too strongly with their corporate counterparts.[17] And finally, a third and more cynical version insists that prosecutors deliberately withhold prosecution because they hope to enter the "revolving door" of a lucrative law firm partnership or general counsel position.[18]

Although the fear-of-losing claim is the most plausible of the three theories, none is completely borne out by the facts. To be sure, a fair amount of empirical literature affirms that prosecutors seek to maximize convictions and avoid trial losses; that's what one might expect of a rational utility-maximizing actor. And it would be hardly surprising to encounter risk-aversion among a group of otherwise successful individuals.[19] But white-collar crimes are not always as difficult to prove as some commentators suggest, and prosecutors can be downright risk-seeking under the right circumstances.

True enough, investigations of crimes like fraud and bribery often require the assistance of forensic accountants and a good grasp of a given industry's practices and terminology. This has never proven intractable, however, for the large federal agencies in New York, California, Boston, and other jurisdictions. When the government feels like it, it mobilizes its extensive resources. Indeed, the very threat of this mobilization is what induces corporations to often self-police and report violations of their own, lest the government find out first and impose much harsher punishments. White-collar crimes may be hard to prove (at least when it comes to demonstrating someone's knowledge or intent to deceive others), but they aren't *impossible* to prove, and aggressive prosecutors who know that have every incentive in the world to ferret out information and make a name for themselves as the prosecutor who successfully convicted Chief Officer X or Powerful Politician Y.

A long history of prosecutions for fraud, bribery, and insider trading proves this point. Prior to the 2008 Financial Crisis, prosecutors in the United States Attorney's Office in the Southern District of New York had been praised for successfully prosecuting Bernie Ebbers, WorldCom's CEO, for perpetrating a billion-dollar fraud on WorldCom's investors. They had successfully prosecuted Martha Stewart, CEO of her own home design and entertaining company, for her participation in obstructing the government's investigation of insider trading.[20] Federal prosecutors in Virginia had successfully convicted Bob McDonnell, the governor of Virginia, in

---

[17] JENNIFER TAUB, BIG DIRTY MONEY: THE SHOCKING INJUSTICE AND UNSEEN COST OF WHITE COLLAR CRIME (2020).

[18] *See* Harvey Silverglate, *The Revolving Door at the Department of Justice*, FORBES (June 22, 2011), www.forbes.com/sites/harveysilverglate/2011/06/22/revolving-door.

[19] On the other hand, one would expect prosecutors' offices to attract litigators who are, by nature, drawn to high-stakes conflicts, either by personality or by personal beliefs. *Cf.* Richard H. McAdams et al., *The Law of Police*, 82 U. CHI. L. REV. 135 (2015) (hypothesizing that those attracted to policing include "those who feel the most intrinsic satisfaction from facilitating the punishment of wrongdoers").

[20] United States v. Stewart, 433 F.3d 273, 281–89 (2d Cir. 2006) (recounting the background of the investigation and the evidence presented at trial).

a tawdry bribery case (although that conviction would eventually be overturned by the Supreme Court).[21] Even in the years *following* the Financial Crisis, the Southern District of New York would proceed to charge at least eighty individuals with violations of insider trading laws, a course of conduct that would eventually lead to an embarrassing reversal by the Court of Appeals for the Second Circuit.[22]

If the government were so *afraid* of losing trials and pursuing white-collar offenses, or so reticent to urge creative interpretations of familiar white-collar statutes, why did this fear manifest *only* in the months and years following the Financial Crisis, and even then, rather unevenly? And how could one say that government prosecutors – including the prosecutors in Main Justice (the DOJ's central division in Washington, DC) and those in the United States Attorneys' Offices, who arguably compete in some fashion for resources, reputation, and high-profile cases – *uniformly* acted in support of one subset of offenders (bank executives who ostensibly committed fraud), while doggedly pursuing a different subset (hedge fund executives who allegedly engaged in insider trading)?

However strongly the sentiment might prevail, "fear of losing" doesn't seem to explain all decisions in federal prosecutions.[23] Sometimes, the government aggressively pursues politicians, wealthy executives, and well-known celebrities. Sometimes, it presses the judiciary to entertain and adopt novel and interpretations of fraud, bribery, and obstruction of justice. And sometimes, the government shows little fear in rounding up professionals and others of "high social status" and parading them before television cameras. If the government is so afraid of losing, why does that fear surface in some white-collar cases and not in others?

The "cushy elites" argument shares similar weaknesses. If prosecutors, due to their elite status, are unable to perceive the wrongfulness of corporate actors' actions, why do they go out of their way to punish certain CEOs and CFOs? Were the prosecutors who pursued Ken Lay and Richard Skilling any less lulled by the "elite" than those who decided not to bring cases against Lloyd Blankfein? And what does it mean to be "elite" in this context anyway? Although federal prosecutors enjoy power and prestige within the legal profession, they do not enjoy the financial perquisites and wealth that corporate elites possess. At best, prosecutors enjoy a sort of academic elite résumé: attendance at top law schools (or very high performance at a regional law school), coveted clerkships after law school, and short stints with top law firms, a state AG's Office, or a federal agency's enforcement wing prior to joining a local United States Attorney's Office. To be sure, this kind of elitism imbues the prosecutor with a certain type of prestige, but it hardly places her on the

---

[21] McDonnell v. United States, 579 U.S. 550, 579–80 (2016).

[22] United States v. Newman, 773 F.3d 438 (2d Cir. 2014), abrogated in part by Salman v. United States, 137 S.Ct. 420 (2016).

[23] Lauren M. Ouziel, *Legitimacy and Federal Criminal Enforcement Power*, 123 YALE L. J. 2236, 2267–68 (2014) (citing a prominent list of high-profile cases that prosecutors have lost).

same socioeconomic plane as the billionaires and multimillionaires who helm major corporate and financial institutions.

That brings us to the revolving door thesis. Perhaps government prosecutors underenforce white-collar crime because they wish to curry favor with future employers, namely the financial institutions, Fortune 500 corporations, and white-shoe law firms that commonly represent corporate interests. In other words, government officials purposely hold their fire with corporate offenders so that they can eventually become law firm partners and general counsels of in-house law departments.

Notice, the revolving door thesis effectively runs headlong into the cushy elites thesis. If prosecutors are biased by their elite status (because they attended top schools, clerked for the right judge, and served a short stint in exclusive law firms), then it seems quite likely that they would be primed for a law firm partnership or a general counsel position *anyway* once their stint at the federal prosecutor's office has ended. The door is going to revolve for them *anyway*. If that's the case, why would they prostrate themselves just to further their ascendance up a mountain they have already scaled?

Moreover, as some have pointed out, the revolving door argument makes little sense as applied to prosecutors and enforcers in highly adversarial settings. As Lauren Ouziel observes, the market for legal representation in high-stakes litigation prizes diligence and *aggressiveness* because aggressive litigators are more apt to win (or at least not lose).[24] Why would a competitive law firm hire someone into its litigation department who has been *soft* on her adversaries? What use is the "soft prosecutor" to a company's in-house law department once the prosecutor has left the government's employ? Empirical work on the matter has all but shredded the theory. According to David Zaring's study of prosecutors in the Southern District of New York, aggressive prosecutors who helmed the hard-fought trials of corporate executives were rewarded for their aggression with partnerships at top firms.[25] Far from harming their prospects, trials and aggressive tactics redounded to the prosecutor's favor and resulted in lucrative job offers. If we were to draw a causative inference from Zaring's findings, we might say that the prospect of returning to private practice likely made prosecutors *more* aggressive with corporate actors, not less.

There may be a complex set of reasons the government fails to charge corporations and the individuals who helm them – and, as Chapter 2 will explain, the government does a relatively bad job explaining its decisions for doing so. Nevertheless, the standard explanations of fear, elitism, and revolving doors all fail to explain the paucity of charges in some instances and a sudden profusion of prosecutions in others. In future chapters, such as Chapters 3 and 5, I will explain why substantive law itself confuses the question of underenforcement even further.

---

[24] "The external market for line prosecutors values trial experience, coupled with evidence of diligence and aggressiveness." Lauren M. Ouziel, *Democracy, Bureaucracy, and Criminal Justice Reform*, 61 B.C. L. REV. 523, 558 (2020).

[25] David Zaring, *Against Being against the Revolving Door*, 2013 U. ILL. L. REV. 44. For more on the revolving door and its prominence in white-collar discourse, see Chapter 6.

1.1.2 *A Failure to Reform*

A second theme that dominates the debate is the government's failure to impose meaningful reforms on the businesses and industries that perpetrate harm. Unlike the charging critique, the reform critique pertains almost exclusively to corporate entities and the broader industry in which they reside.[26]

Much of the reform critique reflects a story of dashed expectations: the government announces, often with great fanfare, that it has struck a multimillion-dollar settlement with a corporation and its executives. The corporation agrees to forfeit or pay hundreds of millions of dollars (or more) and enact various operational reforms under the watchful eye of a government prosecutor, monitor, or regulatory agency. Years later, the same company (often with new executives at the helm) either violates the same law or a different provision of the federal code, triggering the public to question the government's assurances that it had adequately addressed the original misconduct in the first place.

No doubt, "recidivism" is an issue in corporate crime, just as it is an issue in other areas of criminal law. Many contend, however, that corporate recidivism is under-counted and understudied. To some degree, that is clearly correct – in part because of decentralized and relatively lax record-keeping, and in part because companies are fluid and can change form, ownership, and name over time.[27] Corporations also enjoy perpetual life, a feature we ordinary humans lack. Whereas old age dampens the average individual's ability and desire to violate the law, corporations remain as young or old as their employees, managers, and directors.

To understand why the government has been so unsuccessful in reforming corporate offenders (or reforming them as well as it often claims), it helps to understand why people offend in this context in the first place. Most corporate offenses incorporate elements of fraud and deceit, even if they aren't charged formally as fraud crimes. Put simply, why do people in corporate and business contexts cheat and violate known laws?

In the early 1950s, the sociologist Donald Cressey devised what would eventually become known as the "fraud triangle."[28] Under this theory, fraudulent behavior is the product of opportunity, pressure, and rationalizations.

---

[26] *See* Brandon L. Garrett, *Structural Reform Prosecution*, 93 VA. LA. REV. 853 (2007); David M. Uhlmann, *After the Spill Is Gone: The Gulf of Mexico, Environmental Crime, and the Criminal Law*, 109 MICH. L. REV. 1413 (2011); Veronica Root, *The Compliance Process*, 94 IND. L. J. 203 (2019).

[27] *See* Mihailis E. Diamantis, *The Law's Missing Account of Corporate Character*, 17 GEO. J. L. & PUB. POL'Y 865 (2019).

[28] DONALD RAY CRESSEY, OTHER PEOPLE'S MONEY (1971). Cressey theorized the factors that would eventually become the triangle, but the "fraud triangle" term itself was coined by Steven Albrecht. *See* Steven W. Albrecht, *Fraud in Government Entities: The Perpetrators and Types of Fraud*, 7 GOV'T. FIN. REV. 27 (1991). For a historical discussion of the triangle and how it evolved, see Leandra Lederman, *The Fraud Triangle and Tax Evasion*, 106 IOWA L. REV. 1153, 1180–81 (2021) (applying the framework to tax fraud and evasion).

Sophisticated corporate actors participating in highly competitive markets are well acquainted with the triangle. They experience pressures to perform and improve shareholder value; enjoy certain opportunities to quietly flout the law; rationalize that their deceptive behavior is neither harmful nor even truly illegal; and possess the intellect and psychological tools necessary to carry off a given scheme. These concepts apply to other crimes of deceit as well: domestic and foreign bribery; environmental crimes; tax evasion; collusive pricing; and obstruction of justice all reflect elements of opportunity, pressure, rationalizations, and capability.

When the government says it has reformed a given industry or corporation, what it likely means is that it believes it has reduced the company's (or industry's) opportunities to engage in a particular time of crime, often by increasing the likelihood of detection. The problem with this type of reform is that it is often fleeting. Crime operates hydraulically: when you close off one end of the system, the water flows to the other end. Accordingly, the government's claims of reform, even if well-intentioned and made in good faith, are often temporary and eventually proven to be inaccurate. The industry that previously was infamous for violations of Crime A eventually becomes known for violations of Crime B.[29] Or alternatively, a new set of institutions surface to commit Crime A or Crime B, eclipsing the harm caused by an older legacy industry. Those who insisted they fixed the problem eventually lose credibility.

1.1.3 *A Failure to Punish*

As the Varsity Blues prosecutions demonstrate, underenforcement refers to more than a failure to charge offenders for their crimes, and more than a failure to reform offenders. In some instances, it reflects a belief that white-collar defendants walk away with exceedingly light punishments. This "failure to punish" narrative plays out in several ways.

As described through a *comparative* lens, the complaint isn't so much about the absolute amount of time an offender spends in prison, but rather the fact that the wealthy white-collar offender walks away with an exceedingly light sentence, while a less fortunate counterpart suffers a far longer term of incarceration for a comparable or less serious offense. Presumably, one could address this inequality by leveling up the white-collar offender's sentence or instead by leveling down and reducing or eliminating the non–white-collar offender's punishment.[30]

---

[29] *See* Garrett, *supra* note 26; Veronica Root, *Coordinating Compliance Incentives*, 102 CORNELL L. REV. 1003 (2017).

[30] *See* Aya Gruber, *Equal Protection Under the Carceral State*, 112 Nw. U. L. REV. 1337, 166–68 (2018); Levin, *supra* note 14, at 259, 289.

If we adopt a *proportional* perspective, the critique directs its focus to the connections between the harm the offender has caused, the benefits she has reaped from a given offense, and the punishment she should receive. If white-collar offenders receive less punishment than they deserve in light of the great harms they have caused, we consider this outcome an expressive and retributive failure. Moreover, if the criminal justice system repeatedly rewards white-collar offenders with relatively light sentences (and if detection of said offenses remains fairly low), those who contemplate similar misconduct will simply conclude that the benefits of engaging in crime outweigh the personal costs. Disproportionately low sentences send bad signals, to victims and putative offenders alike.

Before exploring these arguments further, it is helpful to keep several points in mind. *First,* criminal law is extremely decentralized.[31] Different jurisdictions can develop stunningly different sentencing systems, and the judges and prosecutors within those systems correspondingly enjoy different levels of power. Comparative critiques tend to gloss over these differences. Instead, it's the "government" that gives Huffman just a few months' imprisonment for fraudulently pumping up her daughter's standardized test scores but imposes a much longer sentence on a poorer person who lied to enroll her daughter in a better-resourced school district. In reality, it is likely *two different systems* that critics are comparing, replete with different prosecutors' offices, different parole and pretrial systems, and very different judiciaries. That's not to deny the fact that Huffman's sentence seems awfully light compared to the many offenders who receive far worse sentences for nonserious crimes. Nevertheless it complicates the remedy one might seek in response to this problem, unless that remedy is to eliminate all systems of criminal punishment across the board.[32]

Second, if we adopt either the retributivist or deterrence-based theories of punishment, then we will also run into problems when we try to assess the "right" amount of punishment for white-collar offenders. The issue is primarily one of translation.[33] The white-collar offender causes several direct and indirect harms. If she defrauds someone of their money or bribes a local official to obtain an unearned advantage, her direct harms can be tabulated easily enough. But someone still must translate that concrete monetary harm into a term of imprisonment. That's where consistency and consensus fade away. If we even agree imprisonment (and not merely a fine or monetary penalty) is necessary, or that one kind of harm (stealing someone's life savings) is worse than another (offering an inspector a $1,000 bribe to ignore a marginal violation), our agreements are likely to break down once our system imposes specific punishments. The calculation grows more fraught once we consider the offender's subjective experience of punishment or the downstream effects

---

[31] *See* John F. Pfaff, Locked In: The True Causes of Mass Incarceration and How to Achieve Real Reform (2017).

[32] On prison abolition generally, see Angela Y. Davis, Are Prisons Obsolete? (2003).

[33] Cass R. Sunstein et al., *Predictably Incoherent Judgments,* 54 Stan. L. Rev. 1153 (2002).

of her misconduct.[34] The more information we feed into our punishment system, the more likely it is to produce results at least some of us find suspect.

Regardless of the philosophy of punishment one embraces, translation issues pose difficult problems for those wishing to assess the criminal justice system.[35] If the purpose of punishment is to condemn in proportion to one's "desert," then the punisher must have some way of translating the currencies of harm into the currencies of imprisonment, collateral consequences, and government-fueled stigma. If punishment's purpose is instead explained primarily in terms of deterrence, one must accomplish the same task by comparing the "harms" the offender has either threatened or imposed on society with the detection-discounted "sanction" the government has meted out in response to those harms. Either way, translation issues skew an observer's assessment of whether the system is functioning effectively or fairly. Moreover, the translation issue continues to confuse us if we imagine more ambitious goals for criminal punishment, such as "restitching" a society that has seen its norms trampled[36] or implementing a reciprocity tool that stabilizes society by assuring its members that nearly everyone follows the rules.[37] No matter what we do, we will always live with possibility that our institutions will inadvertently skew the translation of harm into punishment. And this problem exists even *before* we contemplate the difficulty of detecting and proving certain types of white-collar crime.

Consider the comparatively straightforward goal of deterring wrongdoing. In law and economics terms, we say an offender is optimally deterred when the sanction (S) multiplied by the probability of punishment (p) is just a unit higher than the harm (H) imposed by the offender's offense, or

$$(p) S > H$$

For policymakers, this inequality offers scant guidance. A legislature or court possesses little knowledge of the "p" in the Varsity Blues case. It certainly isn't a probability of 1 (which would mean the offender is always detected and successfully punished) but it also isn't 0. (If it were 0, Huffman would be in the free and clear.) The closer that p falls to 0, however, the larger the sanction must be to counterbalance such a low probability of detection and punishment. Thus, if a court were to think about Huffman's wrongdoing solely in terms of deterrence and probabilities of detection, it might well conclude that Huffman should receive a very *high* sanction

---

[34] *See, e.g.*, Adam Kolber, *The Subjective Experience of Punishment*, 109 COLUM. L. REV. 182 (2009).

[35] For a discussion of incommensurability, see generally Miriam Baer, *Sorting Out White-Collar Crime*, 97 TEX. L. REV. 225, 248–49 (2018) (discussing literature).

[36] Joshua Kleinfeld, *Reconstructivism: The Place of Criminal Law in Ethical Life*, 129 HARV. L. REV. 1485, 1500 (2016).

[37] *See* VINCENT CHIAO, CRIMINAL LAW IN THE AGE OF THE ADMINISTRATIVE STATE (2019).

in order to balance out a relatively low chance of getting caught. But what represents a "high" sanction in this situation and how can we reliability determine the possibility of detection in cases like these?

Similar difficulties ensue when we think about the previous inequality's "H" term. Huffman paid a college counselor roughly $30,000 to assist her in fraudulently boosting her child's expected standardized test scores. The *harm* she caused society – undermining faith in the college application system and eroding the legitimacy and reputation of the standardized testing company and its test scores – is abstract and intangible.[38] No single person could tell us how much it is worth in terms of a prison sentence, or whether it merits a prison sentence at all.

Thus, we encounter a world in which judges have no idea what "p" is and no easy way of documenting "H." Nevertheless, a federal judge claimed that she sentenced Huffman to two week's imprisonment on *deterrence* grounds.[39] A different judge, viewing the same facts and agreeing fully with the sentencing judge's goal of securing deterrence, might well have imposed a sentence twice or three times that long. Prosecutors, meanwhile, sought a term of six months. Which (if any) of these sentences represents too little punishment and which suggests too much?

Notice this problem arises even when the offender's harm is more concrete. Consider the con artist who defrauds an unwitting investor of $50,000. We might agree that the harm amounts to at least $50,000, plus whatever intangible and abstract harms arise out of the con artist's activity, such as decreased faith in markets, excessive self-protection by putative victims, and a reduced sense of well-being by consumers and investors. How do we reliably translate that $50,000 figure into a nonmonetary punishment such as prison? How do we translate the other, less-easy-to-calculate, and more indirect downstream costs? And to add to the confusion, to what extent do we consider the offender's starting point (such as her wealth or status in society) and fall from grace?[40] Should the public stigma of a criminal prosecution *reduce* the offender's concrete sentence or should we just assume that stigma is a useful feature baked into the process?

Years ago, I opined that translation difficulties are actually a boon to enforcement agencies.[41] Since it is all but impossible to reliably translate financial and intangible harms into a cogent punishment regime, punishers enjoy more latitude to make punishment decisions than regulators, who are often limned by highly manipulable

---

[38] It may also cease to be the basis of a wire or mail fraud charge. *See* Michael R. Dreeben, *Insider Trading and Intangible Rights: The Redefinition of the Mail Fraud Statute*, 26 AM. CRIM. L. REV. 181 (1988); Peter J. Henning, *Maybe It Should Just Be Called Federal Fraud: The Changing Nature of the Mail Fraud Statute*, 36 B. C. L. REV. 435 (1995).

[39] *See* Judgment at 2, United States v. Huffman, No. 1:19-cr-10117-IT (D. Mass. Sept. 16, 2019); Joey Garrison, *Felicity Huffman Sentenced; 2 Weeks in Prison, $30,000 Fine for College Admissions Scandal*, USA TODAY (Sept. 13, 2019), www.usatoday.com/story/entertainment/celebrities/2019/09/13/felicity-huffmans-sentenced-college-admissions-scandal/2284438001.

[40] *See generally* Kolber, *supra* note 34.

[41] *See* Miriam H. Baer, *Choosing Punishment*, 92 B.U. L. REV. 577 (2012).

cost-benefit analyses.[42] It should come as no surprise, then, that where regulation and punishment are plausible responses to socially undesirable behavior, the government will lean more in the direction of back-end, specific punishments and less in the direction of front-end, industry-level regulation.[43]

I still believe I was right in terms of an agency's short-term interests; punishment attracts public support and promotes access to the public fisc. But over the long run, I might have been mistaken. Indeed, one might conclude that translation issues ultimately *hamper* prosecutors and criminal justice systems, at least where white-collar crime is concerned. Translation problems make it increasingly difficult for us to say whether a given punishment is too slight, too much, or something in between. With no real guideposts to explain or justify white-collar punishments, commentators focus their attention on distinctions they *can* see, such as Huffman's celebrity status and socioeconomic privilege.

The difficulty in reliably translating harms into punishments grows more important when we consider the inconvenient fact that individuals sometimes derive pleasure from punishing people. Call it schadenfreude, comeuppance,[44] or "altruistic punishment."[45] The psychological literature establishes that many of us experience a forceful desire, under certain circumstances, to punish others. Thus, one cannot help but wonder if white-collar crime's underenforcement thesis reflects a crude desire to lash out more than it reflects a cogent analysis of sentencing and charging data. The problem may not be that *crimes* are going uncharged (or going uncharged more than prior practice). Rather, it might instead be that the game is *legally* rigged, and the public is angry at the people who have rigged it, defended it, and who play it and routinely come out ahead.

✳ ✳ ✳ ✳ ✳

Underenforcement may well be a problem in white-collar crime, but it is less pervasive and less predictable than critics presume. The government doesn't do nearly as good a job ferreting out frauds, corruption, and obstruction as it hopes to, and its claims of industry reform, in retrospect, can sometimes be cringeworthy. Nevertheless, for every blunt allegation of underenforcement, there exists countervailing evidence of aggressive prosecutions, hard-fought convictions, and even eye-popping sentences of punishment. Moreover, there exists numerous instances of cases in which the government has sought to *expand* the meaning of white-collar

---

[42] "[P]unishers draw flexibility from society's inability to define punishment in testable, concrete terms." *Id.* at 581.

[43] *Id.*

[44] *See* WILLIAM FLESCH, COMEUPPANCE: COSTLY SIGNALING, ALTRUISTIC PUNISHMENT, AND OTHER BIOLOGICAL COMPONENTS OF FICTION (2009).

[45] *See* Ernst Fehr & Simon Gächter, *Altruistic Punishment in Humans*, 415 NATURE 137, 137 (2002).

statutes, apply established laws to bit players and nonculpable actors, and incarcerate offenders for far longer than a few months (or even a few years).

1.2 WHITE-COLLAR CRIME'S OVERCRIMINALIZATION

Over the past two decades, critics have reached consensus that criminal law punishes too much conduct, magnifies racial and economic inequality, and often fails to achieve its deterrent, retributive, and rehabilitative aims. Much of this narrative is bound up in a broader critique of mass incarceration, racialized street policing, and excessive prosecutorial discretion. Benjamin Levin incisively divides this critique into two subcategories.[46] The "over" lens criticizes those aspects of criminal law that expose individuals to too much punishment, too much of the time. The "mass" lens decries the phenomenon of mass incarceration visited upon marginalized communities.[47] As Levin's dual framework demonstrates, the two concepts yield different reform approaches. A person concerned with fixing criminal law's "overages" would seek to narrow excessively broad laws, lessen its punishments, and reduce the government's leverage to compel guilty pleas. Those concerned with criminal law's "mass" effects, on the other hand, might well be drawn to structural reforms that aim broadly for decarceration.[48]

White-collar crime does not lend itself easily to the "mass" critique described above. There is no phenomenon of white-collar mass incarceration, although recent work *does* show that white, older males are no longer the prototypical or even predominant targets of white-collar prosecutions.[49] Yet there are numerous examples of laws and punishments that fall easily within Levin's "over" category. Observers frequently cite the fact that the federal criminal code defines thousands of crimes, many of them "regulatory" in nature and only tangentially related to interstate commerce.[50] Others seem to be a variation of the same template, be it fraud, bribery, or obstruction of the government's business. The issue isn't merely one of volume. White-collar crime's statutes are also famously broad and "open textured."[51] They feature language that covers too much conduct, defines the conduct in ambiguous language, or fails to specify a particular state of mind on the part of the offender.[52] For that reason, many say the federal code punishes

---

[46] Levin, *supra* note 14, 259, 259–60.

[47] *Id.*

[48] *Id.* at 262 ("definitional differences yield vastly different policy solutions").

[49] Michael L. Benson et al., *Race, Ethnicity, and Social Change: The Democratization of Middle-Class Crime*, 59 CRIMINOLOGY 10 (2021).

[50] *See* John S. Barker, Jr., *Jurisdictional and Separation of Powers Strategies to Limits the Expansion of Federal Crimes*, 45 AM. U. L. REV. 545 (2005).

[51] On the meaning and implications of an "open-textured" statute, see Dan M. Kahan, *Lenity and Federal Common Law Crimes*, 1994 SUP. CT. REV. 345, 353–54.

[52] *See, e.g.,* William J. Stuntz, *The Pathological Politics of Criminal Law*, 100 MICH. L. REV. 505, 512–19 (2001) ("*Pathological Politics*"); Darryl K. Brown, *Federal Mens Rea Interpretation and the Limits of Culpability's Relevance*, 75 LAW & CONTEMP. PROBS. 109,

behavior many of us would deem inadvertent or nonculpable.[53] And in some notable cases, federal statutes appear to threaten, if not impose, extremely disproportional punishments. Thus, as noted in this book's Introduction, one hears of the fisherman who might be sent to prison for twenty years for trawling for the wrong type or size of fish.[54] Or, the brilliant programmer who reportedly faces at least fifty years' imprisonment for illegally downloading an academic database and making it freely available to the public.[55] And one repeatedly hears of schemes to defraud that come nowhere near fruition but nevertheless are charged and sentenced as if they threatened the public with real harm.[56]

Although white-collar overcriminalization is a systemic problem, critics tend to focus their ire on the system's prosecutors.[57] Prosecutors apply white-collar statutes too aggressively. They seek to punish conduct that many of us would consider noncriminal. They threaten excessive punishments to force defendants, even innocent ones, to accept plea deals. And even worse, federal prosecutors rely on the DOJ's lobbying powers to urge Congress to create new laws and expand old ones. When overcriminalization is the problem, prosecutors are the star villains, with willing judges and legislators relegated to supporting roles.[58] This indeed was the point made by the late Bill Stuntz; like the underenforcement thesis, claims of overcriminalization branch out into distinct arguments, each of which will be discussed and echoed in later chapters.

Outliers

Commentators often have a paradigmatic case in mind when they envision a fraud, a bribery scheme, or a case of obstruction of justice. Cases that trigger claims of overcriminalization tend to fall far enough away from the paradigm to instigate discomfort.[59] We imagine the statute covers some act or set of acts, and that the behavior prosecuted in a given case differs too much from the statute's core

---

112–13 (2012); Samuel W. Buell, *Is the White Collar Offender Privileged?* 63 Duke L.J. 832, 842 (2014).

[53] *See, e.g.*, Stuart P. Green, *Why It's a Crime to Tear the Tag Off a Mattress: Overcriminalization and the Moral Content of Regulatory Offenses*, 46 Emory L.J. 1533 (1997).

[54] Yates was charged with obstruction of justice for destroying or concealing the too-small fish he included in his catch. The purported reason for destroying the fish was that he was attempting to avoid a fine. *See* Yates v. United States, 574 U.S. 528 (2015).

[55] *See* Kim Zetter, *Congress Demands Justice Department Explain Aaron Swartz Prosecution*, Wired (Jan. 29, 2013), www.wired.com/2013/01/doj-briefing-on-aaron-swartz.

[56] *See* United States v. Corsey, 723 F.3d 366, 370 (2d Cir. 2013).

[57] *See* Shon Hopwood, *Clarity in Criminal Law*, 54 Am. Crim. L. Rev. 695 (2017); Ellen S. Podgor, *"What Kind of a Mad Prosecutor" Brought Us This White Collar Case?* 41 Vt. L. Rev. 523 (2017).

[58] *See* Hopwood, *supra* note 57; Stephen F. Smith, *Overcoming Overcriminalization*, 102 J. Crim. L. & Criminology 537 (2012); Stuntz, *supra* note 52.

[59] *See, e.g.*, United States v. Brogan, 552 U.S. 398 (1998).

proscription to place it within the statute's boundaries, notwithstanding the statute's often expansive language. Thus, the term "tangible object" may *technically* seem to cover the destruction of fish as much as it covers the destruction of documents or data, but we feel such discomfort with the prosecutor's application of the statute that we deem it an example of "overcriminalization" and seek correction from either the judiciary or legislative branch.

When we consider these arguments more closely (usually a variant of "X is a far different case than the *ordinary* case of fraud/bribery/obstruction"), a tension emerges. Has the prosecutor breached the paradigm by prosecuting the wrong type of *conduct* or by prosecuting the wrong type of *offender*?

I have spoken already in the Introduction of United States v. Yates, in which the Supreme Court overturned an obstruction of justice conviction lodged against a commercial fisherman who attempted to conceal his catch of illegal grouper.[60] At issue was whether the concealment of the fish constituted the kind of concealment described in the relevant obstruction of justice statute. A minority of the Court thought it clearly did, in part because the statute itself made it illegal to destroy or conceal "any ... tangible object" with the intent of interfering with a federal investigation. But a plurality (joined in the judgment by Justice Alito, who wrote separately) rejected this reading of the statute, insisting that Congress had in mind the destruction of more and less tangible items, such as documents and digital material.[61]

Why so much mental effort to overturn a marginally important prosecution? Perhaps the plurality truly believed Congress intended something other than fish when it employed the words "tangible object." But perhaps the *outlier* issue related more to the defendant's identity and not his actual conduct. Justice Ginsburg mentioned that a defendant in John Yates' position potentially faced a term of twenty years' imprisonment, but as Justice Kagan pointed out in dissent, that was true of *every* defendant charged under that statute. Federal obstruction statutes, unlike statutes one commonly sees in state codes, are generally *ungraded*. As Chapter 3 will explain, there is no such thing as first-, second-, or third-degree obstruction. Instead, the obstruction statutes roughly correspond and often overlap with the type of investigation or activity the obstructive activity was meant to subvert.[62] Thus, as the Court was well aware, even under its new reading of the obstruction statute, the government could charge a commercial fisherman for destroying computer data or physical records indicating how many illegal fish had been caught that day. To put it another way, if Yates' case was an outlier because of the minor nature of his *conduct*, the statute left plenty of room to charge other minor

---

[60] 574 U.S. 528 (2015).

[61] *Id.* at 1079 (citing objects "used to record or preserve information").

[62] *See* Julie R. O'Sullivan, *The Federal Criminal Code Is a Disgrace: Obstruction Statutes as Case Study*, 96 J. CRIM. L. & CRIMINOLOGY 643 (2006).

cases, provided the information sought was contained in a physical document or a computer hard drive that the defendant sought to destroy or conceal.

The more likely aspect of the case that animated its backlash was Yates' socio-economic status. The statute in question had been enacted in the wake of the Enron and Worldcom scandals. It had been intended to shore up problems with the Arthur Andersen prosecution and the shredding of documents and data that took place before Andersen had received its official subpoena.[63] From that perspective, the Yates prosecution seems like a misfire. Congress granted prosecutors a tool to more effectively pursue wayward executives, and prosecutors instead used it to tackle a recalcitrant fisherman.

Imagine the commercial fisherman had in fact been a Goldman Sachs director out on his boat for an afternoon of leisurely enjoyment. And imagine further that our Goldman Sachs director had caught the very same fish that Yates had, in violation of the government's fishing regulations. And now imagine that our director, just like Yates, had also received a visit on his ship from a local coast guard official, and that the local coast guard official had informed the director that his catch was in violation of federal regulations and that he should keep the catch segregated in his ship's hold until he returned to port so that he could be assessed a fine. Had the Goldman Sachs director destroyed the fish before reaching port, would anyone be nearly as offended or concerned by a subsequent prosecution under the federal obstruction of justice statute? Would we even blanch at the prosecutor's argument that the statute's "tangible object" language extended to the very tangible fish?

This is the underexplored problem with outlier arguments. We might complain that the *offense* charged is an outlier, but in some cases, it seems to be the identity of the offender that fuels our discomfort. We would do well to disentangle these two concerns. Charging outlier conduct is a *legal* concern; we rely on courts to tell prosecutors not to stretch statutes beyond their plausible meaning. Charging an outlier offender, however, is in fact a *political* concern; if our prosecutors are spending their limited resources pursuing fishermen instead of corporate executives, we can use multiple tools to question, shame, and perhaps even fire the appointed actors who run the DOJ. The overcriminalization mantra, however, elides these distinctions.

At bottom, Yates' prosecution faltered because he seemed like a terrible target for a law that was devised and amended with an eye toward addressing the issues that arose when Arthur Anderson, the now defunct accounting giant, shredded its Enron documents in advance of its first subpoena.[64] Of course, few are willing to admit this part out loud because to do so is to deny one of the strongest tenets in criminal law: that criminal law punishes *behavior* without regard to a person's status or wealth. So instead, critics of Yates' prosecution were left to argue – in almost amusing fashion – that the words "tangible object" didn't in fact include fish. This neither helped the

[63] *See Yates*, 135 S. Ct. at 1081.
[64] *See id.*

Court (a 5-4 opinion in which Justice Kagan lamented the Court's overreaching is hardly a win) nor the future Yates of the world who would just as surely find themselves charged with some other federal crime.

Panics and "Doing Something"

Another line of criticism focuses not so much on a single case itself so much as a general category of prosecutions. This line of critique, often informed by the political economy literature, posits that white-collar criminal prosecutions represent the government's performative attempt to show the general public it is "doing something," often in the midst of upheaval or some panic.[65] The problem with this stance is that the effort to "do something" is neither meaningful nor productive. And indeed, that is exactly the outcome preferred by corporate executives and other wealthy individuals: to have the government *look* like it is "doing something" even when it really isn't.[66]

Consider the ways the government might approach a potential crisis in a given industry. To prevent the crisis in the first place, it might devise a series of rules and other "front-end" limitations on corporate actors. We might refer to this as front-end regulation. Much of today's front-end regulation pertains to *disclosure* – we direct companies that are public exchanges to register with the SEC and to disclose certain types and degrees of information to their owners and the general public. But apart from disclosure regulation, we can also tell people and corporations how to behave – what we might call "governance" regulation.[67] Depending on the industry, we can impose many *ex ante* requirements (of the disclosure or governance variety), or very few. That is what we mean when we say an industry is lightly or heavily regulated. Command and control regulation delineates positive obligations for regulated entities and often tells them how they can or cannot achieve those obligations. Standards or principles-based regulation focuses on certain standards entities are supposed to achieve (e.g., environmental emissions) without directly telling the entities how to achieve them. And devices like taxes or cap and trade systems effectively permit as much activity of the entity as it likes, provided it pays the costs associated with that activity.[68]

---

[65] See Thomas Joo, *Legislation and Legitimation: Congress and Insider Trading in the 1980s*, 82 Ind. L. J. 575 (2007).

[66] See Vikramaditya S. Khanna, *Corporate Crime Legislation: A Political Economy of Corporate Crime*, 82 Wash. U. L. Q. 95 (2004).

[67] See Peter V. Letsou, *The Changing Face of Corporate Governance Regulation in the United States: The Evolving Roles of the Federal and State Governments*, 46 Willamette L. Rev. 149, 149 n.1 (2009).

[68] "Legal scholars, economists, and political scientists sometimes distinguish among three types of regulation: command-and-control rules; performance-based standards; and incentive-based systems." Jon D. Hanson & Kyle D. Logue, *The Costs of Cigarettes: The Economic Case for*

Front-end regulation is politically and economically costly. It is politically costly to regulators and economically costly to regulated entities and their owners. It requires legislators to debate complex issues and take sides (perhaps against groups who might vote out the legislator the next time she is up for election), and it requires regulators to defend their decision-making in both courts of law and the court of opinion.[69] Regulation is also economically costly to companies. Although some large or well-established companies might prefer regulation when it forms a barrier to entry to new entrants, many seem to prefer less regulation (or certainly, less command-and-control regulation).

By contrast, criminal punishment seems not to endure so much pushback from corporate chieftains. A recent article by Adam Levitin and William Bratton[70] highlights this point: two years after the Financial Crisis first arose, enforcement attorneys and prosecutors sought penalties from financial institutions who had promoted securities and other products based on residential mortgages.[71] Whereas financial institutions fought regulators tooth and nail over new regulations and comprehensive legislation, they were willing to enter into settlement agreements collectively, amounting to more than a billion dollars. Levitin and Bratton observed:

> The enforcers who bring such [enforcement] proceedings wield preemptive power that primary financial and other regulators no longer possess. The same company that defends stoutly and uncooperatively in rulemaking contexts, treats a prosecutor-ial initiative with utmost risk aversion, making a quick deal.[72]

Why are the very institutions that are so confidently dead set against regulation willing to negotiate their way to a punitive settlement? Perhaps it is because the financial institutions themselves prefer paying a penalty, even a massive one, to government incursions on their business decisions.[73] Regulation is seen as interfering in one's autonomy, whereas punishment – particularly punishment in the corporate context – is seen as a one-time hit that hopefully happens to someone else.[74]

---

ex post Incentive-Based Regulation, 107 YALE L.J. 1163, 1173 (1998), citing Susan Rose-Ackerman, *Consensus versus Incentives: A Skeptical Look at Regulatory Negotiation*, 43 DUKE L.J. 1206 (1994).

[69] On the ways in which government actors perceive and internalize costs, see Daryl J. Levinson, *Making Government Pay: Markets, Politics, and the Allocation of Constitutional Costs*, 67 U. CHI. L. REV. 345 (2000).

[70] William W. Bratton & Adam J. Levitin, *A Tale of Two Markets: Regulation and Innovation in Post-Crisis Mortgage and Structured Finance Markets*, 2020 U. ILL. L. REV. 47 (2020).

[71] *See id.* at 77.

[72] *Id.* at 77–78.

[73] *See generally* Vikramaditya S. Khanna, *Corporate Crime Legislation: A Political Economy Analysis*, 82 WASH. U. L. Q. 95 (2004).

[74] The late Larry Ribstein hypothesized a reverse lottery that applied solely to executives of unpopular firms. Larry E. Ribstein, *Agents Prosecuting Agents*, 7 J.L. ECON. & POL'Y 617, 632 (2011).

Thus, the criticism of punishment in this context isn't grounded in theories of desert. To the contrary, it is that the resources we devote to punishing business crimes (particularly crimes that are ascribed to corporations) could be better addressed by directing greater support to civil enforcement and front-end regulation. Punishment might grant us a temporary feeling of well-being, but it is far less clear that it permanently improves private-sector behavior. Moreover, it becomes counter-productive when our primary metric for assessing the government's response to a crisis is the number of top executives sent to jail for long periods of time.

Erosion and Expansion of Mens Rea Distinctions

Finally, another way in which white-collar crime has been overcriminalized is that prosecutors (with an assist from judges) have eroded the law's mental state require-ments. Crimes such as mail, wire, and securities fraud are often referred to as "specific intent" crimes, in that they require offenders to possess a purpose to defraud others.[75] Over a period of decades, however, courts and prosecutors have widened the requisite mental state necessary to prove these crimes.

The paradigmatic fraud scheme is one in which a perpetrator purposely uses false or misleading statements to deceive a victim and obtain her money or property. A purposely devised scheme covers quite a bit of behavior. It includes attempted frauds along with completed ones, and it covers implausible schemes along with ones that are likely to succeed. Courts have nevertheless expanded criminal fraud statutes to cover behavior that might not be purposeful at all. For the most part, this has occurred gradually and in an ad hoc manner.[76]

How has this happened? First, courts have embraced the "willful blindness" doctrine in fraud cases, which allows jurors to conclude that a person possesses knowledge of the falsity of a statement when she deliberately take actions to shield herself from information that would have confirmed the statement's falsity.[77] Thus, if a CEO announces a company's profits, but deliberately fails to look into information that would have demonstrated the material falsity of his announcement, his "willful blindness" can serve as evidence of his "purposeful" scheme to fraud.

If you find yourself confused by the idea that *not* knowing a material fact can constitute knowledge, which can *then* be used to prove purpose, you are not alone. Appellate courts have repeatedly affirmed the concept, only to remind lower courts, and implicitly, juries, that the doctrine should not be read as punishing cluelessness

---

[75] Samuel W. Buell, *Novel Criminal Fraud*, 81 N.Y.U. L. REV. 1971, 1985 (2006).

[76] *See* Baer, *supra* note 35, at 245.

[77] *See* Global-Tech Appliances, Inc. v. SEB S.A., 563 U.S. 754, 766 (2011); United States v. Jewell, 532 F.2d 697, 700 (9th Cir. 2011).

or a lack of due diligence.[78] The fact that lower courts continue to experience so much difficulty defining the concept ought to give us pause.[79]

Willful blindness is controversial, but it at least assumes deliberate behavior.[80] But in some cases, courts have further stretched the meaning of criminal fraud statutes by allowing prosecutors to rely on a person's *reckless* behavior. To be sure, these cases have not equated reckless activity with fraud. Instead, they often disclose that a statement, made with reckless regard of its falsity, can constitute fraud. But here again, we are relying on increasingly thinner boundaries to separate criminal misconduct from socially undesirable behavior. And the more we do that, the more we create the notion that mens rea no longer protects the private sector from overcriminalization.

1.3 OUT OF ONE PATHOLOGY, MANY

Thus far, white-collar crime might sound a lot like the rest of criminal law. Indeed, in one of his most famous and well-cited articles, Stuntz described all of criminal law – federal and state, street crime, and otherwise – as continually expanding in scope and depth. Despite fluctuations in crime and public opinion, criminal *law* proceeded in only one direction:

> If ordinary politics drives criminal law, it will drive it toward more liability here and less there, more liability now but less then. One sees some of that variability in the history of American criminal law, but not much. The more accurate generalization is that criminal law expands in different areas at different times and places, but it always expands.[81]

Not only did Stuntz's critique include federal and white-collar crime, but it also highlighted aspects of the expansive mail and wire fraud statutes that covered what Stuntz referred to as, "marginal middle class dishonesty." The two statutes, Stuntz argued, captured far more "borderline" misconduct than one would expect of a politically savvy and self-interested legislature. ("[O]ne would think borderline dishonesty by middle-class offenders would be the last thing any popularly elected legislature would want to criminalize.")[82] Stuntz attributed this phenomenon, not to

---

[78] *See* United States v. Macias, 786 F.3d 1060, 1062, 1064 (7th Cir. 2015); United States v. Ciesiolka, 614 F.3d 347, 352–53 (7th Cir. 2010); United States v. Carrillo, 435 F.3d 767, 781–82 (7th Cir. 2006).

[79] For experimental evidence supporting the notion that laypeople may be unable to follow fine gradations in knowledge and recklessness, see Matthew R. Ginther et al., *Decoding Guilty Minds: How Jurors Attribute Knowledge and Guilt*, 71 Vand. L. Rev. 241, 244 (2018). For further analysis of willful blindness and the practical and conceptual difficulties it poses, see Kenneth Simons, *The Willful Blindness Doctrine: Justifiable in Principle, Problematic in Practice*, 53 Ariz. St. L. J. 655 (2021).

[80] *See* United States v. Giovannetti, 919 F.2d 1223, 1228 (7th Cir. 1990).

[81] Stuntz, *supra* note 52, at 527–28.

[82] *Id.* at 524–25.

ordinary politics, but instead to a knotty series of institutional arrangements and incentives: "Legislators gain when they write criminal statutes in ways that benefit prosecutors. Prosecutors gain from statutes that enable them more easily to induce guilty pleas. Appellate courts lack the doctrinal tools to combat those tendencies."[83] Stuntz's point was that legislatures (including Congress) possessed all the incentives in the world to draft broadly written criminal laws and then rely on prosecutors to apply them the way the public "really" intended. Prosecutors appreciated the breadth, volume, and overlap of the statutes, because together, these characteristics eased the burden of prosecution and promoted the extraction of easy guilty pleas.

Although Stuntz treated white-collar and street crime as equivalents throughout much of his discussion, he did acknowledge the "special case" posed by federal prosecutors. Unlike state counterparts, the government's head prosecutors (the AG and United States Attorneys) were unelected and therefore more insulated from public opinion.[84] More importantly, their jurisdiction was, for the most part, duplicative of state and local prosecutors. "[T]here is an enormous amount that federal prosecutors can do ... but very little that they must do." From there, Stuntz reasoned that federal prosecutors would choose "interesting" and "professionally rewarding" cases primed to enhance their social and political capital.[85]

Stuntz's article was published in 2001. Less than a decade later, federal prosecutors would receive intense scrutiny for failing to pursue cases against the corporate executives who played prominent roles in precipitating a reckless subprime mortgage boom, followed by a painful financial crisis and recession. If any event suggested weaknesses in Stuntz's otherwise powerful analysis, it was the Financial Crisis. Under Stuntz's framework, prosecutors should have *loved* to have taken on "interesting" and professionally rewarding investigations of fraud and financial misconduct. And if the law was as broad as Stuntz said it was, they also should have experienced few difficulties securing convictions. But, as Chapter 5 highlights, prosecutors lost an early mortgage fraud prosecution, and that loss influenced their decision to steer clear of future cases.[86]

---

[83] *Id.* at 528.

[84] "United States Attorneys are appointed, not elected, and the appointment process is not designed to make them politically accountable to the local population in the way district attorneys are." *Id.* at 542. *See also* Lisa Miller & James Eisenstein, *The Federal-State Criminal Prosecution Nexus: A Case Study in Cooperation and Discretion*, 30 LAW & SOC. INQ. 239, 265 (2005) ("Federal law enforcement agents and prosecutors are less directly accountable to the public than their local counterpart.") As Lauren Ouziel points out, there is a further divide between the federal AG and United States Attorneys, who are politically appointed, and the line prosecutors and investigators who staff prosecutor's offices and enforcement agencies. Ouziel, *supra* note 24, at 537 (observing moments in which the line prosecutors' incentives may not be aligned with that of higher-level appointees). *See also* Leslie B. Arffa, *Note, Separation of Prosecutors*, 128 YALE L. J. 1078 (2019) (arguing that decentralization of prosecutorial authority serves as a useful check on presidential power).

[85] Stuntz, *supra* note 81, at 543.

[86] *See generally* Chapter 5.

My point is not to deny the pathology that causes legislatures to supply prosecutors with a surfeit of statutes and broadly drafted terms, not to mention "proxy" crimes that enable the prosecutor to punish an individual for Crime X by charging an easier-to-prove Crime Y.[87] The legislature's obeisance to the executive branch is clearly responsible for some of white-collar crime's overcriminalization. But more than one pathology is afoot. As we have already seen, white-collar crime does more than overcriminalize; it also underenforces. Given the ways in which the public responds to such underenforcement, it behooves us to interrogate the reasons for this enforcement gap and determine if additional dynamics may be in play. As the rest of this book argues, one can identify *multiple* pathologies in white-collar crime. They pertain to how we make law, how we enforce it, and how we speak about it.

1.4 SUCKING UP AND PUNCHING DOWN?

Overcriminalization and underenforcement narratives are, at bottom, criticisms of federal prosecutors. They imagine the federal prosecutor as a prototypically bad agent: one who stretches the law too far and punishes too much, but who also declines to pursue the wealthy and powerful, thereby allowing corruption and injustice to go unchecked.

One way to rationalize these narratives is to say prosecutors suck up and punch down; that is, they conveniently ignore offenses undertaken by the powerful, and aggressively charge and extract guilty pleas from the power*less*. Although conceptually elegant, the explanation ignores too many inconvenient facts. As the cases described in this book demonstrate, prosecutors *often do* seek out rich and wealthy criminal defendants, and they often are more than happy to publicize those efforts. Sometimes, government prosecutors can and do "punch up" as forcefully and loudly as they can.

As for punching *down*, disproportionate sentences for offenses such as mail or wire fraud are not the norm in federal sentencing. We often hear that defendants "face" up to ten, twenty, or even fifty years in prison if convicted of the charges contained in an indictment, but the actual sentence the defendant receives in many white-collar cases is often far less than that, an issue I discuss in Chapter 3. That doesn't mean we should ignore the statutory maximum sentence imposed by numerous white-collar statutes. To the contrary, they create enormous confusion and fuel charges of overcriminalization that either inaccurate or incomplete. Nevertheless, the story they tell is more nuanced. People don't go to jail for eighty

---

[87] For examples and criticisms of proxy crimes and pretextual prosecutions (which are overlapping phenomena), see Daniel C. Richman & William J. Stuntz, *Al Capone's Revenge: An Essay on the Political Economy of Pretextual Prosecution*, 105 COLUM. L. REV. 583 (2005); RICHARD H. MCADAMS, *The Political Economy of Criminal Law and Procedure*, in CRIMINAL LAW CONVERSATIONS (Paul J. Robinson, Stephen Garvey, & Kimberley Kessler Ferzan, eds., 2007).

years for engaging in garden-variety mail frauds. We just tell everyone they are "facing" that amount at the moment of their arrest.

It should be clear by now that the aim of this book is not to say we have a good system. We clearly don't. At a minimum, it generates too many myths and misunderstandings about the criminal justice system's treatment of white-collar offenses. That is hardly a good story if we care about the system's reform and future sustainability. But it is a reductive and incorrect statement to say that white-collar crime *always* overcriminalizes offenses involving the middle class and the poor, and that it *always* underenforces misconduct of the wealthy. Sometimes, powerful executives and wealthy celebrities find themselves in the government's crosshairs. And sometimes the government's *over*criminalization cases are visited on the politically powerful (including the former governor of Virginia), and not merely those who work in a back office or engage in "borderline" behavior.[88] Sometimes the system works, and sometimes it fails for reasons other than prosecutorial cowardice or corruption.

That brings us to the topic of blame. If we move away from reductive stories of overcriminalization and underenforcement, we begin to identify additional institutions responsible for our confusion and disenchantment. Many of white-collar crime's weaknesses can be traced to Congressional action and inaction. Statutes are "underwritten," and therefore reliant on judges, regulators, and prosecutors to give them meaning (Chapter 4). Many of those same statutes are "ungraded," in that they fail to statutorily subdivide crimes into bad and worse variations (Chapter 3). Those two pathologies, taken together, lead to a world in which we are less able to track what our enforcement agencies are doing (Chapter 2) and misunderstand enforcers' concerns about picking and winning viable cases (Chapter 5). When we find ourselves in the dark long enough, we begin to glom on to certain beliefs, which in time become myths (Chapter 6). That is the irony of white-collar crime's pathologies: however beneficial they may be in the short term to prosecutors, they eventually fuel cynicism and a decline of public support in the long run.[89] Not only does this decline of support leave prosecutors and investigators worse off, but it ultimately impoverishes society as well.

---

[88] For additional examples, see Albert W. Alschuler, *Criminal Corruption: Why Board Definitions of Bribery Make Things Worse*, 84 FORDHAM L. REV. 463 (2015).

[89] *See* Chapters 3 and 4.

2

Unknown Knowns

There are known knowns – there are things we know we know ... We also know there are known unknowns – that is to say, we know there are some things we do not know. But there are also *unknown* unknowns, the ones we don't know we don't know.

Donald Rumsfeld, Secretary of Defense (August 22, 2001)[1]

INTRODUCTION

In 2018, Paul Manafort, President Donald Trump's former campaign manager, was convicted after a federal trial on multiple counts of tax fraud, two counts of bank fraud, and a single count of failure to disclose a foreign bank account. (He subsequently pleaded guilty in a separate case to additional offenses.) At the time of his arrest in 2017, several mainstream media sources reported that Manafort faced as much as eighty years' imprisonment.[2] Technically, this term of years was correct.

[1] Dan Zak, *"Nothing Ever Ends": Sorting through Rumsfeld's Knowns and Unknowns*, WASH. POST (July 1, 2021). For an excellent explanation of "unknown knowns" – information known to a person or group "but that is, for all practical purposes, unknown at the time it is needed" – see Herb Lin, *The Fourth Quadrant: The Unknown Knowns*, LAWFARE (July 9, 2021), www.lawfareblog.com/fourth-quadrant-unknown-knowns (highlighting that Rumsfeld himself never bothered to acknowledge his matrix's fourth quadrant). *See also* Steve Rayner, *Uncomfortable Knowledge: The Social Construction of Ignorance in Science and Environmental Policy Discourses*, 41 ECON. SOC'Y 107 (2012); Daniel Sarewitz, *Unknown Knowns*, 37 ISSUES SCI. & TECH. 18 (2020), https://issues.org/known-unknowns-uncomfortable-knowledge-sare witz/.

[2] Associated Press, *Paul Manafort Faces up to 80 Years in Prison, Millions in Fines*, SYRACUSE. COM (Oct. 30, 2017), www.syracuse.com/politics/2017/10/paul_manafort_rick_gates_indictment.html; David Martosko, *Paul Manafort Faces up to 80 Years in Jail and Is under House Arrest Along with Former Business Partner Rick Gates after Pleading Not Guilty to $75m Money-Laundering Charges – As Trump Insists It Is NOTHING to Do with Him*, DAILY MAIL (Oct. 30, 2017), www.dailymail.co.uk/news/article-5031419/Paul-Manafort-Rick-Gates-told-SURRENDER.html; Lydia Wheeler, *Manafort Faces Maximum of 80 Years in Prison*, THE

Had a district court judge maximized the sentence under each count *and* strung those sentences together consecutively, Manafort *could* have received eighty years' imprisonment. In fact, Manafort faced – and ultimately received – a far shorter sentence, prior to his eventual pardon.[3]

Manafort's prosecution was notable for several reasons. First, it grew out of the investigation of allegations that Russia had interfered in the 2016 presidential election. Second, Manafort was prosecuted by prosecutors working for Robert Mueller, who had been appointed by Rod Rosenstein, the Deputy Attorney General of the Department of Justice (DOJ), to investigate Russia's interference and additional allegations that Donald Trump had obstructed justice. After Manafort's arrest on charges of bank fraud and other crimes, he met with prosecutors on multiple occasions in order to secure a cooperation agreement; prosecutors instead rejected such a path when they determined that he was deliberately withholding information.[4]

Manafort's supporters had every reason to play up the unusual nature of his prosecution, observing that it had arisen out of the Mueller investigation even though it had nothing to do with Russia. and insisting the government used Manafort's mundane bank fraud crimes to induce Manafort's cooperation against Donald Trump. Post-trial, Manafort's attorneys similarly highlighted the overly high sentence he was facing. According to Manafort's lawyers, the prosecutors sought to punish Manafort for failing to cooperate in the prosecution of President Trump.[5]

HILL (Aug. 21, 2018), https://thehill.com/homenews/administration/402935-manafort-faces-maximum-of-80-years-in-prison/; *The Manafort Verdict and How We Got Here*, POLITICO (Oct. 6, 2018), www.politico.com/interactives/2018/paul-manafort-trial-latest-news/.

[3] Following a jury trial and conviction, Manafort was sentenced to just under four years' imprisonment for his bank fraud offenses and then received an additional three years' imprisonment for a separate offense, to which he pleaded guilty. Miles Parks & Ryan Lucas, *Paul Manafort, Former Trump Campaign Chairman, Sentenced to Just under 4 Years*, NPR (Mar. 7, 2019), www.npr.org/2019/03/07/701045248/paul-manafort-former-trump-campaign-chairman-sentenced-to-just-under-4-years; Darren Samuelsohn et al., *Manfort Gets 47 Months in Prison for Financial Fraud*, POLITICO (Mar. 7, 2019), www.politico.com/story/2019/03/07/manafort-gets-47-months-in-prison-for-financial-fraud-1210786 (observing that Manafort initially faced up to eighty years' imprisonment); Sharon LaFraniere, *Paul Manafort's Prison Sentence Is Nearly Doubled to 7½ Years*, N.Y. TIMES (Mar. 13, 2019), www.nytimes.com/2019/03/13/us/politics/paul-manafort-sentencing.html. Manafort eventually was pardoned for all of his crimes by President Donald Trump. *See* Josh Gerstein, *Trump Pardon Unwinds Some Manafort Forfeitures*, POLITICO (Feb. 26, 2021), www.politico.com/news/2021/02/26/trump-manafort-pardon-471785.

[4] On the Mueller investigation generally and its implications, see ANDREW WEISSMANN, WHERE LAW ENDS: INSIDE THE MUELLER INVESTIGATION (2021). For a breakdown of Manafort's investigation, indictment, convictions, and failed cooperation effort with Mueller investigators, see *id.* at 142–62, 174–87, 282–310.

[5] "Before and during the trial, Mr. Trump both sought to defend Mr. Manafort as a victim of prosecutorial overreach." Sharon LaFraniere, *Paul Manafort, Trump's Former Campaign Chairman, Guilty of 8 Counts*, N.Y. TIMES (Aug. 21, 2018), www.nytimes.com/2018/08/21/us/politics/paul-manafort-trial-verdict.html. Trump would rely on this claim when he eventually pardoned Manafort for all of his crimes. Andrew McCarthy, a frequent critic of the Mueller

The prosecutors assigned to Manafort's prosecution remained relatively quiet during this time period. They stressed their voluminous evidence of Manafort's fraud and obstruction and the serious nature of the crimes of which he had been convicted, but they did not cite data showing how many investigations the government had undertaken regarding serious bank frauds in the past three or five years. Nor did they show how many offenders had been charged with such crimes in a given year, or convicted of such crimes, or sentenced for bank-fraud related offenses. As is often the case in federal criminal law, prosecutors relied on *qualitative* descriptions of the defendant's misconduct to justify their decision-making, but provided little *quantitative* data to contextualize their prosecution and reinforce their credibility.

There are good policy reasons why prosecutors would shy away from presenting such data. They might worry it provides a roadmap to putative criminals.[6] They might believe that no amount of data will convince skeptics and critics, in which case the effort to collect the information isn't worth it. They might also believe that presenting such information undermines their position. If prosecutorial charging decisions are truly discretionary, it ought not to matter whether Manafort's prosecution was a one-off or one of many.

These arguments are only partially persuasive. Even if prosecutors maintain discretion in *individual* cases, they still answer to the people they serve. The public has a right to know, in the aggregate, which cases are run-of-the-mine and which ones are outliers. It has a right to question the government's enforcement policies and resource-allocation decisions. It cannot perform this oversight function if it lacks reliable, usable data.

Sometimes reliable granular data is not easily accessible, even to prosecutors. As several of the top criminologists in this field have repeatedly warned, the collection and dissemination of white-collar data is highly fragmented within the federal criminal system.[7] Investigative and arrest data are compiled by the many agencies

---

investigation and former federal prosecutor, criticized the Manafort bank fraud indictment as "overcharged." Andrew C. McCarthy, *The Manafort Indictment: Not Much There, and a Boon for Trump*, NAT'L REV. (Oct. 30, 2017), www.nationalreview.com/2017/10/manafort-indictment-no-signs-trump-russia-collusion/. Even after Manafort was sentenced to a relatively short term on the bank fraud counts, his attorney criticized prison time as "hostile and unnecessary." *Manafort Lawyer Calls Washington Prison Sentence "Hostile," "Unnecessary,"* REUTERS (Mar. 13, 2019), www.reuters.com/article/usa-trump-russia-manafort-lawyer-int/manafort-lawyer-calls-washington-prison-sentence-hostile-unnecessary-idUSKBN1QU2CY.

6 "Badly motivated corporate managers might also use the government's disclosures about how it makes its corporate cases, and how it exercises its charging and sanctioning discretion, as a roadmap for unlawful activities designed to evade legal sanction." Samuel W. Buell, *Why Do Prosecutors Say Anything? The Case of Corporate Crime*, 96 N.C. L. REV. 823, 852 (2018).

7 SALLY S. SIMPSON & PETER CLEARY YEAGER, BUILDING A COMPREHENSIVE WHITE-COLLAR VIOLATIONS DATA SYSTEM, FINAL TECHNICAL REPORT (2015) (report and proposal submitted to Bureau of Justice Statistics). "[O]fficial data on white-collar crime are scattered across a bewilderingly large number of law enforcement and regulatory agencies."

who enforce the criminal code and investigate criminal violations of regulatory laws. At some stage, an enforcement agency's arrest and investigative information will be entered in the National Incident Based Reporting System, or NIBRS.[8] The ninety-plus United States Attorneys' Offices, in turn, record all their "matters" in the LIONS (Legal Information Office Network System) database. The Fraud Department of Main Justice maintains its own additional records. And the United States Sentencing Commission collects information on federal convictions and sentences.[9] Periodically, the Bureau of Justice Statistics (BJS), the DOJ's "primary statistical agency," compiles and releases information on these topics.[10]

Not one of these databases was designed with "white-collar crime" in mind.[11] Moreover, each appears to rely on its own dictionary and systemic classification rules, which further complicates the task of easily sharing, verifying, or replicating information. This problem is magnified by the proliferation of federal agencies who investigate different but often overlapping white-collar matters, as well as varying approaches of the federal prosecutors' offices.[12] To put it another way, there is a lot of redundancy in the federal criminal justice system. But however helpful redundancy may be for investigating and deterring wrongdoing, it hampers the collection

---

MICHAEL L. BENSON ET AL., *White-Collar and Corporate Crime*, in THE HANDBOOK OF MEASUREMENT ISSUES IN CRIMINOLOGY AND CRIMINAL JUSTICE 92, 93 (Beth M. Huebner & Timothy S. Bynum, eds., 2016).

[8] NIBRS is the system that replaced the Uniform Crime Reporting system, which is the system that has measured federal, state, and local crime enforcement since 1930. The FBI administers the NIBRS and UCR systems. It has overseen agencies' migration to NIBRS, which has occurred slowly over the past two decades and was supposed to be complete by 2021. Numerous state and local agencies resisted the changeover because of costs and fears that NIBRS would artificially boost crime statistics. (The UCR imposes a rule whereby only the most serious offense is reported.) Kevin J. Strom & Erica L. Smith, *The Future of Crime Data*, 16 CRIMINOLOGY & PUB. POL'Y 1027, 1035 (2017) ("NIBRS does not impose the hierarchy rule and also captures data on a wider range of criminal offenses.")

[9] Even here one encounters issues. "Compared to most jurisdictions, the federal courts have a lot of sentencing data. The problem is finding it, analyzing it, and putting it to good use." Paul J. Hofer, *Data, Disparity, and Sentencing Debates: Lessons from the TRAC Report on Inter-Judge Disparity*, 25 FED. SENT. REP. 37, 37 (2012).

[10] On the BJS and its mission, see *About BJS*, BUREAU JUST. STAT., https://bjs.ojp.gov/about. For an example, of one its reports, see MARK MOTIVANS, FEDERAL JUSTICE STATISTICS 2010 – STATISTICAL TABLES, Table 57 (2012).

[11] On the evolution of crime reporting and use of statistics, see generally Paul Wormeli, *Criminal Justice Statistics – An Evolution*, 17 CRIMINOLOGY & PUB. POL. 483 (2018); PANEL ON MODERNIZING THE NATION'S CRIME STATISTICS ET AL., MODERNIZING CRIME STATISTICS: REPORT 1: DEFINING AND CLASSIFYING CRIME (Janet L. Lauritsen & Daniel L. Cork eds., 2016), www.nap.edu/catalog/23492. On the difficulties of applying data-collection principles to federal white-collar crime, see CYNTHIA BARNETT, THE MEASUREMENT OF WHITE-COLLAR CRIME USING UNIFORM CRIME REPORTING DATA (2000), https://ucr.fbi.gov/nibrs/nibrs_wcc.pdf.

[12] "The current assortment of federal law enforcement agencies, and the assignment of their respective investigative responsibilities, has come about in a largely random manner." *See* Paul J. Larkin, Jr., *Essay: A New Law Enforcement Agenda for a New Attorney General*, 17 GEO. J. L. & PUB. POL'Y 231, 240 (2019).

and dissemination of data about such wrongdoing. If overlapping enforcement jurisdiction has its many features, data collection is one of its most stubborn bugs.

These issues are hardly new. White-collar criminal data has long been the target of criticism by criminologists and the handful of law professors who study the topic.[13] As criminologist Sally Simpson bluntly explains: "It is difficult to measure white-collar crime because all of the typical sources of crime data (including official data, offender self-reports, and victimization reports) are limited in scope, not collected in a systematic manner, or have unique problems that discourage operationalization and generalization."[14]

Lacking proper measurement tools, we have come to distrust the institutions responsible for enforcing and punishing white-collar crime. Our instinct is to blame the executive branch for these weaknesses, and to try to improve data reporting by centralizing and modernizing white-collar crime's data collection. As I explain toward the end of this chapter, centralization and modernization are misguided ventures. To get at the heart of white-collar crime's data problems, we need to fix our *inputs*. And the best way to do that is to fix the laws that make up our criminal code, a feat I tackle in Chapters 7 and 8.

2.1 DEFINITIONAL CHALLENGES

How much white-collar crime occurred in the past five years? How much of that crime was successfully addressed by our federal enforcement institutions? Have white-collar arrests fallen or increased? What about convictions and punishments? And how do we distinguish (for counting purposes and otherwise) a sub-category such as "corporate crime" from the broader category of white-collar crime?

Each of these questions is difficult to answer, in part because scholars, researchers, and practitioners all adhere to a different definition of white-collar crime.[15] If we assume the term refers to statutorily defined crimes that involve the use deceit to subvert governmental systems or to cheat others out of property (however defined), we will find that many such crimes are either never reported or are instead resolved outside the criminal justice system. Victims might not even realize they are victims until many years later. Obstruction and bribery can go unchecked for months or years. Frauds or similar crimes discovered by corporate employers may be quietly remedied and dealt with without reporting such behavior to the proper authorities.

---

[13] April Wall-Parker, *Measuring White-Collar Crime*, in The Handbook of White-Collar Crime 32 (Melissa L. Rorie, ed. 2020) (describing competing theories underlying the changing definition).

[14] Sally S. Simpson, *Making Sense of White-Collar Crime: Theory and Research*, 8 Ohio St. J. Crim. L. 481, 482–83 (2011).

[15] *See generally* David O. Friedrichs, *Definitional Debates and the Case for a Typological Approach*, in The Handbook of White-Collar Crime 23 (Rorie, ed. 2020) (describing the distinct ideological views underlying the definitional debate).

And government authorities might decide, for political or strategic purposes, to treat corporate transgressions as civil instead of criminal violations. Accordingly, a drop in the number of reported frauds or instances of bribery and obstruction may not be cause for celebration. By the same token, an uptick in reported crimes might reflect improvement in enforcement and not an increase in wrongdoing. *Data* in this case conveys ambiguous information and sends conflicting signals.[16]

Nevertheless, there do exist some indirect methods for surveying citizen perceptions of white-collar crime and its pervasiveness.[17] Hotlines and whistleblower programs can serve as a helpful proxy for the frequency and seriousness of corporate and white-collar crime.[18] So too can publicly and privately funded surveys. The National Public Survey on White Collar Crime was last administered in 1999; it offers useful, if somewhat dated, information on public attitudes toward fraud and bribery compared with other offenses.[19] At least two scholars have extended this type of attitudinal analysis to crimes such as insider trading.[20]

PriceWaterhouseCooper's annual Crime and Fraud Survey, which has been in existence for twenty years, is representative of the types of privately funded surveys one finds on the Internet.[21] It is helpful in capturing a certain mood but is of limited value in tracking the actual incidence of federal crimes. For example, the 2020 survey reports that 56 percent of its respondents experienced "fraud" in the

---

[16] An additional challenge arises in the fact that the offender's state of mind may not be observable to most victims or enforcers. Accordingly, many frauds may go unpunished simply because outsiders are unable to distinguish the negligent loss from the scheme to defraud. "[F]or white collar crime, measurement is an any event elusive, because the definitions of bad action and mental state are always more amorphous and contested than anything that could be captured in a Uniform Crime Index." David Mills & Robert Weisberg, *Corrupting the Harm Requirement in White Collar Crime*, 60 STAN. L. REV. 1371, 1376 (2008).

[17] One could also learn quite a bit from corporate compliance officers and organizations, who are responsible for monitoring and detecting wrongdoing within the workplace. Compliance measurement is itself an emerging field, however, and it remains unclear how likely it is that companies will widely share such information in the absence of legal requirements to do so. *See generally* MEASURING COMPLIANCE: ASSESSING CORPORATE CRIME AND MISCONDUCT PREVENTION (Melissa L. Rorie and Benjamin van Rooij, eds., 2022) (providing extensive overview of measurement issues).

[18] Eugene Soltes, *The Frequency of Corporate Misconduct: Public Enforcement versus Private Reality*, 26 J. FIN. CRIME 923 (2019) (examining internal hotlines for three corporations). Dorothy S. Lund & Natasha Sarin, *Corporate Crime and Punishment: An Empirical Study*, 100 TEX. L. REV. 285 (2021) (using Suspicious Activity Reports, CFPB (Consumer Financial Protection Bureau) consumer complaints, and SEC whistleblower complaint volume as proxies for incidence of white-collar crime).

[19] DONALD REBOVICH ET AL., NAT'L WHITE COLLAR CRIME CTR., THE NATIONAL PUBLIC SURVEY ON WHITE-COLLAR CRIME (2000), www.ojp.gov/pdffiles1/Digitization/181968NCJRS.pdf.

[20] Stuart Green & Matthew Kugler, *When Is It Wrong to Trade Stocks on the Basis of Non-public Information? Public Views of the Morality of Insider Trading*, 39 FORDHAM URB. L.J. 445 (2011).

[21] *PwC's Global Economic Crime and Fraud Survey 2020*, PwC, www.pwc.com/us/en/services/consulting/cybersecurity-risk-regulatory/library/global-economic-fraud-survey-2020.html.

past twenty-four months.[22] The same report goes on to say that the top five types of fraud included "(1) Customer Fraud, (2) Cybercrime, (3) Accounting Fraud, (4) Asset Misappropriation, and (5) Bribery."[23] Notice the breadth of these categories; a term like "customer fraud" could encompass anything from a dangerous act of deception to a relatively modest ethical lapse. Since the surveys are self-reported by nonexperts, it is difficult to know how accurately they reflect actual violations of federal laws.

In addition to mixing high-level misconduct with mid- and low-level petty crime, the workplace surveys underscore the difficulty of disentangling *offense*-based definitions of white-collar crime from *offender*-based conceptions. For years, criminal law's commentators have debated these opposing approaches. Some criminologists still promote the views of Edwin Sutherland, the sociologist who first coined the "white-collar" phrase in a late 1939 speech to the American Sociological Association. Sutherland's aim was to convince his audience that wealthy people of "high social status" could just as easily commit crimes as their poorer, less fortunate counterparts, and that their corporate positions enabled them to promote harmful and illicit schemes, unhampered by serious consequences. Sutherland's definition thus encompassed a category of behavior broader and quite different from the paradigmatic wrongdoing that federal prosecutors and investigators currently associate with the term. A corporate executive's overreach likely fell within Sutherland's definition, regardless of whether it met a criminal statute's technical definition. A con artist's pyramid scheme, however, likely fell outside Sutherland's definition. Even if the scheme involved deceit and money, it did not raise the same class and power issues.[24]

Thus, in defining and setting white-collar crime's boundaries, Sutherland was not merely *describing* a type of behavior. He was arguing for a new approach to that behavior, such as expanding criminal and regulatory penalties for a certain category of *people*, namely those who enjoyed the benefits of high social status and economic power.

Sutherland divided white-collar crime into two basic categories: misappropriation (akin to fraud or "swindles") and the "double cross" (i.e., self-dealing).[25] Today, numerous statutes prohibit and punish conduct that Sutherland would have likely dubbed misappropriation.[26] By contrast, much of the double cross category (or "self-dealing") still eludes criminal law's reach. The strongest success story in this group is

---

[22] *Id.* at 2.

[23] *Id.*

[24] Some refer to these as "contrepreneurial" crimes. *See* Scott Menard et al., *Distribution and Correlates of Self-Reported Crimes of Trust*, 32 DEVIANT BEHAV. 877, 883 (2011).

[25] For a helpful summary of Sutherland's work, see Aleksandra Jordanoska & Isabel Schultz, *The Discovery of White-Collar Crime: The Legacy of Edwin Sutherland*, in THE HANDBOOK OF WHITE-COLLAR CRIME.

[26] *See* discussion generally in Chapters 3 and 7.

the crime of insider trading, which prohibits and punishes trading in securities when the trade is premised on violations of duties to either the corporation or to the information's source. Beyond this offense, examples of true double cross crimes are difficult to find, now that the Supreme Court has cabined "honest services fraud" to the giving or acceptance of bribery or kickbacks.[27] To be sure, a number of statutes punish *public* officials for favoring themselves over the public, but these anti-bribery statutes do so under a very narrow set of circumstances. Moreover, over the past three decades, courts have increasingly *narrowed* the statutes that purport to punish self-dealing.[28] That isn't to say society deems double cross behavior laudable. Nevertheless, experience in this area has shown us to be far less willing to criminalize self-dealing than others types of deception. Accordingly, a lot of behavior many of us deem venal, self-serving, or "corrupt" falls outside fraud law's ambit, and perhaps outside the federal criminal code altogether.

Meanwhile, institutional actors and practitioners – the prosecutors, agency regulators, and judges – perceive and employ the white-collar crime term as a shorthand for a collection of prohibited activities defined by statutes.[29] The most expansive version of this approach has been provided by the BJS, which defines white-collar crime as: "any violation of law committed through non-violent means, involving lies, omissions, deceit, misrepresentation, or violation of a position of trust, by an individual or organization for personal or organizational benefit."[30]

The FBI's definition is more reader-friendly, but it regrettably implies that white-collar crime is merely an umbrella term for fraud:

> [White-collar crime is] synonymous with the full range of frauds committed by business and government professionals. These crimes are characterized by deceit, concealment, or violation of trust and are not dependent on the application or threat of physical force or violence. The motivation behind these crimes is financial – to obtain or avoid losing money, property, or services or to secure a personal or business advantage.[31]

---

[27] Skilling v. United States, 561 U.S. 358 (2010). By defining the "honest services fraud" statute so narrowly, *Skilling* more or less put to bed Justice Scalia's previously voiced concern that the federal code had enabled the judiciary to develop a "common law crime of unethical conduct" that broadly punished self-dealing. *See* Sorich v. United States, 555 U.S. 1204, 1207 (2009) (Scalia, J. dissenting from denial of certiorari).

[28] *See* Aziz Z. Huq & Genevieve Lakier, *Apparent Fault*, 131 Harv. L. Rev. 1525, 1527–28 (2018).

[29] Because my own interest lies in exposing pathologies of enforcement and lawmaking, much of this book follows the offense-based approach.

[30] *White Collar Crime*, Bureau Just. Stat., www.bjs.gov/index.cfm/content/content/dcrp/tables/index.cfm?ty=tp&tid=33.

[31] *White Collar Crime*, Fed. Bureau Investigation, www.fbi.gov/investigate/white-collar-crime.

To my mind, the BJS definition is still valuable in that it comes closest to capturing the behaviors that render white-collar crime so difficult to prevent and detect.[32] As Susan Shapiro observed more than three decades ago, white-collar crimes are violations characterized by their *deceit* and violations of *trust*.[33] They can be undertaken by persons *or* organizations, and they can also harm persons *or* organizations *or* institutions, including the government itself. They are problematic precisely because they *do not* always tie neatly to status or class; people of all walks of life possess the skill, opportunity, and willingness to leverage their relative positions of trust and power to take advantage of others.[34] These are the behaviors, writ large, that threaten our economic and social security, our markets, our ability to engage in reliable business transactions, and our ability to work and thrive.[35]

Once we agree on a working definition, albeit an imperfect one (perhaps the BJS definition, but widened to include crimes other than fraud), we can get to work identifying white-collar crime's subcategories. For example, we might want to track *corporate crime*, which "is typically understood to involve illegal behavior by firms and their agents (executives and managers) in the pursuit of corporate benefit."[36] We might also want to distinguish crimes of deceit that occur within one's occupation, *occupational crime*, and crimes that occur outside one's occupation. We also might want to make clear that we are concerned mostly with federal crimes, and with crimes that – in the aggregate or individually – leave some mark on markets or government systems. I leave the fine details of these boundaries and distinctions for a different day. As the rest of this chapter demonstrates, we are nowhere near an optimal collection of data *even* for the major federal crimes that most agree are white-collar offenses, namely fraud, bribery, and obstruction of justice.

---

[32] The BJS definition mirrors the definition Hebert Edelhertz provided in his landmark 1970 report on white-collar crime for the (then) National Institute of Law Enforcement and Criminal Justice (now named the National Institute of Justice, an agency housed within the DOJ). Edelhertz, a former chief of the DOJ Criminal Division's Fraud Section, defined white-collar crime as, "an illegal act or series of illegal acts committed by nonphysical means and by concealment or guile to obtain money or property, to avoid payment or loss of money or property, or to obtain business or personal advantage." HERBERT EDELHERTZ, THE NATURE, IMPACT AND PROSECUTION WHITE-COLLAR CRIME 3 (1970), www.ojp.gov/pdffiles1/Digitization/4415NCJRS.pdf.

[33] Susan P. Shapiro, *Collaring the Crime, Not the Criminal: Reconsidering the Concept of White-Collar Crime*, 55 AM. SOCIO. REV. 346 (1990). For an attempt to unify these crimes under a moral theory, see STUART P. GREEN, LYING, CHEATING, AND STEALING: A MORAL THEORY OF WHITE-COLLAR CRIME (2007).

[34] Michael L. Benson et al., *Race, Ethnicity, and Social Change: The Democratization of Middle-Class Crime*, 59 CRIMINOLOGY 10, 10 (2020) (observing that "[s]ince the mid-1970's, the percentage of non-White people convicted of white-collar type crimes in the federal judicial system has been growing steadily").

[35] For the sake of this discussion, I limit this definition to federal crimes.

[36] Sally S. Simpson et al., *An Empirical Assessment of Corporate Environmental Crime-Control Strategies*, 103 J. CRIM. L. & CRIMINOLOGY 231, 232 (2013). *See also* Samuel W. Buell, CAPITAL OFFENSES: BUSINESS CRIME AND PUNISHMENT IN AMERICA'S CORPORATE AGE (2016) (focusing primarily on the phenomenon of corporate crime and its enforcement).

2.2 WHAT WE WOULD *LIKE* TO KNOW

Imagine you were an omnipotent figure in charge of planning policy for white-collar crime's enforcement and that you had adopted an "offense-based" definition of the term, and that this term had garnered the support of law enforcement organizations and multiple researchers (i.e., a nonviolent crime of lies, deceit, abuses of trust, or misappropriation). Imagine as well that you had the powers to allocate resources wherever you thought most needed, to create or revise written laws, or to increase or decrease sanctions, or both. Assuming you were principled and inspired by a good faith interest in reducing white-collar crime, which data would you most want to collect as a precursor to making your policy decisions?

Presumably, you would want to know how frequently white-collar crimes take place, as well as their absolute number. You would want to know the comparative frequencies of white-collar offenses as well (i.e., which ones were increasing and which ones appeared to be waning), and you would want to know if particular types of white-collar crimes attracted certain offenders or were targeted at certain victims.

Once you learned more about the incidence of white-collar crime, you would also want to get some sense of its absolute and comparative cost. Many drivers violate the traffic laws by speeding or failing to signal before changing lanes. The costs of those behaviors justify some intervention (fines or perhaps a patrol car parked on a highway), but they do not justify massively expensive or extreme interventions (pulling over every driver who drives even a mile above the speed limit or fails to signal on a sparsely populated road). Comparative and absolute costs give us an idea of how much we should spend on white-collar enforcement and how we should allocate scarce resources.

Tracking Incidence

Alas, much of this information is unknown to our legislators and executive branch, the individuals who make white-collar policy. As noted earlier, the actual *incidence* of white-collar crime is a figure we will never quite grasp. Deceptive behaviors are, after all, difficult to detect *by design*: "[B]ecause white-collar crimes are based on conspiracy, fraud, and deceit, they may go undetected, even by their victims, for long periods of time."[37] We can use various proxies to come up with an approximation of how bad "lying, cheating, and stealing" have become, but we will never arrive at a specific, accurate figure. Moreover, as Chapter 6 discusses in greater detail, the proxies themselves may become the subject of misunderstanding and abuse.

Tracking Cost

By the same token, estimating the *cost* of white-collar crime is a fraught exercise, which I return to as well in Chapter 6. There is no real disagreement that white-

---

[37] Benson et al., *supra* note 7, at 93.

collar crime's annual costs figures in the billions (well, hundreds of billions) of dollars, but the methodologies used to reach and verify those figures are themselves a source of great disagreement.[38] Although "cost," like incidence, ought to play some role in determining white-collar crime's enforcement, the term has become too politicized to meaningfully contribute to enforcement policy. Suffice it to say, white-collar crime costs our society quite a bit of money, year in and year out, but we are unlikely to come up with a figure that is either objective or draws consensus.

Tracking Enforcement

Even if we agree that it is too difficult to reliably track either the incidence of white-collar crime or its corresponding costs, it ought to be easier to track white-collar crime's enforcement, particularly if we limit our oversight to federal enforcement, since the federal system, despite its fragmentation, is still tiny compared to the rest of the enforcement universe.[39] As several prominent criminologists argue:

> Offense-based definitions are relatively easy to operationalize. To do so, researchers need only identify offenses that meet the criteria of being nonphysical property offenses committed by means of deceit or guile, then gather information on offenses of this kind that have come to the attention of authorities.[40]

As this excerpt suggests, data collection might be the activity that breaks white-collar crime's stalemate between offense- and offender-based definitions. Since our systems are designed to track the country's offenses, it makes most sense to embrace an offense-based definition, at least insofar as data collection is concerned.[41]

But the premise of "easy" data collection – even for specific offenses – diverges sharply with experience. As we learn from the remainder of this chapter, the collection of white-collar crime data is, and often has been, balkanized, inconsistent, and sometimes surprisingly spotty.[42]

Start with investigations. To judge government enforcement efforts, one would want to know how many investigations the government opened in a given year for fraud and bribery at a minimum, as well as analogous offenses such as tax evasion, serious regulatory offenses, and certain types of obstruction and

---

[38] For an excellent exploration of white-collar crime's costs and the many ways in which costs are undercounted, see Mark A. Cohen, *The Costs of White-Collar Crime*, in The Oxford Handbook of White-Collar Crime 78 (Shanna R. van Slyke et al., eds., 2016).

[39] "[F]ederal prosecutors have substantially fewer cases to prosecute than their local counterparts." Lauren Ouziel, *Legitimacy and Federal Criminal Enforcement Power*, 123 Yale L.J. 2236, 2267 (2014).

[40] Benson et al., *supra* note 7, at 94.

[41] Barnett, *supra* note 11, at 2–3.

[42] For a very helpful overview of the DOJ's data-collection weaknesses, see Jennifer Taub, Big Dirty Money: The Shocking Injustice and Unseen Cost of White Collar Crime (2020) chapter 2.

perjury.[43] We would want to tag all of those investigations with an indicator that they were in fact white-collar matters, and we would want all of our investigating agencies to adhere to the same rules regarding how they record an investigation and "code" it within a given database. It would be helpful as well to know how long these investigations lasted, how many investigative agents (and/or prosecutors) were assigned to them, whether they bore any fruit and how much fruit.

From there, we would want to know how many offenders were arrested, for which crimes, and in how many counts. And again, to the extent we tagged these arrests and offenses as white-collar crimes, we would want to make sure that all the prosecuting agencies involved used the same coding rules. We would also want to have some sense of a conviction rate (and how many of those were by trial verdict and how many by guilty plea), and we would want to know how many convicted offenders were sentenced to terms of imprisonment (and for how long). Further, reflecting the issues Sutherland raised decades ago when he first coined the phrase, we would want to know where along the socioeconomic spectrum the government's targets, arrestees, and convicted offenders all fell.[44]

Finally, because the government retains discretion to *not* enforce the law, an ideal world would also provide some meaningful insight on the number of instances in which the government declined to file any charges at all ("declinations"), as well as the number of cases that were dismissed on account of a defective legal theory or successful motion to suppress evidence.

Visually, one seeking data might conceptualize the relevant stages of investigation and prosecution as Figure 2.1.[45]

Figure 2.1 represents the ideal. Real-world white-collar data collection, however, meets these metrics incompletely and inconsistently. In the sections that follow, I explore this point by examining this unwieldy system's component parts.

Investigations

Federal agencies do not track investigations so much as they track discrete "incidents," which is the term used by NIBRS and its various marketing materials. Multiple federal enforcement agencies enjoy overlapping authority for investigating these incidents, which include violations of white-collar statutes.[46] Thus, a fraud

---

[43] Consistent with Susan Shapiro's "abuses of trust" analysis, see *supra* note 33, numerous legal scholars place fraud under the same umbrella as bribery, perjury, obstruction, and tax evasion. *See, e.g.*, Stuart P. Green & Matthew Kugler, *Public Perceptions of White-Collar Crime Culpability: Bribery, Perjury & Fraud*, 75 LAW & CONTEMP. PROBS. 33 (2012).

[44] For a useful comparison of sentencing outcomes depending on the white-collar definition one adopts, see Miranda A. Galvin, *Substance of Semantics? The Consequences of Definitional Ambiguity for White-Collar Research*, 57 J. RSCH. CRIME & DELINQ. 369 (2020).

[45] *See also* SIMPSON & YEAGER, *supra* note 7, at 63–66 (proposing a similar but more technically complicated map).

[46] Larkin, *supra* note 12, at 240.

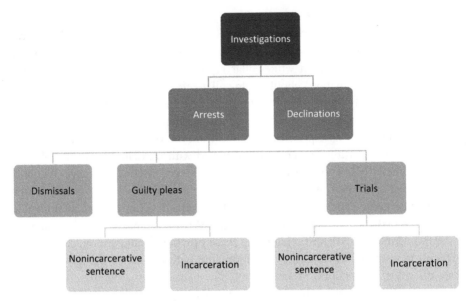

FIGURE 2.1. Idealized data collection for white-collar crime

investigation, depending on the nature of the offense and the identity of the victim, might be housed in the Department of Health and Human Services' Office of Inspector General, or in the FBI, or developed primarily by the SEC's Enforcement Division and referred to the DOJ.

It is unclear the exact moment when, or if, an investigation must be recorded in the government's tracking databases. To the extent an investigation stems from an incident of crime, the investigative agency *should* at some point file its information with the government's centralized reporting system, but that system was originally designed for state and local agencies to report the major index crimes – such as homicide, kidnapping, and rape.[47] Notice the discrete "incident" language makes much more sense in the context of violent index crimes. We can conceptualize a homicide as a single incident with an offender, victim, and completed offense. In comparison, when we consider an ongoing, often hidden crime such as fraud and bribery, whose victims might be institutions instead of identifiable persons, the incident language feels artificial and misplaced.[48]

---

[47] For a historical overview of the system created in 1930 (the UCR) and its migration to the newly created NIBRS system, see FED. BUREAU INVESTIGATION, EFFECTS OF NIBRS ON CRIME STATISTICS (2015), https://ucr.fbi.gov/nibrs/2014/resource-pages/effects_of_nibrs_on_crime_statistics_final.pdf.

[48] For criticism of the UCR and its application to white-collar crime, see BARNETT, *supra* note 11, at 6; Zachary Bookman, *Convergences and Omissions in Reporting White-Collar Crime*, 6 DEPAUL BUS. & COM. L.J. 347, 348–49 (2008).

To upgrade its reporting systems, the government has designed and required agencies to migrate their reporting to NIBRS. Although NIBRS is in many ways an improvement over the previous Uniform Crime Reporting program (UCR), it still features shortcomings in white-collar reporting. It contains more fields (and therefore more information) about white-collar offenses and offenders, but it also employs functional categories and definitions that are confusing. Sometimes, the categories are synonymous with specific federal offenses (e.g., "wire fraud") and sometimes not (e.g., "false pretenses"). Thus, from the very beginning of an investigation, federal reporting agencies will be tasked with translating a federal offense into a specific NIBRS code, an activity likely to raise consistency issues over the long run. To even an expert, it will be far from obvious which behavior qualifies as a "confidence game" and not just wire fraud.[49] (Indeed, given our reliance on the Internet, social media, and digital banking, the two categories should frequently overlap.) Moreover, NIBRS's reliance on these functional categories makes it more difficult to employ NIBRS's data in conjunction with the rest of the government's data on arrest, convictions, or sentencing. The categories may be descriptive, but they are neither self-explanatory nor interoperative.

Because white-collar crime is the responsibility of multiple enforcement agencies, one would hope that they would all employ the same approach in translating the federal code's voluminous white-collar statutes into NIBRS-speak. That, however, does not appear to be the case.

Consider the "Data Declarations and Methodology" section of the FBI's 2018 *Crime in the United States Report* ("CIUS"), a yearly compilation of statistics regarding crimes committed across the United States, which includes a section solely devoted to federal crimes and arrests.[50] The federal section of the CIUS collects, from the FBI and several DOJ enforcement agencies, the lists of federal arrests an agency has made in the prior year and a list of offenses it has classified under various NIBRS codes.

A brief review of the federal CIUS demonstrates both *inter-* and *intra-*component disparities in how agencies translate offenses into NIBRS's language. Let's start with the FBI, which enjoys the broadest enforcement jurisdiction of the federal agencies. The CIUS's list of offenses that the FBI apparently treats as fraud is quite extensive; indeed, it is so extensive that it includes offenses that most would agree are *not*

---

[49] The "offense lookup table" located in the FBI's NIBRS User Manual does not employ federal statutory section numbers and instead speaks of offenses in layperson's language. *See* FED. BUREAU INVESTIGATION, CRIM. JUST. INFO. SERV. DIV., 2021 NATIONAL INCIDENT-BASED REPORTING SYSTEM USER MANUAL, 2.5 Offense Lookup Table (2021), www.fbi .gov/file-repository/ucr/ucr-2019-1-nibrs-user-manua-093020.pdf. The FBI has published *other* materials (see *infra* at notes 50–52) that explicitly cite the federal code's offense sections.

[50] FED. BUREAU INVESTIGATION, CRIME IN THE UNITED STATES (2018), https://ucr.fbi.gov/ crime-in-the-u.s/2018/crime-in-the-u.s.-2018/additional-data-collections/federal-crime-data/fed eral-crime-data.pdf.

white-collar crime. At the same time, it excludes statutes that could easily be bound up in a white-collar investigation.

For example, according to the 2018 CIUS, the FBI classifies marriage fraud as a fraud under NIBRS, even though marriage fraud functions quite differently from commercial and occupational frauds. At the same time, the all-purpose conspiracy statute, 18 USC 371, seems to be missing from the CIUS's list of crimes that fall under NIBRS's fraud codes, as is the all-purpose obstruction of justice statute, 18 USC 1503. Program fraud and embezzlement, the crime that punishes someone for misappropriating money or property from local and state programs that receive minimal federal funding (18 USC 666), is also absent from the 2018 NIBRS list. That might be because Section 666 *also* covers program bribery (which apparently is not treated as a category of NIBRS fraud), or it might be because an administrator assumed Section 666 *only* covers program bribery.

The confusion grows once one considers other agencies. According to the same 2018 CIUS report, the DOJ's Office of the Inspector General (whose jurisdiction is admittedly very narrow) apparently *does* report violations of 18 USC 666 as an incidence of NIBRS fraud, but it classifies its false statements case filed under 18 USC 1001 as an "other" offense under NIBRS's coding system, and not a fraud.[51] One can find additional dissimilarities like these if one spends enough time plowing through several years of CIUS reports.[52]

Now, it may be the case that if we had all the case files in front of us, and the administrators who input these cases, the factual context would explain away the disparities. Perhaps in 2018, there really were no fraud arrests promulgated by the FBI under any of these statutes (at least as a primary offence). But one should be skeptical of any explanation that relies heavily on factual context. It is difficult to believe the false statements offense the FBI classified as a fraud looks all that different from the false statements offense the DOJ's Office of the Inspector General labeled an "other" case. It is additionally strange that the 2018 CIUS report codes an honest services fraud case as fraud, but does not do the same for charges brought under 18 USC 666. And it is positively head-scratching that the FBI's list of charged frauds includes no crimes charged under 18 USC 371 – especially when the DOJ's Office of the Inspector General's list includes such a designation.

As mentioned earlier, this is just a snapshot of the inconsistencies one sees when scrolling through the agencies' lists of offenses and NIBRS's classifications that are included in the FBI's CIUS report. The more agency classifications one reviews, the more classification disparities one encounters. One could blame the executive branch for this confusion, given the hundreds of millions of dollars that were

---

[51] *Id.* at 95–96.

[52] For the 2019 version, see FED. BUREAU INVESTIGATION, CRIME IN THE UNITED STATES (2019), https://ucr.fbi.gov/crime-in-the-u.s/2019/crime-in-the-u.s.-2019/additional-data-collections/federal-crime-data/federal-crime-data.pdf.

allocated to the creation of and migration to NIBRS.[53] But that seems unfair, as the inconsistencies just as easily highlight a different problem: our disorganized federal criminal code.[54] As Chapters 7 and 8 argue, we live in a world in which we have too many statutes, too many statutes that bundle disparate offenses, and too many statutes whose labels imply one set of behaviors quite different from the core behaviors the statute has become synonymous with punishing.[55] Given these inputs, it would be surprising if the coding system *weren't* plagued by disparities and questionable coding choices.

Legal scholars have long argued that a poorly written code undermines criminal justice.[56] Criminologists have powerfully documented weaknesses in the government's data-collection systems. If the previous analysis demonstrates anything, it is that the two problems intersect. A bad code doesn't just fuel bad *cases*; it also fuels the creation of bad data.

Arrests and "Matters"

If one felt NIBRS's incident-based reporting were too unreliable to support research in white-collar crime, one could instead focus on the matters that have been opened by federal prosecutors and their offices. When the United States Attorneys' Office sees fit to open a matter referred to it by an agency, it enters the case in its LIONS (Legal Information Office Network System) reporting system. This system contains arrest, dismissal, conviction, and declination information. To that end, it is the closest thing we have to a case-tracking system for federal white-collar cases. Unfortunately, here again, we encounter translation and classification problems.

First, as David Kwok observes, the manual that directs administrative staff in filling out LIONS is itself obtuse:

> Selection of the lead charge is also at the discretion of DOJ; its purpose is to indicate "the substantive statute that is the primary basis for the referral using the U.S. code." The lead charge may be updated after initial case filing; it is not necessarily the charge in the first count, nor it is necessarily the charge with the greatest potential sentence.[57]

---

[53] *See, e.g.,* FY 2019 NCS-X *Implementation Assistance Program: Support for Local Law Enforcement Agencies,* BUREAU JUST. STAT, https://bjs.ojp.gov/funding/opportunities/bjs-2019-15103.

[54] For the classic evisceration, see Julie R. O'Sullivan, *The Federal Criminal "Code" Is a Disgrace: Obstruction Statutes as Case Study,* 96 J. CRIM. L. & CRIMINOLOGY 643 (2006).

[55] *See* discussion *infra* at Chapters 7 and 8.

[56] Paul H. Robinson & Michael T. Cahill, *The Accelerating Degradation of American Criminal Codes,* 56 HASTINGS L.J. 633 (2005).

[57] David Kwok, *Trends in Prosecution of Federal and State Public Corruption,* 2 STETSON BUS. L. REV. 30, 51 (2022), at 21, citing Case Management Staff, Executive Office for United States Attorneys, Legal Information Office Network System User's Manual, Release 5.4.2,

Notice several problems: LIONS requires the prosecuting office to report the "lead" charge, which is the "primary basis" for the referral, but which may change over time. If an office feels pressure to prosecute a particular type of crime, it is possible that it might designate that crime as the primary basis of a referral, notwithstanding the importance of an underlying white-collar matter. Moreover, although a LIONS case report *can* be updated, there is no guarantee it *will* be updated, which presents a problem for complex crimes whose statutory focus may evolve over the course of an investigation.

Now let's move on to the question of arrests. Here, the information starts to become more accessible and, frankly, more reliable. The United States Attorneys' Annual Statistical Report (or "ASR") aggregates data on all arrests and cases charged annually by the ninety-plus United States Attorneys' Offices, which carve up the United States and its territories by location.[58] However, the ASR takes its information from LIONS. Accordingly, if LIONS undercounts certain crimes, then the ASR, by definition, is undercounting those crimes.

Moreover, the ASR itself provides a frustratingly incomplete snapshot of arrests, convictions, and declinations in federal jurisdictions. On the one hand, it *does* contain detailed tables of:

- *General data, broken out by prosecutors's offices.* All federal cases that have been "filed," are "pending," and "terminated" within a given year, broken out by each United States Attorney's Office.
- *General data, broken out by disposition and prosecutors's offices.* For all cases terminated in a given year, whether the cases were resolved by conviction, dismissal, a verdict of not guilty, or something else. This too, is correlated to each United States Attorney's Office.
- *Category-specific data.* In tables 3A and 3B, one finds aggregate information divided by criminal category. *This* information, however, does not pair up with the location-specific data featured in earlier tables. If you want to know how many bank fraud cases were prosecuted across *all* of the United States Attorney's Offices, you can find a row on tables 3A and 3B. If you would like to know how many of those cases were prosecuted in prosecutors' offices in New York or Louisiana, you need to find something else.[59]

The category-specific data also includes, but does not separate, offenses relevant to the study of white-collar crime. For example, it includes a bundled section on

---

sections 5–10 page 126, www.justice.gov/usao/file/835096/download (for LIONS reporting instructions).

[58] *Annual Statistical Reports*, OFF. U.S. ATT'YS. For the FY 2019 report, see www.justice.gov/usao/page/file/1285951/download.

[59] In addition to the ASR, the DOJ also releases its national caseload data on a monthly and annual basis. These releases form the basis of the ASR, which is far easier to read in a short period of time.

Program Category	Cases		Defendants		Disposition				
	Filed	Terminated	Filed	Terminated	Guilty	Not Guilty	Dismissed	Rule 20	Other
Table 3B (Continued)									
Organized Crime	213	160	592	567	497	5	53	0	12
Terrorism/National Security Critical Infrastructure	225	161	287	230	181	1	38	4	6
Theft									
Checks/Postal	580	570	689	792	733	1	54	1	3
Motor Vehicle Theft	64	49	103	92	84	1	5	0	2
Theft of Government Property	284	277	325	328	301	1	21	2	3
Violent Crime									
Violent Crime in Indian Country	862	875	930	952	862	13	76	0	1
Other Violent Crime	17,476	14,886	21,616	18,413	17,014	103	1,108	60	128
Non-Violent Crime in Indian Country	252	251	330	334	296	4	32	0	2
White Collar Crime									
Advance Fee Schemes	48	65	70	79	72	0	6	0	1
Fraud Against Business Institutions	275	279	432	416	392	1	18	2	3
Antitrust Violations	21	32	29	41	33	3	2	3	0
Bank Fraud and Embezzlement	561	495	802	771	690	2	73	2	4
Bankruptcy Fraud	63	40	93	50	41	0	8	1	0
Commodities Fraud	19	7	33	13	12	1	0	0	0
Computer Fraud	265	168	528	240	215	0	17	5	3
Consumer Fraud	131	111	200	170	157	0	10	2	1
Corporate Fraud	75	63	97	88	80	3	4	1	0
Federal Procurement Fraud	56	44	94	67	53	1	11	0	2
Federal Program Fraud	518	525	628	618	559	6	48	1	4
Health Care Fraud	532	404	878	646	568	9	67	2	0
Insurance Fraud	28	27	37	48	42	0	6	0	0
Other Investment Fraud	87	103	112	131	108	3	19	1	0
Securities Fraud	130	94	197	154	139	1	13	0	1
Tax Fraud	600	512	619	640	586	3	44	5	2
Intellectual Property Violations	29	31	75	41	37	1	1	0	2
Identity Theft	404	345	583	503	471	0	24	7	1
Aggravated Identity Theft	549	563	857	873	815	2	52	4	0
Mortgage Fraud	31	39	47	88	74	1	12	1	0
Other Fraud	1,120	975	1,560	1,448	1,319	9	96	17	7
All Other	2,834	2,636	3,838	3,701	3,340	16	264	33	48

CASEVIEW CAN CAPTURE MORE THAN ONE PROGRAM AREA IN A SINGLE CASE THROUGH THE USE OF MULTIPLE PROGRAM CATEGORY CODES. MULTIPLE CODING RESULTS IN A MORE ACCURATE DEPICTION OF THE NATURE AND COMPLEXITY OF OUR CRIMINAL CASES AND ENABLES THE EXECUTIVE OFFICE FOR UNITED STATES ATTORNEYS (EOUSA) TO IDENTIFY ALL CASES THAT INVOLVE A PARTICULAR SUBJECT MATTER, REGARDLESS OF WHETHER IT IS ENTERED AS A PRIMARY OR SUBSEQUENT CODE. AN ALL OCCURRENCE REPORT SHOWS HOW OFTEN CERTAIN PROGRAM CATEGORY CODES ARE ENTERED WHETHER THEY ARE PRIMARY OR TERTIARY. DATA ON THIS TABLE DOES NOT INCLUDE MAGISTRATE PROCEEDINGS.

FIGURE 2.2. Screenshot of the ASR: White-collar crime offenses[60]

government regulatory offenses, labor management offenses, and official corruption. All of these sections include crimes that could be classified as white- collar crimes, but they also include offenses that likely fall outside the definition.

Finally, the ASR features an additional section labeled "white-collar crime." This final section, however, is in fact a compilation of *fraud* offenses and a single row pertaining to antitrust violations. A screenshot of page 14 of the FY 2019 ASR can be seen in Figure 2.2.

In other word, as Figure 2.2 demonstrates, the ASR's white-collar crime category is, at bottom, no more than a compilation of fraud statutes. If this is the data that commentators have in mind when they decry the severe drop in white-collar prosecutions, then our concerns about white-collar underenforcement may be misplaced; the real problem lies with federal *fraud's* possible underenforcement. The latter is, to be clear, deserving of our attention. But, it is far different from the former, which is the claim that dominates the media accounts discussed in Chapter 6.

2.3 ADDITIONAL SOURCES OF INFORMATION

Aside from the United States Attorneys' Offices, additional prosecutors independently develop and prosecute cases within "Main Justice," as the DOJ's centralized

---

[60] *See supra* note 58, at 14.

unit is often called. One of Main Justice's groups is the Fraud Section, whose mission includes the prosecution of complex white-collar crimes. The Fraud Section compiles its *own* year-in-review document that includes charging and conviction statistics.[61] But if you were hoping to mesh this report with the ASR, you are out of luck. The Fraud Section's report does not contain the same categorical information as the ASR. Instead, the Fraud Section's compilation reports summary information for each of its three units. Thus, we again encounter as interoperability problem, where it becomes impossible to cross-check one source of information with another.

2.4 SENTENCING DATA

The United States Sentencing Commission aggregates information from the district courts regarding the sentencing guideline under which a criminal defendant was sentenced and compiles this information in its annual *Sourcebooks of Federal Sentencing Statistics*.[62] The commission also releases periodic reports on data gathered under specific guidelines.

Although the commission's information is helpful and perhaps the most usable of all the data sources described in this chapter, it adds another layer of complexity to the study of white-collar crime.[63] Whereas the rest of the government's data are keyed either to an activity ("advance fee schemes") or to a specific statute ("18 USC 1341"), the commission's sentencing data are tagged to the primary guideline under which a given defendant was sentenced.

Moreover, because the fraud and bribery guidelines both hinge on several "specific offense characteristics," the data the Sentencing Commission collects is very much tied to those offense levels. For example, it is relatively easy to track the number and percentage of fraud convictions by the amount of money involved. But even here, the data are somewhat misleading. The fraud guideline's loss amount information pertains to *intended* loss amounts. Accordingly, if I attempt to defraud you of some fantastical amount of money (say, $20,000,000), but there is little likelihood I could ever pull off the scheme, the case may still be coded as one involving $20,000,000. The judge, recognizing the implausibility of the scheme, might sentence me to a lesser sentence, but the "loss amount" may still be coded at that amount.

Thus, even the Sentencing Commission's reports – which are arguably more accurate than arrest data – paint a misleading portrait of white-collar enforcement.

---

[61] DEPT. JUST., FRAUD SECTION: YEAR IN REVIEW 2019 (2019), www.justice.gov/criminal-fraud/file/1245236/download.

[62] U.S. SENT. COMM'N, 2021 ANNUAL REPORT AND SOURCEBOOK OF FEDERAL SENTENCING STATISTICS (2021), www.ussc.gov/research/sourcebook-2021.

[63] Bookman, *supra* note 48, at 349 (raising similar issues with the USSG's sentencing data and pointing out that it does not extend back past 1995).

Perhaps the DOJ has benefitted from a system that equates "actual" loss with "intended loss" insofar as prosecutors prefer leverage in plea bargaining and easier sentencing hearings. The conventional complaint with the intended loss approach is that it overpunishes implausible and nascent frauds.[64] But as the foregoing discussion demonstrates, it also undermines data collection.

To repeat: defective sentencing and statutory regimes do more than create bad punishment outcomes. They also contribute to bad information systems, which in turn makes it even more difficult to see where our legal systems are failing in the first place.

2.5 UNENFORCED OR HIDDEN?

If we wanted to summarize visually the systems this chapter has discussed, we might devise Figure 2.3.

In terms of reliability and usability, the sentencing data maintained by the BJS is probably the best repository we have. The systems maintained by LIONS and NIBRS, by comparison, are more prone to coding and translation errors that undermine our ability to reliably track and understand white-collar crime's enforcement, particularly if some reports (e.g., the ASR) equate white-collar crime with a narrow category of fraud statutes and nothing more. That is, incidentally, why I have not spent much time in this chapter discussing reports released by the Transactional Records Access Clearinghouse (TRAC) at Syracuse University, a nonprofit organization that has taken on the Herculean task of obtaining and analyzing the government's enforcement information and releasing summary reports of interest to the public.[65]

In recent years, TRAC has released several reports that are critical of a sharp drop in white-collar crime arrests and prosecutions.[66] Their use of the "white-collar" term is consonant with the ASR's narrow usage – i.e., "white-collar" equals "fraud" – depicted in the screenshot in Figure 2.2. Multiple scholars have premised their policy reform and theoretical work on TRAC's reports.[67]

---

[64] For a representative example, see United States v. Corsey, 723 F.3d 366, 377 (2d Cir. 2013) (Underhill, J., concurring) (arguing that the guidelines' analysis premised on intended loss amount is "valueless" because the fraud scheme at issue was "more farcical than dangerous").

[65] Others have recognized the shortcomings in TRAC's data. "TRAC data relies upon the United States Attorneys' offices to properly code cases." Kwok, *supra* note 57, at 20. "[TRAC] does useful and creative work, but is still relegated to using DOJ data." Bookman, *supra* note 48, at 349.

[66] *Corporate and White-Collar Prosecutions at All-Time Lows* , TRAC REPORTS (Mar. 3, 2020), https://trac.syr.edu/tracreports/crim/597/; *White Collar Prosecutions Fall to Lowest in 20 Years*, TRAC REPORTS (May 24, 2018), https://trac.syr.edu/tracreports/crim/514/; Stewart Bishop, *White Collar Cases Continue Long-Term Slump, Report Says*, LAW 360 (Aug. 9, 2021), www .law360.com/articles/1411151/white-collar-cases-continue-long-term-slump-report-says.

[67] *See, e.g.*, Kwok, *supra* note 57 (using, but still warning of shortcomings in TRAC data); Trung Nguyen, *The Effectiveness of White-Collar Crime Enforcement: Evidence from the War on Terror*, 59 J. ACCT. RSCH. 5 (2021) (using TRAC research to show correlation between drop in

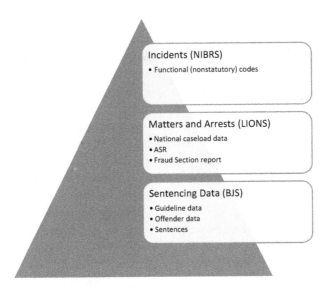

FIGURE 2.3. Our world in white-collar data

I concur in TRAC's general claim (and therefore share the emergent concern) that *fraud* cases have fallen as a percentage of the federal government's docket.[68] Whereas they once took up approximately 15 percent of the federal sentencing docket, they register more in the range of 10 percent today. But a drop in *fraud* prosecutions isn't necessarily the same thing as a drop in *white-collar enforcement*. That's not to say I believe the entire drop in fraud prosecutions can be explained by a move to prosecute more time-consuming economic, political, or regulatory crimes, but I do think we need far more granular data before we equate fraud with white-collar crime for data-collection purposes. The story may still be a negative one, but it may be negative in a way that is different than we assume. And that matters a lot for how we approach questions of policy and reform.

2.6 THE MISGUIDED EMPHASIS ON CENTRALIZATION AND MODERNIZATION

I began this chapter with Secretary Donald Rumsfeld's famous statement about the differences between known unknowns, unknown unknowns, and known knowns. Many criticisms of white-collar crime's data systems unconsciously echo Rumsfeld's

---

"white-collar" crime's enforcement and increase in antiterrorism funding in the wake of the 9/11 terrorist attacks).

[68] One could reach the same conclusion by reading the annual Federal Justice Statistics reports, which also import data from LIONS and include a category for "fraudulent property" offenses. MARK MOTIVANS, FEDERAL JUSTICE STATISTICS 2020 2 (May 2020), https://bjs.ojp.gov/content/pub/pdf/fjs20.pdf.

matrix. Michael Benson, Jay Kennedy, and Matthew Logan argue, for instance, that white-collar crime "confront[s] four main challenges or issues," which include "(1) The problem of how to define these concepts; (2) the hidden nature of both white collar and corporate crime; (3) the lack of consistent, readily available, centralized data sources; and (4) the technical complexity of many of the offenses."[69] Many of these would easily fit the category of known knowns (technical complexity) or known unknowns (knowledge that white-collar and corporate crimes remain hidden).

Rumsfeld famously left out the fourth category of his imaginary matrix, unknown knowns, which are things one *thinks* one knows, but in fact does not really know at all. This problem of veiled ignorance aptly explains white-collar crime's data-collection issues. As Benson, Kennedy, and Logan demonstrate, we *know* we are missing some data, and we rightly *fear* we are missing additional information. But in focusing so intently on the unknowns, we fail to recognize the problems with the facts we already think we know. It is this failure to revisit our "knowns" – the criminal states upon which we rely to shape and generate data – that hampers policy improvements in this arena.

Surveying the Suggestions

For at least two decades, criminologists and legal scholars have called for the collection and dissemination of more and better data pertaining to the government's enforcement of white-collar crime.[70] Many of the most prevalent critiques call for a "centralization" and "modernization" of systems.

For example, Paul Larkin argues that we should streamline the number of federal agencies that investigate violations of the federal code. He isn't wrong about the fragmentation of enforcement power; more than thirty federal agencies enjoy the power and responsibility to "investigate crimes, execute search warrants, serve subpoenas, make arrests,"[71] and most importantly for this chapter's purposes, report information to the public and to other government agencies. The chances all thirty agencies will adopt uniform reporting practices for white-collar cases appear to be slim to none, and given the way NIBRS has been created and thus far used, no one should be surprised by that outcome.

Larkin's critique is aimed primarily at questions of enforcement; he contends that a reorganization of the federal enforcement arena would eliminate costly inefficiencies. He makes no mention of data collection, but his streamlined approach would almost certainly impact it.[72] It is arguably easier to create uniform reporting practices among four or five agencies than it is to compel that kind of compliance from

---

[69] Benson et al., *supra* note 7, at 107.
[70] *See, e.g.*, SIMPSON & YEAGER, *supra* note 6; BARNETT, *supra* note 11; Bookman, *supra* note 48; TAUB, *supra* note 42; Kwok, *supra* note 57.
[71] Larkin, *supra* note 12, at 239.
[72] *Id.* at 241.

twenty-nine or thirty. When we streamline enforcement, we arguably improve our data-collection efforts.

But the data-reporting issue runs deeper than simple lack of uniformity. The problem is also a lack of common language. The federal code employs one lexicon, the NIBRS system employs another, and the LIONS and Sentencing Commission's systems each employ something slightly different. As a result, administrators must engage in the difficult task of "translating" suspected and charged legal violations into "incidents" and "matters," and later, into sentencing categories. Streamlining the field of enforcement agencies from thirty to, say, five, isn't going to solve this translation problem.

Zachary Bookman, the CEO and founder of Opengov Inc., lays out a more complicated approach. In a 2008 article, he argues for the creation of a "white-collar index," a special section of the UCR (now NIBRS) that would aggregate data on "the already existing categories of fraud, forgery and counterfeiting, bribery, and embezzlement."[73] I like Bookman's proposal. The idea of a white-collar index provides the pathway for more informed policymaking, better allocations of resources, and a ready source of information to evaluate the claim that someone's prosecution represents an unusual use of resources. But there are again limits to how much this index can do. It *might* result in greater attention paid to how federal agencies fill out the NIBRS codes (which is good), but it might not, in which case the index will only be as good as the information that populates its fields. And of course, the creation of this index cannot solve the lack of interoperability between the NIBRS, LIONS, and BJS sentencing data systems.

For a proposal for an integrated system, one can take heart from the 2015 final report submitted to the DOJ, *Building a Comprehensive White-Collar Violations Data System*. In this thorough and sober report, criminologists Sally Simpson and Peter Yeager survey the weaknesses in the current system and then argue that the federal BJS would be best positioned to build and maintain an integrated, systematic database of white-collar crime data. The data system Simpson and Yeager have in mind seems immense; it purports to cover not only criminal violations but also regulatory and administrative transgressions, and it tracks matters from beginning to end. Moreover, it tracks offender information as well as characteristics of specific offenses: "From the federal agencies and departments that enforce laws against white-collar offenses, it would systematically and regularly collect enforcement case data on key factors: sources of identification of cases of offenses, characteristics of offenses and offenders, and case outcomes."[74]

To their credit, Simpson and Yeager bluntly recognize the hurdles to erecting such a system. From their own experience putting together the report, the criminologists acknowledge that information varies across agencies, and that some agencies

---

[73] Bookman, *supra* note 48, at 387.
[74] SIMPSON & YEAGER, *supra* note 6, at 3.

are reluctant to share data. They also agree that there would be difficulty in determining how broadly to define certain terms while preserving enough specificity to make the categories useful.[75] Simpson and Yeager further acknowledge that their project requires agencies to reach consensus on data fields and crime definitions, and to embed links that would allow for the tracking of investigations, matters, and cases.[76] But most of all, Simpson and Yeager's ambitious project would *cost money*.[77] No surprise, then, that the government appears not to have acted on their recommendations. If anything, an integrated data project is even *less* likely today than it was in 2015, as the BJS's annual budget has *declined* in recent years.[78]

Others have lodged additional modernization proposals, with little outward success. One can readily understand why. An expensive data-modernization project presents the classic problem of temporal inconsistency: the project's costs are concrete and register immediately, and the benefits are contingent, and likely to occur in future time periods.[79] Even if the discounted benefits outweigh the immediate costs, many policymakers will delay long-term renovations and instead convince themselves that the information the government already provides is more than good enough.[80] And let's be clear, even if we adopted the most state of the art, internally consistent data-collection system, a good portion of information would be lost to prosecutorial discretion and plea bargaining, both of which take place within a legally constructed black box.[81]

---

[75] *Id.* at 13.

[76] *Id.* at 14.

[77] *Id.* at 77, 90 (speculating that communications with federal agencies regarding a data-sharing project stalled when budgetary costs became an issue).

[78] Ted Gest, *Alarming Staff Shortages Linked to Delays in Fed Crime Data* (Mar. 16, 2020), https://thecrimereport.org/2020/03/16/alarming-decline-in-workforce-linked-to-delays-in-fed-crime-data-collection/; JANE WISEMAN, STATE OF THE NATION'S FEDERAL JUSTICE STATISTICS (2021), https://scholar.harvard.edu/files/janewiseman/files/state_of_the_nations_federal_cj_statistics_2021.pdf.

[79] Although rational individuals would assess "immediate costs or benefits more strongly than equivalent costs or benefits that arise in later periods," the hyperbolic discounter (e.g., person with an immediacy bias) "place[s] a much greater premium on the near-term." Miriam H. Baer, *Confronting the Two Faces of Corporate Fraud*, 66 FLA. L. REV. 87, 105 (2014). For an overview of literature, see Christine Jolls et al., *A Behavioral Approach to Law & Economics*, 50 STAN. L. REV. 1471, 1539–40 (1998); Ted O'Donoghue and Matthew Rabin, *Doing It Now or Later*, 89 AM. ECON. REV. 103, 106 n.7 (1999).

[80] On temporal inconsistency's implications for actors within the criminal justice system (e.g., prosecutors), see Miriam H. Baer, *Timing Brady*, 115 COLUM. L. REV. 1 (2015).

[81] "The initial decision to prosecute, determination of preliminary charges, charge reductions, and plea negotiations all precede final sentencing determinations and hold the potential to exert powerful influences on criminal punishments." *See* Lauren O'Neill Shermer & Brian D. Johnson, *Criminal Prosecutions: Examining Prosecutorial Discretion and Charge Reductions in U.S. Federal District Courts*, 27 JUST. Q 394, 295 (2010). *See also* Jenia I. Turner, *Transparency in Plea Bargaining*, 96 NOTRE DAME L. REV. 973 (2021) (examining lack of transparency within plea-bargaining process).

Perhaps this is why Jennifer Taub's proposal, although less technical, is the most eye-catching. Her book attempts to centralize the responsibility for white-collar reporting in the DOJ and advocates the creation of an "elite division" within Main Justice to prosecute high-level corporate crime.[82] If such a division existed, its data reporting would be simpler, since the enforcement effort would be singularly focused on a type of crime (complex frauds, bribery, and perhaps similar violations) and offender (corporations and high-level executives). As we have already seen, the shape and design of an enforcement institution indelibly alters its data collection. And yet, one cannot help but wonder if this newly created elite unit would simply release yet another report (much like the DOJ's Fraud Section) that used its own metrics and its own data and spoke to none of the other reports. Elite units sound good on paper, but they don't necessarily fix complex problems, and they cannot come close to addressing the data-collection issues that white-collar criminologists have patiently outlined for years.

Taking a Step Back

As of this writing, the DOJ is unlikely to undertake *any* of the discussed proposals. Although an agency's recalcitrance is rarely a cause for celebration, it might be in *this* case. The reason is that investing money in a massive modernization and integration system doesn't make much sense at this juncture. A data system is dependent on its inputs, and the inputs in this case are the federal code's white-collar statutes. That is where we should turn our attention, especially before we invest hundreds of millions of dollars in a data-collection upgrade.

Because our federal code fails to statutorily grade its white-collar crimes, it effectively increases the difficulty of tracking charged offenses (Chapter 3). Because our statutes are purposely "underwritten," and rely on prosecutors and the judiciary to define major terms, their open-endedness imposes additional downstream effects on our data-collection efforts (Chapter 4). And when we create broadly written "umbrella" statutes that house several offenses under the same statutory house, we all but ensure a breakdown in reliable tracking (Chapters 3, 7, and 8).

For all these reasons, my counterintuitive advice is that we should defer modernization efforts to a future day. Let's instead rewrite and revise the laws that purport to define fraud, bribery, obstruction, and the many other crimes that pertain to deception and abuses of trust. One cannot cure an enforcement system of its data deficiencies without first fixing its inputs. When we fix white-collar crime's statutes (as proposed in Chapters 7 and 8), then we can move on to addressing white-collar crime's data-collection problems.

---

[82] TAUB, *supra* note 42, at 218–19. Taub also calls for better data collection and centralized tracking of cases. *Id.* at 222.

3

Flat Laws

INTRODUCTION

In early August 2018, reporters breathlessly announced that Chris Collins, a Republican congressman representing the district that includes the city of Buffalo, had been indicted on several counts of insider trading.[1] From the face of the indictment, the charges appeared quite serious. Collins had given his son material nonpublic information that the senior Collins had acquired as a result of his position on a pharmaceutical company's board of directors. Collins had reportedly alerted his son and a third person, minutes after learning that one of the company's most promising drugs had failed an FDA trial. This information, in turn, enabled Collins's coconspirators to sell their stock in advance of a public announcement.[2]

Following the congressman's arrest, the government's press release described, in its usual straightforward way, the factual allegations described in the grand jury indictment, the legal charges that had been lodged against Collins and his coconspirators, and finally, the maximum sentence Collins and his coconspirators might face if convicted.[3] In regard to this last piece of information, the government helpfully summarized each of the charges in a table and then listed the maximum sentence Collins permitted by each of those charges. This table, which was released to the public and can still be found on the Department of Justice's (DOJ's) website, is reprinted in Figure 3.1.

---

[1]   *See, e.g.,* Alan Feuer & Shane Goldmacher, *New York Congressman Chris Collins Is Charged with Insider Trading,* N.Y. Times (Aug. 8, 2018), www.nytimes.com/2018/08/08/nyregion/chris-collins-insider-trading.html.

[2]   *See* Indictment at ¶¶10–42, United States v. Collins, 409 F. Supp. 3d 228 (S.D.N.Y. Aug. 18, 2018) (No. 18 Cr. 567), superseded on Aug. 6, 2019.

[3]   *See* Press Release, Dep't of Justice, Congressman Christopher Collins and Others Charged in Manhattan Federal Court with Insider Trading and Lying to Federal Law Enforcement Agents (2018), www.justice.gov/usao-sdny/pr/congressman-christopher-collins-and-others-charged-manhattan-federal-court-insider.

Count	Charge	Defendants	Maximum Penalty
1	Conspiracy to commit securities fraud (18 U.S.C. § 371)	All	5 years in prison
2	Securities fraud (15 U.S.C. §§ 78j(b) & 78ff; Title 18 U.S.C. § 2)	CHRISTOPHER COLLINS; CAMERON COLLINS	20 years in prison
3	Securities fraud (15 U.S.C. §§ 78j(b) & 78ff; Title 18 U.S.C. § 2)	All	20 years in prison
4	Securities fraud (15 U.S.C. §§ 78j(b) & 78ff; Title 18 U.S.C. § 2)	CHRISTOPHER COLLINS; CAMERON COLLINS	20 years in prison
5-7	Securities fraud (15 U.S.C. §§ 78j(b) & 78ff; Title 18 U.S.C. § 2)	All	20 years in prison
8	Securities fraud (15 U.S.C. §§ 78j(b) & 78ff; Title 18 U.S.C. § 2)	CHRISTOPHER COLLINS; CAMERON COLLINS	20 years in prison
9	Conspiracy to commit wire fraud (18 U.S.C. §§ 1349)	All	20 years in prison
10	Wire fraud (18 U.S.C. §§ 1343 & 2)	All	20 years in prison
11	False Statements (18 U.S.C. §§ 1001 & 2)	CHRISTOPHER COLLINS	5 years in prison
12	False Statements (18 U.S.C. §§ 1001 & 2)	CAMERON COLLINS	5 years in prison
13	False Statements (18 U.S.C. §§ 1001 & 2)	STEPHEN ZARSKY	5 years in prison

FIGURE 3.1. DOJ press release table excerpt announcing indictment of Christopher Collins[4]

4   *Id.*

Not surprisingly, several news outlets noted each of the maximum terms attached to the charges that had been lodged against Representative Collins, aggregated them, and announced that he faced "150 years" in prison if convicted.[5]

The problem with this reporting is that Collins wasn't facing anything close to 150 years' imprisonment. No question, his crime was a serious one, and it would eventually cost him his job and, for a period of time, his liberty. (He ultimately obtained a last-minute presidential pardon from Donald Trump.) But a term of imprisonment so severe is rarely imposed on white-collar offenders, and rarer still when the offender is a first-time offender.[6] How did the media reach the conclusion Collins was facing such a long term of imprisonment?

The reason it appeared that Collins was facing such a severe sentence was that the statutes he was charged with violating encompass a wide range of conduct. Crimes like wire fraud and insider trading can cover garden-variety schemes involving $20,000 or complex machinations that threaten systemic consequences because they involve billions of dollars. As a result, statutory sentencing ranges in this area can be extremely broad. Any person charged with a single count of federal wire fraud faces between *zero* and *twenty* years of imprisonment.[7] That doesn't mean everyone, or even most defendants, will receive the latter punishment. And this becomes even more important when criminal defendants are charged in multiple counts that, only in rare circumstances, will be constructed consecutively to place the defendant in jail for an even longer period of time.

That Collins had been charged in so many counts was hardly unusual. Fraud schemes often trigger multiple charges: a defendant's accounting fraud scheme might easily constitute securities fraud (because it pertains to shares of a company) while also violating the wire fraud statute (because the scheme employs interstate wires, including emails and telephone calls). Even though a series of representations may be part of an overarching scheme, the law often treats each use of the mails or

---

[5] "He could face up to 150 years in prison if convicted on all counts, according to Nick Biase, a spokesman for the United States Attorney's Office of the Southern District of New York." Erica Orden, *New York Republican Rep. Chris Collins Won't Step Aside, Calling Insider Trading Charges "Meritless,"* CNN (Aug. 8, 2018), www.cnn.com/2018/08/08/politics/chris-collins-indicted-insider-trading/index.html.

[6] There are offenders who have received severe sentences for securities fraud and similar crimes, but most of these cases still fall far short of 150 years' imprisonment. *See* Ken Belson, *WorldCom Chief Is Given 25 Years for Huge Fraud*, N.Y. TIMES (July 14, 2005), www .nytimes.com/2005/07/14/business/worldcom-chief-is-given-25-years-for-huge-fraud.html. On white-collar sentencing generally, see Courtney Semisch, *What Does Federal Economic Crime Really Look Like?* U.S. SENT'G COMMISSION (Jan. 2019), www.ussc.gov/sites/ default/files/pdf/research-and-publications/research-publications/2019/20190130_Econ-Crime .pdf. *See also* Mark W. Bennett, Justin D. Levinson, & Koichi Hioki, *Judging Federal White-Collar Fraud Sentencing: An Empirical Study Revealing the Need for Further Reform*, 102 IOWA L. REV. 939 (2017).

[7] *See* 18 U.S.C. § 1342 (2018).

wires as a separate substantive offense.[8] Plus, if the offender acts in concert with others, the conspiracy is a separate count. Thus, the potential number of charges pile up quickly.[9]

All of this means that the "facing" language tells us very little about the person who has been charged with a federal fraud crime. Someone who is "facing" twenty-five years' imprisonment for a fraud scheme has not necessarily been charged with an overly serious offense and will almost certainly receive a sentence far less than twenty-five *years*; we know that because the average sentence for fraud hovers somewhere closer to twenty-five *months*.[10] Nevertheless, because our federal fraud code fails to subdivide frauds into lesser and more serious degrees, *all* frauds ostensibly "face" the same, extremely harsh-sounding maximum sentence. And because the unit of a fraud offense is often measured by the offender's use of a given medium (e.g., how many times she used the mails or sent something in interstate wires), the government can prosecute a single scheme in multiple counts, with each count representing a different mailing or use of a different medium. Thus, it is not uncommon to hear that a criminal defendant has been charged in a 10, 50 or even 150 count indictment. To the layperson, the inflated count implies: (a) that the offense was very serious; (b) that the offender has generated great harm and is deserving of a profound degree of punishment; and (c) that the government seeks to impose a rather harsh, if not draconian, punishment. Indeed, in some instances, the multiple count indictment will sound like overkill.

Although a federal sentencing statute technically permits a judge to sentence a defendant to consecutive terms of punishment (i.e., forcing him to serve one term after the other), the legal and normative default is in fact concurrent sentencing.[11] Thus, in *most* cases, when a defendant is sentenced for violating several fraud statutes, her sentences for those crimes will be served concurrently. Being charged in "five counts" of mail fraud is not inclined to produce a longer sentence than a single count charge of mail fraud, particularly if all five counts pertain to the same

---

8   "Each separate use of the mail in furtherance of such a scheme constitutes a separate crime." United States v. Blankenship, 746 F.2d 233, 236 (5th Cir. 1984).

9   "Charge-stacking, the process of charging defendants with several crimes for a single criminal episode, likewise induces guilty pleas, not by raising the odds of conviction at trial but by raising the threatened sentence ... [T]he effect is to make convictions cheaper." William J. Stuntz, *The Pathological Politics of Criminal Law*, 100 MICH. L. REV. 505, 520 (2001). *See also* Michael L. Seigel & Christopher Slobogin, *Prosecuting Martha: Federal Prosecutorial Power and the Need for a Law of Counts*, 109 PENN ST. L. REV. 1107 (2005).

10   *See* U.S. SENT'G COMMISSION, SOURCEBOOK OF FEDERAL SENTENCING STATISTICS, at S-32 table 13 (2018), www.ussc.gov/sites/default/files/pdf/research-and-publications/annual-reports-and-sourcebooks/2017/2017SB_Full.pdf.

11   *See* 18 U.S.C. § 3584(a) (2018); RICHARD S. FRASE, *Principles and Procedures for Sentencing of Multiple Current Offenses*, in SENTENCING MULTIPLE CRIMES 189, 189–90 (Jesper Ryberg et al. eds., 2018).

scheme.[12] Although a judge can diverge from this default, she must publicly enunciate her reasons for doing so and explain how this decision coheres with the general sentencing factors laid out in Title 18 United States Code Section 3553.[13] That is, for a judge to effectively extend someone's term of imprisonment by issuing consecutive sentences, the judge must find that the offense is serious enough to warrant divergence from concurrent sentencing.[14] Moreover, the judge who sentences an offender to consecutive terms must address Section 3553(a)'s directive to sentence an offender to "no more time than necessary" to achieve the purposes of punishment.[15] If the goal is to sentence the offender to the *minimum* sentence that achieves punishment's ends, consecutive sentencing ought to be rare, and in the federal system, it usually is.[16]

Nevertheless, the few cases in which judges sentence consecutively are also the most salient ones. Bernie Madoff's 150-year term of imprisonment was made possible by the sentencing judge's decision to impose both the maximum term recommended by the guidelines *and* to string that term out across multiple counts consecutively.[17] As Judge Denny Chin explained at Madoff's sentencing, the reason he did this was that Madoff's behavior – running a massive Ponzi scheme for decades that left organizations and individuals bereft of their wealth while enriching Madoff several times over – was so egregious that it warranted this type of treatment.[18] But Madoff was very much the outlier, both in terms of his behavior and the sentence he received.

Chris Collins was no Bernie Madoff. To be sure, his misconduct was flatly illegal and an abuse of power, but it did warrant a century of imprisonment. The amount of documented gain in Collins' case – less than $1,000,000 – dictated a definite but modest term of imprisonment.[19]

---

[12] The default to concurrent sentencing when the counts pertain to a single scheme is also consistent with the United States Sentencing Guidelines, which remain a starting point for judges, even though their sentencing ranges are advisory. *See* USSG 3D1.2 Groups of Closely Related Counts ("All counts involving substantially the same harm shall be grouped together into a single Group").

[13] 18 U.S.C. § 3553 (2018).

[14] 18 U.S.C. § 3553(a) (2018).

[15] *Id.*

[16] *See* Lauren O'Neill Shermer & Brian D. Johnson, *Criminal Prosecutions: Examining Prosecutorial Discretion and Charge Reductions in U.S. Federal District Courts*, 27 JUST. Q 394, 408–9 (2010) (observing that consecutive sentences make up only 4 percent of the entire federal sentencing population).

[17] Transcript of Sentencing Hearing 42–49, United States v. Madoff, 626 F. Supp. 2d 420 (S.D.N.Y. 2009) (No. 91 Cr. 213).

[18] *See id.*

[19] *See* Jerry Zremski, *Chris Collins' Recommended Prison Sentence? A Year and a Day*, BUFFALO NEWS (Dec. 22, 2020), https://buffalonews.com/news/local/crime-and-courts/chris-collins-rec ommended-prison-sentence-a-year-and-a-day/article_e32f5e45–86cd-5f84-b4ec-45f547ac5ff6 .html.

Collins' case demonstrates the ways in which the federal code generates so much confusion – and ultimately fuels simultaneous claims of overcriminalization and underenforcement. At the outset of a case, when the government first announces its charges, the media reports the defendant "faces" 150 years' imprisonment.[20] This either implies that Collins is one of the greatest masterminds in insider trading or that the government is out to "get" him because of his political leanings (highly unlikely). And since Collins is a first-time offender, the outlandish sentence leaves his attorney plenty of leeway to gripe in the press that the government is treating his client unfairly and aggressively (still no).

Later, the defendant and the prosecutor reach a deal. The defendant almost assuredly won't plead guilty to all the counts. In fact, there is no reason to have him plead guilty to so many counts because many of them are redundant and the judge would likely order his sentences to run concurrently. Accordingly, the defendant instead pleads guilty to a single count.

Once a defendant like Collins agrees to plead guilty, his attorney will negotiate a plea agreement that spells out the sentencing range that applies to his case.[21] That range will look *tiny* in relation to the original term of "150 years" Collins was allegedly "facing" at the time of his arrest. Most of the public won't remember this original number, but a few commentators will – including those who believe our criminal justice institutions are biased or incompetent. Among this group, the gap between the 150 years a defendant reportedly faced and the paltry sentence he is slated to receive will trigger further backlash. It will highlight the system's inequity between street and white-collar crimes and burnish the conclusion that prosecutors have welshed on their obligation to punish and incapacitate the wealthy and well-connected who are intent on harming others. And you can't really blame observers for feeling that way. After all, with such a gap, one can only conclude that prosecutors were either bluffing all along or that they cut the defendant a special deal in order to avoid an arduous criminal trial. Neither of these conclusions generates good feelings about the state of federal criminal enforcement.

3.1 A PROBLEM OF STATUTORY DESIGN

It's easy to blame the DOJ and federal prosecutors for this spectacle. *Were they only more transparent; if they told us the truth at the outset, we wouldn't run into this problem!* is the takeaway most commentators are apt to draw from the Collins

---

[20] *Cf.* John Carreyrou, *U.S. Files Criminal Charges against Theranos's Elizabeth Holmes, Ramesh Balwani*, WALL ST. J. (June 15, 2018), www.wsj.com/articles/u-s-files-criminal-charges-against-theranoss-elizabeth-holmes-ramesh-balwani-1529096005?mod=article_inline.

[21] *See* Stephen J. Schulhofer & Ilene H. Nagel, *Plea Bargaining under the Federal Sentencing Guidelines*, 3 FED. SENT'G REP. 218 (1991); Barry Boss & Nicole L. Angarella, *Negotiating Federal Plea Agreements Post-Booker*, 21 CRIM. JUST. 22 (2006).

episode.[22] The criticism is a variation of a theme: that prosecutors are faithless agents; they favor their own interests at the expense of the general public; and that this translates into easier convictions and harsher sentences for those least likely to complain, and slaps on the wrist for anyone with money or power.[23] But the problem goes far deeper than labeling prosecutors "bad agents."[24] It's also a problem of system-wide legitimacy.

In a very helpful article comparing federal and state enforcement of street crime, Lauren Ouziel argues that the factor that makes federal enforcement agencies more powerful is the federal government's legitimacy. Legitimacy, in turn, is influenced by what Ouziel calls the system's "moral credibility." When the government's punishment for a given crime vastly mismatches the public's assessment of the underlying offense, a "moral credibility gap" forms.[25]

Many of white-collar criminal enforcement's problems can be traced to its statutes, its judicially created doctrines, and the design of its code. Some scholars focus on statutes and doctrine, but few contemporary scholars focus on the federal code's holistic overall *design*.[26] The aim of this chapter is to foreground the design issue and focus on one aspect, namely the code's failure to statutorily subdivide and grade its white-collar offenses. The federal criminal code is overly flat. This flatness, I will argue, fuels the kind of "moral credibility gap" that Ouziel has described in other contexts. And this, gap, in turn, helps erode the legitimacy of not only the criminal justice system, but of prosecutors' offices in particular.

Chapter 2 highlighted the various ways in which statutory labels stunt our ability to measure white-collar crime's enforcement frequency and distribution. Flatness contributes to our data-collection problems. Undifferentiated prohibitions of wrongdoing (e.g., treating all mail fraud violations as a singular offense, regardless of seriousness) subvert our attempts to determine just how many cases have been opened, prosecuted, and convicted over a given period of time. The criminal code's flatness not only fails to reflect principled and considered distinctions in variations of the same offense, but it also buries information deeper in an offender's case file.

---

[22] *See* BRANDON L. GARRETT, TOO BIG TO JAIL: HOW PROSECUTORS COMPROMISE WITH CORPORATIONS 254–55, 274–75 (2014); Jennifer Taub, BIG DIRTY MONEY: THE SHOCKING INJUSTICE AND UNSEEN COST OF WHITE COLLAR CRIME 13–26 (2020).

[23] On prosecutors and agency costs, see Stephanos Bibas, *The Need for Prosecutorial Discretion*, 19 TEMP. POL. & CIV. RTS. L. REV. 369, 373–75 (2010).

[24] For more on agency theory and the notion of prosecutors as suboptimal agents of the people they serve, see Stephanos Bibas, *Transparency and Participation in Criminal Procedure*, 81 N.Y.U. L. REV. 911 (2006); Stephanos Bibas, *Prosecutorial Regulation versus Prosecutorial Accountability*, 157 U. PENN. L. REV. 59 (2009.

[25] Lauren M. Ouziel, *Legitimacy and Federal Criminal Enforcement Power*, 123 YALE L.J. 2236, 2301–16 (2014).

[26] For scholarship critiquing the judiciary's expansive interpretation of criminal statutes, see, e.g., Shon Hopwood, *Clarity in Criminal Law*, 54 AM. CRIM. L. REV. 695 (2017) (arguing for an invigorated approach to lenity); Stephen F. Smith, *Overcoming Overcriminalization*, 102 J. CRIM. L. & CRIMINOLOGY 537 (2012).

Agency reporting is only the top layer of the problem. Below that layer lie additional issues of code design. I pick up this point later in Chapters 7 and 8, but in addition to flat statutes, we also encounter compound and mislabeled statutes, statutes that bundle together an almost haphazard mixture of crimes, and statutes that punish one kind of offense (bribery) while bearing the label of another (fraud). Statutes that flatten *and* bundle *and* mislabel easily lead to general confusion, and that confusion is not what we want if we are trying to preserve (or grow) our system's credibility with the general public.

Years ago, Julie O'Sullivan published an influential article examining the federal code's obstruction of justice statutes. The title of this piece memorably declared the federal criminal code a "disgrace."[27] The characterization was harsh but on the mark. The obstruction statutes, much like the federal statutes that delineate fraud, were overly broad and often overlapped.[28] To these criticisms, O'Sullivan easily could have added the federal criminal code's failure to rigorously grade its white-collar offenses. This lack of gradation isn't simply an additional problem. Rather, it is one of *the* primary stumbling blocks to improving white-collar crime and its enforcement.

3.2 GRADED CODES: A WORLD OF STEPS

For the remainder of this chapter, it will be helpful to keep two images in mind: steps and umbrellas. State criminal codes are full of steps; that is they feature statutory *grading*. These legislatively enacted prohibitions are arrayed in a series of steps or degrees, with each step representing a more serious offense that either permits or requires a judge to impose more serious punishment.

These statutory steps uphold several functions: First, they invest defendants with certain rights. I have referred elsewhere to these rights as "proof rights" and "ceiling rights."[29] The proof right is the right not to be convicted of a given offense unless the prosecutor proves every material element beyond a reasonable doubt. The ceiling right is the right not to be punished above a certain statutory maximum, which usually increases with each degree of an offense.[30] In a graded system, the two concepts enjoy a reciprocal relationship: When proof rights are weak, ceiling rights are strong, and vice versa.[31]

---

[27] *See* Julie R. O'Sullivan, *The Federal Criminal Code Is a Disgrace: Obstruction Statutes as Case Study*, 96 J. Crim. L. & Criminology 643 (2006).

[28] "Federal statutes consistently and seriously err on the side of over-inclusiveness." *Id.* at 655.

[29] Much of this discussion can be found in Miriam H. Baer, *Sorting Out White-Collar Crime*, 97 Tex. L. Rev. 225, 257–60 (2018).

[30] ("The graded regime creates a ceiling right by guaranteeing that the defendant's punishment will fall at or below some legislatively prescribed ceiling"). *Id.* at 257. *See also* Shermer & Johnson, *supra* note 16, at 408 ("The statutory maximum trumps the sentencing guidelines and establishes an absolute ceiling for the most severe punishment possible").

[31] Baer, *supra* note 29, at 228.

Imagine a death caused by an individual's poor driving. Depending on the circumstances (the nature of the offender's driving, the reasons for such driving, the way the car accident occurred), the offender might be charged with criminally negligent homicide, voluntary manslaughter, or a much more serious crime like depraved mind murder. Let's compare criminally negligent homicide with depraved mind murder. To prove criminally negligent homicide, the government need only prove a mental state of negligence (in some states, "gross" negligence). Compared to other statutes, the defendant's proof right is weak; the only mental state the government has to prove is negligence. But the defendant's corresponding ceiling right is strong: statutes such as criminally negligent homicide feature relatively low statutory maxima. When the statutory ceiling is low, the government can secure its conviction easily but it cannot dole out too much punishment.

In contrast, a serious crime like depraved mind murder features a higher statutory maximum. Judges can sentence the depraved mind driver to a far longer sentence of imprisonment than the criminally negligent driver. But to secure a conviction, the prosecutor either must demonstrate a specific mindset (as is the case in New York) or instead prove a series of objective factors that demonstrate a particularly "depraved" disposition (most other states). The person accused of depraved mind murder thus enjoys weak ceiling rights (which is why she faces a relatively high punishment), but relatively strong proof rights.

Proof rights and ceiling rights provide the defendant some degree of protection from strategic overcharging. If I accuse you of depraved mind murder, I'm going to have to prove more than I would have to if I charged you with negligent homicide. And if I charge you with a strict liability offense (e.g., an environmental misdemeanor), the punishment the judge metes out will be tempered by that misdemeanor's statutory ceiling.

In other words, proof rights and ceiling rights modestly restrain prosecutorial gamesmanship. The grand jury *might*, despite its much-criticized deference to prosecutors, blanch when a prosecutor's proof of a particular element appears to be lacking. A defense attorney *might* successfully lodge a pretrial motion to dismiss or successfully demand a "lesser included offense" instruction when the case goes before a jury.[32] And a judge *might* dismiss a charge with a higher ceiling if that judge is persuaded that evidence is lacking *and* knows that the jury will have the opportunity to decide a lesser charge. Prosecutors who recognize these contingencies will be more careful in her investigation, her charging practices, and perhaps her plea-bargaining stances.

It is important not to overstate these points. Prosecutors can still successfully "overcharge" defendants by indicting them for more serious crimes than the underlying facts warrant and then dropping the more serious charges during the plea-

---

[32] Andrew Manuel Crespo, *The Hidden Law of Plea Bargaining*, 118 COLUM. L. REV. 1303, 1364–66 (2018).

bargaining stage.[33] It is beyond debate that prosecutors benefit from and often rely on this strategy. Nevertheless, proof rights and ceiling rights are still worth *something*. Even if the absolute number is small, *some* defendants will take their cases to trial or seek a lesser included offense instruction, and some defendants will win these challenges. If prosecutors know this (and there is every reason to believe they do), they can be modestly deterred from engaging in the worst of strategic overcharging behaviors.

Graded systems are also important because they convey important information to the general public. It matters to many of us how a state labels its prohibited offenses.[34] A criminally negligent homicide implies a different set of morally meaningful factors than a second-degree depraved mind murder. Imagine instead if the state simply labeled all homicides "killings" and allowed a sentencing court to decide, based on a preannounced set of factors, how much punishment an offender should receive. Would it be problematic if we attached an identical label to a teenager who killed someone because she foolishly texted a friend while driving and a sociopath who brutally murdered his parents and children? Both, after all, would be guilty of "killing." If the notion of affixing the same vague label to all of these offenses sounds outlandish or intuitively wrong, then we should be just as concerned with federal statutes that place the least and worst versions of fraud and obstruction of justice (and to a lesser extent, bribery) all under the same label.[35]

Statutory steps are valuable because they distinguish offenders and they do so saliently. Put another way: they efficiently and effectively convey information about a given offense, and by extension, the person convicted of that offense; that is the "retail" value of a given label. Those same labels are also valuable at a wholesale level.[36] Particularly when attached to easy-to-follow degrees, they enable the public to exercise oversight over its enforcement institutions. Imagine two nearby

---

[33] For an excellent attempt to empirically document federal charging and plea bargaining practices and their effects on sentencing outcomes, see Shermer & Johnson, *supra* note 16, at 409 (explaining methodology) and 413 (finding that "property crimes" were more than twice as likely to exhibit charge reductions than "violent crimes"). Readers familiar with Chapter 2 will notice again that Shermer and Johnson's study, however meticulously carried out, is still stymied by the categorical limitations already baked into the government's arrest and sentencing data.

[34] On criminal law and labeling, see Stuart P. Green & Matthew B. Kugler, *When Is It Wrong to Trade Stocks on the Basis of Non-public Information? Public Views of the Morality of Insider Trading*, 39 Fordham Urb. L.J. 445, 451 (2011) (embracing fair labeling as "the idea that 'widely felt distinctions between kinds of offences and degrees of wrongdoing are respected and signaled by the law, and that offences are subdivided and labeled so as to represent fairly the nature and magnitude of the law-breaking'") (quoting Andrew Ashworth, Principles of Criminal Law 88 [5th ed. 2006]).

[35] "[L]abels matter, and in criminal law, offense grades happen to be the mechanisms we most commonly use to convey those labels." Baer, *supra* note 29, at 256 (citing authorities).

[36] *Cf.* Kenworthey Bilz, *We Don't Want to Hear It: Psychology, Literature and the Narrative Model of Judging*, 2010 U. Ill. L. Rev. 429, 482 (2010) (contrasting the "retail, trial level" with the "wholesale, legislative level" in criminal law).

jurisdictions, both of which convict 500 fraud cases over a two-year period. Wouldn't we want to know how many of those fraud cases are serious and how many are relatively hum-drum? And wouldn't we also want to know how many of those cases were originally portrayed as serious offenses, only to be pleaded out and sentenced as run-of-the-mill scams? Statutory gradation simplifies this task. Within minutes, we can figure out how many convictions in each offense family were first-degree offenses and how many were the far less serious third- and fourth-degree versions. Gradation *democratizes* the arduous task of tracking prosecutorial charging practices and determining ultimate sentence lengths.[37]

By contrast, in the ungraded system, oversight is more costly and therefore more difficult. The ubiquitous concept known as "overcharging" loses its meaning because *all* crimes of a certain family type are charged under a single, all-encompassing statute. You can't accuse the government of overcharging Chris Collins on an insider trading case because there is no statutorily defined "lesser" insider trading felony.[38] Thus, overcharging is really another way of saying someone has been *overpunished*. But to know how harshly a federal fraud defendant was punished, we need to analyze historical sentencing data reflecting a judge's application of highly technical and complex sentencing guidelines. *Then* we need to consider the discretion the judge used to derive a sentence at, above, or below the recommended guideline range. These extra steps increase the public's cost of monitoring its enforcement institutions. It takes more effort to discern how much or little punishment has been and will be doled out.

From this vantage point, we can see how the "steps" built into graded statutes perform several functions. First, they convey information about a given offender, about the differences between worse and merely bad variations of the same crime, and about our enforcement institutions. Second, they also provide modest protection to defendants in the form of proof rights and ceiling rights. These steps are far from a panacea, however. They do not bring about greater deterrence, which hinges far more on someone's likelihood of getting caught. Nor do they ensure proportionality, fairness, or equity. We can think of numerous states, whose codes are far more graded than the federal code, whose offenders serve wildly inequitable

---

[37] As noted earlier, Shermer and Johnson have published an excellent study of charging and sentencing lengths within the federal system. *See supra* note 16. Among their findings is that offenders charged with "fraud" who are also college graduates are *less* likely to benefit from sentence reductions. *Id.* at 418.

[38] The federal statute distinguishing different classes felonies and misdemeanors, 18 USC 3559, has little relevance for white-collar crimes. Most of the federal statutes that define fraud, bribery, and obstruction authorize a punishment of at least one year's imprisonment and are therefore felonies. The other classifications ("Class A" or "Class B") have little bearing on the offender's ultimate sentence, except in circumstances not relevant to this discussion. *See, e.g.,* Kaley Ree Jaslow, *Note, Life in Jail for Misbehavior: Criminal Contempt and the Consequence of Improper Classification*, 71 FLA. L. REV. 599, 606 (2019) (citing potential importance of classification for revocation of supervised release); Daniel N. Marx & Michael J. Licker, *Deepening a Split and Adding to a Consensus*, 31 CRIM. JUST. 20 (Fall 2016).

and extremely long sentences. Moreover, one need not be a statistician to conclude that graded codes play little to no role in preventing mass incarceration. Steps are fine, but they are hardly sufficient to make a criminal justice system fair or effective.

Nevertheless, graded codes serve an additional function. Because they are written and enacted by a legislature, they are more likely to reflect the public's viewpoint that certain factors render one version of an offense more serious (and therefore more deserving of condemnation) than another; that is, grades either are – or at least can be – more responsive to public opinion. They promote democratic values along two axes. First, the graded statute itself reflects principled decision-making among democratically elected representatives; it is a product of democratic deliberation. Second, gradation enables us to more easily track what enforcement institutions do on a daily basis. We can more easily determine which crimes they charge and the ultimate convictions they pursue. Grading thus reinforces democratic monitoring. When we can better track our enforcement bureaucracy, we can more effectively engage with it and promote reforms that enhance its overall legitimacy.[39]

3.3 THE FEDERAL CODE: UMBRELLAS EVERYWHERE

Unlike state codes, the federal code's white-collar offenses, particularly those that relate to fraud and obstruction, feature little to no grading – and certainly, none of the explicit "degree" labels that characterize state codes.[40] Federal criminal law instead relies on a series of overlapping umbrella-type statutes: broadly worded prohibitions against fraud, bribery, extortion, and obstruction that cover multiple variations of the same offense, and whose statutory sentence windows cover an expanding range of outcomes.

It's important to point out that although the federal code features *many* variations of fraud, bribery, and obstruction (as discussed in Chapter 2), these variations should not be confused with the graded offenses we see in state codes. Manslaughter isn't just a *distinct* offense from murder, it is in fact a *lesser* offense. By contrast, there is nothing morally (or statutorily) meaningful about the various fraud, bribery, and obstruction statutes one encounters in the federal code. To use fraud as an example,

---

[39] On the intersection of democracy and bureaucracy and its implications for criminal justice reform, see Lauren M. Ouziel, *Democracy, Bureaucracy and Criminal Justice Reform*, 61 B.C. L. REV. 523 (2020).

[40] One exception is the code's distinction between domestic bribery and the giving and receiving of gratuities. *See* 18 U.S.C. § 201(b) and (c). The former carries a twenty-year maximum penalty, whereas the latter carries one of just two years. *See* STUART P. GREEN, *Official and Commercial Bribery: Should They Be Distinguished?* in MODERN BRIBERY LAW: COMPARATIVE PERSPECTIVES 40–42 (Jeremy Horder & Peter Allridge, eds. 2013) (describing and distinguishing major bribery statutes in federal code). Even here, the federal code does not label the lesser offense "bribery in the second degree" and the more serious one "bribery in the first degree." It instead covers both crimes under the same statutory umbrella and labels one "bribery" and the other "gratuity."

there are fraud statutes that punish the use of the mails or the wires to carry out schemes, or which punish schemes designed to victimize health care companies or the United States government.[41] There is also an all-purpose federal bribery statute, a foreign bribery statute, an honest-services statute, a Hobbs Act bribery statute, and a bribery statute keyed to federal-funded programs.[42]

With the possible exception of the federal bribery statute, which contains a lesser punishment for the provision or receipt of an illegal gratuity, no morally meaningful statutory line differentiates these crimes.[43] The fact that some statutes happen to have higher statutory maximum ceilings is largely a reflection of accident. Indeed, the United States Sentencing Guidelines direct the sentencing judge to calculate a defendant's sentence for *any* of the fraud statutes under the identical economic fraud guideline. Accordingly, assuming all facts are equal, a $50,000 fraud scheme charged under the mail fraud statute will receive roughly the same sentence as the same scheme charged under the health care fraud statute.[44] The statutory maximum term of imprisonment for the latter (fifteen years) is less than the former (twenty years), but the judge who imposes a guideline sentence will impose the *identical* sentence because that is how the guidelines have been written (and frankly, rightly so). Insiders – prosecutors, defense attorneys, guidelines commissioners, and judges – appreciate this fact. Outsiders – including first-time defendants, commentators, and even academics unfamiliar with the federal system – are more likely to focus on a statute's statutory maximum.

While federal prohibitions on fraud and obstruction eschew statutory gradation, the federal bribery statute is slightly different. It subdivides bribery and the giving and acceptance of "gratuities" or a reward for official behavior already accomplished. Even here, the code's gradation falls far short of the ladder/step system we see in state codes.[45] The umbrella is an apt metaphor because federal statutes cover not only a broad array of behavior, but they also proscribe broad statutory sentencing ranges of zero- to ten-, fifteen- or twenty-years' imprisonment. And for the most part,

---

[41] *See* 18 U.S.C. § 371 (2018); 18 U.S.C. § 1031 (2018); 18 U.S.C. § 1341 (2018); 18 U.S.C. § 1343 (2018); 18 U.S.C. § 1347 (2018).

[42] 18 USC 201; 18 USC 1346; 18 USC 666; 15 USC 78dd-1 et seq.; 18 USC 1951. Commercial bribery schemes can also be prosecuted under the Travel Act, 18 USC § 1952, when they take place in interstate commerce and violate the laws of one of the states in which they take place.

[43] Whereas a bribe contemplates an official will engage in certain action in exchange for money or property, a gratuity is a gratuitous gift or reward provided to someone "because of" her decision or action. United States v. Sun-Diamond Growers of California, 526 U.S. 398 (1999). On the contestable distinctions between bribery and gratuities, see Randall D. Eliason, *Surgery with a Meat Axe: Using Honest Services Fraud to Prosecute Federal Corruption*, 99 J. Crim. & Criminology 929 (2009); Sarah N. Welling, *Reviving the Federal Law of Gratuities*, 55 Ariz. L. Rev. 417 (2013).

[44] They will receive the same *recommended* sentence range under the Guidelines, but judges are not bound by these ranges.

[45] *See* Baer, *supra* note 29, at 228.

these federal statutes have expanded over time to include a wider range of conduct while simultaneously threatening a wider range of punishments.

3.4 SPACE AND TIME

The comparison of graded and ungraded codes unfolds along two axes. *Spatially*, the state code subdivides wrongdoing into graduated steps, with each "higher" step representing more culpable or more harmful conduct. The federal system, by contrast, contents itself with using broad, open-textured umbrella statutes to define and punish different variations of the same offenses of deception.[46]

Temporally, the state system engages in some degree of "up front" sorting of its defendants. At the moment of charging, some defendants know they are facing the most serious consequences under a state's code, while others know they have been charged with lesser offenses.[47] That information alone improves the defendant's plea-bargaining stance insofar as it reduces the uncertainty and fear associated with more serious charges and higher sentencing ranges.[48] The federal system, by contrast, delays its sorting. Rather than subdividing offenses up front in meaningful statutory categories, the federal system relies primarily on judges and sentencing guidelines to tease apart distinctions at the back end of the criminal justice system.

In previous work, I have referred to these mechanisms respectively as "front-end sorting" and "back-end sorting" systems.[49] Front-end systems require legislatures to debate and agree upon the abstract factors that distinguish a related set of offenses. To be sure, this front-end system *still* relies on actors other than legislators to define and implement a given grading scheme. Prosecutors must initially decide how to charge an offense under a higher or lower grade. As a case unfolds, they will decide again whether a given case can be pled out under a lower charge.[50] Plea-bargaining, and all of its unfortunate baggage, clearly impacts the front-end system's ceiling and proof rights.

Moreover, as we know from homicide law, front-end systems rely heavily on statutory interpretation. Judges must interpret the statutory language that purports to distinguish the more serious variation of a crime from the less serious one. And

---

[46] There are exceptions to this rule. Federal drug laws are "graded," albeit not in the same manner as state statutes. The federal homicide statutes also feature two grades. Baer, *supra* note 29, at 235 and n. 35. Computer and identity fraud offenses are also punished according to complex statutory rubrics that even insiders struggle to comprehend. *Id.* at 228 n. 6 and 269.

[47] None of this is to deny the existence of "overcharging," which Jeffrey Bellin has defined as "charging the defendant with an offense or enhancement that is not 'readily provable,' or an offense for which the jury should not convict." Jeffrey Bellin, *Theories of Prosecution*, 108 CALIF. L. REV. 1203, 1225 (2020).

[48] *See* Jeffrey Bellin, *Plea Bargaining's Uncertainty Problem*, 101 TEX. L. REV. 539 (2023).

[49] *See* Baer, *supra* note 29, at 230–31.

[50] *See* Ronald F. Wright & Rodney L. Engen, *Charge Bargaining and Theories of Prosecutors*, 91 MARQ. L. REV. 9, 17–18 (2007).

jurors must decide whether a prosecutor has proven the existence of certain factors – be they related to culpability, risk, or actual harm – that warrant more the more serious offense.[51] All of these actors play important roles, but the legislature still remains central to this exercise.

By contrast, the legislature's role is more tangential where back-end sorting is concerned. Once it defines a proscribed activity in rather general terms (e.g., a "scheme to defraud" that employs either the mails or interstate wires), it delegates the remainder of the system's sorting to judges and regulatory experts, such as the United States Sentencing Commission. And whereas front-end sorting envisions an abstract debate ("what is 'provocation' in the homicide context?"), back-end sorting is inevitably intertwined with an offender's specific circumstances and characteristics.

These distinctions illuminate some of the federal criminal justice system's legitimacy problem. A system of umbrellas and back-end sorting may sound rather favorable to prosecutors and investigators. Who wouldn't embrace the leverage of threatening a Representative of Congress with 150 years' imprisonment? But as we will see, the whipsaw effect of threatening such a fanciful sentence and then committing to a far less punitive plea agreement drives the very cynicism and frustration at the heart of white-collar crime's critiques.

3.5 HISTORICAL DETOUR[52]

Before we go further, it might be helpful to explain why state codes feature gradation and why the federal system is much flatter.

The first graded offense dates to 1794, when Pennsylvania's legislature divided its homicide statute into two degrees of murder and manslaughter.[53] Other states soon followed course, in part to chip away at the then prevailing common law rule that subjected all murder convictions to capital punishment.[54] Eventually, the intuition

---

[51] *See* Crespo, *supra* note 32, at 1360.

[52] Portions of this section are adapted from my article, *Sorting Out White-Collar Crime. See* Baer, *supra* note 29, at 233–40.

[53] *See* Paul J. Larkin, Jr., *The Demise of Capital Clemency*, 73 WASH. & LEE L. REV. 1295, 1301 (2016) (citing McGautha v. California, 402 U.S. 183, 198 (1971), which traces society's "rebellion against the common law rule imposing a mandatory death sentence on all convicted murderers"); see also Model Penal Code Sentencing § 210.2 (Am. Law Inst. 1980); Guyora Binder, *The Origins of American Felony Murder Rules*, 57 STAN. L. REV. 59, 119 (2004). On capital punishment's early application to crimes other than homicide, see Lauren Ouziel, *Beyond Law & Fact: Jury Evaluation of Law Enforcement*, 92 NOTRE DAME L. REV. 691, 713 & n.84 (2017) (noting that "[d]eath was the sentence for many felonies"); Kathleen "Cookie" Ridolfi & Seth Gordon, *Gubernatorial Clemency Powers Justice or Mercy?* CRIM. JUST. (Fall 2009), at 26, 29 ("At the time of the Declaration of Independence in 1776, more than 200 crimes carried mandatory death sentences in England").

[54] "[J]uries ... disliked seeing a mandatory death sentence in cases where the offender did not deserve to die and would refuse to convict a defendant if doing so would send him to the gallows." Larkin, *supra* note 53, at 1301; see also Ouziel, *supra* note 53, at 714 ("Second degree murder was developed ... largely as a concession to capital-averse juries").

to subdivide crimes and label them by degree spread beyond homicide.[55] Today, gradation in state codes is the norm.[56]

The federal criminal code, laid out in title 18, and in additional titles such as title 21, all but ignores the convention of labeling crimes by degree.[57] Why so little grading for federal crimes? One might start with the fact that federal criminal law barely existed in the years following the Revolution. As Kate Stith and Steve Koh have observed, "The first criminal statute was enacted in 1789 (even before the lower federal courts were established)."[58] Although other statutes would eventually follow[59] – most notably the mail fraud statute in 1872 – federal criminal law focused predominantly on protecting the federal government and its processes.[60] Accordingly, the preoccupation that drove early state law reform, namely, the fear that juries would reject felony prosecutions that exposed too many targets to capital punishment, was absent in the federal sphere. Few federal crimes existed, and the ones that did exist threatened relatively weak punishments.

Moreover, because the judiciary decisively rejected the concept of a federal code bound by common law,[61] the federal legislature could approach federal criminal law as a blank slate, unrestrained by common law expectations and norms. Congress

---

[55] Ouziel, *supra* note 53, at 713–14 (detailing the effort, first in Pennsylvania and then in other states, "to reduce the number and scope of capital crimes, and to enact criminal laws that offered more nuanced degrees of guilt and punishment").

[56] *See* Sam Kamin & Justin Marceau, *Vicarious Aggravators*, 65 FLA. L. REV. 769, 776 (2013) ("[T]oday, nearly every state uses degrees of murder as the first slice at determining which murderers should live and which should die").

[57] Federal drug crimes are statutorily subdivided by drug weight but make no mention of the familiar "degree" language. *See* 21 U.S.C. 841 et seq.

[58] Kate Stith & Steve Y. Koh, *The Politics of Sentencing Reform: The Legislative History of the Federal Sentencing Guidelines*, 28 WAKE FOREST L. REV. 223, 226 n.7 (1993).

[59] *See* David S. Schwartz, *A Question Perpetually Arising: Implied Powers, Capable Federalism, and the Limits of Enumerationism*, 59 ARIZ. L. REV. 573, 643–44 (2017) (describing the Act's criminalization of "counterfeiting, treason, piracy, felonies on the high seas").

[60] STEPHEN F. SMITH, *Overfederalization*, in 1 REFORMING CRIMINAL JUSTICE: INTRODUCTION AND CRIMINALIZATION 39, 40 (Erik Luna, ed. 2017) (describing federal criminal law in the early period following the nation's founding). Criminalization of mail fraud was consistent with "the expansion of federal authority that came about in the wake of the Civil War" and reflected a concern with the growth in "large scale swindles and frauds" made possible by a more sophisticated economy. Mark Zingale, *Fashioning a Victim Standard in Mail and Wire Fraud: Ordinarily Prudent Person or Monumentally Credulous Gull?* 99 COLUM. L. REV. 795, 802–3 (1999). The new economy, in turn, created opportunities for deception and exploitation: "An integrated national economy generated a higher percentage of commercial and financial transactions taking place at a distance, often between strangers." EDWARD J. BALLEISEN, FRAUD: AN AMERICAN HISTORY FROM BARNUM TO MADOFF 108 (2017).

[61] "It was settled early in our history that prosecutions in the federal courts could not be founded on any undefined body of so-called common law." Screws v. United States, 325 U.S. 91, 152 (1945) (Murphy, J., dissenting) (citing United States v. Hudson, 11 U.S. (7 Cranch) 32 (1812), which held that Congress "must first make an act a crime [and] affix a punishment to it" and United States v. Gooding, 25 U.S. 460 [1827]).

could shape its laws and punishments however it liked and did not have to worry that a "felony" designation would portend capital punishment.[62] Early federal criminal statutes featured generic sentencing caps of ten years' imprisonment and, within those caps, federal judges could sentence according to their discretion.[63]

From the late 1800s to the 1980s, white-collar sentencing remained a relatively lenient affair. The mail fraud statute's statutory maximum sentence of imprisonment remained rather low, at just five years until 2002, when Congress increased it to twenty.[64] And until the late 1980s, judges often declined to impose prison sentences on white-collar offenders, and even when they did, those sentences were not particularly onerous.[65]

Federal criminal law grew substantially during the twentieth century. Narrow at first, it broadened during the first half of the 1900s,[66] owing in part to Congress's enactment of substantive laws that overlapped state codes.[67] Many of these statutes represented "cheap" political reactions to singular events or scandals of the day.[68] Eventually, the common problems associated with federal criminal law in the modern era came to be its breadth, its overlap with state law, and its internal incoherence.[69]

---

[62] "Because the field is almost entirely optional, Congress is free to use criminal law in innovative ways." DANIEL J. RICHMAN ET AL., DEFINING FEDERAL CRIMES 25 (1st ed. 2014) (citing and praising federal criminal law's creativity).

[63] Stith and Koh, *supra* note 58, at 290; see also Mistretta v. United States, 488 U.S. 361, 364 (1989) ("Congress early abandoned fixed-sentence rigidity ... and put in place a system of ranges within which the [judge] could choose the precise punishment").

[64] Wire fraud's maximum sentence was similarly increased. Peter Henning, *The Changing Atmospherics of Corporate Crime Sentencing*, 3 J. BUS. L. & TECH. 243, 246 (2008).

[65] *See* Daniel Richman, *Federal White Collar Sentencing in the United States: A Work in Progress*, 76 LAW & CONTEMP. PROBS. 53, 55 (2013) (describing white-collar sentencing practices in the 1970s). "Congress was especially concerned that prior to the Sentencing Guidelines, '[m]ajor white collar criminals often [were] sentenced to small fines and little or no imprisonment.'" United States v. Martin, 455 F.3d 1227, 1240 (11th Cir. 2006) (quoting S. Rep. No. 98–225, at 76 (1983), *as reprinted in* 1984 U.S.C.C.A.N. 3182, 3259). For challenges to this claim, see Samuel W. Buell, *Is the White Collar Offender Privileged?*, 83 DUKE L.J. 823, 833 n.22 (2014) (citing studies).

[66] *See* Stuntz, *supra* note 9, at 515. "[The] expansion of federal criminal law generally focused on vice in the first third of the twentieth century, regulatory crimes and racketeering in the second third, and violence and drugs (plus yet more white-collar offenses) in the last third" (citations omitted).

[67] For more on federal criminal law's growth and consequent overlap with state law, see DANIEL RICHMAN, *The Changing Boundaries between Federal and Local Law Enforcement* in 2 CRIMINAL JUSTICE 2000: BOUNDARY CHANGES IN CRIMINAL JUSTICE ORGANIZATIONS 81, 83–84 (Charles M. Friel, ed. 2000).

[68] Stuntz, *supra* note 66, at 531–32 (describing "symbolic stands" legislators take by enacting redundant statutes in response to particularly notable or upsetting crimes).

[69] *See, e.g.,* Rachel E. Barkow, *Clemency and Presidential Administration of Criminal Law*, 90 N.Y.U. L. REV. 802, 822 & nn.119–20 (2015) (citing commonly voiced criticisms of federal criminal code's bloat); SMITH, *supra* note 60, at 41 ("[T]he loose collection of statutes known as 'federal criminal law' is sprawling and virtually limitless in its reach"); Stuntz, *supra* note 66, at 525 (observing that "anyone who studies contemporary state or federal criminal codes is

Even in the modern era, federal and state criminal law continue to travel different paths. State codes (and state legislatures) have benefitted from the insights incorporated in the American Law Institute's 1962 Model Penal Code (MPC). The oft-praised MPC proved highly influential and led to the reformation of over thirty state codes.[70] Whereas the MPC streamlined[71] state codes by adopting uniform vocabulary and four basic mental states (purpose, knowledge, recklessness, and negligence), it left intact the practice of legislatively articulating more and less serious variants of the same offense. Indeed, its opening section explicitly includes as one of its "general purposes" the "differentiat[ion] . . . between serious and minor offenses."[72]

The federal code, meanwhile, remained politically impervious to the MPC's reforms. Ronald Gainer's discussion of this episode is highly instructive.[73] According to Gainer, for years, members of both houses sought reforms along the lines suggested by the MPC.[74] Had this effort succeeded, the federal code might have incorporated the MPC's explicit embrace of statutory gradation. A decade-long effort to revise the federal code ultimately collapsed, however, and in its stead, Congress enacted a statute focused predominantly on sentencing, which is how we ended up with the back-end sorting system we encounter today.[75]

The 1984 Sentencing Reform Act sought to eliminate sentencing disparities, to guarantee a definite but modest prison sentence for white-collar offenses, and to correct the variance between a sentencing court's formal judgment and the amount of time a prisoner actually served in prison.[76] The Act created and vested in the

---

likely to be struck by their scope, by the sheer amount of conduct they render punishable"); O'Sullivan, *supra* note 27, at 643 (declaring the "code" a "haphazard grabbag of statutes").

[70] This section is adapted from Baer, *supra* note 29, at 238–39. *See also* Gerard E. Lynch, *Towards a Model Penal Code, Second (Federal?): The Challenge of the Special Part*, 2 BUFF. CRIM. L. REV. 297, 302 (1998) (observing the MPC's success in colonizing state penal codes). Despite its initial success, the MPC's influence has waned over the years. *See* Paul H. Robinson & Michael T. Cahill, *The Accelerating Degradation of American Criminal Codes*, 56 HASTINGS L.J. 633, 635–44 (2005).

[71] The MPC was not the only instance in which jurists sought to consolidate or streamline statutes. Stuart Green has written extensively of the twentieth-century consolidation of theft crimes into a more workable set of statutes. *See generally* STUART P. GREEN, THIRTEEN WAYS TO STEAL A BICYCLE: THEFT LAW IN THE INFORMATION AGE (2012).

[72] In its opening section, the MPC identifies as one of its "general purposes" the definition of offenses in order to "differentiate on reasonable grounds between serious and minor offenses." Model Penal Code § 1.02 (1)(e) (Am. Law Inst. 1985).

[73] On the history of federal code reform and of its ultimate failure in 1982, see Ronald L. Gainer, *Federal Criminal Code Reform: Past and Future*, 2 BUFF. CRIM. L. REV. 45, 111–29 (1998) (tracing a twelve-year effort to revise federal code).

[74] *See id.*

[75] *See id.*

[76] "The sentencing reforms of the past twenty-five years have had several goals, including 'truth in sentencing,' control of prison populations, and reduction of unwarranted disparity." Paul J. Hofer et al., *The Effect of the Federal Sentencing Guidelines on Inter-Judge Sentencing Disparity*, 90 J. CRIM. L. & CRIMINOLOGY 239, 239–40 (1999) (arguing that of the three goals, the "truth in sentencing" objective was most successful).

United States Sentencing Commission the responsibility for managing the federal government's punishment apparatus.[77] Eliminating parole, the Act eclipsed the federal code's broad, indeterminate sentencing ranges with a highly regimented administrative sentencing regime, encapsulated by the Sentencing Guidelines.[78]

3.6 THE SIGNALING VALUE OF GRADES

So much for history. Why should we care so much whether a system sorts its offenders at the front end or the back end? After all, a well-run system ought to produce the same results for roughly similar offenses. And, as we well know, gradation offers little to no protection from the worst excesses of the criminal justice system. The most meticulously graded criminal code can be paired with racist policing, cynical plea-bargaining tactics, and draconian sentence ranges. Why then, should we care so much about statutory grades?

Consider the following: anyone who has ever watched an episode of "Law and Order," followed a state homicide trial closely in the newspapers, or has read true crime books is probably quite familiar with terms such as "manslaughter" and "murder," and terms such as first and second degree. Moreover, that person also likely understands that "first degree" suggests a more serious transgression than fourth or fifth degree. These aren't esoteric facts. Rather, they form a language that has been successfully incorporated into our popular culture.

By contrast, unless someone has studied or worked within the federal criminal system, that person likely knows very little about the Sentencing Guidelines or its associated "offense level." Only experts and insiders would immediately recognize the "special offense characteristics" that increase a fraud offender's potential sentence, such as the offender's "intended loss amount" or her use of "sophisticated means" to pull off a scheme. And only insiders would know that Chris Collins – or anyone accused in twenty counts of violating the insider trading laws –isn't going to jail for 150 years if the amount of money involved is in the low seven-figure range.

---

[77] *See* Rachel E. Barkow, *Separation of Powers and the Criminal Law*, 58 STAN. L. REV. 989, 1028 (2006) (Congress purposely created "a federal criminal agency modeled in crucial respects after traditional administrative agencies"); Paul H. Robinson, *One Perspective on Sentencing Reform in the United States*, 8 CRIM. L.F. 1, 13–14 (1998) (describing the Commission's history, resources and intended function); Ronald F. Wright, *Sentencers, Bureaucrats, and the Administrative Law Perspective on the Federal Sentencing Commission*, 79 CALIF. L. REV. 1, 9–10 (1991) (citing early preferences for creation of sentencing commission). On the political economy of shifting to a commission model, see Dhammika Dharmapala et al., *Legislatures, Judges, and Parole Boards: The Allocation of Discretion Under Determinate Sentencing*, 62 FLA. L. REV. 1037, 1084 (2010) (explaining how "legislatures acting in their own self-interest may be motivated" to move toward a determinate sentencing regime overseen by a sentencing commission).

[78] Although the federal guidelines system is the most famous of the guideline regimes, its administrative approach can be traced to earlier state practices. *See* Robinson, *supra* note 77, at 10 ("The sentencing reform movement began at the state, not the federal, level").

Grades create easy-to-understand signals, and the public uses those signals to track individual cases and monitor law enforcement activity in general.[79] When grades work well, they promote personal accountability among the punished and professional accountability among the punishers.

One of the reasons graded statutes convey salient signals to the public is that statutory gradations distinguish crimes that fall within the same family of offenses. State statutes carefully parse distinctions between "armed" robbery and other types of robberies, between "aggravated" rape and less serious transgressions of sexual autonomy. Concededly, the *terms* of those gradations can be arbitrary or highly contested. Not everyone will agree with a court's definition of "aggravated" and prosecutors will inarguably benefit from a graded statute's indeterminacy. But the presence of these terms in graded statutes provides the public an opportunity to debate, learn, and revise its beliefs.

I don't mean to downplay the ways in which a graded scheme can go awry. Legislatures can construct silly or arbitrary distinctions; prosecutors can withhold exculpatory evidence relevant to the statutory element that elevates an offense; and juries can ignore the entire system and simply vote according to vague notions of right or wrong. Grading schemes can degrade or lose their relevance.

But over time, the blunt categories and their terms take on both legal and *social* meaning. Legislatures *do* consider the difference between a lesser offense and a more serious one, as do the many other criminal justice actors who occupy the courthouse. Grading is far from perfect, but when it reflects salient, morally meaningful distinctions, it helps citizens and experts construct a joint understanding of which offenses are more deserving of condemnation, fear or incapacitation and which ones are less deserving of those feelings.

3.7 BACK-END SORTING BACKFIRES

The foregoing discussion illuminates the distinction between two types of systems. One system sorts its criminal defendants early in the process by distinguishing worse and less worse versions of an offense in easy-to-comprehend statutory degrees. The alternative system is the one that sweeps its defendants under a broad umbrella statute that later sorts its offenders during the sentencing phase.

Theoretically, the two systems could produce similar punishment outcomes. If a Chris Collins receives a sentence of sixty-seven months' imprisonment for insider trading under the Sentencing Guidelines, it is quite possible he would receive some facsimile of that sentence under a front-end graded regime.

The graded system's additional benefit is that it conveys salient, easy-to-digest information. Outsiders learn that the defendant has been charged with second- or third-degree homicide. Insiders debate the meaning of "depraved indifference" and

---

[79] *See* Baer, *supra* note 29, at 281.

"aggravated" assault. A graded system forces its *insiders* to debate and clarify its major terms, but it also enables *outsiders* to better track and understand the system's overall behavior.

By contrast, the ungraded system sorts its cases much later in time, at the sentencing stage. Legislatures play almost no role here, other than enacting a series of overlapping umbrella statutes. Sentencing commissions, prosecutors, and judges are left to decide where along a spectrum a given offender's case ought to fall. In this ungraded system, the sorting of offenses is inextricably intertwined with the sorting of offenders. That is, the judge will examine the offense characteristics at the same time the judge learns of the offender's background and history. Tracking and understanding this system, if it happens at all, will be left solely to sophisticated insiders and researchers.

Because the federal lacks grades, it ironically is more amenable to the kinds of substantive and punitive expansion that critics find so concerning.[80] Imagine the code were laid out in a series of degrees. A decision to suddenly enact a "new" securities fraud statute (which Congress in fact did in the Dodd–Frank Act's wake) would invite complicated questions about grading. Commentators would invariably ask, "Is this new offense a first-degree offense or a second-degree offense?" The prospect of such a question, and of the fights that would accompany it, would likely discourage criminal lawmaking except in those instances where a pressing enforcement gap truly existed.

In sum, grading increases the cost of promulgating new criminal laws, and that is a good thing. When grades are absent, Congress faces few constraints on its tendency to symbolically append a statute to its code. It doesn't need to announce how serious the new offense is; nor does it need to decide how that offense intersects with existing offenses. It can leave the details to the legal system's other actors. Such "outsourcing" is the focus of Chapter 4.

---

[80] Stuntz, *supra* note 9.

4

Outsourcing

INTRODUCTION

Matthew Martoma was a second-year law student at Harvard Law School. Desiring better grades to improve his candidacy for a highly sought-after judicial clerkship, he apparently altered his law school transcript.[1] After his fraudulent behavior came to light, he was expelled from Harvard, only to bounce back and eventually attend Stanford Business School several years later.[2]

Martoma graduated Stanford and eventually became a highly ranked analyst and portfolio manager at a hedge fund.[3] That fund, SAC Capital, was itself controversial for the "edgy" trading methodology its analysts employed.[4] They collected private bits of information and then reassembled those bits into a "mosaic" that allowed them to better understand – and bet on – the future performance of publicly held corporations.[5]

To a layperson, Martoma's behavior almost certainly sounds like insider trading. But as it turns out, the black letter law of insider trading diverges quite a bit from

---

[1] Nate Raymond et al., *SAC's Martoma Tried to Cover Up Fraud at Harvard, Documents Show*, REUTERS (Jan. 9, 2014), www.reuters.com/article/us-sac-martoma-harvard/sacs-martoma-tried-to-cover-up-fraud-at-harvard-documents-show-idUSBREA081C720140109.

[2] It is unclear whether Stanford ever learned of Martoma's expulsion. Michelle Celarier, *Martoma May Have Lied to Stanford – As Well as Harvard*, NEW YORK POST (Jan. 14, 2014), https://nypost.com/2014/01/14/martoma-was-expelled-from-harvard-then-lied-to-stanford/?utm_source=url_sitebuttons&utm_medium=site%20buttons&utm_campaign=site%20buttons.

[3] United States v. Martoma, 894 F.3d 64, 68–69 (2d. Cir. 2018) (Martoma "managed an investment portfolio with buying power of between $400 and 500 million" and reported directly to Steven Cohen, the founder and manager of SAC Capital).

[4] Nate Raymond, *SAC's Steinberg Wanted "Edgy" Information, Ex-analyst Says*, REUTERS (Nov. 27, 2013), www.reuters.com/article/sac-steinberg-idUSL2N0JC1EQ20131127.

[5] Peter J. Henning, *The Gray Line of "Confidential" Information*, NEW YORK TIMES (Aug. 5, 2013), https://dealbook.nytimes.com/2013/08/05/the-sometimes-gray-line-of-confidential-information/?_r=0.

what the lay person might assume it to be.[6] Nevertheless, the United States Attorney's Office for the Southern District of New York (SDNY), helmed at the time by the very popular Preet Bharara, would eventually arrest and prosecute numerous hedge fund analysts (including Martoma) for collecting information (tips) from insiders (tippers) and trading on that information for their own benefit.[7] Coming on the heels of the 2008 Financial Crisis, the SDNY's crackdown was cited as evidence that the government's enforcement bureaucracy was awakening from its slumber.[8] Moreover, it seemed poised to wipe out the clubby networks whose multimillionaires and billionaires had profited off of unfair access to valuable information.[9]

Years later, it's difficult to say if the initiative was a success. In its earliest stages, the government's efforts bore real fruit: approximately eighty traders either pleaded guilty or were convicted at trial, and SAC Capital itself negotiated a guilty plea that effectively put it out of business.[10] Later appellate court decisions, however, over-turned a number of the SDNY's insider trading convictions and inspired more questions than answers about the status of *tippers* (individuals who wrongfully disclose material confidential information) and *tippees* (the individuals who proceed to trade on such information).[11]

Some might say the government's insider trading offensive left us with a *weaker* understanding of insider trading's boundaries, and that this weaker understanding undermined internal compliance efforts within hedge funds and publicly traded companies.[12] And as for Steven Cohen, SAC's founder? His company may have disappeared, but the government declined to charge *him* with any crime, an event he apparently celebrated by purchasing a Picasso.[13]

---

[6] *See, e.g.*, Chiarella v. United States, 445 U.S. 222, 223 (1980) (rejecting "general duty" among market participants "to forgo [trading] on material, nonpublic information").

[7] Michael Bobelian, *As Preet Bharara Drops Seven Insider Trading Charges, Some Enforcement Might Move Out of New York*, Forbes (Oct. 23, 2015), www.forbes.com/sites/michaelbobe lian/2015/10/23/as-preet-bharara-drops-seven-insider-trading-charges-some-enforcement-might-move-out-of-new-york/?sh=515350f93680.

[8] Commentators nevertheless questioned and criticized the prosecutions as pretextual. *See* Justin Fox, *SAC and the Strange Focus on Insider Trading*, Harvard Business Review (July 26, 2013), https://hbr.org/2013/07/sac-and-the-strange-focus-on-insider-trading.html.

[9] *See* John Anderson, Insider Trading Law, Ethics & Reform 91 (2018).

[10] Sam Gustin, *SAC Capital Pleas Deal Ends Long Wall Street Saga*, Time (Apr. 11, 2014), https://time.com/59119/sac-capital-guilty-plea/.

[11] *See* discussion *infra* at text and notes 67–72.

[12] For evidence that insider trading increased during this time period, see Menesh S. Patel, *Does Insider Trading Law Change Behavior? An Empirical Analysis*, 53 UC Davis L. Rev. 447 (2019).

[13] *SAC's Cohen Buys $155M Picasso after Settling Trading Probe*, Page Six (Mar. 26, 2013), https://pagesix.com/2013/03/26/exclusive-sacs-cohen-buys-155m-picasso-after-settling-trading-probe/?utm_source=url_sitebuttons&utm_medium=site%20buttons&utm_campaign=site%20buttons.

4.1 LAWMAKING BY OUTSOURCING

From an enforcement perspective, Martoma's prosecution is notable because it represents an instance in which prosecutors pursued individuals who exploited their social and economic networks to secure lasting advantages in the stock market. This type of enforcement is hardly new.[14] Prosecutors have often relished the opportunity to protect the markets from the predations of the wealthy and well-connected.[15] Indeed, insider trading's aggressive enforcement partially rebuts the oft-repeated mantra that federal prosecutors are disinclined to pursue high-status offenders. As Bharara's pursuit of SAC aptly demonstrates, sometimes the government *likes* to play the role of white knight, particularly if that means creatively stretching a criminal statute to cover morally objectionable behavior.

More relevant to this chapter, the government's pursuit of insider trading underscores a brewing debate over which institutions should enjoy power to "make" criminal law in the United States. Whereas Chapter 3 focused on pathologies present in our criminal code, the present chapter focuses on a different set of pathologies that arise when the legislature leans too heavily on other branches to generate criminal law's content and set its boundaries.

We often say criminal law is "statutory" to distinguish it from first-year law school subjects such as contracts or torts.[16] This recitation carries both descriptive and normative components. First, criminal law usually *can* be traced to a specific statute. This is particularly the case in federal criminal law, where it has been "long settled" that there exists no such thing as "federal criminal common law."[17] Second, the mantra that "criminal law-is-statutory" reflects a normative aspiration embodied in the legality principle.[18] The principle tells us that criminal law must be the product of a democratically elected legislature, that prohibitions should be prospective, and that penal laws should be well-defined, written down, and interpreted narrowly. The overall purpose of these rules is simple: to provide advance notice of what is

---

[14] For earlier examples, see ANDERSON, *supra* note 9, at 92 (citing prosecution of Ivan Boesky in the 1980s).

[15] Donald C. Langevoort, *Rereading Cady, Roberts: The Ideology and Practice of Insider Trading Regulation*, 99 COLUM. L. REV. 1319, 1328–29 (1999).

[16] "Statutes created by Congress are the basis of charges brought by prosecutors." Hon. Robert J. Conrad & Katy L. Clements, *The Vanishing Criminal Jury Trial: From Trial Judges to Sentencing Judges*, 86 GEO. WASH. L. REV. 99 (2018).

[17] "The definition of the elements of a criminal offense is entrusted to the legislature, particularly in the case of federal crimes, which are solely creatures of statute." Liparota v. United States, 471 U.S. 419, 424 (1985). "It is the legislature, not the Court, which is to define a crime, and ordain its punishment." United States v. Wiltberger, 18 U.S. (Wheat) 76, 95 (1820). Absolute statements such as these have led contemporary courts to declare, "No federal criminal common law exists." United States v. McLean, 802 F.3d 1228, 1230 (11th Cir. 2015).

[18] On the legality principle and its implications, see John Calvin Jeffries, *Legality, Vagueness, and the Construction of Penal Statutes*, 71 VA. L. REV. 189 (1985).

wrongful and to restrain the government from arbitrarily depriving us of our liberty.[19]

Notwithstanding these teachings, life on the ground often diverges from the ideal. Even at the federal level, the Executive and Judiciary branches play a significant role in "making" criminal law, even if they avoid writing statutes from whole cloth. Some crimes require the judiciary to interpret open-ended terms.[20] Some invite jurists to add background terms.[21] And some (okay, many) explicitly depend on administrative agencies to engage in fact-finding or promulgate a set of rules and regulations.

Some crimes rely more than others on these nonstatutory lawmaking modalities. Insider trading is clearly one of them. It has relied far more heavily on judges, prosecutors, and regulators to define its meaning than it has on Congress. Ironically, the same could be said of the legal doctrines the government relied upon to prosecute *SAC Capital*, the entity that employed, compensated, and encouraged its analysts' trading activity.

We should not be overly surprised that crimes that fall upon the wealthy and powerful are also the crimes that Congress has chosen to leave open-ended and underdefined. It's difficult enough to draft a criminal statute when everyone agrees what should be prohibited and who should be punished. It is far more taxing to accomplish that goal when the proscribed behavior is more ambiguous and complicated, and when the law's putative offenders enjoy the power to lobby Congress and aggressively fight prosecutions in court.[22] When behavior and norms are in flux, outsourcing becomes the legislature's go-to strategy.

In response to this phenomenon, the judiciary has employed different mechanisms to rein in such outsourcing. When Congress drafts statutes whose prohibitions are truly unintelligible, or which place unreviewable discretion in government

---

[19] United States v. Hudson and Goodwin, 7 Cranch 32 (1812) (holding that Congress "must first make an act a crime [and] affix a punishment to it"); United States v. Wiltberger, 18 U.S. 76, 95, 5 Wheat. 76, 5 L.Ed. 37 (1820) (setting forth the "plain principle that the power of punishment is vested in the legislative, not in the judicial department").

[20] Dan M. Kahan, *Lenity and Federal Common Law Crimes*, 8 SUP. CT. REV. 345, 347 (1994) ("federal criminal law, no less than any other statutory domain, is dominated by judge-made law crafted to fill the interstices of open-textured statutory provisions").

[21] *Compare* Neder v. United States, 571 U.S. 1, 23 (imputing "materiality" to federal bank fraud statute) *with* United States v. Oakland Cannabis Buyers' Coop, 532 U.S. 483, 490 (2001) (casting doubt on federal courts' ability to recognize a legal defense "not provided for in statute").

[22] On insider trading's controversial standing among academics and practitioners, see Stephen M. Bainbridge, *Insider Trading Law?* 70 BUS. LAWYER 751 (2015) (summarizing arguments); Michael P. Dooley, *Enforcement of Insider Trading Restrictions*, 66 VA. L. REV. 1, 1–2 (1980); Peter J. Henning, *What's So Bad about Insider Trading Law?* 70 BUS. LAW. 751, 751–52 (2015) ("United States insider trading law seems to be about as popular as the flu, at least from the perspective of legal academics").

prosecutors and agents, courts will declare them unconstitutionally vague.[23] A step down from this extreme is when a statute features an ambiguous term whose meaning cannot be deduced from secondary sources. In cases such as these, a court may rely on the rule of lenity to interpret the disputed language in the defendant's favor.[24] Concepts such as lenity and vagueness limit the executive branch's ability to "make" law. When courts police these concepts aggressively, prosecutors and regulators respond by treading more carefully. When courts apply these brakes infrequently, prosecutors and regulators feel freer to push the envelope.[25]

Courts can further constrain Executive lawmaking by narrowly construing statutes. A narrow interpretation is often heralded as necessary in order to prevent the vagueness problems that would otherwise ensue. Thus, in Yates v. United States, the Court interpreted an obstruction of justice statute to apply only to a person's corrupt and purposeful destruction of data.[26] Not too long before that, it held that "honest services fraud" applies only to a fiduciary's undisclosed bribe or kickback, and not to her undisclosed self-dealing transactions.[27] And in roughly the same time period, it held that the federal bribery statute applied only to agreements to perform "official acts," and that those "acts" did not include giving a person enhanced access to meetings or parties.[28] For each of these cases, the Court invoked vagueness concerns to justify embracing a narrower interpretation of the relevant statute.[29] Or to put it another way, it put the kibosh on prosecutorial lawmaking – at least in *these areas*.

---

[23] Kolender v. Lawson, 461 U.S. 352, 358 (1983). *See, e.g.,* City of Chicago v. Morales, 527 U.S. 41, 56 (1999) (finding impermissibly vague a Chicago ordinance prohibiting street gang members from loitering in public places).

[24] The version of lenity that predominates is one that awards a tiebreak to the defendant after courts have exhausted all methods of statutory interpretation. As a result, lenity is believed not to play a major role in federal criminal law. *See, e.g.,* Zachary Price, *The Rule of Lenity as A Rule of Structure,* 72 FORDHAM L. REV. 885, 899 (2004) ("The rule of lenity today has very little practical effect in decisions interpreting criminal statutes in either state or federal courts"). *See also* Lawrence M. Solan, *Law, Language and Lenity,* 40 WM. & MARY L. REV. 57, 59–60 (1998). Lenity could become stronger were courts to require the narrowest possible construction, reduce deference to government prosecutors, and limit potential sources of statutory interpretation. For more on these more muscular version of lenity, see Shon Hopwood, *Restoring the Historical Rule of Lenity as a Canon,* 95 N.Y.U L. REV. 918, 921 (2020); *cf.* Carissa Byrne Hessick & Joseph Edward Kennedy, *Criminal Clear Statement Rules,* 79 WASH. U. L. REV. 351, 357–58, 368 (2019) (addressing lenity's practical shortcomings and proposing clear statement rules as an alternative).

[25] Notwithstanding this freedom, Congress can less visibly shape the government's enforcement policies through its purse-strings and its committee oversight powers. *See* Daniel C. Richman, *Federal Criminal Law, Congressional Delegation, and Enforcement Discretion,* 46 UCLA L. REV. 757 (1999).

[26] Yates v. United States, 574 U.S. 528, 546 (2015).

[27] Skilling v. United States, 561 U.S. 358, 408–9 (2010).

[28] McDonnell v. United States, 579 U.S. 550, 572–74 (2016).

[29] McDonnell, 579 U.S. at 576; Skilling, 561 U.S. at 410; Yates, 574 U.S. at 546.

Although these "narrow construction" cases attract attention, their spillover effects remain relatively modest.[30] Interpreting *one* criminal statute narrowly does not necessarily mean the judiciary will treat different statutes the same way. Moreover, Congress can always respond by enacting a clearer, broader law if it disagrees with the judiciary's narrow interpretation.[31]

By contrast, the so-called nondelegation doctrine, a largely dormant rule that prohibits Congress from "delegating" its lawmaking powers to other branches, has the potential to wipe out multiple statutory frameworks in one sitting, should the Supreme Court decide to breathe life into it.

Before going further, it is helpful to consider what we mean by "delegation" or "nondelegation." When political scientists and economists speak of delegation, they often are referring to the legislature's reliance on other actors to refine a statute's on-the-ground meaning.[32] Much of the early public choice literature explains delegation as Congress's way of preserving its political capital while also providing the public with popular (if overdetermined) legal prohibitions.[33] This is the behavior I have in mind when I use the term "outsourcing." Congress paints with broad strokes and relies on other legal actors to fill in the details.

For administrative and constitutional law scholars, "nondelegation" denotes a specific doctrine that enforces the Constitution's separation of powers. Under this doctrine, Congress can ask its correspondent branches to enhance a statute by doing *their* jobs, but not by asking them to do *its* job. That's the idea – but it has had little practical effect (up until now) on the administrative state.

For nearly a century, the Supreme Court has afforded Congress wide discretion in relying on administrative agencies to flesh out the meaning of constitutive and open-ended statutes, including penal prohibitions. If Congress writes a law that says it shall be a crime to intentionally pollute the waters, it can leave it to the Environmental Protection Agency (EPA) to define terms like pollution and waters. So long as the legislature includes in its statute an "intelligible principle" to guide the EPA (or any other delegee), the statute has not run afoul of the nondelegation doctrine.[34] True, the Court *has* hinted that a higher degree of intelligibility might

---

[30] Stephen F. Smith, *Yates v. United States: A Case Study in Overcriminalization*, 163 U. PA. L. REV. 147, 149 (2014) ("It is a gross oversimplification to view the interpretive question in Yates as whether a fish is a 'tangible object'"); F. Andrew Hessick & Carissa Byrne Hessick, *Constraining Criminal Laws*, 106 MINN. L. REV. 58–59 (2022).

[31] William J. Stuntz, *The Pathological Politics of Criminal Law*, 100 MICH. L. REV. 505, 560 (2002) ("Barring vague statutes does little about breadth [a]nd breadth is much harder for courts to regulate").

[32] Kahan, *supra* note 20, at 347 ("The historic underenforcement of lenity, I will argue, reflects the existence of another largely unacknowledged, but nonetheless well established, rule of federal criminal law: that Congress may *delegate* criminal lawmaking power to courts").

[33] *See, e.g.*, Daniel C. Richman, *Old Chief v. United States: Stipulating Away Prosecutorial Accountability?* 83 VA. L. REV. 939, 959 n.69 (1997).

[34] J. W. Hampton, Jr., & Co. v. United States, 276 U.S. 394, 409 (1928).

be necessary for criminal statutes, but even there, it has granted the legislature a fair degree of latitude.[35]

That deferential stance may be changing. A few years ago, several Supreme Court justices signaled their discontent with this framework and their willingness to revisit the doctrine in Gundy v. United States, a case that challenged the Sex Offender Registration and Notification Act (SORNA).[36] Only a plurality of the Court (led by Justice Kagan) adopted the deferential stance predicted by the nondelegation doctrine.[37] Of more interest was Justice Gorsuch's dissent, which lamented Congress' abdication of its lawmaking authority to the executive branch. It was one thing to ask another branch to engage in true factfinding, Gorsuch wrote, but a far different matter to punt policy decisions to the Attorney General. In Justice Gorsuch's view, SORNA was over the line, and so were many other statutes.[38]

Should Justice Gorsuch persuade the Court to tighten its delegation rule, his efforts will work profound impacts on numerous enforcement agencies. Before we reach that point, it's helpful to ask whether outsourcing produces uniformly bad outcomes in the white-collar context or whether we would prefer to witness its eventual erosion or demise.

4.2 OUTSOURCING AND UNDERWRITTEN CRIMES

According to Dan Richman, administrative delegation is not all that different from expansive judicial interpretation; both are a form of outsourced lawmaking.[39] According to administrative crime's critics, administrative outsourcing problematically enables regulators to sidestep deliberative hurdles embedded in the legislative process.[40] On the other hand, excessive reliance on judges to fill legislative blanks is equally undesirable when it yields too much power to judges and prosecutors. That some critics get more worked up about delegation than they do about open-ended

---

[35] US v. Touby, 909 F.2d 759, 765 (1990).

[36] Gundy v. United States, 113 S.Ct. 2116 (2019).

[37] SORNA required sex offenders to register with a national registry or otherwise face federal criminal sanctions. Because pre-Act offenders could not register overnight, the Act directed the Attorney General to develop implementation rules. Relying on its own previous interpretation of the Act, the Court's plurality concluded that SORNA, "easily passe[d] constitutional muster" with the nondelegation doctrine's 'intelligible principle' requirement because the statute directed the Attorney General to develop these registration requirements 'as soon as feasible.'" Gundy, 139 S.Ct. at 2129–30.

[38] *Id.* at 2143 (Gorsuch, J., dissenting).

[39] Daniel Richman, *Defining Crime, Delegating Authority – How Different Are Administrative Crimes?* 39 YALE J. REG. 304 (2022) (arguing that administrative crimes, as examples of outsourcing, are more normatively desirable than other, well-accepted forms of legislative outsourcing).

[40] Brenner M. Fissell, *When Agencies Make Criminal Law*, 10 U.C. IRVINE L. REV. 855, 905 (2020); Andrew Hessick & Carissa Byrne Hessick, *Nondelegation and Criminal Law*, 107 VA. L. REV. 281, 311 (2021).

statutes (notwithstanding Justice Gorsuch, who has complained about both)[41] highlights contemporary society's discomfort with regulatory power.

Outsourcing's defenders contend that there simply is no way for a legislature to successfully address contemporary problems without relying on administrative experts, interpretive judging, and enforcement discretion.[42] Outsourcing's critics don't deny these points, but they observe the many ills that can arise when elected representatives rely too heavily on others to do the heavy lifting of crafting and refining legal prohibitions.[43]

The constitutional debate adopts a more absolutist tone. Delegation's archest critics contend that the Court's lax approach violates the Constitution's separation of powers principle, particularly where criminal laws are concerned.[44] Delegation's critics aren't concerned merely with the degree of criminal law's outsourcing. They are concerned that it happens *at all*.[45]

Since this is a book about white-collar crime and its pathologies, the remainder of this chapter sidesteps the constitutional debate and instead focuses on the policy implications of Congress's outsourcing habit. In doing so, I hope I can shed some light on this debate by demonstrating that not all outsourcing is the same. To be sure, outsourcing carries real tradeoffs – which I discuss in the sections that follow – but it generates distinctly *different* problems depending on the type of crime – and outsourcing – involved. Matthew Martoma's prosecution, discussed at the beginning of this chapter, nicely elucidates this point. Martoma was eventually convicted by a jury of insider trading. His employer, SAC Capital, eventually pleaded guilty to a set of crimes premised on corporate criminal liability. Each of these crimes rely in great degree on institutions other than Congress to obtain their meaning. At the same time, each doctrine has travelled a far different trajectory than one might predict from reading criminal delegation's most recent critiques.

The insider trading offense owes its existence to a very generous reading of the Securities Exchange Act of 1934 and rule 10b-5, the SEC's all-purpose securities antifraud rule. Corporate criminal liability, on the other hand, is a theory of vicarious liability, formally known as *respondeat superior*, that holds the corporation

---

[41] *See, e.g.*, Wooden v. United States, 142 S.Ct. 1063, 1081–85 (2022) (Gorsuch, J., concurring in judgment) (arguing for a more muscular rule of lenity).

[42] "[I]n our increasingly complex society, replete with ever changing and more technical problems, Congress simply cannot do its job absent an ability to delegate power under broad general directives." Mistretta v. United States, 488 U.S. 361, 372 (1989); *see also* Kahan, *supra* note 20, at 352; Richman, *supra* note 39 (defending administrative crimes); *see also* Rachel E. Barkow, *Separation of Powers and the Criminal Law*, 58 STAN. L. REV. 989, 1009–10 (2006) (observing that "the Court has been highly receptive to functional arguments about the need for government flexibility").

[43] Carissa Byrne Hessick, *The Myth of Common Law Crimes*, 105 VA. L. REV. 965, 992 (2019).

[44] *See, e.g.*, Gundy, 139 S.Ct. 2116, 2141 (Gorsuch, J., dissenting).

[45] Fissell, *supra* note 40, at 857.

liable for its employees' crimes.[46] Both are what this chapter calls "underwritten" crimes.[47] The underwritten crime helps us understand where outsourcing can go wrong, how outsourcing can create starkly different results, and how we can best remedy its excesses.

Insider trading and *respondeat superior* liability rely heavily on the common law's familiar case-by-case method to flesh out their meaning. You will not learn the definition of insider trading's famous misappropriation theory from reading a statute; and you will not find *respondeat superior*'s contours embedded in title 18 of the federal code.[48] If you want to know anything about either topic, you will need to study the judicial opinions that give meaning to these doctrines.

But that's where the similarities end. Insider trading has generated numerous trials, countless appellate and Supreme Court opinions, many clarifying regulations by the SEC, and a rich body of doctrinal law purporting to define and interpret key elements.[49] The familiar claim that delegation instills too much power in the executive branch is difficult to square with this cache of material.

The vicarious rule of corporate criminal liability, by contrast, has barely registered on courts' radar since the Supreme Court's initial announcement of *respondeat superior* in the first decade of the twentieth century.[50] Yes, there have been several appellate cases of note; they nicely fill out the Court's initial framework and eliminate the kinds of defenses one might expect a corporation to raise.[51] But the handful of cases that address corporate crime head-on have ossified. The common law of corporate criminal liability is much the same today as it was in 1970.

---

[46] The federal code's dictionary statute partially codifies criminal liability by equating corporations and other business entities as legal persons. *See* 1 U.S.C. § 1 (2018) (except as otherwise indicated by context, terms such as "persons" and "whoever" include "corporations, companies, associations, firms, partnerships, societies, and joint stock companies, as well as individuals"); *see also* 18 U.S.C. § 18 (2018) (defining "organization" to mean "person" other than an individual).

[47] For an excellent discussion of *both* areas of law and their intersection, see ANDERSON, *supra* note 9, at 108–17 (discussing corporate criminal liability in insider trading cases).

[48] See discussion at note 34, *supra*.

[49] See, e.g ., ANDERSON, *supra* note 9, at chapter 2 (describing relevant regulatory provisions) and 3 (surveying common law elements); Zach Lustbader, *Note, Title 18 Insider Trading*, 130 YALE L.J. 1828, 1836–40 (2021) (charting the judicial and administrative development of insider trading doctrine).

[50] MIRIAM H. BAER, *Corporate Criminal Law Unbounded*, in OXFORD HANDBOOK OF PROSECUTORS AND PROSECUTION 8 (Ronald Wright, Kay Levine, and Russell Gold, eds., 2021); Sara Sun Beale, *The Development and Evolution of the U.S. Law of Corporate Criminal Liability and the Yates Memo*, 46 STETSON L. REV. 41, 56 (2016).

[51] *See, e.g.*, United States v. Hilton Hotels, 467 F.2d 1000, 1004, 1006–7 (9th Cir. 1972) (acknowledging corporate crime's "implied" nature and further advising that the corporation may be liable despite employee's violation of corporate policy); Standard Oil v. United States, 307 F.2d 120, 128–29 (5th Cir. 1962) (requirement that employee act with "a purpose" to benefit corporation brings employee's behavior within the scope of employment); U.S. v. A&P Trucking Co., 358 U.S. 121, 126 (1958) (extending *respondeat superior* liability to partnerships).

That's not to say corporate *prosecutions* have remained stagnant. Prosecutors in the 1990s created nonbinding charging guidelines to guide prosecutors in their treatment of corporate offenders.[52] These charging guidelines enabled corporate defendants to enter side agreements (so-called deferred [DPAs] or nonprosecution agreements [NPAs]) with government prosecutors.[53] Whereas prosecutors are constrained in how and when they can advance different theories of insider trading, they enjoy almost absolute power to decide which errant corporations to charge, which ones to extend DPAs or other extrajudicial agreements, and how many commitments to extract through the DPA process.

Thus, outsourcing produces dramatically different outcomes depending on the crime and institutional context. Insider trading is an apt example of *fractured* delegation, featuring iterative interactions between and within different branches of government. Corporate prosecution, by contrast, is a case of *unitary* delegation that has enabled federal prosecutors to craft and implement a shadow law of corporate responsibility. I discuss these two examples in greater detail in the next sections.

4.3 INSIDER TRADING

To the layperson, insider trading signifies the act of trading on a public stock exchange using private information – what many might see as yet another example of how the wealthy benefit from an unfair advantage. As legal experts are well-aware, the "unfair advantage" theory is neither the law nor even the primary rationale for the prohibition on insider trading.[54] Instead, courts have conceptualized it as a violation of fiduciary duty while also claiming that market confidence would fall apart if the general public thought insiders could trade in violation *of that duty*.[55]

---

[52] On the Sentencing Guidelines' evolution and structure, see Mistretta v. United States, 488 U.S. 361, 379 (1989); Frank O. Bowman, III, *Mr. Madison Meets a Time Machine: The Political Science of Federal Sentencing Reform*, 58 STAN. L. REV. 235, 243–45 (2005); Ronald L. Gainer, *Federal Criminal Code Reform: Past and Future*, 2 BUFF. CRIM. L. REV. 45, 111–29 (1998). Regarding the organizational sentencing guidelines and their unique weaknesses, see Jennifer Arlen, *The Failure of the Organizational Sentencing Guidelines*, 66 U. MIAMI L. REV. 321, 325–26 (2011).

[53] CINDY R. ALEXANDER & JENNIFER ARLEN, *Does Conviction Matter? The Reputational and Collateral Effects of Corporate Crime*, in RESEARCH HANDBOOK ON CORPORATE CRIME AND FINANCIAL MISDEALING 92–96 (Jennifer Arlen, ed. 2018); Jennifer Arlen & Marcel Kahan, *Corporate Governance Regulation through Non-prosecution*, 84 U. CHI. L REV. 323, 332–33 (2017).

[54] *See* Samuel W Buell, *What Is Securities Fraud?* 61 DUKE L. J. 511, 562 (2011) (arguing that such an equal access rule would "sweep too broadly"). On the ways in which the SEC has nevertheless invoked the "level playing field" narrative to generate public support, see Langevoort, *supra* note 15, at 1324–26.

[55] John Anderson, *Insider Trading and the Myth of Market Confidence*, 56 WASH. U. J.L. & POL'Y 1, 3–4, 13 (2018).

Insider trading law is thus a method of protecting investor confidence; it is not intended to ensure equal knowledge among investors.

Insider trading is also an excellent example of an underwritten, and therefore outsourced, crime. Neither the Securities Exchange Act of 1934 nor rule 10b-5 say anything specific about insider trading. Section 10(b) criminalizes the use of "any manipulative or deceptive device or contrivance"[56] and Rule 10b-5 prohibits "any person" (including corporate entities) from directly or indirectly using any "device, scheme, or artifice to defraud" in connection with the purchase or sale of a security.[57] And finally, the 1934 Act's penalty provision states that any person who "willfully" violates the law is criminally liable and subject to a maximum term of twenty years' imprisonment.[58]

From a trio of Supreme Court cases, we learn far more. For example, we know from reading the Court's 1980 decision in *Chiarella* and its 1993 follow-up decision in *O'Hagan*, that there are in fact two major theories of insider trading.[59] The classic insider is an officer, director of employee who trades on her company's material, nonpublic information and does not publicly disclose her knowledge in advance of the trade.[60] The misappropriation theory extends the prohibition on trading to a company outsider. The outsider violates the law when she receives confidential information from a source and then traded in the shares of some company to which she otherwise owes no duty.[61] The violation here is not to the company's shareholders but rather to the source of the confidential information.

Insider trading law has inspired a rich body of criticism, eliciting charges that it is overbroad, underinclusive, incoherent, and misguided.[62] Its defenders insist it is necessary, wholly justified, and far more coherent than critics would have us believe.[63] Under the best circumstances, Congress would hold hearings, deliberate

---

[56] 15 U.S.C. § 78j(b).

[57] 17 C.F.R. § 240.10b-5 (2021).

[58] 15 U.S.C § 78ff(a). This provision further provides that a person who proves he had no knowledge of the relevant rule or law can avoid imprisonment, but not a finding of guilt.

[59] Chiarella v. United States, 445 U.S. 222 (1980); United States v. O'Hagan, 521 U.S. 642 (1997). On the Supreme Court's case-by-case development of insider trading, see, e.g., Jill E. Fisch, *Constructive Ambiguity and Judicial Development of Insider Trading*, 71 SMU L. REV. 749, 752–57 (2018); Donald C. Langevoort, *"Fine Distinctions" in the Contemporary Law of Insider Trading*, 2013 COLUM. BUS. L. REV. 429, 434–35, 439–40.

[60] Chiarella, 445 U.S. at 230.

[61] O'Hagan, 521 U.S. at 652.

[62] HENRY G. MANNE, INSIDER TRADING AND THE STOCK MARKET 77–91 (1966); ANDERSON, *supra* note 9, at 89–118; Bainbridge, *supra* note 22, at 176–89.

[63] Donna M. Nagy, *Beyond Dirks: Gratuitous Tipping and Insider Trading*, 42 J. CORP. L. 1, 6–8 (2016); Fisch, *supra* note 59, at 752; Michael Guttentag, *Selective Disclosure and Insider Trading*, 69 FLA. L. REV. 519, 525 (2017). Those in the middle might include Donald Langevoort, who has specifically noted the ways in which insider trading's straddling of criminal and civil liability creates problems for courts and ultimately muddles its meaning. *See* Donald C. Langevoort, *Words from on High about Rule 10b-5: Chiarella's History, Central Bank's Future*, 20 DEL. J. CORP. L. 865, 885–87 (1995).

on these issues and devise language that captures the behavior a majority views as harmful and morally wrongful. More importantly, as I have argued elsewhere, Congress might devise *more* than one prohibition on insider trading, opting to subdivide the crime into a series of offenses, some more serious and some less.[64]

Congress has yet to seriously engage these efforts, however, and seems disinclined to do so in the future. In 2021, the House passed the Insider Trading Prohibition Act, whose stated goal was to "codify" the already existing law of insider trading (whatever that means).[65] The Act cast little new light on the offense and never made it out of committee in the Senate.

Nevertheless, some areas of insider trading have become fairly settled. The officer who trades in an employer's stock, aided by the employer's nonpublic information, knows full well he or she is violating the law. The Martoma prosecution, however, is emblematic of a more vexatious category of cases, in which one person discloses information and another person trades on it. This bifurcation of knowledge and trading continues to cause inconsistency among federal courts.

Consider this easy example: If Al and Bee agree in advance that Al will disclose his employer's private information, and that Bee will trade on it and split the proceeds with Al, everyone agrees that Al and Bee are guilty.[66] But not all scenarios are so clear cut. Al and Bee may not share nefarious goals. Al's disclosure may be inadvertent, or Al may disclose information for altruistic reasons, such as to expose wrongdoers. When Al reveals information for a *corporate* purpose, even a misguided one, Al arguably has not violated his fiduciary duty. And if Al has not violated his fiduciary duty, then it is implausible to say Bee has violated such a duty.

Readers will recognize this hypothetical as a version of the Supreme Court's decision in Dirks v. SEC.[67] In Dirks, the Court rejected a rule that would have required *all* tippees to abstain from trading on inside information.[68] Instead, Dirks examined the initial tipper's purpose. If the purpose was altruistic, breach was absent

---

[64] *See* Miriam H. Baer, *Insider Trading's Legality Problem*, 127 YALE L.J. F. 129, 145 (2017) ("Besides providing citizens some advanced indication of what is forbidden, statutory proscription's less-heralded benefit is its ability to subdivide criminal behavior").

[65] Insider Trading Prohibition Act, H.R. 2534, 116th Cong. (2019). For a discussion on the Act's advantages and shortcomings, see Kayla Quigley, *The Insider Trading Prohibition Act: A Small Step towards a Codified Insider Trading Law*, 26 FORDHAM J. CORP. & FIN. L. 183, 208–14 (2021).

[66] A substantive crime and the conspiracy to commit that crime are separate offenses. Iannelli v. United States, 420 U.S. 770, 777 (1975) ("Traditionally, the law has considered conspiracy and the completed substantive offense to be separate crimes").

[67] Dirks v. S.E.C., 463 U.S. 646 (1983).

[68] "The SEC's position as stated in its opinion in this case is that a tippee 'inherits' the [obligation not to trade] whenever he receives inside information from an insider." Dirks, 103 S.Ct. at 3262. Although Dirks involved a tipper who was a classic insider, later cases have extended its reasoning to misappropriation cases. Martoma, 894 F.3d 64, 73 n. 5 (2nd Cir. 2017) (citing authorities).

and the tippee was in the clear.[69] Thus, the Court wrote: "[T]he test is whether the insider personally will benefit, directly or indirectly, from his disclosure."[70] The benefit could be "a pecuniary gain" or "a reputational benefit that will translate into future earnings."[71] The Court then buried a landmine:

> For example, there may be a relationship between the insider and the recipient that suggests a quid pro quo ... or an intention to benefit [the recipient]. The elements of fiduciary duty and exploitation ... also exist when an insider makes a gift of confidential information to a trading relative or friend.[72]

If ever there existed an exemplar of the dangers of relying on the judiciary to "write" criminal law, Dirks is it. The quote sets forth three separate concepts – quid pro quo, unadorned intent to benefit, and the gift to a relative or friend – of varying levels of generality. These three prongs casually intertwine substantive and evidentiary concepts ("a relationship ... that *suggests* a quid pro quo") while leaving major terms (relative, friend, benefit) undefined.

Because Dirks's personal benefit test is phrased so broadly, it is hopelessly overdetermined; each court that encounters it can extract whichever rule it likes best. This Second Circuit demonstrated as much in United States v. Newman.[73] In Newman, the Second Circuit held that Dirks could be satisfied solely through evidence of a "meaningfully close personal relationship" whose exchange was "objective, consequential, and represents at least a potential gain of pecuniary or similarly valuable nature."[74] In other words, tippee liability appeared to require *an exchange* or quid pro quo, *even between family members*. Newman drew plaudits from the white-collar bar and howls from nearly everyone else. Even worse, for a short period, it apparently touched off an *increase* in insider trading.[75]

The Supreme Court subsequently undid some of the Second Circuit's damage by clarifying in its *Salman* decision that a gift among family members satisfied the personal benefit test, with no need for an exchange or quid pro quo.[76] But *Salman* did not direct lower courts on how to handle cases in which a family exchange was missing, or in which the tippee's knowledge of a tipper's fiduciary breach was less obvious. Nor did it ever address, outside the family context, which aspects of a relationship might inherently "sugges[t] a quid pro quo," as outlined in Dirks.

---

[69] Dirks was decided before the SEC's enactment of Regulation FD (Regulation Fair Disclosure), which more broadly regulates disclosures of information. *See* Nagy, *supra* note 63, at 36–41.

[70] Dirks, 463 U.S. at 662.

[71] *Id.*

[72] *Id.*

[73] United States v. Newman, 773 F.3d 438 (2d Cir. 2014), *abrogated by* Salman v. United States, 137 S.Ct. 420 (2016).

[74] *Id.* at 452.

[75] Patel, *supra* note 12, at 480.

[76] Salman v. United States, 137 S.Ct. 420, 428 (2016).

Meanwhile, Martoma's case was making its way through the courts. Martoma's conviction arose out of information provided to him by a medical expert who relayed – for a lucrative consulting fee of $1,000 per hour – confidential information about the progress of an experimental drug developed to combat Alzheimer's disease.[77] Thanks to the expert, Martoma received confidential information that the drug's efficacy was questionable and urged SAC to reduce its positions in two companies developing the drug. Martoma's advance warning netted $80 million in gains and averted $194 million in losses for SAC, contributing to a personal bonus of $9 million.[78]

Complicating Martoma's case was the fact that the trial court directed his jury on *two* theories of tipper-tippee liability: the quid pro quo theory as well as the gift theory.[79] Martoma's trial concluded prior to the Second Circuit's Newman decision. Under *Newman's* reasoning, Martoma's jury should have been instructed on the "meaningfully close relationship" and "objective, consequential exchange" the Newman court envisioned between the tipper and tippee, even when the tip was intended as a gift. But post-*Salman*, the Supreme Court's streamlined definition obviated the need to show anything more than family members gratuitously passing information to each another that they knew would subsequently become the source of trades.[80]

Taking advantage of the Supreme Court's latest decision (and confusing the general public even more), *Martoma's* prosecutors insisted in their appellate brief that *Salman* had "fully abrogated" Newman's requirement that there be a "concrete" exchange of benefits between the tipper and tippee.[81] Although a divided Second Circuit panel initially embraced this view in *Martoma I*, it backtracked a bit in *Martoma II*, reasoning that "we need not decide whether Newman's gloss on the gift theory is inconsistent with *Salman*." Since the trial had adduced evidence Martoma paid the tipper $70,000 in consulting fees, the government had clearly established its *second* theory of tipper-tippee trading, namely a quid pro quo. In other words, there was no need to revisit the Second Circuit's gift theory language because Martoma was clearly guilty under *Dirks's* quid pro quo language.[82]

Post-*Martoma*, scholars and enforcement officials have cited alternative mechanisms to punish insider trading. Title 18, section 1348, the all-purpose securities fraud

---

[77] The consulting fee potentially represented payment for *legitimate* consulting services as well as illegitimate tipping. United States v. Martoma, 894 F.3d 64, 78 (2d Cir. 2017).

[78] *Id.* at 70.

[79] *Id.*

[80] *Salman*, 137 S. Ct. at 427–28.

[81] Reply Brief at 1, United States v. Martoma, 894 F.3d 64 (2017) (No. 14-3599).

[82] As the Martoma II decision observed, the Second Circuit had previously accepted far less evidence of the tipper's expectation of a personal benefit. *See* Martoma II, 894 F.3d 64, 74 (2d Cir. 2017) (citing cases and examples). Dissenting from Martoma II, Judge Rosemary Pooler expressed skepticism the trial testimony had established a quid pro quo. *Id.* at 87–88 (Pooler, J., dissenting).

statute that was enacted as part of the Sarbanes–Oxley Act, is one candidate; it says nothing about insider trading, but a recent Second Circuit opinion suggests prosecutors might be able to lodge prosecutions that are unconstrained by the judiciary's rule 10b-5 precedents.[83] In other words, prosecutors might be able to avoid the whole *Newman, Salman, Dirks* trio mess by charging an insider trader under section 1348 instead of section 10(b) of the Securities Exchange Act.

Consider that for a moment. Section 1348's language says nothing about insider trading.[84] If courts permit insider trading prosecutions to proceed under Section 1348 while untethering the statute from Rule 10b-5's judicial precedents, they will destroy the very guardrails earlier courts erected to restrain prosecutorial power. The resulting crime will be broad, vulnerable to claims of arbitrary enforcement, and very likely lack uniformity across different United States Attorneys' offices. In other words, it will vindicate outsourcing's strongest critics.

This outcome was foreseen over a decade ago. Writing of the Sarbanes–Oxley amendments and Section 1348's enactment, Professors Weisberg and Mills warned that its language was so broad that it could become an all-purpose antidistortion statute.[85] Until recently, their concern seemed premature. But as Section 1348 grows in popularity, so too does the prescience of their warning. Through this little noticed

---

[83] United States v. Blaszczak, 947 F.3d 19 (2d Cir. 2019) (hereinafter "Blaszczak I"), *cert. granted, judgement vacated*, 141 S.Ct. 1040 (2021); Brett Atanasio et al., *Insider Trading Case to Watch: The Second Circuit to Revisit Blaszczak*, JDSupra (Feb. 18, 2021), www.jdsupra.com/legal news/insider-trading-case-to-watch-the-3483251/. The Second Circuit subsequently revisited the case in United States v. Blaszczak, 56 4th Cir. 230, 2022 WL17926047 (2d Cir. Dec. 27, 2022) (hereinafter "Blazsczak II") and vacated the conviction on alternative grounds (namely that the confidential information at issue did not constitute "money or property" under the relevant fraud statutes). Judge Walker, in a concurring opinion joined by Judge Kearse, voiced the concern that *Blasczak II* ignored the question posed earlier: whether Section 1348's conception of insider trading was broader than Rule 10b-5. If Section 1348 was truly unencumbered by prior insider trading precedent, Walker reasoned, then prosecutors would find it easier to pursue criminal charges under Section 1348 than civil charges under Rule 10b-5. "Traditional notions of fair play are offended by the present incongruence . . . . It should not require fewer elements to prove a criminal conviction than to impose civil penalties for the same conduct." United States v. Blaszczak, 56 F.4th 230 (2d Cir. 2022) (Walker, J., concurrence).

[84] The "new" statute broadly prohibits obtaining or selling securities using false or fraudulent pretenses:

Whoever knowingly executes, or attempts to execute, a scheme or artifice –
(2) to obtain, by means of false or fraudulent pretenses, representations, or promises, any money or property in connection with the purchase or sale [of] . . . any security of an issuer with a class of securities registered under section 12 of the Securities Exchange Act of 1934 (15 U.S.C. 78*l*) or that is required to file reports under section 15(d) of the Securities Exchange Act of 1934 (15 U.S.C. 78o(d)).

18 U.S.C. §1348. On Section 1348's implications for insider trading law and its enforcement, see Karen E. Woody, *The New Insider Trading*, 52 Ariz. St. L.J. 594 (2020).

[85] David Mills and Robert Weisberg, *Corrupting the Harm Requirement in White Collar Crime*, 60 Stan. L. Rev. 1371, 1435–38 (2008).

and little debated "sleeper provision," Congress might have finally achieved the outcome the SEC sought and the Supreme Court rejected for years: the prohibition and punishment of anyone trading securities according to an "unfair informational advantage."[86]

A final caveat is in order: Section 1348 was enacted in 2002. Mills and Weisberg surfaced their concerns in 2008. That the judiciary *still* has yet to uniformly embrace such an aggressive interpretation of Section 1348 is a testament to outsourcing's slow pace. As we see from the corporate crime example, this pace can be both a feature and a bug.

4.4 CORPORATE CRIME

In addition to SAC Capital's employees, prosecutors indicted SAC Capital, and secured its conviction under the standard definition of corporate crime. Like insider trading, corporate criminal liability relies on nonlegislative actors to give it meaning. Nevertheless, even though corporate criminal liability is as "outsourced" as insider trading, it has developed in a dramatically different manner.

Whereas the law of insider trading features numerous doctrinal twists and turns, the doctrinal law of corporate criminal liability has remained nearly unchanged since the Supreme Court first articulated it in *New York Central.*[87] In that case, the Court addressed the constitutionality of the Elkins Act, an early price-fixing statute that made railroad carriers responsible for their employees' misconduct. The *New York Central* case affirmed Congress's ability to hold a corporation criminally responsible for the crimes of its employees.[88]

Since then, a handful of appellate opinions have fleshed out *respondeat superior.* It applies beyond statutes that explicitly designate liability.[89] It is triggered whenever an employee, acting within the scope of her actual or apparent authority, and with *an* intention to benefit the corporation, violates the law.[90] It applies regardless of the employee's place within the company, and even when the employee acts in direct contravention of the company's written rules or policies.[91] Finally, it applies to partnerships and limited liability companies as well as corporations.[92]

---

[86] *Id.* at 1435 ("Does this provision . . . now effectively allow prosecutions based on the notion that the defendant simply had an unfair informational advantage?").

[87] N.Y. Cent. & Hudson River R.R. v. United States, 212 U.S. 481 (1909).

[88] *Id.* at 491.

[89] United States v. Hilton Hotels Corp., 467 F.2d 1000, 1004–5 (1972) (imputing *respondeat superior* to Sherman Act even though statute includes no express provision for corporate criminal liability); Albert W. Alschuler, *Two Ways to Think about the Punishment of Corporations*, 46 AM. CRIM. L. REV. 1359, 1363 (2009) (citing additional applications).

[90] *See* RICHARD GRUNER, CORPORATE CRIMINAL LIABILITY AND PREVENTION (2004).

[91] *Hilton Hotels*, 467 F.2d at 1004.

[92] U.S. v. A&P Trucking Co., 358 U.S. 121, 126–27 (1958) (extending *respondeat superior* to partnerships).

Each of *respondeat superior's* elements – the scope of the employee's authority, the intention to benefit the entity, and the lack of any organizational compliance defense – has been developed over the years in federal district and appellate court decisions.[93] Congress has effectively ratified the doctrine insofar as it has defined a "person" for purposes of title 18 as a corporation or business organization, but that is pretty much all it has explicitly said about corporate criminal liability.

If federal prosecutors desired, they could fill their dockets prosecuting corporations for all of their employees' crimes, but prosecutors have elected *not* to do this. Instead, they have constructed their own shadow law of liability while employing their discretion to decline cases.[94] Under the Federal Principles for Charging Business Organizations, first promulgated by then Deputy Attorney General Eric Holder in 1999 and now a fixture of the Justice Department's internal Justice Manual, prosecutors are advised to evaluate corporate wrongdoing by considering over ten different factors. The factors include the extent of wrongdoing, the corporation's efforts to prevent it, its efforts to remedy it once found, voluntary disclosure of the wrongdoing, cooperation with the government's investigation, and the collateral effects a criminal prosecution might place on innocent third parties.[95]

This preoccupation with third parties indirectly explains the government's reluctance to charge corporations criminally. Because of the rich layer of regulation that applies across numerous industries, there is a general view that many corporations cannot survive a criminal prosecution, much less a conviction.[96] The poster boy for this analysis is Arthur Andersen, the Enron accounting firm that was charged with obstruction of justice.[97] In the wake of Andersen's indictment, thousands of employees lost their jobs and the company eventually folded.

[93] Miriam H. Baer, *Three Conceptions of Corporate Crime (and One Avenue for Reform)*, 83 LAW & CONTEMP. PROBS. 1, 9 (2020).

[94] "[C]orporate criminal practice lies almost solely within the prosecutor's discretion, shaped in large part by the language of his or her settlement agreements. The *prosecutor* decides which corporations will pay for their employees' harms, the content of the settlement agreement the corporation will sign, and the effective quasi-sentence the corporation will suffer for its employees' harms." Baer, *supra* note 93, at 11. *See also* Cindy R. Alexander & Mark A. Cohen, *The Evolution of Corporate Criminal Settlements: An Empirical Perspective on Non-prosecution, Deferred Prosecution, and Plea Agreements*, 52 AM. CRIM. L. REV. 537, 538 (2015) (describing growth of NPAs and DPAs); Gordon Bourjaily, *DPA DOA: How and Why Congress Should Bar the Use of Deferred and Non-prosecution Agreements in Corporate Criminal Prosecutions*, 52 HARV. J. LEGIS. 543, 547 (2015) (critiquing growth of a shadow law of corporate liability).

[95] On the evolution of these factors and their content, see Gideon Mark, *The Yates Memorandum*, 51 U.C. DAVIS L. REV. 1589, 1592–602 (2018).

[96] Gregory M. Gilchrist, *The Special Problem of Banks and Crime*, 85 COLO. L. REV. 1, 25–27 (2014); David Zaring, *Litigating the Financial Crisis*, 100 VA. L. REV. 1405, 1444 (2014) (quoting DOJ officials' justifications for failing to file charges against corporate entities).

[97] Arthur Andersen LLP v. United States, 544 U.S. 696, 704–6 (2005). "The criminal conviction of Arthur Andersen [for shredding its Enron audit documents] destroyed that firm by ruining its reputation, even though the actual sentence it received was relatively minor and even though

Even prior to Andersen's demise, various US Attorney's offices began to experiment with extrajudicial resolutions. Instead of seeking an indictment and guilty plea, the government sought instead to work out a "deferred" (DPA) or "non" prosecution agreement (NPA) with the corporate offender.[98] The agreement usually stated that the government would hold off prosecuting the company provided it made certain improvements, paid certain fines, and avoided wrongdoing for a two- to three-year period of probation.[99]

At first, these types of agreements were viewed quite positively. Several scholars argued that they demonstrated an innovative and experimental governance approach.[100] Others, however, warned that the government's policy could founder, causing corporations to enter into a series of agreements that promised cosmetic improvements that fell short of their promise.[101] Still others (including me) fretted that corporate crime's shadow law reduced government transparency and enabled prosecutors to impose corporate remedies that were faddish and surveillance-heavy but not necessarily effective.[102]

Although early agreements required little of the corporate offender other than the payment of a fine and a promise to do better, contemporary and later-generation DPAs impose what Jennifer Arlen has referred to as "corporate mandates."[103] These mandates included a spectrum of obligations: the imposition of an outside monitor, explicit admissions of wrongdoing, and potentially major changes in the corporation's operations.[104] As they became more elaborate, the DPAs triggered questions about the judiciary's power to supervise and regulate them. Could a court, for example, weigh in on whether a monitor's reports should be released to the public? Could it comment on whether the agreement itself adequately served the public's interest?

District courts appeared willing to wade into these murky waters. One could even imagine, in 2014 or thereabouts, the development of a common law of DPA

---

its conviction was later reversed by the Supreme Court." SANFORD H. KADISH ET AL., CRIMINAL LAW AND ITS PROCESSES: CASES AND MATERIALS 764 (11th ed. 2022).

[98] On the differences between the DPAs and NPAs, see Alexander & Cohen, *supra* note 94, at 545.

[99] *Id.* at 538.

[100] *See* Cristie Ford & David Hess, *Can Corporate Monitorships Improve Corporate Compliance?* 34 J. CORP. L. 679, 698 (2009).

[101] Kimberly D. Krawiec, *Cosmetic Compliance and the Failure of Negotiated Governance*, 81 WASH. U. L. Q. 487, 487, 522–23 (2003); *see also* Brandon L. Garrett, *The Metamorphosis of Corporate Criminal Prosecutions*, 102 VA. L. REV. ONLINE 1, 10–11 (2016).

[102] Jennifer Arlen, *Prosecuting Beyond the Rule of Law: Corporate Mandates Imposed through Deferred Prosecution Agreements*, 8 J. L. ANALYSIS 191, 192 (2016); Baer, *supra* note 93, at 14–15.

[103] Arlen, *supra* note 102.

[104] Baer, *supra* note 93, at 2.

oversight by federal district courts.[105] The DC and Second Circuits, however, put a stop to this movement in two opinions announced in 2016 and 2017. In United States v. Fokker BV, the DC Circuit rejected the lower court's attempt to gauge whether a DPA met the public interest in deterring wrongdoing, remediating its causes, and condemning violations of law.[106] Since the DPA was merely an expression of the prosecutor's charging power, the judiciary enjoyed little authority to second-guess the prosecutor's charging decision.[107]

The Second Circuit continued this theme in United States v. HBSC Bank. *HBSC* overturned a relatively narrow lower court opinion that purported to make a corporate monitor's report available to the public, over the government's objection. The Second Circuit overturned the lower court's ruling, citing its limited ability to comment on or oversee DPAs.[108]

Thus, the "law" of the DPA remains a series of policy positions written and implemented by the Department of Justice (DOJ). Prosecutors periodically clarify their charging principles, or issue additional guidance and policies relating to specific corporate offenses. None of these are binding.[109] The next administration could just as easily retire the principles if it desired. This admittedly would create *political* responses, but corporate offenders would have no *legal* recourse in court if the DOJ eliminated or replaced its policies.

4.5 FRACTURED OR UNILATERAL?

The insider trading and corporate crime examples teach us something about legislative outsourcing. Both doctrines rely heavily on the common law's lawmaking modality, on administrative agencies (assuming one treats the DOJ as a quasi-administrator in the corporate crime context), and both concepts can be traced to profoundly underwritten statutes.

From a functional perspective, this is where the commonalities end. For insider trading, law is largely the product of two cross-checking branches, the Executive and Judiciary. And even within those branches, institutions deliberate and disagree with each other. The SEC can adopt one stance while the DOJ pushes the law in a slightly different direction. The appellate courts can offer one gloss on tipper-tippee

---

[105] Congress, by contrast, has shown little interest in getting involved, despite certain legislative efforts. Bourjaily, *supra* note 94, at 565–66 (describing a piece of 2014 proposed legislation purporting to empower judges to review DPAs to ensure they were in the "interest of justice").

[106] United States v. Fokker Servs, B.V., 818 F.3d 733, 738 (D.C. Cir. 2016).

[107] *Id.* ("[T]he fundamental point is that [charging] determinations are for the Executive – not the courts – to make.")

[108] United States v. HSBC Bank USA, 863 F.3d 125, 129 (2d Cir. 2017).

[109] W. Robert Thomas, *Corporate Criminal Law Is Too Broad – Worse It Is Too Narrow*, 53 Ariz. St. L. J. 199, 218–19 (2020). *See, e.g.*, US Department of Justice, Justice Manual §9-28.000; Paula Desio, An Overview of the Organizational Guidelines, United States Sentencing Cmm'n (2016).

trading and the Supreme Court can respond by rejecting it. Skirmishes of these types generate multiple entry points for access and debate.[110]

Where corporate crime is concerned, delegation has been sequential and unilateral. The Supreme Court got the ball rolling in *New York Central* by approving a theory of corporate criminal liability that was unbelievably broad. The practical realities of corporate prosecution led the DOJ to create a workaround concept that relies primarily on prosecutors to define and apply. *Respondeat superior* is the judiciary's creation, but DPAs, NPAs, and declinations remain the products of prosecutorial discretion and, therefore, prosecutorial power.

Corporate crime accordingly serves as a striking example of unilateral delegation. Power that once rested with the legislature has been ceded to the courts and then ceded once again to prosecutors.

4.6 TESTING OUTSOURCING'S CRITICS

Reformers have cited numerous problems outsourcing.[111] These arguments reflect the following four themes.

- *It renders lawmaking too easy.* Because criminal law punishes and deprives us of liberty, we desire a system that renders criminal lawmaking difficult. We *want* our criminal laws to be the product of deliberation, negotiation, and even some gridlock. Accordingly, we are fearful of any modality that renders it too easy for the government to criminalize and punish.[112]
- *It creates an imperial prosecutor.* When Congress enacts a law that is open-textured or/and dependent on administrative rulemaking, it enhances the prosecutor's power, which to many is already too great.[113]
- *It sidesteps the community.* If criminal law channels condemnation and reaffirms communal norms, its laws should be the product of the community – that is, an elected legislature operating according to majority rule. Because it yields authority to nondemocratic actors, delegation sidesteps the community and undermines law's expressive value.[114]
- *It subverts notice.* The legality principle holds that criminal laws should be duly enacted by a legislature, written down and freely accessible to the

---

[110] Scholars disagree on how the uncertainty of insider trading law. *Compare* ANDERSON, *supra* note 9, at 117 (arguing that insider trading "gives insufficient notice of criminal liability") *with* Michael A. Perino, *Real Insider Trading*, 77 WASH. & LEE L. REV. 1647, 1656–57 (2020).

[111] *See* Hessick & Hessick, *supra* note 40, at 306; Fissell, *supra* note 40, at 905.

[112] *See, e.g.,* Barkow, *supra* note 42, at 1012–13 ("Because the state could potentially go after any citizen in a criminal proceeding, the normal course of politics should act as a threshold check on the passage of laws that criminalize too much ordinary conduct").

[113] Hessick, *supra* note 43, at 992.

[114] Fissell, *supra* note 40, at 858.

public. When statutes are unclear, the government exposes its subjects to unexpected losses of liberty.[115]

Collectively, the concerns listed yield strong reasons for vesting the legislature, and only the legislature, with criminal lawmaking. Nevertheless, as this chapter's two examples demonstrate, these fears are not fully realized by either insider trading or corporate criminal liability. For both of these crimes, the actual on-the-ground experience differs from the predicted outcome.

For example, say what you will about insider trading, but its evolution as a body of law could not fairly be described as "easy" or solely in service of prosecutorial power.[116] It has taken the judiciary *decades* to affirm and develop its two major theories of insider trading liability, and the Supreme Court has forcefully *rejected* the SEC's broad conception of what constitutes an offense. For that reason, it is difficult to view insider trading as an exemplar of unchecked regulatory or prosecutorial overreach.

But outsourcing's critics rely on additional arguments: they contend that non-democratic lawmaking fails to include communal deliberation and voice. How does insider trading fare in this regard? The question of communal voice is a tricky one. Most would agree that even a democratically enacted statute can fail to fully reflect the "community's" views.[117] Federal criminal provisions may be the product of compromise and haggling enacted in haste in response to a particular scandal, or may be widely misunderstood.[118]

Perhaps we are less worried about actual preferences and more concerned about democratic participation and legitimacy. Brenner Fissell, for example, has argued that simply because an administrative rule happens to coincide with the community's preferences, that happy accident does not alter the institution's illegitimacy in the eyes of a political theorist.[119] Even so, it is unclear that communal voice – and the legitimacy it extends – can *only* arise from laws that have been enacted by elected representatives.

As we have already seen, insider trading's lawmaking process permits a fair amount of outside commentary. Because of its overlap with civil enforcement, insider trading is partially the product of SEC regulation, which enables affected parties to challenge arbitrary and capricious rules in court.[120] Moreover, because the

---

[115] Hessick & Hessick, *supra* note 40, at 313.

[116] "[I]nsider trading actions were relatively rare before 1986, the number of civil and criminal actions has since increased markedly." John P. Anderson et al., *Public Perceptions of Insider Trading*, 51 SETON HALL L. REV. 1035, 1075 (2021).

[117] Aliza Plener Cover, *Supermajoritarian Criminal Justice*, 87 GEO. WASH. L. REV. 875, 877 (2019).

[118] *Id.* at 903–4.

[119] Fissell, *supra* note 40, at 892.

[120] From the surveys that have already been performed, we know the general public supports the regulation and prosecution of some version of insider trading, although we could do a lot more to determine what it is the public believes is wrongful when someone trades on inside

targets of insider trading prosecutions and enforcement actions are, on balance, wealthier and enjoy better access to legal resources than even the average white-collar defendant, they also enjoy the ability to press the government to prove its civil and criminal cases in court.[121] To the extent these cases result in jury trials, that too creates an opening for community involvement.[122] And finally, to the extent negative jury decisions reverberate in government offices and alter the ways in which prosecutors and regulators choose and develop their cases, this, too, reflects a degree of community feedback.[123]

Now let's compare *respondeat superior*. For decades, the law of *respondeat superior* has been so stable that it has ossified. Neither Congress[124] nor the federal courts have shown any real interest in revisiting or adjusting *respondeat superior*, despite the fact it fails to describe a workable theory of corporate culpability.[125] But the DOJ has created a series of shadow rules that it can revise at will. Because the department itself is in no way bound in how it promulgates and enforces these policies, its "lawmaking" has been remarkably easy, except that the department is not really writing any laws at all.

Prosecutorial power nears its legal apex when corporate crime is its focus. The judiciary can only rarely second-guess the prosecutor's charging authority. Accordingly, in most instances, the prosecutor's bargain – whether it suits the public interest or not – is almost always beyond the judge's power to review.[126] Moreover, because DPAs, NPAs, and declination agreements are side bargains, prosecutors need not reveal their reasoning, their decision-making process, or even the pertinent facts underlying that process.[127]

---

information. Anderson et al. *supra* note 116, at 1058; Stuart P. Green & Matthew B. Kugler, *When Is It Wrong to Trade Stocks on the Basis of Non-public Information? Public Views of the Morality of Insider Trading*, 39 FORDHAM URB. L.J. 445, 455–57 (2011).

[121] Cara Salvatore, *SEC Loses Insider Trading Trial against Ex-software Worker*, LAW360 (Mar. 28, 2019), www.law360.com/articles/1143723/sec-loses-insider-trading-trial-against-ex-software-worker; Jean Eaglesham, *SEC Loses Second Insider-Trading Case in Seven Days*, WALL STREET JOURNAL (Jun. 6, 2014), www.wsj.com/articles/BL-LB-48269; Bruce Carton, *SEC Increasingly Taking Cases to Trial, but Recent Record Is Dismal*, COMPLIANCE WEEK (Feb. 10, 2014), www.complianceweek.com/sec-increasingly-taking-cases-to-trial-but-recent-record-is-dismal/14158.article.

[122] "The jury's unreviewable power to acquit gives it the ability to check both the legislative and executive branches." Barkow, *supra* note 42, 1015 (arguing that the jury "is a key component of the separation of powers in the criminal law"). Akhil Amar, *Sixth Amendment First Principles*, 84 GEO L J. 641, 684 (1996).

[123] Anna Offit, *Prosecuting in the Shadow of the Jury*, 113 Nw. U. L. REV. 1071, 1088–90 (2019).

[124] "Congress has played a remarkably small role in the overall development of corporate criminal law." Baer, *supra* note 93, at 4–5.

[125] Thomas, *supra* note 109, at 202–3.

[126] Fokker Servs, B.V., 818 F.3d 733, 741–42 (D.C. Cir. 2016).

[127] Miriam H. Baer, *Governing Corporate Compliance*, 50 B.C. L. REV. 949, 977 (2009) ("[T]here is no judicial review of corporate compliance regulation because courts have long held unreviewable the prosecutor's discretion not to file an indictment").

That brings us to the question of communal authority. Does the prosecutor's DPA reflect the community's interests? For many, the answer is a clear "no." Those who subscribe to the underenforcement thesis believe prosecutors have advanced corporate offenders far too much forbearance.[128] At the other end of the political spectrum, critics contend that prosecutorial reforms are faddish, noneconomic, and counterproductive.[129] A third (and overlapping) group worries that corporate liability effectively shields individual offenders from punishment and legal comeuppance.[130]

And what about notice? Corporate defendants within the white-collar bar often say they lack the benefit of notice because *respondeat superior* is itself so broad and prosecutorial guidelines are just that – guidelines.[131] But prosecutors, in turn, respond that they have bent over backward to provide corporations with some idea of the behavior that triggers an investigation, that is met with a DPA, or that results in criminal charges.[132] Perhaps the best we can say here is that notice is *fluid*. Because the quasi-law of corporate criminal liability is bound up in prosecutorial charging decisions, and because those decisions are themselves discretionary, the best we can say is that the government gives as much notice as it feels it politically is obligated to do so. Thus, if we were to compare the two areas of law on each of these metrics, we might arrive at Figure 4.1.

Figure 4.1 yields different conclusions about criminal outsourcing. Insider trading law may be messy, but it has not resulted in a massive transfer of power to prosecutors. Nor has it created an insuperable notice gap for most defendants. The executive branch shares its insider trading lawmaking authority with trial and appellate judges, as well as the Supreme Court. As a result, a rich doctrinal framework paves the way for spirited litigation and the occasional jury trial.

By contrast, the government's end run around *respondeat superior* creates none of these opportunities. Prosecutors unilaterally decide what is and is not worthy of corporate prosecution and leverage that power to obtain promises from selected corporate offenders. Since the DOJ has the power to write, revise, and implement its

---

[128] David M. Uhlmann, *The Pendulum Swings: Reconsidering Corporate Criminal Prosecution*, 49 U.C. Davis L. Rev. 1235, 1241–43 (2016) ("When criminal violations occur but are ignored or addressed by non-criminal alternatives, we obscure the line that the criminal law draws between acceptable and unacceptable behavior").

[129] Arlen & Kahan, *supra* note 53; Jennifer Arlen, *Prosecuting beyond the Rule of Law: Corporate Mandates Imposed through Deferred Prosecution Agreements*, 8 J. Legal Analysis 191–234 (2016).

[130] Gregory Gilchrist, *Individual Accountability for Corporate Crime*, 34 Ga. State U. L. Rev. 335, 335 (2018); Brandon L. Garrett, *The Corporate Criminal as Scapegoat*, 101 Va. L. Rev. 1789, 1793–95 (2015).

[131] Peter Reilly, *Negotiating Bribery: Toward Increased Transparency, Consistency, and Fairness in Pretrial Bargaining under the Foreign Corrupt Practices Act*, 10 Hastings Bus. L. J. 347, 349 (2014).

[132] Samuel W. Buell, *Why Do Prosecutors Say Anything? The Case of Corporate Crime*, 96 N.C. L. Rev. 823 (2018).

Type of crime	Type of delegation	Ease of lawmaking	Increase Prosecutorial Power?	Communal deliberation?	Notice to offenders?
Insider trading	Simultaneous, fractured	Moderate to low	No	Some	High in core cases, lower in marginal cases
***Respondeat Superior* and corporate prosecution**	Sequential, unitary	High (particularly for soft law policies)	Yes	Low	Formally high, but as an enforcement matter, lower

FIGURE 4.1. Comparing outsourcing outcomes

charging policies, it comes far closer to exercising imperial power scholars so rightfully fear. To date, the DOJ has largely restrained itself in accordance with its highly prized norms of independence and nonpartisan nature. But norms don't last forever, and we might appreciate the pitfalls of this shadow law more keenly when another norm-busting president takes office.

4.7 UNDERWRITTEN CRIMES, POORLY DRAFTED CODES

Outsourcing produces divergent outcomes. Some types of outsourcing enable the prosecutor to unilaterally call the shots while others result in a fractured transfer of authority. Outsourcing is also rarely complete. Congress has, over the years, enacted laws that tangentially acknowledge and support insider trading's prohibited status, and which also support corporate criminal liability. The "community" has enjoyed the periodic opportunity to weigh in on these matters. Accordingly, it is wrong to characterize insider trading or corporate crime as *unwritten*. Rather, they are *underwritten*, and functionally, that poses a problem, albeit one distinct from those raised by outsourcing's critics.

When an underwritten law's definition is left primarily to institutions other than Congress, the resulting debate focuses exclusively on law's *external boundaries* (i.e., the line between innocent and guilty conduct) while ignoring its potential *internal boundaries* (the lines that separate a family of similar but distinct offenses). This is hardly unique to the crimes discussed in this chapter. When we rely on courts, regulators, and prosecutors to "fill out the details" of a given crime, the resulting debates eclipse important issues such as subdivision and differentiation of wrong-doing. To take the example of the *Dirks, Newman, Salman* trio, we are still waiting for a definitive approach to tipper-tippee insider trading liability.[133] A better approach might have been for a legislature to consider "gift insider trading" along-side "quid pro quo insider trading" and come up with a graded rubric to capture

---

[133] Baer, *supra* note 64, at 141–43 (contrasting common law lawmaking, which develops in a piecemeal way, with statutory lawmaking, which at least enables a legislature to holistically "consider a set of crimes deliberately and all at once").

both crimes, albeit with different language, different treatment (e.g., first versus second degree), and a different range of punishments. Then again, as Chapter 3 observed, this is something the federal code simply does not do for most white-collar crimes.

Similar criticisms arise out of corporate criminal liability. In the years following *New York Central*, the judiciary embraced and developed an extremely broad rule of criminal liability. During the same time period, regulatory bodies and state legislatures adopted a series of rules that severely inhibit indicted companies from continuing as a going concern. It is difficult to believe that the public affirmatively prefers a world in which nearly *all* employee offenses are imputable to corporations. No one really believes that all corporations should be prosecuted any time an employee violates one of the thousands of federal criminal statutes with *an* intent to benefit their employer. Nor do most citizens desire the disruption *en masse* that arises out of the so-called corporate death penalty.[134]

Recognizing these sentiments, prosecutors have constructed alternative mechanisms to deter and hold corporations accountable for their wrongdoing. The problem is while the courts continue to tell the public that the law of the land is one thing, prosecutors apply something else. And just like insider trading, the corporate crime framework has never included room for *graded* liability. If some forms of corporate behavior are worse than others, we ought to be able to locate the abstract principles and language that says as much. But the opportunity to craft a meaningful and democratically resonant theory of graded corporate wrongdoing will never materialize so long as prosecutors adhere to open-ended and virtually unchallengeable charging guidelines.[135]

In sum, the underwritten criminal statute is undesirable, but not simply because someone other than an elected representative plays a role in "writing" it. Legal actors other than legislators have always played some role in adapting and teasing out law's meaning, and that is unlikely to change. But outsourcing becomes a net negative when it contributes to the federal code's flatness and lack of a gradation, an issue I explore in Chapters 3, 7, and 8.

In an ideal world, we would prefer a corporate crime statute that reflects and incorporates extant knowledge about markets, psychology, and corporate

---

[134] "If the trigger for criminal liability is the 'wrongful accumulation of power,' corporate crime ceases to be crime. It instead morphs into something quite different, namely a status crime for being too large, too powerful, and too prone to contribute to widening income and welfare gaps throughout society." Baer, *supra* note 93, at 10. *See also* Gerard E. Lynch, *RICO: The Crime of Being a Criminal, Parts III & IV*, 87 Colum. L. Rev. 920, 932–33 (1987) ("Fundamental to our traditional law of crimes, criminal procedure and evidence is a conception of crime that is transaction-bound").

[135] Miriam Baer, *To Fix Corporate Crime, Write a Statute*, N.Y.U. Comp. Enforce. Blog (Apr. 16, 2021), https://wp.nyu.edu/compliance_enforcement/2021/04/16/to-fix-corporate-crime-write-a-statute/, extracting relevant points from Baer, *supra* note 50, and Baer, *supra* note 93.

organizations. But we instead make do with charging policies that only partially reflect such learning. We almost certainly would prefer a series of insider trading laws that recognize distinctions between insiders, misappropriators, and gift tippers and tippees. But we instead rely on courts to interpret a single, undifferentiated fraud statute to encompass *all* insider trading. A reflective legislature would ask *why* these activities are wrong, *how* much harm they cause collectively and relative to one another, and how much culpability they reflect, as both an absolute and relative matter. A well-designed legislative code wouldn't punt these distinctions to a prosecutor's office or a sentencing judge; it would incorporate these principled distinctions into the code itself, signaling to both citizens and legal actors alike that these distinctions matter. To be sure, charging discretion and plea bargaining would gradually blur these distinctions, as they always do, But the distinctions would still matter, and they would still place some constraints on legal actors. That's a far better world than the one we currently have.

Thus, instead of seeking to radically rewrite the nondelegation doctrine, we might instead use the examples featured in this chapter as an opening for examining crimes that are "underwritten." A law becomes underwritten when its paucity of language:

(1) creates *excessive back and forth* between and among courts and regulators;
(2) permits a *"shadow law" of liability* to develop alongside the actual law of liability; or
(3) directs legal actors to focus exclusively crime's *outer boundaries* – that is, the line between criminal and innocent behavior – at the expense of a crime's internal boundaries.

One could argue that when even *one* of these three characteristics surfaces, Congress should pay greater attention to the statute that nominally defines an offense. But when *all three* arise in concert, Congress should task itself with revising its statutes, and doing so in a way that explicitly differentiates meaningful variations of an offense. This might not satisfy all of outsourcing's critics, but it would at least place us on a path to figuring out how best to fill white-collar crime's widening holes and how best to improves its enforcement, a subject of Chapter 5.

5

Gap Management

INTRODUCTION

It is impossible to discuss white-collar crime without delving into the 2008 subprime mortgage crisis ("2008 Financial Crisis") and the recession it produced. The story by now is well known: In response to an extended housing bubble, bankers bundled, securitized, and marketed housing loans that were severely inflated in terms of value.[1] Eventually, the bubble popped, causing housing prices to plummet and foreclosures to accelerate. Mortgage securities became toxic assets on the books of the institutions (mostly banks and insurance companies) who had purchased them. Employment and consumer markets buckled, and the government eventually bailed out the banking industry to the tune of billions of dollars while ordinary Americans lost their homes, jobs, and savings.[2]

Previous disasters, such as the 1980s Savings and Loan (S&L) scandals,[3] had reportedly generated hundreds of successful prosecutions.[4] Several decades later, the

---

[1] "The financial crisis began with a housing bubble. A glut of cheap financing enabled buyers to bid up home prices across the U.S. above fundamental values." William W. Bratton & Adam J. Levitin, *A Tale of Two Markets: Regulation and in Post-crisis Mortgage and Structured Finance Markets*, 2020 U. ILL. L. REV. 47, 54 (2020). *See also* Kathryn Judge, *Fragmentation Nodes: A Study in Financial Innovation, Complexity, and Systemic Risk*, 64 STAN. L. REV. 657, 659–60 (2012).

[2] "Americans lost $9.8 trillion in wealth as their HOME values plummeted and their retirement accounts vaporized." Renae Merle, *A Guide to the Financial Crisis – 10 Years Later*, WASH. POST (Sept. 10, 2018), www.washingtonpost.com/business/economy/a-guide-to-the-financial-crisis–10-years-later/2018/09/10/114b76ba-af10-11e8-a20b-5f4f84429666_story.html.

[3] The S&L scandals involved a series of local banking institutions (thrifts) that failed in the 1980s, and whose failures were caused by a mixture of bad judgment and criminal misconduct. *See generally*, Bruce Green, *After the Fall: The Criminal Law Enforcement Response to the S&L Crisis*, 59 FORDHAM L. REV. S155, S161 (1990), https://ir.lawnet.fordham.edu/flr/vol59/iss6/7/.

[4] *But cf.* Daniel C. Richman, *Corporate Headhunting*, 8 HARV. L. & POL'Y REV. 265, 266–67 (2014) (pointing out that S&L prosecutions encountered their own roadblocks and

corporate accounting fraud scandals of the early 2000s produced numerous convictions, including those of notable titans such as Kenneth Lay and Jeffrey Skilling
(Enron), as well as Bernie Ebbers (Worldcom), Dennis Kozlowski (Tyco), and John
and Timothy Rigas (Adelphia).[5] *In the past*, the conventional wisdom argued,
enforcers responded to widespread scandal by punishing a core of elite figures
responsible for society's harm. *Now*, however, corporate elites appeared to be
completely in the clear.[6] Financial institutions eventually paid massive fines pursuant to so-called deferred prosecution agreements, but few high-level officers were
subjected to criminal charges, much less convictions.[7]

The government's overall enforcement record from this time period is admittedly
ambiguous. The criminal piece of it, however, is painfully clear. The
2008 Financial Crisis produced few criminal trials and fewer victories. After years
of hemming and hawing, the federal government's premier enforcement arm, the
Department of Justice (DOJ), all but admitted that corporate executive prosecutions
would not be forthcoming.

This setback continues to impact white-collar crime's discourse in profound ways.
Commentators simply cannot fathom why federal prosecutors were unable to mount
cases against the architects of the subprime crisis, a crisis that is commonly described
as one big scam.[8] Criticisms of the DOJ's Financial Crisis response tend to fall
within two categories. The first focuses on the government's alleged failure to devise
and press innovative theories of fraud.[9] The DOJ was simply too cautious, too old-
fashioned, and too sclerotic to creatively pursue the legal arguments that would have
saved the day (or at least punished a few bad men). Let's call this the *legal* critique
because it rests upon the belief that the DOJ should have exercised its *de facto*
lawmaking power to push the statutory envelope to capture a wider range of
wrongdoers. Among the legal critique's greatest shortcomings is its failure to

---

disappointments); Green, *supra* note 3, at 3 (contemporaneous article citing frustrations with
slow pace of S&L investigations).

[5] www.justice.gov/archive/opa/pr/2006/May/06_crm_328.html (Department of Justice [DOJ]
announcing jury convictions of lay and skilling); www.cnbc.com/2020/02/03/bernard-ebbers-
ex-ceo-convicted-in-worldcom-scandal-dies.html (announcing Ebbers conviction); https://
money.cnn.com/2005/06/20/news/newsmakers/rigas_sentencing/ (describing father and son
sentences in Adelphia fraud cases); https://money.cnn.com/2005/09/19/news/newsmakers/
kozlowski_sentence/ (describing Dennis Kozlowski's sentence).

[6] For the seminal article posing this contrast (framed as a question, but indubitably intended as a
critique), see Hon. Jed S. Rakoff, *The Financial Crisis: Why Have No High-Level Executives
Been Prosecuted?* New York Rev. Books (Jan. 9, 2014), www.nybooks.com/articles/2014/01/
09/financial-crisis-why-no-executive-prosecutions/.

[7] On post-Crisis fines and sanctions, see Bratton & Levitin, *supra* note 1, at 80–81.

[8] Popular treatments include *The Big Short*, which eventually was made into a well-received
movie. Michael Lewis, The Big Short: Inside the Doomsday Machine (2010).

[9] *See e.g.*, Jeffrey Madrick & Frank Partnoy, *Should Some Bankers Be Prosecuted?* New York
Rev. Books (Nov. 10, 2011), www-nybooks-com.ezp-prod1.hul.harvard.edu/articles/2011/11/
10/should-some-bankers-be-prosecuted/. *See also* Bratton & Levitin, *supra* note 1, at 80 (observing prosecutors' lack of creativity).

recognize the difficulty of developing a "new" theory of legal wrongdoing that is convincing, supported by evidence, and reflects a plausible interpretation of extant law.[10]

The second type of critique is more prevalent. It insists prosecutors failed to track down important leads and use them to build conventional narratives of wrongdoing. By overlooking the falsehoods and misstatements contained in certain financial institutions' books and records, the government failed to prove the traditional fraud cases that were there for the picking, and which would have been winnable had investigators employed a bit more elbow grease.[11] One might denominate this the *factual* critique as it faults legal actors for failing to obtain and use the requisite facts necessary to win a criminal prosecution.[12]

Together, these two critiques fuel the normative claim that far less fraud was prosecuted than should have been in the Crisis's wake. This conventional wisdom continues to cast fault on the DOJ, blaming prosecutors for being too cowed by fancy defense counsel, too unwilling to allocate proper resources to major investigations, and too biased by self-interest and the prospect of eventual work in private-sector law firms.[13] In response, the DOJ's defenders have reasoned that the true

[10] Madrick and Partnoy's formulation appeared to embrace a theory of fraud premised on a state of mind best described as negligence. Madrick & Partnoy, *supra* note 9 (proposing a rule that requires the government to "merely prove that bankers should have known rather than actually did know they were deceiving their clients").

[11] *See, e.g.*, JOHN C. COFFEE, JR., CORPORATE CRIME AND PUNISHMENT: THE CRISIS OF UNDERENFORCEMENT 23–27 (2020).

[12] JENNIFER TAUB, BIG DIRTY MONEY: THE SHOCKING INJUSTICE AND UNSEEN COST OF WHITE-COLLAR CRIME (2020); RENA STEINZOR, WHY NOT JAIL? (2015); JESSE EISINGER, THE CHICKENSHIT CLUB: WHY THE JUSTICE DEPARTMENT FAILS TO PROSECUTE EXECUTIVES (2017); Rakoff, *supra* note 6. Other critics attacked the government's few convictions, which were (at best) tangential to the crisis itself. *See, e.g.*, Todd Haugh, *The Most Senior Wall Street Official: Evaluating the State of Financial Crisis Prosecutions*, 9 VA. L. & BUS. REV. 153 (2015) (analyzing the prosecution of Kareem Serageldin, a former Credit Suisse executive punished for defrauding his employer). For more measured analyses, see Robert Quigley, *The Impulse towards Individual Criminal Punishment After the Financial Crisis*, 22 VA. J. SOC. POL'Y & L. 103 (2015) (arguing that most cases of criminal behavior were orthogonal to the causes of the crisis); David Zaring, *Litigating the Financial Crisis*, 100 VA. L. REV. 1405, 1413–15 (2014) (citing reasons government was reluctant to prosecute cases).

[13] Jesse Eisinger was an early proponent of the claim that prosecutors were hesitant to file charges because they sought private-sector employment (also known as the "revolving door" argument). EISINGER, *supra* note 12, at 188. Subsequent empirical analyses have challenged aspects of the revolving door assertion. *See, e.g.*, David Zaring, *Against Being against the Revolving Door*, 2013 U. ILL. L. REV. 507; Wenton Zheng, *The Revolving Door*, 90 NOTRE DAME L. REV. 1265, 1268, 1272–75 (2015). Nevertheless, scholars continue to invoke concerns that prosecutors have been captured by corporate elites. *See* Mary Kreiner Ramirez, *Criminal Affirmance: Going beyond the Deterrence Paradigm to Examine the Social Meaning of Declining Prosecution of Elite Crime*, 45 CONN. L. REV. 865, 900–3 (2013).

causes of the crisis – poorly conceived regulations paired with bedrock beliefs that the real estate market would never fall – lie largely outside criminal law's reach.[14]

This now-famous debate illuminates an underexplored paradox. On the one hand, courts, legislatures, and prosecutors have implemented remarkably broad language to capture, in very general terms, crimes such as fraud, bribery, and obstruction of justice.[15] These are the tools that have led many critics to proclaim that white-collar crime, like the rest of criminal law, is overcriminalized. It punishes too much behavior, too indiscriminately, and extends prosecutors far too much discretion to pick and choose their targets.

At the same time, crimes of this nature continue to be the most difficult to prove, particularly when they arise in corporate settings and cause substantial, lasting, and diffuse harm. This is the characteristic that makes white-collar crime different from the rest of criminal law. Life within corporate settings is remarkably compartmentalized and siloed. Information and responsibility fractures among multiple units and departments, allowing criminal targets to claim that the left hand did not know what the right hand was doing, or at very least, that an intent to harm or deceive was absent. When losses arise out of opaque and abstruse schemes, criminal convictions become difficult to achieve.

Thus, we end up with the problem that white-collar crime is both overcriminalized and underenforced. To further unpack this problem, we might say that white-collar crime operates across two thresholds. The first is the well-trod line between innocence and liability. Thanks to our broad laws, many cases of wrongdoing advance past this threshold. And at least in some instances, they can do so precipitously. The moment an individual hits the "send" button on a fraudulent email, devises a scheme to take someone else's money under false pretenses, or even *agrees* to participate in someone *else's* criminal scheme, that person becomes guilty of an offense. Unlike those offenses that follow a sliding scale matching the size of deviation with the degree of sanction, crimes such as fraud, bribery, and obstruction often follow a rather sudden trajectory.[16]

But the line between innocence and guilt isn't the only line that counts. The second and more important tipping point distinguishes liability from the viable prosecution. The temporal space between these two thresholds, the *gap* between liability and viability, is the space in which the fraud scheme (or bribery or obstruction) hides and festers. If we care at all about this gap, then we need to think more

---

[14] *See, e.g.*, Gregory M. Gilchrist, *Individual Accountability for Corporate Crime*, 34 GA. ST. U. L. REV. 335, 335 (2018); Richman, *supra* note 4, at 266–67.

[15] On the problems presented by outsourcing and underwritten crimes, see Chapter 4.

[16] On law's bumpiness, see Adam J. Kolber, *Smooth and Bumpy Laws*, 102 CAL. L. REV. 655 (2014). For an examination of legal thresholds and their effect on behavior throughout numerous domains, see LEE ANNE FENNELL, SLICES & LUMPS: DIVISION AND AGGREGATION IN LAW AND LIFE (2019).

deeply about the relationship between these two thresholds and how our government manages it.[17]

The remainder of this chapter foregrounds this analysis in a discussion of government's ill-fated prosecution of two Bear Stearns hedge fund executives during the early months of the Financial Crisis. The jury's full acquittal of Bear Stearns's two executives instantiates the difficulty of prosecuting schemes that look and feel different from the "prototypical" fraud case the jury has in mind.

The chapter's second half conceptualizes the gap between the liability and viability. Realists might ask whether the liability threshold even matters when viability is the real line that determines whether a prosecution will take place. But liability matters precisely because individuals often realize, at some point, that they have "crossed a line." And they often realize this long before anyone in charge or with the power to punish has knowledge of their offense. Thus, it is crucial to disentangle the two thresholds because the gap that forms between them bedevils our enforcement agencies. To be sure, some space between liability and viability is desirable. But an overly wide gap enables just-formed schemes to grow in complexity, risk, and harm. More perniciously, as evidenced by the post-Financial Crisis fallout, an intractably wide gap erodes society's trust.

Traditionally, prosecutors have attempted to manage this problem by deploying *gap-minding* strategies. These strategies operate within a framework that trades leniency or money in exchange for information. Whistleblowing and cooperation both fit easily within this framework, as the information they provide ultimately pushes a few more cases across the viability threshold. By contrast, an alternative approach I call *gap-narrowing* is more ambitious; it directly attacks the gap between the liability and viability and attempts to bring the two thresholds closer together. It is more risky, but it also promises greater, more lasting rewards.

5.1 AN EARLY LOSS

In 2008, the US Attorney's Office for the Eastern District of New York charged two hedge fund managers at Bear Stearns with wire and securities fraud for failing to timely inform their investors that two subprime-related funds were precipitously losing value.[18] The issue was whether the two managers were purposely withholding information or whether they truly believed the funds were in solid shape barring a few market hiccups. After a several-week trial, the jury acquitted the managers of all counts.[19]

---

[17] *See generally* Samuel Buell, *The Upside of Overbreadth*, 83 N.Y.U. L. Rev. 1491, 1507–12 (2008) (unpacking detection avoidance and exploring its attendant ills).

[18] Coffee, *supra* note 11, at 20–23 (providing overview of the case).

[19] Quigley, *supra* note 14, at 106 (summarizing prosecution and government loss).

Relying primarily on the managers' emails, prosecutors attempted to weave a narrative of purposeful concealment. The jury acquitted, however, because defense attorneys were able to draw doubt from those very emails.[20] Thus, the acquittal illuminated the difficulties of building a retrospective case of fraudulent intent based primarily on a written record whose evidence was ambiguous.

A prospective investigation records evidence in real time, relying on wiretaps and cooperating informants to surreptitiously record conversations and telephone calls. The government substantially controls the investigation when it acts prospectively, setting up meetings through its informants, prompting discussions of certain subjects, and introducing (temporarily false) fears of apprehension.[21] No wonder, then, that the undercover investigation often produces a flashy cascade of guilty pleas and trial convictions.[22]

By contrast, a retrospective case relies on evidence of actions already taken and observed. For some cases, the actions themselves will suffice to prove the basic elements of a fraud or bribery case. But the retrospective case becomes more difficult when the crime itself requires the government to prove a "high" mental state such as "specific intent to defraud." When norms are unclear, and transactions are themselves complex and difficult to understand, proving intentional deceit becomes more difficult.

Retrospective cases pose an additional problem. Consider the role prototypes play in criminal prosecutions. Linguists contend that individuals do not perceive abstract objects by defining them constructively, but rather by comparing what they see to a paradigmatic example. Thus, if I ask you if a bench-like seating area is a "chair" (or better yet, whether the chair is a piece of furniture), your answer will hinge on how closely the seating area resembles the paradigmatic elevated platform with a back, a seat, and four legs.[23]

---

[20] COFFEE, *supra* note 11.

[21] On the ways in which these tools have enabled the government to combat organized crime, see John C. Jeffries, Jr. & John Gleeson, *The Federalization of Organized Crime: Advantages of Federal Prosecution*, 46 HASTINGS L.J. 1095, 1103–9 (1995).

[22] *See, e.g.*, Susan Pulliam, *Wired on Wall Street: Trader Betrays a Friend*, WALL ST. J. (Jan. 16, 2010), www.wsj.com/articles/SB10001424052748703657604575005043589755402 (describing use of undercover informants to catch insider trading). *See also* Richman, *supra* note 4, 266 (describing the value of contemporaneous information).

[23] An early account of the theory and its connection to cognition can be found in Dirk Geeraerts, *Prospects and Problems of Prototype Theory*, 27 LINGUISTICS 587 (1987) (contending that "prototype theory has become one of the cornerstones of cognitive linguistics, which tries to account for the interaction between language and cognition"). For an extended discussion of how the theory illuminates statutory interpretation and juror decision-making (and for the many examples culled from the linguistics literature, including the proper classification of a chair), see Lawrence M. Solan, *Law, Language, and Lenity*, 40 WM. & MARY L. REV. 57, 65–69 (1998); Lawrence M. Solan, *Learning Our Limits: The Decline of Textualism in Statutory Cases*, 1997 WIS. L. REV. 235, 274 (1997). On prototype theory's implications for criminal codes, see Stuart P. Green, *Prototype Theory and the Classification of Offenses in*

This concept imbues a more nuanced account of why prosecutors may be inclined to pursue some fraud cases more than others. Most of us have some scheme in mind (i.e., a prototype) when we hear the term fraud. That paradigm, in turn, helps a legal actor decide not only which schemes are illegal, but which ones will be most easy to prove. The sticking point for many fraud cases is *mens rea* or the "specific intent" to deceive. For schemes that take place within so-called legitimate business settings, *mens rea* is often the element that distinguishes the reckless loss of money from the prosecutable (and prohibited) scheme to deceive.[24]

If you think about a fraud case from an elemental (definitional) perspective, you might find yourself making a mental checklist. Were there "misstatements" designed to deprive someone of money or property? Were they "material"? Did someone use the mails or wires to further their scheme? Did they "purposely" make these misstatements or omissions with the "specific intent to deceive"? These are the components of a typical jury instruction.[25]

According to prototype theory, however, the elemental approach is not how most laypeople define abstract terms. Instead, we have a paradigmatic case in mind, and then mentally inquire how closely the case before us resembles the paradigm. In a courtroom setting, the paradigm helps the fact-finder determine whether the prosecution has met its burden. The account is consistent with the popular "story model" account of decision-making, in which "jurors reach verdicts by assembling the most sensible and easy-to-construct 'story' out of the evidence."[26]

For something as elusive as an offender's state of mind, the paradigm also helps fill the gaps. The garden-variety confidence scheme is easy to prove because the actions themselves imply maleficence. If a smooth talker promises to invest an elderly person's money in a real estate transaction and instead uses the funds to purchase his own Picasso, juries can ably infer fraudulent intent.[27] They don't need

---

A Revised Model Penal Code: A General Approach to the Special Part, 4 BUFF. CRIM. L. REV. 301, 303 (2000).

[24] Samuel Buell argues that certain "badges of guilt" play a role in helping courts distinguish the sharp business practice from the criminal fraud. *See* Samuel W. Buell, *Novel Criminal Fraud*, 81 N.Y.U. L. REV. 1971, 2000 (2006) ("An inquiry relying on badges of guilt is concerned with an actor's outward behavior that manifests consciousness of wrongdoing").

[25] *See, e.g.*, 2 MODERN FEDERAL JURY INSTRUCTIONS-CRIMINAL P 44.01 (mail, wire, health care fraud jury instructions setting forth elements of offense).

[26] Kenworthey Bilz, *We Don't Want to Hear It: Psychology, Literature and the Narrative Model of Judging*, 2010 U. ILL. L. REV. 429, 436 (2010) (citing and discussing the work of Nancy Pennington and Reid Hastie, the story model's developers). For early work establishing the model, see Nancy Pennington & Reid Hastie, *Explaining the Evidence: Tests of the Story Model for Jury Decision Making*, 62 J. PERSONALITY SOCIAL PSYCH. 189 (1992)

[27] "The intent of the crime … [may be] shown by the scheme itself." Peter Henning, 1 CORPORATE CRIMINAL LIABILITY, 3D § 8:10, *citing* United States v. Bruce, 488 F.2d 1224, 1229 (5th Cir. 1973).

a wiretap or written confession to know what's going on. The purchase of the Picasso does all the work.[28]

When the scheme diverges too far from a conventional prototype, however, the case becomes an uphill battle.[29] Consequently, a taped conversation or strong evidence of a cover-up and concealment can make all the difference between an acquittal and a conviction. And here's a further paradox: The more prosecutors rely on these familiar tools, the more they become a part of the paradigmatic fraud prosecution and of the popular consciousness that feeds the juror's "story" expectations. In other words, the prosecutor's understanding of what the prototype *is* plays an essential role in what it comes *to be*. So, even though a fraudster's concealment or purchase of a million-dollar painting are hardly *legal* requirements for a conviction, they nevertheless become *practical* components of the paradigmatic case. And in the prosecutor's mind, it is the paradigmatic case that is most likely to secure a conviction.

In the Bear Stearns cases, the government enjoyed few of the factual elements that make a fraud case "easy." There were no wiretaps or surreptitiously taped conversations, no examples of egregious accounting practices, and not nearly enough evidence of concealment (although one defendant had quietly transferred some of his own money to a separate fund).[30] The two managers refused to testify against each other, forcing the government to rely primarily on a cache of conflicting emails. And there was a plausible story to be told, which was that the defendants were merely *overly optimistic* about the funds' ability to recover from a momentary setback.

It is accordingly unsurprising that the government failed to prosecute more high-level executives once the Bear Stearns loss was in the rearview mirror. What the acquittal taught them was that they should err on the side of caution.[31] Moreover,

---

[28] In other words, we have a sense of what fraud looks like, and the Picasso purchase reaffirms our intuition. *Cf.* Solan, *Law, Language, and Lenity, supra* note 23, at 66 ("when we use the word rain, we have some idealized sense of what it means for it to be raining").

[29] Consider the litany of concerns laid out by a former prosecutor and his coauthors:

> The financial instruments and arrangements at issue in the credit crisis investigations are highly complex ... [T]here simply may not have been intentional misconduct or criminally reckless behavior, but rather plain bad judgment on the part of market actors. Even in situations where there was wrongdoing, the time and resources required to mount investigations and the burden of proving intent to defraud are formidable obstacles for prosecutors and regulators to surmount, except in the most straightforward of fraud cases.

Andrew J. Ceresney et al., *Regulatory Investigations and the Credit Crisis: The Search for Villains*, 46 AM. CRIM. L. REV. 225, 227–28 (2009) (Ceresney was a cochief of the SEC's Enforcement Division).

[30] FINANCIAL CRISIS INQUIRY COMMISSION, *The Unraveling* at 238.

[31] "Ever since the acquittal of the failed Bear Stearns hedge fund managers ... federal prosecutors have been remarkably reluctant to go after Wall Street or the mortgage industry criminally for actions related to the way financiers treated their customers." Zaring, *supra* note 12, at 1410.

what the government prosecutor was likely to consider a paradigmatic case was already informed by the Enron and Worldcom accounting scandals that were prosecuted during the early aughts.[32] *Those* cases included all sorts of bells and whistles that were missing in the Bear Stearns case, including damning voice mails, fired whistleblowers, and patently improper accounting practices buoyed by almost laughable concealment tactics. Even if it meant overlooking some likely instances of wrongdoing, it would hardly be a bad prosecutorial strategy to decline future cases that were missing such obvious badges of misconduct.

5.2 THRESHOLDS IN WHITE-COLLAR CRIME

The preceding discussion highlights an important paradox. Scholars who insist that fraud is difficult to prove have acknowledged in other work that federal criminal law is also extremely broad.[33] The open-ended language of the mail, wire, and securities fraud statutes permit an enormous amount of punishment for everything from the most serious to most mundane of schemes.[34] At the same time, we often say that crimes like fraud and bribery are difficult to prove. How can it be that the statutes prohibiting fraud and bribery are simultaneously broad and yet so difficult to establish? The answer lies in the study of two thresholds.

The first threshold – the liability threshold – is objectively defined by the law. It is a threshold we often study in law school and criminal law classes – albeit in a very artificial fashion. In the law school casebook, if your behavior and state of mind meet the elements of a crime such as fraud, the final element you satisfy constitutes a sudden tipping point from innocence to guilt.[35] That is, you leap suddenly from the category of "no crime" to "crime." And because fraud itself is an inchoate offense (i.e., one that can be prosecuted while it is still a scheme and before it has achieved its aim), the liability threshold's tipping point may be reached before any harm has occurred.

[32] "[B]ecause prototypes are formed, reinforced, and at times changed as the result of cumulative experience, experts often refer to prototype theory as a probabilistic model of conceptualization." Solan, *Law, Language, and Lenity, supra* note 23, at 66. "[A]s we seek to place new stimuli into already-established mental categories, we compare the new input with prototypical examples of each category." Note, *War, Schemas, and Legitimation: Analyzing the National Discourse about War*, 119 HARV. L. REV. 2099, 2101 (2006).

[33] *Compare* Richman, *supra* note 4, at 268 ("a financial collapse is not itself evidence of criminal conduct") with Daniel C. Richman, *Political Control of Federal Prosecutions: Looking Back and Looking Forward*, 58 DUKE L.J. 2087, 2092 (2009) ("The reach of the mail and wire fraud statutes ... is enormous, as is the risk their misuse could chill socially and economically valuable conduct and even threaten longstanding political norms").

[34] "The words 'to defraud' as used in some statutes have been given a wide meaning, wider than their ordinary scope. They usually signify the deprivation of something of value by trick, deceit, chicane, or overreaching." Hammerschmidt v. United States, 265 U.S. 182, 188 (1924).

[35] For extended examination of this dynamic, see Kolber, *supra* note 16, and Adam J. Kolber, *The Bumpiness of Criminal Law*, 67 ALA. L. REV. 855 (2016).

For example, the elements of a criminal mail or wire fraud case are often described as:

(1) A scheme to defraud,
(2) the defendant's "specific intent" to defraud,
(3) materiality, and
(4) contemplated use of the mails or interstate wires.[36]

Although a criminal case requires the false or misrepresentative statement to be "material" (capable of influencing the body to whom it is addressed), it does not require actual loss (damages) or reliance, two of the elements of a civil action.[37] Nor is there a precise definition of what constitutes a "scheme," except courts all seem to agree it implies the deprivation of "something of value" by trick or deceit, and is therefore much broader than the common law's definition of fraud.[38] Because damages and reliance are nonelements in the criminal context, the liability threshold for a *criminal* fraud counterintuitively arises earlier than the threshold for a civil case.[39] Further, all "schemes" satisfy the various fraud statutes, regardless of their plausibility or stage of planning.

Two other legal concepts slide more individuals over the liability threshold. First, to be guilty of a conspiracy, one need only agree to join someone else's scheme. If I know you are cooking the company's books and I reluctantly agree to help you hide what you are doing (and defraud our employer), I become your coconspirator – your *partner*. Legally, I am as guilty as you are, even though you might have done all the work.[40] The same is true of the law of complicity. If I intentionally aid or abet your scheme (by, for example, forwarding documents that I know to be fraudulent or filling in fraudulent numbers on a spreadsheet), I become complicit in your

---

[36] Some courts collapse the "scheme" and "materiality" elements. United States v. Spalding, 894 F.3d 173, 181 (5th Cir. 2018). Others treat materiality as a separate requirement. United States v. Raza, 876 F.3d 604, 619 (4th Cir. 2017). On materiality generally, see Neder v. United States, 527 U.S. 1 (1999) (affirming requirement). Materiality usually envisions an untrue statement or omission that causes someone to part with their money or property or assume "actual significance" in the deliberations of the investor. On securities fraud's materiality element, see TSC Indus Inc. v. Northway Inc., 426 U.S. 438, 449 (1976). *See also* United States v. Williams, 934 F.3d 1122, 1128 (10th Cir. 2019) (advising that materiality is "identical" for bank fraud, mail fraud, wire fraud, and false-statement offenses).

[37] Neder, 527 U.S. at 25 (federal fraud statutes require neither reliance nor proof of loss).

[38] Durland v. United States, 161 US 306 (1896) (statute's breadth and extension to future promises of performance). "[T]he words 'to defraud' commonly refer 'to wronging one in his property rights by dishonest methods or schemes,' and 'usually signify the deprivation of something of value by trick, deceit, chicane or overreaching.'" McNally v. United States, 483 U.S. 350, 358 (1987) (quoting Hammerschmidt v. United States, 265 U.S. 182, 188 [1924]).

[39] *See* Christine Hurt, *The Undercivilization of Corporate Law*, 33 J. Corp. L. 361 (2008).

[40] "And so long as the partnership in crime continues, the partners act for each other in carrying it forward." Pinkerton v. United States, 328 U.S. 640, 646 (1946).

scheme. As an accomplice, I am legally as guilty as you, the principal.[41] Finally, federal fraud law permits no unringing of the bell; you can withdraw from a conspiracy and blunt future liability, but you cannot undo your previous actions so far as the law is concerned.[42]

No wonder, then, that observers often highlight white-collar crime's breadth. When all facts are known, the law *is* quite powerful and the liability threshold is remarkably easy to surpass, even when one sincerely desires to avoid it.

5.3 THE PERCEPTION OF A WINNABLE CASE

Many of those who work within business settings will at some point cross the liability threshold. "Liability," as used in this context, reflects a person's guilt if all relevant facts were known to an omniscient fact-finder.

Over a certain time period, it is a certainty that many employees will become technically guilty of a federal crime, and not just the silly regulatory crimes that critics sometimes invoke to demonstrate overcriminalization.[43] And at some point, they will realize they have committed an offense, even if they are unsure of its specific title or statutory designation. That is perhaps the greatest irony of the liability threshold: If you are a person with a conscience, *you* will know you have crossed a line and you will suffer, albeit often in silence.

In both physical and practical dimensions, crimes like mail and wire fraud aren't that difficult to commit. All one need do is alter a few aspects of their daily office routine to enter the familiar territory of lying, cheating, or covering up wrong-doing.[44] And as the research on "ethical fading" establishes, many corporate employees move in the liability threshold's direction without realizing it. Only when it's too late do they realize they have ended up on the wrong side of the line.[45]

---

[41] 18 USC 2 (equating principals and accomplices). Rosemond v. United States, 575 US 65, 79–80 (2014) ("The law does not, nor should it, care whether [the accomplice] participates with a happy heart or a sense of foreboding"). Joshua Dressler, *Reforming Complicity Law: Trivial Assistance as a Lesser Offense*, 5 OHIO ST. J. CRIM. L. 427, 428–29 (2007) (arguing that American accomplice law is a "disgrace" because it treats the accomplice as the equivalent of a perpetrator regardless of her culpability or degree of involvement in the offense).

[42] "The federal law of conspiracy does not recognize a defense of renunciation." R. Michael Cassidy & Gregory I. Massing, *The Model Penal Code's Wrong Turn: Renunciation as a Defense to Criminal Conspiracy*, 64 FLA. L. REV. 353, 372 (2012) (criticizing renunciation and urging jurisdictions to abandon it).

[43] Stuart P. Green, *Why It's a Crime to Tear the Tag Off a Mattress: Overcriminalization and the Moral Content of Regulatory Offenses*, 46 EMORY L.J. 1533 (1997).

[44] Crimes such as fraud and bribery occur "in the midst of activities that are not only unobjectionable but are also socially welcome." Samuel W. Buell, *Culpability and Modern Crime*, 103 GEO. L.J. 547, 553 (2015).

[45] For ethical blind spots, see MAX H. BAZERMAN & ANN E. TENBRUNSEL, BLIND SPOTS: WHY WE FAIL TO DO WHAT'S RIGHT AND WHAT TO DO ABOUT IT (2011); Ann E. Tenbrunsel & David M. Messick, *Ethical Fading: The Role of Self-Deception in Unethical Behavior*, 17 SOC. JUST. RES. 223, 227–28 (2004). On behavioral ethics and individual's

That's the bad news for business employees. The good news is that many of them will never be caught. Regardless of how many people transgress the law's boundaries, far fewer commit these crimes in a manner that is observable enough to get them into serious trouble. Accordingly, despite the number of people who are technically *liable* of violating white-collar statutes, many offenders remain comfortably far from the *viability* threshold.

Viability is a perceptual and predictive concept. It reflects the point at which the government believes it has collected enough information to prove and win its case.[46]

Viability occasionally reflects predictions about how a given legal argument will fare in district and appellate courts. But far more often, it reflects intuitions about how defendants will behave once arrested (i.e., cooperate, plead guilty, or seek trial), and how jurors will respond to a given set of facts. For that reason, it hinges on the prosecutor's prior experiences, on the prosecutor's relationship with the lead investigator and the investigator's agency, on salient wins and losses, and on what society deems a prototypical case.[47] To be sure, the viability line is derived partially from the underlying statute and its requisite elements, but it rises and falls on the prosecutor's view of how much and which categories of evidence are necessary to make a case winnable.[48] Moreover, it relies as well on the prosecutor's taste for risk as filtered through her moral obligation to pursue wrongdoing and "do justice."[49] It is difficult to define and test, and it is also dynamic and contingent on past experiences and personal and social values.

Whereas the liability threshold is the product of multiple institutions (e.g., the legislature, prosecutors, judges), the viability threshold is maintained almost exclusively by prosecutors and their respective offices. In federal court, prosecutors enjoy a

general inability to assess their own ethicality, see YUVAL FELDMAN, THE LAW OF GOOD PEOPLE: CHALLENGING STATES' ABILITY TO REGULATE HUMAN BEHAVIOR (2018). Finally, for a vivid description of how corporate lawyers and other gatekeepers get caught up in their own biased motivations, see Donald C. Langevoort, *Chasing the Greased Pig Down Wall Street: A Gatekeeper's Guide to the Psychology, Culture, and Ethics of Financial Risk Taking*, 96 CORNELL L. REV. 1209, 1214 (2011) ("gatekeepers who are inclined – indeed motivated – to infer that nothing is amiss so long as the people they meet and the behaviors they observe show none of the visible markings of disloyalty: extreme selfishness, sloth, dishonesty, etc").

[46] Prosecutors can still lose viable cases. See, e.g., Lauren M. Ouziel, *Legitimacy and Federal Criminal Enforcement Power*, 123 YALE L. J. 2236, 2267–68 (2014) (citing high-profile cases that prosecutors have lost).

[47] On the relationship between prosecutor and her agents, and the ways in which each group serves a check on power, see Daniel C. Richman, *Prosecutors and Their Agents, Agents and Their Prosecutors*, 103 COLUM. L. REV. 749 (2003).

[48] The prosecutor's responsibility for developing and maintaining this line finds its partial expression through plea bargaining. See, e.g., Gerard E. Lynch, *Our Administrative System of Criminal Justice*, 66 FORDHAM L. REV. 2117, 2123 (1998); Marc L. Miller & Ronald F. Wright, *The Black Box*, 94 IOWA L. REV. 125 (2008).

[49] *See* Bruce Green and Fred Zacharias, *The Uniqueness of Federal Prosecutors*, 88 GEO. L.J. 207, 227 (2000) (citing federal prosecutors "overarching duty to seek justice – a duty recognized for well over a century").

monopoly over the ability to seek criminal charges.[50] Regulators can refer cases to the DOJ or urge certain lines of reasoning, but they cannot pursue criminal prosecutions themselves. Interested citizens can file whistleblowing reports with agencies, but they too enjoy little ability to ignite federal criminal law's machinery.[51] Only the prosecutor can trigger criminal liability.[52] Thus, *her* understanding of viability is the understanding that governs insofar as the initial charging decision is concerned.

Now, it is true that if the prosecutor has a *more* expansive view of viability than either the jury, trial judge, or appellate court, these alternative institutional actors will all have their chance to weigh in. Thus, when the prosecutor is overly aggressive or more willing to take her chances, other actors can cross-check the prosecutor's expansive notions of viability. Moreover, this predictive expectation of how these actors will behave is partially what drives prosecutors to hold a case in abeyance while seeking more evidence.[53] But once the prosecutor decides *not* to prosecute, or to offer a particularly generous plea deal, her say is final.[54] When the prosecutor is overly risk averse, judges, hypothetical juries, and even legislators enjoy far less power to tell the prosecutor how to behave.[55]

A final point is in order: Whereas the criminal justice system's legality principle insists on prior notice of what is and is not legal, it does not require the government to advise where it thinks the viability line falls.[56] Indeed, prosecutors have good reason *not* to introspectively interrogate (much less communicate) that line. First, as supplicants for political and budgetary support, prosecutors enjoy no incentive to admit their risk aversion to the public. Second, many prosecutors subscribe to the notion that silence instills just enough fear and uncertainty to increase deterrence. To admit one's fears about viability is to communicate weaknesses in law enforcement. Particularly where white-collar offenders are concerned, this is the last cue a prosecutor wants to send.

Thus, silence is both strategic and self-preservative. For the prosecutor, it makes overwhelming sense to say as little as possible about where the government's viability

---

[50] Richman, *supra* note 477, at 758 ("Prosecutors are the exclusive gatekeepers over federal court, but they need agents to gather evidence. Agencies control investigative resources, but they are not free to retain separate counsel. If agents want criminal charges to be pursued ... they will have to convince a prosecutor to take the case").

[51] The grand jury could theoretically investigate *sua sponte*, but as a practical matter, it cannot easily investigate complex white-collar cases by itself.

[52] Richman, *supra* note 477, at 780 (describing the prosecutor's unique panoply of "coercive tools").

[53] *See generally* Anna Offit, *Prosecuting in the Shadow of the Jury*, 113 Nw. L. Rev. 1071 (2019).

[54] On declinations generally, see Jessica A. Roth, *Prosecutorial Declination Statements*, 110 J. Crim. & Criminology 477 (2020) (constructing rubric to guide prosecutors in their announcement of their reasons for declining cases).

[55] U.S. v. Fokker Services, B.V., 828 F.3d 733 (2d Cir. 2016).

[56] Tom Baker et al., *The Virtues of Uncertainty in Law: An Experimental Approach*, 89 Iowa L. Rev. 443 (2004).

line falls. It is preferable instead to offer vague bromides about the difficulties of investigating and proving complex schemes. This strategy may work for prosecutors, but it also widens the knowledge gap between the criminal justice system's insiders and outsiders. Outsiders learn little about the viability line because the government refuses to say anything substantive. Insiders, meanwhile, develop a feel for where the line falls through their experience. No wonder, then, that the wealthiest white-collar offenders prefer to hire former prosecutors as their defense counsel. If anyone would know where the viability line is, it is the person who most recently worked for the prosecutor's office.

5.4 NOT AN ENDPOINT BUT A GAP

To review so far: Two thresholds impact white-collar crime's enforcement. The liability threshold is the moment guilt would become a near certainty *were all relevant facts observable to a fact-finder*. The viability threshold is the moment a prosecutor concludes she has a viable case and decides to move forward by seeking a grand jury's indictment or a magistrate's arrest warrant. Her decision, in turn, is based on her personal experience, her taste for risk, the collective experience of her peers and her office, the evidence she has amassed, her classification of the case into a certain family of cases, and how well similar cases have fared within a certain time period.

One might expect the two thresholds to intersect at roughly the same moment. Indeed, many of the hypothetical vignettes described in criminal law casebooks give the false impression that the two thresholds arise concurrently. *Jane lies to her investors about the returns certain investments have earned over the past quarter. Here are the statements Jane made to her investors. Evaluate Jane's liability.* To answer such a question is to assume that liability and viability arise simultaneously. In fact, the two points occupy different points on a timeline, separating the moments of technical guilt from the filing of a complaint or return of a grand jury indictment. This is what I refer to as "the gap."

5.5 ON THE DESIRABILITY OF A MODEST GAP

We should begin with the concession that *some* gap between the two thresholds is desirable. The space between liability and viability protects us from government abuse. When laws are open-textured and capture behavior that is on its face ambiguous, a gap between liability and viability is essential. Thresholds that arise in tandem would otherwise invest the prosecutor with an enormous degree of power and chill socially desirable interactions.

Nor would we want the viability threshold to be met *in advance* of the liability threshold. If that were the case, prosecutors could simply target certain populations for crimes they had not actually committed. This concern is graphically described in

FIGURE 5.1. Scenario #1: No gap, wrongful convictions

FIGURE 5.2. Scenario #2: Underenforcement gaps

Figure 5.1, which shows the potential for wrongful convictions when there exists no gap at all.

But false convictions are not the primary concern of white-collar crime. As Figure 5.2 makes clear, underenforcement is the more pressing problem, particularly among the wealthy and powerful. And underenforcement arises when liability thresholds are met and exceeded well in advance of viability thresholds. Under this scenario, numerous individuals violate the law, but they nevertheless evade detection, prosecution or punishment. They either do so for a very long time, or they do so permanently.

It bears repeating that a modest threshold gap is desirable. We *want* the government to expend time and effort investigating what occurred, gathering evidence, and developing its case. That is, after all, how we ensure accuracy. For that reason, we ought not be too concerned when a prosecutor's office sets its viability threshold high. High viability thresholds ameliorate the risk of improvident rushes to judgment and reduce the risk of abuse.

We also want our prosecutors to use their discretion to decline technical but otherwise nonculpable cases of liability. If the executive branch knows that Congress has purposely written its fraud laws in overly broad terms, prosecutors may respond by prosecuting only the "important" cases they assume Congress "really" wants to pursue.[57]

Along a similar vein, Samuel Buell has argued that statutory overbreadth is one of the state's primary tools for redressing the practical and resource-based difficulties of identifying intentional corporate wrongdoing.[58] If prosecutors realize laws are purposely and necessarily overbroad, they can adjust them on the margins by

---

[57] According to Michael Gilbert, lawmakers purposely write overly broad laws in order to induce compliance and improve outcomes in evidentiary disputes. Michael D. Gilbert, *Insincere Rules*, 101 VA. L. REV. 2185 (2015) and Michael D. Gilbert & Sean P. Sullivan, *Insincere Evidence*, 105 VA. L. REV. 1115 (2019). For a less optimistic perspective, see William J. Stuntz, *The Pathological Politics of Criminal Law*, 100 MICH. L. REV. 505 (2001).

[58] Buell, *supra* note 17, at 1507–12. *See also* Lynch, *supra* note 48, at 2137–38 ("Criminal statutes are clearly written in the expectation that prosecutors will proceed only in 'appropriate' cases").

implementing soft rules of nonenforcement. The law induces compliance while also avoiding the worst consequences of overcriminalization.

Thus, we should expect to find two groups of people in our gap:

(1) Guilty offenders for whom most legislators (and the general public) would desire prosecution *if all facts were known* and

(2) guilty offenders for whom most legislators (and the general public) would desire *no* prosecution, *even if* all facts were known.

Let's call the first group "pre-viability cases." A pre-viability case is one that has not *yet* crossed the viability threshold. Were the prosecutor to amass enough evidence, however, she would prosecute the case with alacrity. The second group, meanwhile, is what we can refer to as one of "normative exclusions." For a "normative exclusion" case, the prosecutor has no inclination to prosecute, regardless of how much evidence she amasses.

The pre-viability case is a story of effort, information, and a bit of luck. The normative exclusion, by contrast, is embedded in prosecutorial discretion and normative views of how broadly (or narrowly) Congress intends its prosecutors to interpret its laws. *Both* groups populate the liability/viability gap, even though normative exclusions are conceptually and politically quite different from pre-viability cases.

When the gap is relatively small, neither group poses that much of a problem. After all, sorting and screening potential cases is an integral part of the prosecutor's job.[59] So too, is collecting evidence and gauging when to pull the trigger on a difficult-to-prove case.

When the gap grows *too* wide, however, several problems emerge.

First, it becomes more difficult to distinguish the technically guilty from the guilty-but-not-sufficiently-proven. Or to put it another way, normative misgivings intermix with predictive fears, and prosecutors have very little incentive to disentangle these concepts for themselves, much less a broader audience.[60] Rather than admit outright that one is making a normative exclusion, one can say instead that "we just don't have enough evidence." Savvy defense attorneys know full well how to exploit such predictive and normative uncertainty, both in the prosecutor's office and with the press.[61]

---

[59] Ronald Wright & Marc Miller, *The Screening/Bargaining Tradeoff*, 55 STAN. L. REV. 29 (2002).

[60] I thank Professor Michelle Dempsey for helping me see and understand this normative/predictive distinction.

[61] Judge Lynch, a former federal prosecutor, elaborates on this process:

> The typical investigation of an allegation of past white-collar misconduct is essentially overt. The materials that the prosecutor needs to examine to determine the facts – typically, financial and business records – usually cannot be obtained without the knowledge of the subjects of the investigation, since they must either be produced in

FIGURE 5.3. Scenario #3: Detection avoidance

Second, the longer people remain in the gap, the more likely the public will wonder why it is that the government ignores the vast group of executives who *seem* to be guilty of "fraud" or "corruption" (or who have at least caused a significant amount of loss) but have otherwise not suffered the indignity of a single criminal charge. Even if the prosecutor truly is searching for more evidence, she may find herself *accused* by the public of waffling under pressure or excluding certain elites from prosecution. The intermixture of normative exclusions and pre-viability cases thus undermines the public's trust in government enforcement.

Third, among the pre-viability group, the gap facilitates detection avoidance, which is visually depicted in Figure 5.3. When the formal and informal punishments for a given crime are high, guilty individuals want to make sure their cases *never* reach viability. Concealing evidence, bribing or threatening witnesses, and lying to investigators are all excellent examples of this phenomenon.[62] The longer a previability case lingers, the more harm its proponents can inflict.

One of the (few) benefits of detection avoidance is that it increases the offender's expected costs. In addition to whatever cost an offender expends executing her original scheme, she must now expend additional energy (and sometimes money) concealing her behavior. If a would-be offender is rational, she may decide that avoidance's costs outweigh crime's benefits and therefore refrain from violating the law.[63] But not everyone will forecast the costs of concealing a crime or forecast them accurately. Some will conclude there are no alternatives. And some offenders will simply externalize those costs onto others.[64] In sum, even if detection avoidance poses a theoretical benefit to society, that benefit can be eclipsed by avoidance's costs.

---

response to a subpoena or seized pursuant to a search. Once an investigation becomes overt ... defense counsel can try to influence the prosecutor's conclusions.

Lynch, *supra* note 48, at 2126. *See also* Gerald E. Lynch, *The Role of Criminal Law in Policing Corporate Misconduct*, 60 LAW & CONTEMP. PROBS. 23 (1997) (describing familiar "pitches" by white-collar attorneys).

[62] Buell, *supra* note 17, at 1507–8; Chris William Sanchirico, *Detection Avoidance*, 81 N.Y.U. L. REV. 1331 (2006); Avraham D. Tabbach, *The Social Desirability of Punishment Avoidance*, 26 J. L. ECON. ORGAN. 265 (2009). Tabbach includes "legal" types of avoidance (aggressively challenging subpoenas) in his description of avoidance techniques.

[63] Tabbach, *supra* note 62 at 265–66.

[64] *See generally* Miriam H. Baer, *Linkage and the Deterrence of Corporate Fraud*, 94 VA. L. REV. 1295 (2008) (explaining how later lies are necessary to cover up earlier ones and therefore result in larger, more harmful frauds).

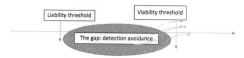

FIGURE 5.4. Scenario #4: Gap-minding

5.6 HOW THE GOVERNMENT USUALLY RESPONDS: GAP-MINDING

To deal with the gap between liability and viability, the government adopts a series of "gap-minding" mechanisms. These tools do not necessarily narrow the gap between liability and viability. But they *do* move a small percentage of previability cases across the viability threshold, as shown in Figure 5.4. This is what I mean by gap-minding.

Numerous programs fall within this category, but three stand out:

Whistleblowing. A whistleblower is an individual – often a member of a group or organization – who voluntarily discloses material violations of law to a government authority.[65] Whistleblowers can alert the government to a completely unknown scheme or provide the missing link between a known scheme and undetected offenders.

When whistleblowing becomes normatively acceptable, it increases the flow of information within and outside of organizations.[66] Moreover, "it convinces some would-be wrongdoers to avoid the proscribed conduct altogether; (ii) introduces a costly element of distrust within extant conspiracies; and (iii) enables the federal government to punish, incapacitate, and seek disgorgement from those who remain undeterred."[67]

Despite efforts to make it more economically and socially palatable, whistleblowing remains a fraught exercise. In addition to revealing an employer's subpar

---

[65] Whistleblower statutes "generally [fall] into one of two categories: those that afford financial incentives to whistleblowers and those that protect them from retaliation." Justin W. Evans et al., *Reforming Dodd-Frank from the Whistleblower's Vantage*, 58 AM. BUS. L.J. 453, 458–59 (2021). *See also* David Freeman Engstrom, *Whither Whistleblowing? Bounty Regimes, Regulatory Context, and the Challenge of Optimal Design*, 15 THEORETICAL INQUIRIES L. 605 (2014).

[66] On whistleblowing's potential for deterring crime, see BENJAMIN VAN ROOIJ & ADAM D. FINE, *Preventing Corporate Crime from Within: Compliance Management, Whistleblowing, and Internal Monitoring*, in THE HANDBOOK OF WHITE-COLLAR CRIME (Melissa Rorie, ed. 2020). As Usha Rodrigues recently observed, how vulnerable one views financial markets to fraud and misconduct will likely impact one's view of whistleblowing and its importance to enforcement agencies. Usha R. Rodrigues, *Optimizing Whistleblowing*, 94 TEMP. L. REV. 255, 263 (2022) ("[t]he importance of whistleblowing protections and policy depends in part on how much one thinks fraud is a problem").

[67] Miriam H. Baer, *Reconceptualizing the Whistleblower's Dilemma*, 50 U.C. DAVIS L. REV. 2215, 2235 (2017).

performance, it can inflict enormous costs on the whistleblower.[68] The common nickname for whistleblowing – snitching – hints at some of those costs.[69] To overcome them, the government not only has to promise to curb the likelihood of retaliation, but also to offer the putative whistleblower a bounty. The higher the bounty, the greater the likelihood the government will attract not only real information but also a lot of unhelpful noise.[70] Thus, like many gap-minding strategies, whistleblowing is an imperfect technique.

Criminal cooperation. Cooperation is the formal name prosecutors use to describe what occurs when a charged offender agrees to disclose information and testify against another offender, often in the hope of receiving a more lenient sentence.[71] Some refer to this colloquially as "flipping" a criminal defendant, but the term understates the enormous power that cooperation as an *institution* confers on government investigators.

Prosecutors maintain discretionary, unreviewable power to decide whom they select as cooperators. They therefore can manipulate competition for valuable cooperation status.[72] Out of a group of six offenders, four may decide to proffer information, but only one might become a formal cooperator who receives leniency at sentencing. Regardless of how few offenders become official cooperators, the government still benefits from the information it receives from the other, would-be cooperators.[73] The prosecutor harbors no legal obligation to "pay" the auditioning defendant for her information. The benefits of cooperation thus run broader and deeper than a specific "cooperation agreement" implies. Writ large, "failed" cooperation benefits the government as much as, if not more than, successful cooperation.

Unlike whistleblowing, criminal cooperation does not include a monetary payoff. Instead, the primary currency the government trades in is the likelihood for less severe punishment.[74] For this trade to work, the offender must perceive a high likelihood of conviction and severe punishment if the offender *doesn't* cooperate. In other words, "the government must first obtain evidence of one type (or level) of wrongdoing to secure [a complicit individual's] admission of another type (or level)

---

[68] Evans et al., *supra* note 65, at 462 ("Whistleblowing is unavoidably jarring").

[69] "Society's view of whistleblowers is complicated, to say the least." Rodrigues, *supra* note 66, at 261 (describing contrasting views of whistleblowers as "rats" or heroes).

[70] *Id.* at 2280, citing Yehonatan Givati, *A Theory of Whistleblower Rewards*, 43 J. LEGAL STUD. 56–57 (2016). *See also* Anthony J. Casey & Anthony Niblett, *Noise Reduction: The Screening Value of Qui Tam*, 91 WASH. U. L. REV. 1169, 1175 (2014).

[71] *See generally* USSC 5K1.1 (government's motion for downward departure in recognition of defendant's substantial assistance); Miriam H. Baer, *Cooperation's Cost*, 88 WASH. U. L. REV. 903 (2011).

[72] Baer, *supra* note 711, at 921.

[73] Baer, *supra* note 711, at 921–23.

[74] Under DOJ policy, the sole "benefit" the prosecutor is authorized to offer is the prospect of sentencing leniency upon the prosecutor's recommendation to the court. *See generally* U.S. Dep't of Justice, Justice Manual §9-27.400.

of wrongdoing."[75] In sum, the government cannot "flip" offenders at will. It needs leverage to make cooperation a viable strategy in the first place.

Corporate cooperation. Finally, government agents can lean on corporations and business entities to self-police and voluntarily disclose information in exchange for a prosecutor's leniency in charging the entity ("charging leniency") or a judge's leniency at sentencing ("sentencing leniency").[76] Given the collateral consequences that attach to criminal convictions, most corporations would prefer the avoidance of criminal charges to a formal charge paired with a weaker sentence. (Then again, sentencing leniency is better than nothing.)

Two phenomena enable the government to pressure corporations to investigate themselves. First, as discussed in Chapter 4, the substantive rule of corporate criminal liability is extremely broad. Under the common law of *respondeat superior*, a corporation is vicariously liable for any crime undertaken by its employee or agent, provided the employee or agent was acting within the scope of employment and harbored a partial intention of benefitting the firm (e.g., improving its profits or maintaining its stock price). Many crimes therefore can easily be attributed to an entity.[77]

Second, corporations, unlike natural persons, enjoy some constitutional rights but not others. They enjoy due process, property, and contractual rights, but they are not endowed with Fifth Amendment's privilege against self-incrimination. Moreover, although they enjoy limited Fourth Amendment rights from unreasonable searches and seizures, they have little ability to challenge documentary subpoenas, other than to claim they have been filed in bad faith or with the intention of harassment.[78]

Collectively, these rules endow the government with sufficient leverage to pressure corporations to monitor themselves and "voluntarily" report their employees' wrongdoing.[79] Consider the common pattern that arises: The government threatens the corporation with criminal prosecution. It signals its intentions by serving subpoenas and obtaining search warrants. The corporation, seeking to avert the costs of

---

[75] Baer, *supra* note 67, at 2247.

[76] On the differences between corporate and individual cooperation, see Baer, *supra* note 67, at 914–15. Corporations can also seek plea agreements that bind the court to a prearranged sentence. See Fed. R. Crim. P. 11(c)(1)(C) (forcing court to choose between agreed upon sentence and rejection of guilty plea). For a devastating critique of this type of corporate plea, see United States v. Aegerion Pharms., Inc., 280 F. Supp. 3d 217 (D. Mass. 2017) (Young, J.).

[77] *See generally* Chapter 4 and MIRIAM H. BAER, *Corporate Criminal Law Unbounded*, in THE OXFORD HANDBOOK OF PROSECUTORS AND PROSECUTION (Ronald Wright, Kay Levine, & Russell Gold, eds., 2021) at 475.

[78] Miriam H. Baer, *Law Enforcement's Lochner*, 105 MINN. L. REV. 1667, 1690–708 (2021). Jennifer Arlen & Samuel W. Buell, *The Law of Corporate Investigations and the Global Expansion of Corporate Criminal Enforcement*, 93 S. CAL. L. REV. 697 (2020).

[79] Admittedly, not all cooperation is fueled by fear or cost-benefit analysis: "Cooperation [also involves] a more general, attitudinal willingness to aid law enforcement's efforts." Jacob T. Elberg, *Health Care Fraud Means Never Having to Say You're Sorry*, 96 WASH. L. REV. 371, 407 (2021).

a protracted investigation, promises to investigate its employees, pay a fine, and commit to a series of reforms. *Other* corporations, meanwhile, duly report instances of wrongdoing to demonstrate their bona fides. The government learns more easily of wrongdoing and does so on the corporation's dime.

It sounds quite rosy until one realizes that some wrongdoing is likely to be so embedded and difficult to detect that the company never even considers disclosing it, much less redressing its effects. And in some instances, the company's market power may be so great that everyone knows the prosecutor will never file criminal charges, lest it put a purveyor of essential goods or services out of business. Anyone with even passing familiarity of the General Motors,[80] Volkswagen,[81] and HSBC[82] cases will recognize this problem.[83]

5.7 MINDLESS GAP-MINDING

These tools envision an exchange between government actors and private citizens. Whistleblowing promises a monetary payout to induce reports of wrongdoing. Criminal and corporate cooperation use the promise of leniency to induce confessions and disclosures. All three techniques rely on, to varying degrees, third-party intermediaries such as lawyers. And all require the government's verification of the information it has received. Because verification is costly and itself unreliable, the government ultimately pays for information that is false, incomplete, or simply unhelpful.[84]

Gap-minding is administratively costly; it requires the government to develop an apparatus to verify information, communicate with would-be cooperators and whistleblowers, and calibrate the amount of "benefit" to trade in exchange for assistance. The responsibility for running these programs falls primarily on the executive branch. Even in those instances where Congress has authorized or funded a program, it devolves to prosecutors and regulators.

---

[80] Stavros Gadinis & Amelia Miazad, *The Hidden Power of Compliance*, 103 Minn. L. Rev. 2135, 2142 (2019) (discussing the General Motors case).

[81] Press Release, Eastern District of Michigan, U.S. Attorney's Office, U.S. Department of Justice, Volkswagen AG Sentenced in Connection with Conspiracy to Cheat U.S. Emissions Tests (Apr. 21, 2017), www.justice.gov/usao-edmi/pr/volkswagen-ag-sentenced-connection-conspir acy-cheat-us-emissions-tests. See also J. S. Nelson, *Disclosure-Driven Crime*, 52 U.C. Davis L. Rev. 1487, 1489–91 (2019).

[82] Dorothy S. Lund & Natasha Sarin, *Corporate Crime and Punishment: An Empirical Study*, 100 Tex. L. Rev. 285, 330 (2021).

[83] On the diffuse and fractured nature of corporate knowledge, see Mihailis Diamantis, *Functional Corporate Knowledge*, 61 Wm & Mary L. Rev. 319 (2019). On diffusion's effect on corporate compliance and ongoing investigations, see Veronica Root Martinez, *Complex Compliance Investigations*, 120 Colum. L. Rev. 249 (2020).

[84] On the implications of cooperator testimony that is untruthful, see Jessica A. Roth, *Informant Witnesses and the Risk of Wrongful Conviction*, 53 Am. Crim. L. Rev. 737 (2016)

Gap-minding can also translate into opaque practices. Whistleblowing is perhaps the most transparent. Pursuant to Dodd–Frank, the SEC files annual reports reveal how many tips it has received, how many of those tips have been converted into "covered actions," and how much money it has awarded to successful whistle-blowers under its whistleblowing program.[85] But the program could provide more meaningful guidance if Congress and the SEC so desired, especially to putative whistleblowers and their attorneys.[86]

From there, transparency diminishes significantly. Criminal cooperation is dependent on the policies and practices of the office where the prosecutor practices. The public may eventually learn of a defendant's cooperation, but it will not learn of the prosecutor's decision-making process. As for corporate cooperation, the DOJ has spent two decades issuing policy guidance on when prosecutors should offer corporations leniency and which factors they should consider.[87] Despite these missives, the DOJ has never explained – to prosecutors or outside attorneys – how decisionmakers will weigh each factor.

At its best, gap-minding allows the prosecutor to condemn misconduct, deter future crimes, and reduce detection avoidance. But gap-minding is itself costly. It bestows windfalls on a few lucky actors. And it distorts the law enforcement agency's mission. It requires the creation of an infrastructure to analyze tips, distribute bounties, and oversee cooperation. Once that infrastructure is built, it marshals its energies in a singular direction, toward the improvement and expansion of the gap-minding process. The means to an end becomes its own end.

5.8 AN ALTERNATIVE APPROACH: GAP-NARROWING

What if instead of *minding* the gap we asked the government to somehow *narrow* the gap between liability and viability? Could we even do such a thing? As I argued earlier, prosecutors almost exclusively control where the viability line falls. Still, other actors and institutions can influence where prosecutors draw that line. Do we want those other actors to weigh in?

If we are serious about maintaining criminal law's statutory backdrop, then we should strongly consider a gap-narrowing approach, especially if it enables more constituents to say where *both* liability and viability lines should be set. A narrower gap is also valuable insofar as it reduces the incentive to engage in detection avoidance. Finally, the actual process of gap-narrowing – of trying to figure out how to move *both* the viability and liability lines – might pave the way for more

---

[85] See Baer, *supra* note 78, at 2227–31.

[86] See Evans et al., *supra* note 68, at 517 (proposing an SEC tracking system that would redress "at a lack of communication between the SEC and whistleblowers").

[87] For an overview of such guidance, see Samuel W. Buell, *Why Do Prosecutors Say Anything? The Case of Corporate Crime*, 96 N.C. L. REV. 823, 832 (2018).

honest discussions about case prototypes and their effect on white-collar enforcement.

How could the government move from a gap-minding approach to a gap-narrowing one? Consider the following reformative approaches:

Moving the liability threshold forward. It may sound counterintuitive but the government could narrow the gap by making it *more difficult* for someone to violate white-collar crime. One way to do this is create practical or regulatory hurdles that make it difficult for individuals to engage in the underlying activity. If a company automates much of its procurement, for example, it might find employees less likely to commit bribery. The automation eliminates the opportunity – and therefore makes it less likely to that someone will find themselves on the wrong side of the liability threshold.[88]

The more controversial way to move the liability line "forward" is to narrow the definition of certain crimes – that is, to make it more difficult to prove an individual guilty of fraud, bribery, or obstruction. If fewer people are guilty of a federal crime, their incentives to engage in detection avoidance ought to abate.[89] There are, however, political, practical, and conceptual drawbacks to this strategy.

First, if we make it *legally* more difficult to commit a given crime, any reduction in detection avoidance is apt to be accompanied by a reduction in deterrence. Thus, the change in liability rule makes sense only if the reduction in (costly) detection avoidance exceeds the reduction in (valuable) deterrence.[90]

Second, liability and viability thresholds do not operate independently of each other. They are, in some ways, tethered. Depending on how the government alters the liability standard, it might *also* end up altering the viability standard. For example, if Congress alters the mental state for a given offense from "purposeful" to "purposeful with time for reflection," it not only narrows the number of people who are technically guilty, but it may make it even *more* difficult to prove guilt among those who continue to fall under the narrower definition.

On the other hand, if Congress alters liability in a way that leaves the viability of a prosecution constant, it successfully narrows the gap. Take the crime of conspiracy or the doctrine of accomplice liability. If Congress narrows these doctrines to require a greater deal of *behavior* (and not just a mere "agreement" or a smidge of trivial "aid"), then the gap between constitutive liability and viability narrows. It becomes more difficult for the offender to commit the crime, but easier for the prosecutor to prove it after the fact. If the additional behavior is more visible, it will be more detectable and therefore easier to prove.

---

[88] Miriam H. Baer, *Confronting the Two Faces of Corporate Fraud*, 66 Fla. L. Rev. 87, 131–32 (2014) (describing devices that make criminal outcomes more difficult to achieve).

[89] Of course, civil and administrative sanctions still create incentives for detection avoidance, but those incentives should be weaker than the prospect of criminal prosecution and punishment.

[90] To be precise, we would want the benefits of reduced detection avoidance to exceed the cost-increase associated with reduced deterrence.

Move the viability threshold backward. Another strategy focuses solely on the viability line. Congress can't tell prosecutors how to do their jobs. (Well, not directly.) But it can make cases more viable by removing one or more of the law's constitutive requirements (i.e., make it easier to prove certain crimes by removing or weakening elements) or by altering the burden of proof.[91]

This is, effectively, what proposals for a "negligent fraud" doctrine accomplish. Along a similar vein, judicial enlargements of the terms "intent" and "knowledge" make questionable fraud cases more viable. But the same tethering problem we encountered when we attempted to move the liability threshold forward rears its ugly head: If the only way to make a case more viable is to water down or hollow out a legal requirement, we will end up yet again altering the liability threshold. More people will be technically guilty of an offense, and more people will occupy the gap.

The more targeted option is to alter the prosecutor's burden. In the American system, there are effectively two ways to do this. First, Congress might enact a series of statutes that are easier to prove than fraud or bribery, but which serve as "proxies" for certain underlying harms.[92] This practice is controversial, in part because proxy statutes reflect unproven assumptions about the relationship between the proven activity (the proxy) and the unproven offense (in this case fraud or bribery).[93]

Another way to alter viability is to pursue *civil* liability instead of criminal prosecution. That is, after all, the only constitutional way to alter the government's burden of proof. Civil cases must be proven by a preponderance of evidence, which is less exacting than the criminal trial's proof beyond a reasonable doubt.[94] The tsunami of pharmaceutical claims pursued by State Attorneys General, in which formerly powerful corporations have been held to account primarily under civil

---

[91] "Federal and state legislatures may reallocate burdens of proof by labeling elements as affirmative defenses … or they may convert elements into "sentencing factor[s]" for consideration by the sentencing court." United States v. Gaudin, 515 U.S. 506, 525 (1995) (Rehnquist, J. concurring) (internal citation omitted).

[92] The creation and use of such offenses (e.g., the possession of burglar's tools as a proxy for burglary) as well as the mounting of pretextual prosecutions (e.g., prosecuting the money launderer for a different crime because the latter is more easily proven) remain controversial strategies. *See, e.g.*, Piotr Bystranowski & Murat Mungan, *Proxy Crimes*, 59 AM. CRIM.L. REV. 1 (2022). Daniel Richman & William Stuntz, *Al Capone's Revenge: An Essay on the Political Economy of Pretextual Prosecutions*, 105 COLUM. L. REV. 610 (2005). RICHARD H. McADAMS, *The Political Economy of Criminal Law and Procedure*, in CRIMINAL LAW CONVERSATIONS (Paul H. Robinson, Stephen Garvey, & Kimberley Kessler Ferzan, eds., 2011).

[93] *See generally* Ronald L. Gainer, *Federal Criminal Code Reform: Past and Future*, 2 BUFF. CRIM. L. REV. 45, 63 (1998) (describing the urge, among prosecutors and legislators, to "draft statutes that focus upon peripheral conduct").

[94] In re Winship, 397 U.S. 358 (1970). Moving from criminal to civil liability alters not only the burden of proof but also the elements that must be proven, the resources available to enforcement agencies, and the government's access to certain procedural tools (such as the ability to secure a search and execute a warrant). I explore these differences at greater length in Chapter 7.

laws, instantiates the benefits of such a category change. Many assume this shift signals a form of retreat or weakness. Perhaps we should reexamine this assumption. Civil liability can never substitute perfectly for criminal liability, but it does enable prosecutors and regulators to build complex and sophisticated cases against wrongdoers, stripping them of their clout, their money, and their reputation.[95]

Alter the government's taste for risk (or introduce more prototypes). If viability is determined in part by risk and by the prosecutor's sense of what constitutes a paradigmatic case, then one way to alter that viability line is to increase the prosecutor's taste for risk.

Scholars have long argued that prosecutors are loss averse, as they prefer not to lose cases in an embarrassing way. Skilled and knowledgeable defense attorneys know how to exploit these fears and convince prosecutors in advance that their client's case falls too far to the side of the viability line.

For many cases, the conversation is likely to take on a binary tone, in that the case either falls over the line or it doesn't. This is partially attributable to the fact that federal fraud laws are flat and feature no gradation (e.g., "first degree" or "second degree").[96] All of this means that the serious but marginally viable case can result in a situation in which it receives *no* response by federal criminal enforcement authorities.

Imagine instead that there existed several tiers of fraud. Would the presence of such statutory gradation alter the prosecutor's taste for risk? Might the presence of more and less serious versions of the same offense make way for a wider array of prototypes? It certainly seems plausible enough that we should at least return to the question in Chapters 7 and 8, which mount a more comprehensive case for statutory gradation.

Additional resources. One last means of improving viability is to make crimes more observable. Regulatory disclosure requirements, government-friendly rules of constitutional criminal procedure, and mass surveillance tools all enhance the government's ability to observe a person's actions and potentially prove a person's corrupt state of mind. Whatever their instrumental value, these tools are *also* the tools of an all-powerful state, one that could easily abuse its powers if insufficiently restrained. As I have written elsewhere, it is unclear the judiciary will continue to allow the government unencumbered access to these tools.[97]

In lieu of panoptic resources, we might instead substantially increase the financial resources we allocate to enforcement institutions, allowing for the profusion of more

---

[95] For an evocative discussion on the ways in which civil sanctions can shame and punish, see Donald C. Langevoort, *On Leaving Corporate Executives "Naked, Homeless and Without Wheels": Corporate Fraud, Equitable Remedies, and the Debate over Entity versus Individual Liability,* 42 WAKE FOREST L. REV. 629 (2007).

[96] *See generally* Chapter 3; Miriam H. Baer, *Sorting Out White-Collar Crime,* 97 TEX. L. REV. 225 (2018).

[97] Baer, *supra* note 78.

investigators, more prosecutors, more investigations, and (hopefully) more worthy prosecutions. This is, after all, what critics like Professor Coffee contend is necessary if we are to get serious about corporate and white-collar crime.[98]

How does an increase in resources differ from gap-minding programs such as cooperation and whistleblowing? The latter programs are themselves costly and require the government to build out a procedural infrastructure. An infusion of cash, by contrast, is just more money that can be used to hire more investigators and take on new and more cases. A major infusion of resources also enables the investigator and prosecutor to experiment a bit, since everyone has more time to work on and develop more cases. An institution freed of having to prove its worthiness to miserly congressional budgeting committees may extend its employees greater support in making qualitative enforcement choices.[99]

Resources are also important for the signals they emit. When Congress noisily earmarks a large amount of money specifically for "white-collar" enforcement, the DOJ can reassure its prosecutors that it will stand by them as they sift through evidence and untangle complicated schemes. A huge influx of resources doesn't just enable *more* work, but also enables *more risky* work.

Still, one of the drawbacks of such an approach is that it requires a long-term commitment. The payoff, if it occurs at all, will happen in the future and will be difficult to quantify. A short-horizon landscape that favors quick fixes and popular programs is not likely to support the "increased resources" strategy, particularly in times of austerity.

For all these reasons, gap-narrowing seems to be best addressed in times of prosperity and political equanimity. Miss either of those two windows and we are apt to find ourselves stuck in gap-minding purgatory.

5.9 DISTRIBUTING VIABILITY

Whether we like it or not, two thresholds dominate white-collar crime, and when the gap between those thresholds grows too wide and too deep, it erodes society's trust in its enforcement institutions and encourages costly layers of detection avoidance. That lack of trust, in turn, can create profound implications for government enforcement in the future.[100]

Much as we are inclined to blame prosecutors, they are neither responsible for the gap's emergence nor equipped to fully redress it. The gap is the product of a system of interlocking institutions and embedded dynamics. For that reason, a complex set of remedies is needed, not just to mind the gap, but also to narrow it.

---

[98] COFFEE, *supra* note 11.

[99] On the ways in which budgeting impacts government enforcement institutions, see Richman, *supra* note 33, at 2093.

[100] *Cf.*, Ouziel, *supra* note 46, at 2301–2 (describing the "moral credibility gap" that arises when there exists "a significant gap between federal penalties and public and judicial views").

Gap-minding is primarily the work of the executive branch. Gap-narrowing relies on a broader set of legal actors. Gap-narrowing may be riskier and prone to failure, but it also promises more meaningful and lasting rewards. Accordingly, the policymaker who cares deeply about white-collar crime's enforcement will explore *both* sets of strategies, notwithstanding gap-narrowing's political risks.

6

Broken Discourse

INTRODUCTION

Preceding chapters have identified the various pathologies in lawmaking and enforcement that hamper our understanding of white-collar crime and its enforcement institutions. The laws that purport to describe white-collar crime's prohibitions are flat, overly broad, and underwritten (Chapters 3 and 4). Our enforcement institutions often get caught up in prototypes and convince themselves certain cases are nonviable. As a result, prosecutors rely heavily on so-called gap-minding policies; these programs shore up weaknesses in individual investigations here and there, but they fail to meaningfully narrow the gap between criminal law's liability and viability thresholds. As a result, detection avoidance increases while the general public loses trust in its enforcement institutions (Chapter 5).

The present chapter focuses on a different but related pathology: white-collar crime's discourse. The public's reaction to crimes of fraud, bribery, and obstruction has evolved over the past two centuries, although not in a straight line. In the post-Civil War period, Congress enacted the mail fraud statute's precursor with an aim toward protecting farmers and distant investors from fly-by-night schemers who had discovered the utility of the public mail system for exploiting information asymmetries that facilitated numerous swindles and confidence schemes.[1] First enacted in

---

[1] EDWARD J. BALLEISIEN, FRAUD: AN AMERICAN HISTORY FROM BARNUM TO MADOFF (2017) 77–89 (examining discourse throughout the 1800s) and 96–101 (describing public reactions to nineteenth-century fraudsters and their victims); and 108 ("Recognition of pervasive information asymmetries encouraged adjustments in how the American state tried to resolve the tension between honoring entrepreneurial freedom and discouraging marketing practices that played fast and loose with the truth"). On the development of pre– and post–Civil War mail-order businesses and the frauds that followed, see id. at 128–30. Before "mail fraud" became an established criminal offense, it was primarily the subject of an administrative sanction (exclusion from using the mails) investigated and administered by the Postal Service. See Jerry L. Mashaw, *Federal Administration and Administrative Law in the Gilded Age*, 119 YALE L.J. 1362, 1454–55 (2010).

1872, mail fraud was a misdemeanor punishable by no more than eighteen months' imprisonment. The eighteen-month cap remained in place when Congress revised the statute in 1889. It finally grew into a felony with a five-year maximum term of imprisonment in 1909, which remained intact until 2002, when Congress inflated the maximum to twenty years' imprisonment.[2]

Over the next century, federal criminal law and its white-collar subset grew substantially. Today, one can find tens of statutes that purport to criminalize fraud, bribery, or obstruction. That figure doesn't even include the many statutes that purport to punish regulatory violations, which skyrockets the number of white-collar statutes into the thousands.[3] At the same time, the statutory maxima for many of these statutes have ballooned as well, from merely five years' imprisonment to as much as twenty or thirty. Thus, with a few notable exceptions, white-collar crime's legislative breadth and punishment have ratcheted largely in one direction – up.[4]

The public's attitudes toward white-collar crime are more difficult to track. Edwin Sutherland coined the phrase in a 1939 speech to the American Sociological Association, followed by Donald Cressey's work in the 1950s, which purported to explain fraud and embezzlement as the product of a triangle of pressure, opportunity, and rationalizations.[5] Despite these breakthroughs, white-collar crime seemingly remained the province of experts rather than the general public during the immediate post–World War II period.[6]

[2] On the mail fraud statute's origins and legislative history, see BALLEISIEN, *supra* note 1 at 130–32, and Norman Abrams, *Uncovering the Legislative Histories of the Early Mail Fraud Statues: The Origins of Federal Auxiliary Crimes Jurisdiction*, 2021 UTAH L. REV. 1079, 1084–105 (2021). On the growth of mail fraud's enforcement in the early twentieth century and the divergent public responses it triggered, see BALLEISIEN, *supra* note 1, at 208–24.

[3] For general criticism of white-collar crime's breadth, see Paul J. Larkin, *Essay: A New Law Enforcement Agenda for a New Attorney General*, 17 GEORGETOWN J. L. & PUBLIC POL'Y 231, 235 (2019).

[4] Concededly, the judiciary's treatment of white-collar statutes has been more uneven. For more on this, see Chapter 4, and compare Aziz Z. Huq & Genevieve Lakier, *Apparent Fault*, 131 HARV. L. REV. 1525, 1546–64 (2018) (describing recent cases in which the Supreme Court has ruled against the government) *with* Dan M. Kahan, *Lenity and Federal Common Law Crimes*, 1994 THE SUPREME COURT REVIEW 345 (1994) (analyzing judiciary's deference to Congress).

[5] *See generally* ALEKSANDRA JORDANOSKA & ISABEL SCHOULTZ, *The "Discovery" of White-Collar Crime The Legacy of Edwin Sutherland*, in THE HANDBOOK OF WHITE-COLLAR CRIME (Melissa Rorie, ed. 2020) at 3–15 (contextualizing Sutherland's work); Leandra Lederman, *The Fraud Triangle and Tax Evasion*, 106 IOWA L. REV. 1153, 1156 (2021) (discussing Donald Cressey's study of embezzlement and subsequent development of the fraud triangle concept and term by later scholars).

[6] Francis Cullen, Jennifer Hartman & Cheryl Jonson, *Bad Guys: Why the Public Supports Punishing White-Collar Offenders*, 51 CRIME, LAW AND SOCIAL CHANGE 31 (2009) (contending that the American public was "inattentive" to corporate and white-collar crime until the 1960s).

Some of that began to change in the late 1960s and 1970s.[7] Congress enacted the Foreign Corrupt Practices Act (FCPA) in the wake of the Watergate investigation, which revealed that President Nixon's acolytes presided over a slush fund used to bribe foreign officials. The FCPA imposed criminal penalties on individuals and corporations who bribed foreign officials for any "business advantage" and further required companies to keep track of foreign expenditures (the "books and records" provision).[8] But despite the enactment of this law, the Department of Justice (DOJ) did not routinely indict individuals for FCPA-related crimes until the early 2000s, when it created a prosecutorial unit for that purpose.[9]

White-collar crime emerged yet again as a matter of importance during the 1980s, as thousands of savings and loans institutions failed due to mismanagement and fraud. The public railed, the DOJ mobilized its prosecutors, and eventually, the government obtained convictions for over 1,000 bankers.[10]

Finally, white-collar crime mounted another assault on the public psyche during the late 1990s and early 2000s, when the emergence of new technologies and an overheated stock market eventually led to a meltdown, followed by numerous revelations of accounting fraud. Here again, public reaction married itself to government action, resulting in a string of mostly successes for government prosecutors.[11]

And now we get to the story that has been told and retold many times: In 2008, major financial institutions caused a near-meltdown of our economy arising from their employees' reckless creation, marketing, and investment in subprime mortgage securities. I have already discussed this story in Chapter 5. The short version is that the government tried (depending on whom you ask), but ultimately failed to successfully convict the cabal of executives most responsible for the meltdown and its ensuing crisis. As discussed in Chapter 5, several of the major banks paid quite a

---

[7] Clinard and Yeager explain the public's renewed interest as "due largely to consumer groups and others who strongly emphasized the need for more social responsibility." MARSHALL B. CLINARD & PETER C. YEAGER, CORPORATE CRIME xi (2006).

[8] 15 U.S.C. §§ 78dd-1, *et seq.*; *Foreign Corrupt Practices Act: An Overview*, DEPT. OF JUSTICE, www.justice.gov/criminal-fraud/foreign-corrupt-practices-act.

[9] *See* Priya Cherian Huskins, *FCPA Prosecutions: Liability Trend to Watch*, 60 STAN. L. REV. 1447, 1449 (2008). "Although enacted in 1977, the FCPA was a very sleepy statute – in terms of enforcement – until the 2000s." Karen E. Woody, *No Smoke and No Fire: The Rise of Internal Controls Absent Anti-Bribery Violations in FCPA Enforcement*, 38 CARDOZO L. REV. 1727, 1733 (2017) (tracking the rise in FCPA enforcement actions).

[10] Bruce Green, *After the Fall: The Criminal Law Enforcement Response to the S&L Crisis*, 59 FORDHAM LAW REVIEW S155 (1991).

[11] "Since the Department of Justice's Corporate Fraud Task Force was formed in 2002 in the wake of Enron, it has charged over 1300 defendants and obtained over 1000 guilty pleas and convictions." John C. Coffee, Jr., *Law and the Market: The Impact of Enforcement*, 156 U. PA. L. REV. 229, 276 (2007) (citing DOJ press release and noting larger number of convictions and prison sentences for financial fraud stretching back several decades).

bit in financial sanctions.[12] The executives who caused a lengthy and unevenly-felt recession, however, emerged financially and socially unscathed.

The public's reaction to this lack of comeuppance is well known. Numerous journalists, politicians, and scholars concluded that white-collar crime's premier enforcement institutions – from the FBI to the DOJ to the SEC and the prosecutors of the vaunted Southern District of New York (SDNY) – had become corrupt, overly risk-averse, or simply incompetent. And this narrative of prosecutorial *power* paired with prosecutorial *failure* attached to the Obama administration as easily as it characterized the Trump administration. It surfaced again when Robert Mueller's Office of the Special Counsel investigated the president of the United States, his campaign, his associates, and several family members in connection with certain election-related crimes and irregularities.[13] Mueller's Office secured numerous prosecutions – several of them high-profile – but his failure to forcefully accuse Donald Trump of specific crimes, or to bring charges against Trump's son or son-in-law, ultimately branded his office a failure in the eyes of many.[14] Over the past two decades, underutilized power has become the salient characterization of federal white-collar prosecution. And the explanations for such underutilization are grounded either in ineptitude or outright corruption.

In the shadow of this narrative of enforcement failure, white-collar crime's discourse has grown in its frequency and intensity. Journalists, pundits, and academics have weighed in repeatedly on the topic. Their critiques have been indelibly shaped by nationwide concerns with inequality, political corruption, and societal breakdown and malaise. At some point, it becomes difficult to discern whether white-collar crime's failures are a primary cause of our social, political, and economic breakdowns, or whether they merely serve an unhealthy reflection of these cleavages.

This chapter's purpose is not to rebut these feelings, as they arise out of a series of concerns that are indeed valid. If the preceding chapters have been the least bit persuasive, readers *should* worry about the shape of our laws, the tunnel vision our enforcers display, and the information holes that make consensus on supposedly basic facts nearly impossible. Moreover, what little empirical evidence we have is far from reassuring. Scholars and oversight groups have detected a weakening of the

---

[12] Dorothy S. Lund & Natasha Sarin, *Corporate Crime and Punishment: An Empirical Study*, 100 TEX. L. REV. 285, 300 (2021) (citing "record-breaking fines against financial institutions" in the financial crisis's wake).

[13] REPORT ON THE INVESTIGATION INTO RUSSIAN INTERFERENCE IN THE 2016 PRESIDENTIAL ELECTION VOLS 1 & II, March 2019 ("Mueller Report"). For an insider's recollection and critical analysis, see ANDREW WEISSMAN, WHERE LAW ENDS: INSIDE THE MUELLER INVESTIGATION (2022).

[14] Jeffrey Toobin, *Why the Mueller Investigation Failed*, NEW YORKER (June 29, 2020). *See also* Robert J. DeNault, *Not a King: President Trump and the Case for Presidential Subpoena Reform*, 16 DUKE J. CONST. L. & PUB. POL'Y SIDEBAR 146, 173 (2021) (citing complaints).

federal enforcement of fraud,[15] antitrust cartel activity,[16] corporate crime,[17] environmental law,[18] and health care violations.[19] Concededly, this weakening may be temporary and politically driven, or in fact reflect a lower incidence of crime (although that seems unlikely), It may also partially reflect a displacement of federal enforcement to more effective institutions such as state AGs, local DAs, or private tort claimants.

It may also be the case, as some have argued,[20] that the government is focusing more intently on longer and more complex prosecutions, but recent data from the United States Sentencing Commissions (excerpted in screenshots in Figure 6.1) doesn't fully support this hypothesis.[21] Reductions in fraud cases, for example, are broad and diffuse and show no discernable pattern. On the other hand, the lack of such a pattern may in fact be good news, insofar as it rebuts the theory that the government is in the corporate bar's pocket. If prosecutors were seeking only to cut liability for the wealthy and powerful, we would expect to see reductions among the most serious cases and not among the least serious, but that's not what we see either. Instead, we see a random extended fall in white-collar prosecutions that no one can quite explain.[22]

For all these reasons, it is admittedly difficult to register much confidence in white-collar crime's enforcement. Nevertheless, the way many observers approach this topic could be more nuanced and constructive. As of now, the way we talk about enforcement veers toward caricature. Our discourse oversimplifies a complex, if admittedly dysfunctional, system and makes white-collar crime's problems more difficult to solve.

6.1 MYTHS AS OVERCONFIDENCE IN BELIEFS

In his insightful piece on the "myths" lawyers often tell themselves in practice, Donald Langevoort deftly synthesizes the literatures on behavioral and social cognition to show how lawyers (and everyone else) often fall prey to certain

---

[15] *White Collar Prosecutions Fall to Lowest in 20 Years*, TRAC REPORTS (May 24, 2018), https://trac.syr.edu/tracreports/crim/514/.

[16] Vivek Ghosal & D. Daniel Sokol, *The Rise and (Potential) Fall of U.S. Cartel Enforcement*, 2020 U. ILL. L. REV. 471.

[17] Brandon L. Garrett, *Declining Corporate Prosecutions*, 109 AM. CRIM. L. REV. 35 (2021).

[18] David Uhlmann, *Prosecutorial Discretion and Environmental Crime Redux: Charging Trends, Aggravating Factors, and Individual Outcome Data for 2005–2014*, 8 MICH. J. ENVTL. & ADMIN. L. 297 (2019 (citing "dramatic drop" in prosecutions in preceding year).

[19] *Health Care Fraud Prosecutions Down 23 Percent*, TRAC REPORTS (May 4, 2016), https://trac.syr.edu/tracreports/crim/424/.

[20] Joseph McGrath & Dierdre Healy, *Theorizing the Drop in White-Collar Prosecutions: An Ecological Model*, 23 PUNISHMENT & SOCIETY 164 (2021).

[21] Figure E-2, 2020 *Sourcebook of Sentencing Statistics*; Figure E-2 2019 *Sourcebook of Sentencing Statistics*.

[22] Screenshots from 2020 *Sourcebook of Sentencing Statistics* and 2019 *Sourcebook of Statistics*.

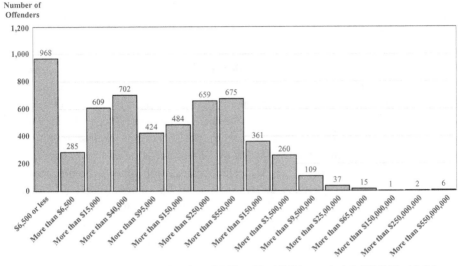

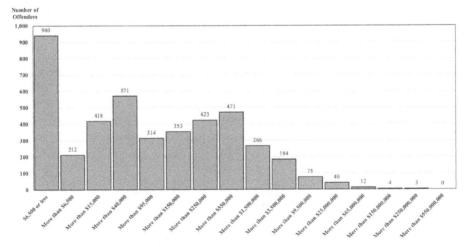

FIGURE 6.1 Screenshots of USSC sentencing data, 2019 and 2020

illusions.[23] Life is messy and ambiguous. A series of biases and heuristics help us "make sense" of that messiness and buffer us from the anxiety that would otherwise accompany complex decision-making tasks. A myth is thus, "something, usually of high cultural or personal significance, that is strongly believed in the face of limited knowledge."[24]

Group dynamics further cement these myths, convincing us that our beliefs are accurate, even when the limited empirical evidence that exists suggests otherwise. Thus, a myth isn't always false, but our adherence to it reflects our overoptimism in the accuracy of our views. And as some of the later work in this area shows, group beliefs can become that much more prone to misplaced confidence when people of like ideologies trade beliefs with each other.[25] The listener thinks she is hearing "new" information that confirms her prior beliefs but is instead simply hearing a fellow traveler's recitation of the same fact. Conformity norms, in turn, replace dissent and skepticism. Myths therefore become far more difficult to dislodge, especially when groups operate within a polarized climate. Even when the holders of myths receive conflicting information, they are likely to discount the information (if it came from an opposing group) or cherry-pick those strands that support their priors.[26]

Hence, the depressing conclusion: Myths are endemic and a natural outgrowth of our need for order and assurance. They are difficult to dispel, and they become more ossified and more extreme from our reliance on, and participation in, groups.

My aim here is to ask how this literature illuminates white-collar crime's discourse. However oversimplified and polarized it has been in the past, it clearly has grown more one-sided in recent years, reflecting a widening gulf between the common understandings of white-collar crime's insiders (practitioners who work within the field, and some scholars) and everyone else.

The corollary to this narrative is that white-collar crime's enforcement institutions, who have the most to lose from the profusion of myths and should therefore be most invested in rebutting them, have demonstrated an almost maddening inability to even acknowledge these narratives. We either get "spin" (an apt description of many a DOJ press release) or inscrutable calls for patience and respect (usually from the Attorney General or a deputy). Neither of these stances go very far.

---

[23] Donald C. Langevoort, *Taking Myths Seriously: An Essay for Lawyers*, 74 CHI. KENT. L. REV. 1569 (2000).

[24] *Id.* at 1569 n.1.

[25] *See generally* Edward L. Glaeser & Cass R. Sunstein, *Extremism and Social Learning*, 1 J. LEGAL ANALYSIS 263 (2009). For a less technical treatment, see CASS R. SUNSTEIN, GOING TO EXTREMES: HOW LIKE MINDS UNITE AND DIVIDE (2009).

[26] *See* Cass R. Sunstein et al., *How People Update Beliefs about Climate Change: Good News and Bad News*, 102 CORNELL L. REV. 1431 (2017); Edward Glaeser & Cass R. Sunstein, *Does More Speech Correct Falsehoods?* 43 J. LEGAL. STUD. 65 (2014).

6.2 BELIEFS ABOUT PROSECUTORS

Federal prosecutors have been a major topic of journalistic and scholarly interest for years. They can be portrayed as heroes or as villains and ruthless bureaucrats. When Robert Mueller, the former head of the FBI and longtime federal prosecutor, took on the Trump election interference investigation, commentators described him in glowing terms. A couple of years later, when Mueller declined to prosecute any member of the Trump family and issued a report that some would say punted on questions of whether the president obstructed justice, Mueller lost a good deal of his social and political capital.

When prosecutors vanquish celebrities and extremely wealthy and powerful opponents, they attain the status of a folk hero, even if appellate courts overturn their trial victories. When they lose or decline to bring cases, they are, at best, ignored, or worse, vilified. Mary Jo White was widely respected when she led the United States Attorney's Office for the SDNY during the late 1990s, producing numerous securities and white-collar convictions. That respect weakened a decade later, however, when she became chair of the SEC; there, she became the target of the progressives' ire, channelled most effectively by Senator Elizabeth Warren. What is most interesting for our purposes is how White's portrayal in the press so dramatically metamorphosed. Once upon a time, she had been seen as a steadfast and independent public servant. *Now,* she was characterized as an aloof *private* lawyer; someone too beholden to corporate behemoths to bring them to heel.[27] The irony is that White's newly constructed identity overshadowed her agency's performance relative to its situational constraints. According to at least one account, White's SEC was *more* aggressive than its predecessor, but White's tenure was still viewed as disappointing and suggestive of regulatory capture.[28] The narrative eclipsed the data regarding the SEC's actual performance. A more nuanced account of White's tenure accordingly failed to surface and take hold.

White's experience is instructive because it shows the effects of personifying enforcement policy. When supervising prosecutors lose or decline to bring major cases, contemporary accounts are quick to assume a loss of will or lack of desire to move forward. If the prosecutor has a history of employment in the private sector (as White famously did as a partner at the law firm of Debevoise and Plimpton), then her private employment fuels the following thought process: The prosecutor *could* have brought a case but chose *not* to bring a case because she was too loyal to her friends in private industry (or even worse, she was expecting a quid pro quo from the defendant company or its white-collar defense firm). I unpack and challenge these inferences in the sections that follow.

---

[27] White hired me as an assistant United States Attorney for the SDNY during the summer of 1999. I entered the office in the fall and remained there through 2004.

[28] *See, e.g.,* Laurence Tai, *Harnessing Industry Influence*, 68 ADMIN. L. REV. 1, 48 (2016).

6.3 THE PLENARY PROSECUTOR

For years, criminal justice scholars have eloquently documented severe and pervasive failures of process within the criminal justice system. Prosecutors, benefitting from massive, menu-like criminal codes, retain the power and ability to pick and choose the cases and charges they prefer.[29] Many of the defendants they charge are too impoverished or unfamiliar with the system to benefit from legal counsel, especially overburdened counsel supplied by the government. Moreover, the system is so sclerotic that it deprives defendants of their right to a speedy trial, causing those in cash-bail jurisdictions to languish in pretrial detention. When "the process is the punishment,"[30] the prosecutor enjoys enormous power – some might say plenary – with few political or legal constraints.[31]

I don't mean to rebut this claim's core argument, much less its most important normative implications. A world in which facts and law don't very much matter and in which a "going price" develops and becomes entrenched within a courthouse working group[32] that ultimately incarcerates and separates poor communities from their loved ones is not one I'm particularly eager to defend. The problem with this narrative, however, is that it ignores unique characteristics of federal criminal law and white-collar crime. As John Pfaff and others have argued, there is no such thing as a single criminal justice system.[33] There in fact exist many such systems across our country. The federal system (the focus of this book) functions quite differently from the generic system that serves as the basis of the plenary power myth.[34]

---

[29] *See* William J. Stuntz, *The Pathological Politics of Criminal Law*, 100 MICH. L. REV. 505, 519 (2001). For a contemporary view of federal criminal law that prefigures some of Stuntz's thesis, see Gerard E. Lynch, *Our Administrative System of Criminal Justice*, 66 FORDHAM L. REV. 2117, 2137 (1998). For a recent affirmation and extension of Stuntz's analysis, see Albert W. Alschuler, *Plea Bargaining and Mass Incarceration*, 76 N.Y.U. ANN. SURV. AM. L. 205, 220 (2021).

[30] MALCOLM FEELEY, THE PROCESS IS THE PUNISHMENT: HANDLING CASES IN A LOWER CRIMINAL COURT (1979).

[31] *See, e.g.*, I. Bennett Capers, *Against Prosecutors*, 105 CORNELL L. REV. 1561, 1564 (2020) (describing and critiquing "the enormous, monopolistic power public prosecutors wield"); Carissa Byrne Hessick, *The Myth of Common Law Crimes*, 105 VA. L. REV. 965 (2019) (tracing the connection between broadly written statutes to prosecutorial power).

[32] STEPHANOS BIBAS, THE MACHINERY OF CRIMINAL JUSTICE (2012).

[33] John F. Pfaff, *Why the Policy Failures of Mass Incarceration Are Really Political Failures*, 104 MINN. L. REV. 2673, 2674 (2020) ("What we have, however, is not a system but a set of systems – plural – that span city, county, state, and federal governments"). *See also* Rachel E. Barkow, *Federalism and Criminal Law: What the Feds Can Learn from the States*, 109 MICH. L. REV. 519, 519 (2011) ("Criminal law enforcement in the United States is multi-jurisdictional"). Indeed, there are some who would say there not only is no singular "system," but also no "justice" to justify calling it a "criminal justice system." *See, e.g.*, Benjamin Levin, *Rethinking the Boundaries of "Criminal Justice"*, 15 OHIO ST. J. CRIM. L. 619, 620 (2018) ("some scholars and activists have begun to challenge the use of [the criminal justice term]").

[34] Some disagree with this view of the prosecutor's office and power. *See, e.g.*, Jeffrey Bellin, *The Power of Prosecutors*, 94 N.Y.U. L. REV. 171, 174 (2019) (criticizing "longstanding and

Federal prosecutors enjoy a surfeit of legal and practical powers.[35] They can pick and choose among thousands of crimes, many of which are broadly drafted and unbound by meaningful monetary or jurisdictional limitations. Federal prosecutors also enjoy a deep well of financial resources and a series of procedural rules that enable them to demand large amounts of information from business entities, be they targets or subjects. And they have the legal and practical leverage to force corporate actors to erect sophisticated workplace monitoring functions and carry out extended "private" investigations.[36] But there are important limits to their power, and some of these limits can be traced to the federal justice system's unique characteristics.

First, the federal system – although much larger than it used to be – is still much smaller than most state systems. Its prosecutors carry a lower caseload and so do many of its defense attorneys.[37] Federal judges have far more time to focus on the criminal cases on their dockets than state counterparts, which means they have more time and incentive to complain on the record when they think a prosecutor has made a bad decision, been too lenient, or overreached. For those who cannot afford an attorney, the system's federal defenders provide talented attorneys hired from a highly competitive pool of applicants.[38] And for those who can, the system features an array of aggressive, well-heeled attorneys who often benefit from having previously worked within the SEC, the DOJ, and the various United States Attorneys' offices.[39]

Moreover, despite their jurisdictional breadth, federal criminal statutes are not unlimited in their application. Prosecutors' offices have learned over the years that district and appellate judges are not always supportive of the broadest application of the fraud, bribery, or obstruction laws. And even if a defendant pleads guilty, a district court judge may not be so inclined to punish a defendant in accordance with the Sentencing Guidelines, whose recommendations for fraud cases are now advisory and therefore increasingly discounted. Prosecutors are also well aware of the

increasingly frenetic claims about prosecutorial preeminence"). Others continue to view the prosecutor as the most important actor within the criminal justice system. "[P]rosecutors are critical actors – probably the most important actor, if we had to choose just one – in administering criminal justice policy in America." Rachel E. Barkow, *Can Prosecutors End Mass Incarceration? Book Review of Emily Bazelon, Charged: The New Movement to Transform American Prosecution and End Mass Incarceration*, 119 MICH. L. REV. 1365 (2021).

[35] For praise of such powers, see John C. Jeffries, Jr., & John Gleeson, *The Federalization of Organized Crime: Advantages of Federal Prosecution*, 46 HASTINGS L.J. 1095 (1995). For recent criticisms of federal prosecutorial power, see Ellen S. Podgor, *White Collar Shortcuts*, 2018 U. ILL. L. REV. 925.

[36] Jennifer Arlen & Samuel W. Buell, *The Law of Corporate Investigations and the Global Expansion of Corporate Criminal Enforcement*, 93 SOUTHERN CAL. L. REV. 697 (2020).

[37] Adam M. Gershowitz & Laura R. Killinger, *Essay, the State (Never) Rests: How Excessive Prosecutorial Caseloads Harm Criminal Defendants*, 105 NW. U. L. REV. 261, 278 (2011).

[38] On the history of the federal defender and federally funded representation, see David E. Patton, *The Structure of Federal Public Defense: A Call for Independence*, 102 CORNELL L. REV. 335 (2017).

[39] Samuel W. Buell, *Is the White Collar Offender Privileged?* 63 DUKE L. J. 67 (2014).

First Amendment and federalism issues that lurk in the background of certain cases, which additionally induces them to tread lightly. And finally, prosecutors understand that juries may blanch when the evidence demonstrating an actor's guilty state of mind is missing.[40] Collectively, these factors promote varying degrees of external and internal restraint. Several of these restraints are strong enough to feed the pathologies described in Chapter 5. They may be uneven, difficult to predict, or distributed in ways many of us dislike, but limits on prosecutorial power nonetheless *exist*.

Accordingly, the image of an imperial or plenary prosecutor is illusory in the federal white-collar context. To be sure, federal prosecutors enjoy leverage and often a deep well of resources, but they are not all-powerful. Their offices can come down quite hard on some offenders, but they may well leave others untouched despite her sincere wishes to the contrary. One can only wonder if this was the case for Robert Mueller, who declined to prosecute Donald Trump Jr. for taking a meeting with a foreign attorney who promised to provide negative information regarding then-presidential candidate Hillary Clinton. A prosecutor with plenary power would have indicted Trump Jr. for accepting a thing of value from a foreign national, regardless of any reservations the Mueller team had about the underlying statute and legal doctrine. That is, after all, what true *plenary* power means: that legal weaknesses and public opinion are irrelevant because the prosecutor is slated to win anyway.

In her metaphoric description of the penal system, Professor Alexandra Natapoff invites her readers to picture a pyramid.[41] At the bottom of the pyramid, one encounters state-level cases, where misdemeanors abound, and administrative bloat and dysfunction are common. It is at the bottom where the "system approaches lawless chaos" and where "[h]undreds of thousands of suspects are railroaded into guilty pleas with little or no legal assistance."[42] At the top of the pyramid, however, we find the "world of federal offenses, serious cases, and well-resourced defendants" where "rules dominate" and the process is "sensitive to evidence" as well as "transparent, accountable, and hyper-visible." At the pyramid's top, "changes in the rules matter and outcomes are authentically contested."[43]

One of Natapoff's lessons is that observers should pay close attention to the pyramid's bottom, where mass injustice festers, and not assume the broad applicability of the pyramid's top, which assumes an idealized rule-of-law system. It's a good lesson, and one that many scholars have taken to heart. But it tends to overshadow Natapoff's implicit acknowledgment, which is that in *some* corners of the criminal justice world, rules *do* matter. It is certainly reasonable to decry the inequality baked into this pyramid, but it is unhelpful to pretend the top slice doesn't

---

[40] Anna Offit, *Prosecuting in the Shadow of the Jury*, 113 Nw. L. Rev. 1071 (2019).

[41] Alexandra Natapoff, *The Penal Pyramid*, in The New Criminal Justice Thinking 71 (Sharon Dolovich & Alexandra Natapoff, eds., 2017).

[42] *Id.* at 71.

[43] *Id.* at 72.

exist, particularly when we think about the prosecutor's role in addressing white-collar crime.

6.4 THE REVOLVING-DOOR NARRATIVE

In addition to the plenary prosecutor myth, a corollary revolving-door narrative focuses specifically on the enforcers who move seamlessly between the federal government and high-end private legal practice.[44] According to the different strands of this "revolving-door" theory, prosecutors either deliberately or subconsciously extend corporate defendants unwarranted leniency in order to secure personal benefits such as partnership positions in white shoe law firms. In Chapter 1, I proffered some reasons to be skeptical of this claim. Here, I explore how the narrative itself has become difficult to dislodge.

Although the plenary prosecutor and revolving-door concepts are distinct, the former relies on the latter. That is, the plenary prosecutor myth *needs* a revolving-door narrative to explain the many instances in which prosecutors have failed to bring cases against executives and corporations. The fact that prosecutors have failed in prosecuting the powerful and wealthy *must* be ascribable to something other than institutional design. Instead, it *must* be the case that prosecutors have shortchanged the public for the prospect of personal gain. The revolving-door thus reinforces myths about prosecutorial power while aggravating the public's distrust of government enforcement agencies.

The revolving-door theory arises out of a common observation: Over time, a certain group of lawyers rotate between federal positions to elite corporate law firms and in-house counsel positions.[45] In the federal enforcement world, the line between prosecuting attorneys and white-collar and corporate defense counsel is admittedly thin and porous. Many federal prosecutors come to the job after having served several years as an associate at a Manhattan or DC law firm, and many of those same prosecutors return to those firms (or to their competitors or corporate clients) after a five- or six-year stint in public service.

Having followed this career track myself prior to entering academia, I cannot deny its existence. Nor do I deny its shortcomings. Traveling in the same circles of attorneys who attended top schools, took jobs with a small cadre of big-name firms, and then reported to the same group of high-level prosecutors and law firm partners

---

[44] "For those enraptured by capture and public choice theory, the revolving door is the epitome of the problem with regulation and government more generally." David Zaring, *Against Being Against the Revolving Door*, 2013 U. ILL. L. REV. 507, 546.

[45] Miriam H. Baer, *Compliance Elites*, 88 FORDHAM L. REV. 1599, 1602–3, n. 15 (2020), citing James D. Cox & Randall S. Thomas, *Revolving Elites: The Unexplored Risk of Capturing the SEC-107*, GEO. L. J. 845 (2019). This circularity of movement isn't true of *all* classes of lawyers. Alexander I. Platt, *The Non-revolving Door*, 46 J. CORP. L. 751, 755 (2021) (presenting evidence of a lack of movement through "the door between the SEC and the plaintiffs' bar").

generates understandable degrees of cynicism and distrust among outsiders. It's a dynamic acute enough to cause Professor Jennifer Taub to declare in her popular and widely read book, "From prep school and beyond, the elite cover for each other."[46] Such "covering" hardly generates trust in the DOJ or its enforcement agencies. Moreover, *within* the circle of revolving prosecutors, network dynamics generate a series of blind spots that undermine one's effectiveness, one's empathy for others, and eventually, one's detection of wrongdoing.[47]

But fluidity is hardly a uniformly negative phenomenon. In many instances, prior experience in either the public or private sector can be highly valuable to a client. Associates trained in high-stakes litigation by law firms might be particularly adept in fighting major legal battles once they switch sides. They might also be better at predicting how the other side will react. (That is often the reason corporate clients give for hiring former prosecutors as their defense counsel.) And porosity might also lay the groundwork for a less ideological, more tonally neutral, problem-solving orientation. Adversaries are more apt to find common ground and plow a path to "yes" when they share common values, beliefs, and norms – and when they view each other as human beings and not enemies.

Moving back and forth between government and private service is thus a mixed bag. It carries risks but it also promotes benefits. And it is far from clear that a *non*revolving door would produce better outcomes. But "revolving-door" claims tend to ignore such nuance. Instead, commentators mechanically claim "capture" (and worse, deliberate corruption) even when the empirical literature suggests otherwise. For example, Professor David Zaring's work in this area demonstrates that *more* aggressive prosecutors, not lenient ones, are the ones who walk away with partner positions at law firms.[48] And there is every reason to believe that a law firm in a highly competitive market would favor the *more* aggressive former prosecutor than the one who immediately caves and offers leniency to a corporate offender.

Theoretically, the government could rebut this myth, and it *is* a myth insofar as critics assume nearly *everyone* revolves, or that every prosecutor's return to a law firm *inevitably* breeds capture or corruption. The easiest way to unravel this claim would be to demonstrate that rotation isn't as prevalent as the media suggests, and that it does not correlate with more lenient outcomes. The government could do this by publishing data and enabling follow-up analyses similar to the one Professor Zaring conducted a decade ago.

But here's the catch: *Even if* the data demonstrated a low correlation between government leniency (however defined) and the prevalence of government-to-law firm pipelines, it is doubtful this finding would dispel the public's belief in the

---

[46] Jennifer Taub, Big Dirty Money: The Shocking Injustice and Unseen Cost of White-Collar Crime 96 (2020).

[47] Baer, *supra* note 45.

[48] Zaring, *supra* note 44. See also Wenton Zheng, *The Revolving Door*, 90 Notre Dame L. Rev. 1265 (2015).

revolving door. Moreover, if the information were just a bit ambiguous or hazy, commentators would instead glom on to the portions of the report that most confirmed their beliefs. That is, after all, what we mean when we talk about myths and sticky belief systems.

6.5 MYTHS ABOUT HARM, OFFENDERS, AND VICTIMS

For years, scholars have attempted to discern the pervasiveness and cost of white-collar and corporate crime. Most accounts seem to agree that "fraud" of various types runs in the hundreds of billions of dollars annually, causing downstream harms to employees, consumers, and the general public.[49] On a more concrete level, a team of corporate finance scholars (Alexander Dyck, Adair Morse, and Luigi Zingales, or "DMZ") has estimated that frauds within publicly traded companies extend into the hundreds of billions of dollars on an annual basis.[50] April Wall-Parker writes in her thorough and informative chapter, "Measuring White Collar Crime," that "occupational fraud and theft can be upwards of $800 billion."[51] Everywhere one looks, there seem to be billions in annual losses.

The picture looks just as bleak from a different angle, which is the frequency of misconduct. Professor Eugene Soltes' more recent paper on financial crime reports that "misconduct is a ubiquitous phenomenon" among Fortune 500 companies. Specifically, Soltes finds:

> Using data from three Fortune 500 companies – none of which faced recent criminal or serious civil sanctions – I show that misconduct is a ubiquitous phenomenon. *These three firms have a substantiated violation every three days per firm on average* ... I provide aggregated data from the largest corporate hotline provider about the number of substantiated claims. Within these statistics, the median number of violations would indicate 124 cases of corporate malfeasance per year.[52]

---

[49] "Mounting empirical evidence suggests that harm to nonshareholders dwarfs that suffered by defrauded shareholders." Urska Velikonja, *The Cost of Securities Fraud*, 54 Wm. & Mary L. Rev. 1887, 1887–88 (2013) (cataloguing costs of fraud felt by investors and noninvestors).

[50] I. J. Alexander Dyck, Adair Morse & Luigi Zingales, *How Pervasive Is Corporate Fraud?* (2021), https://papers.ssrn.com/abstract=2222608 [hereinafter "DMZ"]; Alexander Dyck, Adair Morse, & Luigi Zingales, *How Pervasive Is Corporate Fraud?* (2020), http://faculty.haas.berkeley.edu/ morse/research/papers/DyckMorseZingalesPervasive.pdf; https://pages.business.illinois.edu/ accountancy/wp-content/uploads/sites/12/2014/11/Audit-2010-Dyck-Morse-Zingales.pdf; https://pages.business.illinois.edu/accountancy/wp-content/uploads/sites/12/2014/11/Audit-2010-Dyck-Morse-Zingales.pdf.

[51] April Wall-Parker, *Measuring White Collar Crime*, in The Handbook of White-Collar Crime (Melissa Rorie, ed. 2020).

[52] Eugene Soltes, *The Frequency of Corporate Misconduct: Public Enforcement versus Private Reality*, 26 J. Fin. Crime 923, 924 (2019) (emphasis added).

Violations so frequent that they occur every three days sounds horrendous, particularly when one considers the comparatively low figure for annual SEC enforcement proceedings and federal fraud and bribery prosecutions.

But the narrative of ubiquitous corporate misconduct paired with government passivity isn't quite as airtight as we think. A closer look at Soltes' paper, along with DMZ's calculations, tells a slightly different story. To be sure, it is still a *bad* story, and the costs and pervasiveness of fraud are still unacceptably high. Nevertheless, the way in which we discuss these findings and compress them into easy-to-repeat soundbites often overstates the case that the government is purposely ignoring serious and easy-to-prove malfeasance.

Let's start with the now-famous estimate of how much fraud pervades large, publicly traded companies. That estimate, which has morphed into a slogan that corporate fraud costs the public $400 billion or more annually, is derived from the ongoing study of publicly held companies from 1996 to 2004 by DMZ, the most recent of which was published in the *Review of Accounting Studies* in 2023.[53]

The work of DMZ arises out of a natural experiment. The authors collected information on a data set of companies who had been forced to switch auditors following Arthur Andersen's demise in 2001. The switch to new auditors led to increased scrutiny and eventual discoveries of misconduct and fraud.[54] Thus, DMZ were able to exploit this data set to compare known misconduct with previously *unknown* misconduct and then to extrapolate their findings to all companies that traded on major stock exchanges. As DMZ openly noted, their fraud analysis was not grounded in a rigorous examination of statutory fraud law and its elements.[55] Their model does not distinguish civil fraud from criminal fraud, much less look for evidence of specific intent to deceive. Thus, any critique of *criminal* enforcement that relies on DMZ's figures may be overstating the degree of criminal fraud the government has failed to detect and prosecute. To be sure, the degree of under-enforcement is likely large, but it may not be *as* large as the DMZ figures suggest.

To determine fraud's frequency, DMZ began by attempting to estimate the probability of fraud's detection. Leveraging their data set's post-Enron auditing experience, they used several measures to come up with an estimate of detection, which ranged from 27 to 33 percent (meaning fraud is detected a third of the time).[56] They then examined the number of firms in the data set who had *actually*

---

[53] Alexander Dyck, Adair Morse, & Luigi Zingales, *How Pervasive Is Corporate Fraud?* REV. ACCOUNT. STUD. (Jan. 5, 2023), https://link.springer.com/article/10.1007/s11142-022-09738-5#article-info. For earlier versions, see *supra* note 52 at 50. Unless otherwise stated, the remaining footnotes to DMZ's work are to their 2021 revision available on SSRN, https://papers.ssrn.com/sol3/papers.cfm?abstract_id=2222608.

[54] *Id.* at 1 (admitting that they are using the term "fraud loosely, since what we measure is some form of misconduct or alleged fraud").

[55] *Id.*

[56] *Id.* at 1–2 (authors estimate likelihood of detection by auditors generally as a result of accounting restatements, for securities fraud "at large," and for securities enforcement releases).

been caught engaging in fraud during the same time period (again, broadly defined). That number was 4 percent. From there, DMZ "grossed up" the number of publicly held firms that could be expected to be engaging in fraud. (To use easy numbers: If the probability of detection was 25 percent and 4 percent of the data set companies had been revealed to have engaged in fraud, the authors would have concluded that fraud occurred in 16 percent of all publicly traded companies.)

Once they arrived at a frequency estimate, DMZ engaged in additional calculations to derive the cost of fraud per firm ("X percent of equity value"). This required them to isolate the cost of fraud from other costs (e.g., the market's realization that the company's fundamentals were weak). They then multiplied the frequency times the per-firm cost to come up with an "expected annual cost of fraud ... of the total equity value of U.S. public firms," a figure that they *then* multiplied against the known aggregate value of large, publicly held firms in 2004. They first published their findings as a working paper in 2013. As indicated in footnote 50, they have updated their estimations numerous times since then, arriving at final figures of a third (the degree to which fraud is detected), 10 percent (the prevalence of fraud in publicly held companies), and over $800 billion (the annual cost of fraud among publicly held companies).

One need not be a finance specialist to recognize that DMZ's takeaway number – that is, the annual aggregate cost of accounting fraud – rests upon a series of contingent estimations. Indeed, over the years, the authors have adjusted their estimations, altering their conclusion as to the annual cost of corporate fraud. *All* of these estimations place the overall "fraud" number in the billions, but the variance – often in the hundreds of billions – is nevertheless worthy of discussion.[57] As even a superficial comparison of DMZ's working papers indicates, a small change in the estimated likelihood of detection creates a cascading effect that impacts the "annual social cost" of fraud. For example, when the estimated likelihood of detection *increases*, DMZ's estimated fraud frequency among publicly held firms *decreases*. (In other words, there are fewer undetected frauds we have to worry about.) That in turn reduces the annual cost of fraud. So too does DMZ's

---

[57] The figures mentioned in this discussion are derived in part from the following:

(1) February 2021: pages 2–3 of I. J. Alexander Dyck, Adair Morse, & Luigi Zingales, *How Pervasive Is Corporate Fraud?* (2021), https://papers.ssrn.com/abstract=2222608.

(2) May 2020: pages 2–3 of the version available here: http://faculty.haas.berkeley.edu/morse/research/papers/DyckMorseZingalesPervasive.pdf.

(3) February 2013: pages 4, 5, 13, 24, & 25 of the version available here: https://haas.berkeley.edu/wp-content/uploads/DyckMorseZingales20130306.pdf.

(4) August 2014: page 3 of the version available here: www-2.rotman.utoronto.ca/facbios/file/Pervasive.pdf.

(5) April 2017: pages 2–4 & 30–31 of the version available here: www.law.nyu.edu/sites/default/files/upload_documents/Adair%20Morse%20How%20Pervasive%20is%20Corporate%20Fraud.pdf.

reevaluation of the "cost per firm," a figure that changes substantially between the 2014 and 2017 iterations.

Moreover, as DMZ's papers make clear, the "cost" expressed in these analyses is not analogous to out-of-pocket theft whereby a distinctive villain benefits and a sympathetic victim loses. If you hear "400" or "800 billion" and imagine rich, greedy people taking money from poor people's pockets, you're imagining a different paper. The estimation of DMZ of firm-level and aggregate social cost are premised in part on the reputation costs and loss of access to capital that firms suffer when their fraud is revealed, which is then reflected in the public company's drop in equity. Whatever this cost is, it is highly diffuse. Rich shareholders experience a portion of it; so too do hedge funds and massive pension funds; and so, too, do foreign shareholders and sovereign wealth funds.[58]

Any reader of DMZ's work is apt to agree that undetected corporate accounting fraud is a vexatious and important problem. The findings of DMZ (including the more recent ones) strongly indicate the need for more robust enforcement, well-resourced enforcement agencies, improved internal compliance programs, and stronger disclosure laws. But it would be a mistake for readers to mechanically take DMZ's bottom-line number and plug it into an "elites-looting-the-people" narrative.[59] And it would be even more questionable if DMZ's estimations were to become the fodder for critiques of federal criminal enforcement institutions. By DMZ's own admission, it is questionable how much of DMZ's *estimated* fraud would be *provable* fraud under federal criminal law. If that's the case, we need to look beyond federal prosecutors as we search for better solutions to curbing the incidence of corporate fraud.

As for Wall-Parker's work, her discussion of billions of dollars of fraud covers "occupational fraud," or what is more commonly referred to as employee theft and embezzlement.[60] These are indeed white-collar crimes insofar as they are deceptive nonviolent offenses, but they are offenses perpetrated by low- and mid-level employees and often targeted at *corporate* or organizational victims such as hospitals and schools. Some argue that this kind of behavior shouldn't be criminally prosecuted by *any* authority, much less the federal government.[61] If frauds undertaken by mid- and lower-level employees are so minor that we should decline their prosecution, then

---

[58] Velikonja, *supra* note 49, at 1946 ("shareholders may be the theoretical residual owners, but because of diversification and the fraud discount, their exposure to securities fraud is quite limited").

[59] Michael Hobbes' feature article in the Huffington Post appears to draw on DMZ's work without explicitly saying as much: "In 2017, researchers estimated that fraud by America's largest corporations cost Americans up to $360 billion annually between 1996 and 2004." Michael Hobbes, *The Golden Age of White Collar Crime*, Huff. Post (Feb. 10, 2020).

[60] Wall-Parker, *supra* note 51.

[61] "[P]etty workplace offenses need addressing, but they should not be priorities at the federal level." Taub, *supra* note 46, at 19.

presumably, their harms should *also* be categorized separately when we tell the world how much "fraud" or "white-collar crime" costs the general public on an annual basis.

Moreover, the fact that employees embezzle from corporate employers (to the tune of billions, apparently) undermines the standard claim that government actors serve *solely* the interests of corporate actors, or that the wealthy always escape with their wallets intact. Employers-as-victims clearly give up a fair share of money to embezzlement and theft – and they do it without always seeking federal recourse. If the government were acting solely to please corporate interests, one would expect employee embezzlement crimes to occupy more or all of the federal docket, but that is far from the case. Not every federal white-collar defendant is a "smaller-time freelance business croo[k]."[62] Far from it.

And finally, what about Soltes' findings, that publicly held firms frequently commit violations for which they are never investigated or criminally punished? Like DMZ's estimations, Soltes' findings are disturbing. But Soltes himself adds an important caveat:

> One important note in interpreting this analysis is that, compared to the conduct subject to enforcement and regulatory action, *much of the internal firm misconduct that is not detected by regulators or identified in public databases is less egregious in nature, even when it includes acts of bribery or financial reporting fraud.* Thus, it would be inappropriate to extrapolate that the damages from the average case prosecuted by the DOJ or disciplined by the SEC are indicative of the scope or damages of the average case that arises internally within firms without being detected or sanctioned by regulators.[63]

This bears repeating: Soltes himself warns other researchers that "it would be inappropriate" to assume that the average DOJ/SEC enforcement action involves the same "scope or damages" as the average case reported on a company's hotline. In other words, to the extent companies are handling certain matters in-house or solely through civil lawsuits, they may be doing so because the amounts or type of behavior reflect exactly the kind of behavior the public would deem normatively ineligible for criminal prosecution.[64] If that's the case, prosecutors, regulators, and the compliance personnel who screen cases at private firms might actually be doing something *right.*

---

[62] Taub, *supra* note 46, at 36 (voicing concern that the federal government pursues the smaller-time crooks and ignores the wealthy and powerful). For counterpoints to this claim, see generally Chapter 1.

[63] Soltes, *supra* note 52, at 925 (emphasis supplied).

[64] *See* Jessica A. Roth, *Prosecutorial Declination Statements*, 110 J. CRIM & CRIMINOLOGY 477, 499–500 (2020). *See also* Josh Bowers, *The Normative Case for Normative Grand Juries*, 47 WAKE FOREST L. REV. 319 (2012). *See also* the discussion of normative exclusions in Chapter 5.

6.6 OFFENDERS AND VICTIMS

As scholars discovered decades ago, the image of the prototypical white-collar offender as an elite, white, businessman is oversimplified. Women, members of marginalized communities, and individuals and organizations outside the United States all perpetrate crimes of deception, sometimes on institutions and sometimes on other members of the American public.[65] Moreover, corporations can sometimes be victims, as can wealthy investors.

Massive government institutions are also the victims of costly scams perpetrated by offenders large and small. Health care fraud costs the government and taxpayers anything from $68 billion annually to more than $100 billion (especially regarding Covid-related funds), but not all of the offenders enjoying that loot are corporations or their wealthy executives.[66] And some of the victims of fraud are almost certainly private health care companies. But if one believes that all private health insurers are *by definition* "criminals," one is not apt to view United HealthCare and Aetna as victims, regardless of the facts on the ground.

No reasonable person would argue that the government should invest all its enforcement might in protecting the nation's private health care insurers from primary doctors and their patients. Private companies possess the wherewithal to implement their own highly effective antifraud and antitheft protections. But the presence of wealthy victims and unwealthy and unpowerful offenders should alert readers that a simplified narrative of corporations-as-bad-guys and everyone else-as-good-guys is inaccurate. Further, our unwillingness to admit these inconvenient ambiguities renders us underprotected. If many *non*elites commit crimes of deception that cause harm, we place ourselves at much greater risk if we ignore these crimes or their antecedents.

6.7 PUNISHMENT MYTHS

In April 2021, the DOJ announced it had indicted Moishe Porat, the former dean of Temple University's Fox Business School on two grounds of wire fraud and conspiracy to commit wire fraud.[67] The indictment alleged that Porat and two Temple employees conspired to provide false information to the US News ranking authorities and thereby "deceive the school's applicants, students, and donors into believing that the school offered top-ranked business degree programs, so they would pay tuition and make donations to Temple."[68]

---

[65] On white-collar crime's expansion beyond familiarly narrow categories of wrongdoers, see Wall-Parker, *supra* note 51, at 34.

[66] *Id.*

[67] Press Release, US Attorney's Office East District Philadelphia (Apr. 16, 2021), www.justice .gov/usao-edpa/pr/former-temple-business-school-dean-indicted-fraud.

[68] *Id.*

The case was notable for its focus on higher-education rankings fraud and for its target, a seventy-four-year-old former dean with no criminal record. In the past, someone like Porat might have lost his deanship and suffered criticism in the national newspapers and social ostracism. But the United States Attorney's Office in Philadelphia decided to make an example of Porat's behavior and prosecute it. The DOJ's press release was quite open in its pursuit of this goal: to place "leadership" at institutions of higher learning on notice that they owed the public a duty to refrain from deceptive behavior.[69] The press release wrapped up with the following statement:

> The team from the FBI, the US Department of Education Office of Inspector General, and the Postal Inspection Service, spent several years working together to unravel this fraud. Today, thanks to their investigation, we are holding one of those individuals who engaged in this destructive conduct responsible and accountable.[70]

Notice the relevant facts: the investigation took "years" to unravel and necessitated the joint work of several agencies. But because they were holding accountable a high-level executive individual "engaged in this destructive conduct," the effort was worth the cost.

One can't help but wonder if the "effort was worth it" language rests as well on the prospect of sending a well-respected figure to jail. After Porat was indicted by a grand jury, the DOJ did not hesitate to state (as it nearly always does in its press releases) that Porat faced "a maximum possible sentence of 25 years in prison" if convicted.[71] That number was derived by adding the twenty-year maximum sentence for the substantive wire fraud count, and then another five years for the conspiracy count. But as Chapter 3 makes clear, Porat was never realistically facing twenty-five years' imprisonment. Even after his trial, aggressive prosecutors contended at sentencing that Porat's conduct met the guidelines range for 108–35 months' imprisonment. To be sure, 108 months' imprisonment is a long sentence, especially for a seventy-four-year-old. But it still is not twenty-five years, and the court ultimately sentenced Porat to just fourteen months' imprisonment, a fraction of the fraction the government pursued at sentencing.[72]

Porat's situation is far from unique. Every time the DOJ announces a major white-collar arrest, it also announces the maximum term of imprisonment the defendant is supposedly facing. For purposes of this discussion, let's call this figure the aggregated statutory maximum (ASM). The ASM is simply an aggregate of

---

[69] The message resonated with its intended audience. *See, e.g.*, John Byrne, *A Warning Shot for Deans Who Game College Rankings*, FORBES (Apr. 17, 2021), www.forbes.com/sites/poetsand quants/2021/04/17/a-warning-shot-for-deans-who-game-college-rankings/?sh=740c95a726c5.

[70] Press Release, *supra* note 67.

[71] *Id.*

[72] Kristy Bleizeffer, *Moshe Porat, Former Temple Fox Dean, Sentenced to 14 Months in Prison for Rankings Fraud*, POETS & QUANTS (Mar. 11, 2022), https://poetsandquants.com/2022/03/11/ moshe-porat-former-temple-fox-dean-sentenced-to-14-months-in-prison-for-rankings-fraud/.

punishment the offender can receive for each count charged. The guidelines themselves ignore or downplay the number of counts charged for a single event, as does the judiciary in most instances. Accordingly, the ASM rarely describes a person's actual prison sentence. Nevertheless, one almost always hears the ASM when the government announces an arrest or indictment. For the general public and media, the ASM is a large, easily remembered number expressed in decades of years of imprisonment. And in almost all white-collar prosecutions, the ASM is exceptionally misleading.

Repeated invocation of the ASM reinforces downstream claims of overcriminalization. Why shouldn't it? If you believe the feds are eager to lock up the seventy-four-year-old dean of a business school for twenty-five years, you will be more inclined to accept claims *either* that the federal government is too meddlesome and interferes in local situations where it doesn't belong (the libertarian view), *or* that it is so addicted to mass incarceration that it is willing to place a seventy-four-year-old in jail for twenty-five years (the mass incarceration view).

Now, the ASM may be misleading and farcically inflated, but it still *matters* to the criminal defendant. In fact, if social science is to be believed, it may be a far more important factor than we realize.

According to the literature mining the connection between probability and emotion, we know that individuals have trouble calculating expected costs when low probabilities are paired with terrible outcomes in high-stakes, emotional settings. Cass Sunstein labels this effect "probability neglect."[73] Simply put, "when intense emotions are engaged, people tend to focus on the adverse outcome, not on its likelihood."[74] At the time Sunstein published his essay (2002), the "adverse outcomes" on everyone's mind were a terror attacks and plane crashes. For the white-collar offender charged in a four- or five-count indictment, it could just as easily be the ASM.

The import of probability neglect is that decision-makers ignore low probabilities when considering extremely adverse events. Thus, even if an attorney informs his client truthfully that

- the statutory maximum for a given offense is twenty years,
- and the ASM for the current indictment is **100 years** because the defendant was charged in five counts, *but*
- the Sentencing Guidelines recommend a **thirty-six- to forty-eight-month** range of imprisonment, *and* that
  - district court judges typically sentence fraud offenders to a sentence within and at the very bottom of this range roughly 60 percent of the time, *and*

---

[73] Cass R. Sunstein, *Probability Neglect: Emotions, Worst Cases, and Law*, 112 YALE L. J. 61 (2002).

[74] *Id.* at 63.

○ they sentence some fraud offenders to sentences substantially *below* the range (e.g., to twelve months' imprisonment) 33 percent of the time, *and*

○ they sentence other fraud offenders to sentences *above* the guidelines range (e.g., to sixty months' imprisonment) 7 percent of the time,

the offender is not going to aggregate weighted probabilities.[75] Instead, the offender who suffers probability neglect will glom on to the most salient and adverse figures, which is likely to be "100 years." Given the emotions responsible for probability neglect, one wouldn't be surprised if defendants did everything in their power to reassert some degree of certainty over an inherently uncertain sentencing process.

Concededly, it is possible that defense lawyers – particularly seasoned attorneys with expertise in the area – could successfully ameliorate probability neglect's effect on their clients. Law and economic scholars have demonstrated that lawyers and other experts can sometimes reduce or prevent their clients' cognitive errors.[76] It seems quite reasonable, then, that lawyers would play a positive role in reducing their clients' probability neglect. But that point merely opens a Pandora's box of additional concerns. Timing and access to good counsel will differ. So, too, will an individual's vulnerability to probability neglect. For all these reasons, we should strongly desire a system that reduces the myth that most white-collar offenders are "facing" anything close to twenty, forty, or sixty years' imprisonment. If there are universal design tools that reduce *everyone's* exposure to probability neglect, we should embrace them.

6.8 ON THE DIFFICULTIES OF DISPELLING MYTHS

The aim of this chapter has been to highlight and explore a series of myths and misunderstandings that prevail in white-collar discourse. There are widely circulated myths about prosecutors, punishment, white-collar crime's harms, and the identities of those who commit and suffer those harms. To be sure, major kernels of truth lie at the bottom of these narratives, but the narratives oversimplify the facts and become incredibly sticky. Collectively, these narratives eviscerate trust in our enforcement

---

[75] If the sentencing outcomes were random, then the weighted average would be: $(0.60 \times 36) + (0.33 \times 12) + (0.07 \times 60) = 29.76$ months' expected imprisonment. Thus, assuming random outcomes, the defendant is better off in this jurisdiction than one in which the sentence is a mandatory thirty-six months. For an interesting look at weighted probabilities in the securities and investment fraud context, see QUICK FACTS: SECURITIES AND INVESTMENT FRAUD OFFENSES, FY 2020, UNITED STATES SENTENCING COMMISSION at 2 (showing that 58 percent of offenders were sentenced within the guideline range, and of the remaining 42 percent, 86 percent received a lower sentence than the recommended range, and 14 percent received a higher sentence).

[76] Jennifer Arlen & Stephan Tontrup, *Does the Endowment Effect Justify Legal Intervention? The Debiasing Effect of Institutions*, 44 J. LEGAL STUD. 143 (2015) (finding that the presence of legal counsel either mitigates or eliminates endowment effect bias).

institutions most directly, as well as in our regulatory and political institutions, and our economic institutions. Enforcer-driven excess, arbitrariness, selfishness, and overall incompetence rule the day. According to the narratives, we live in a gilded age on steroids.

If I were the chief enforcer of any major regulatory or law enforcement institution, the first thing I would want to do is dispel these myths and replace them with a more accurate and nuanced portrayal of white-collar crime and its enforcement. I would want to acknowledge the sober facts (corporate crime occurs quite a bit and is caught far less often than it should be), but also highlight improvements. And like any wonky lawyer of my generation, I'd want to avoid an absolutist "us versus them" orientation and stress an optimistic, problem-solving and experimentalist orientation.

But sticky narratives are usually sticky for good reasons. Our society finds reductive stories irresistible because they are simple to digest and help us make sense of a complicated world. Moreover, we know from social science that outrage plays a huge role in how we perceive large-scale crises. When outrage is high, our desire to punish, and to punish harshly, climbs.[77]

Not surprisingly, the standard policy suggestions that have been promoted in this area rest upon dual concerns of transparency and aggression. When corporate and white-collar malfeasance is apparent, commentators want the government to both *say* more and *do* more. Thus, writers as diverse as journalist Jesse Eisinger, law professor Jack Coffee, and federal judge Jed Rakoff all think the government is, for whichever set of reasons, too soft on corporate and white-collar criminals.[78] And in the "say more" domain, one can find any number of scholars who urge the government to explain its decision-making on the record. Brandon Garrett has eloquently argued for the government to release and verify reforms and compliance efforts that arise from corporate prosecutions.[79] Jessica Roth has articulated an

---

[77] *See* Cass R. Sunstein, *On the Psychology of Punishment*, 11 SUP. CT. ECON. REV. 171, 173–75 (2003) (observing that individuals' punitive preferences are based on intuitions that are inconsistent with deterrence and instead "grounded in outrage"); Paul H. Robinson & John M. Darley, *Intuitions of Justice: Implications for Criminal Law and Justice Policy*, 81 S. CAL. L. REV. 1 (2007); Cass. R. Sunstein, Daniel Kahneman, David Schkade, & Ilana Ritov, *Predictably Incoherent Judgments*, 54 STAN. L. REV. 1153, 1164–65 (2002) (finding that punitive damages "are an expression of indignation or outrage on a scale of dollars"). Although much of this literature pertains to punitive damage awards, scholars have identified similar dynamics among criminal juries. *See* Jeffrey J. Rachlinski & Forest Jourden, *The Cognitive Components of Punishment*, 88 CORNELL L. REV. 457, 485 (2003).

[78] *See, e.g.*, JOHN C. COFFEE, JR., CORPORATE CRIME AND PUNISHMENT: THE CRISIS OF UNDERENFORCEMENT (2020); Veronica Root Martinez, *The Government's Prioritization of Information over Sanction: Implications for Compliance*, 83 LAW & CONTEMP. PROBS. 85 (2021).

[79] BRANDON L. GARRETT, TOO BIG TO JAIL: HOW PROSECUTORS COMPROMISE WITH CORPORATIONS 16 (2014) (criticizing opacity of corporate DPAs and the process that generates them).

extremely thoughtful taxonomy and guide for the government's explanation and publication of its declination decisions.[80] And Jennifer Taub's book demands both a massive increase in the collection of white-collar enforcement statistics and the creation of a fraud registry, a proposal that intertwines informative and punitive elements.[81]

With perhaps the exception of Taub's fraud registry, all of these proposals assume a world in which the intended audience takes the information and consumes it as any rational Bayesian might. But we know how unrealistic this assumption is. When people are already polarized into groups with competing views of the world, they assimilate new information in predictably irrational ways. If they mistrust the source, they discount information that challenges their previous world view.[82] Social scientists call this "biased assimilation." Thus, it is unclear that *new* information, especially information disseminated by an already distrusted source, is apt to move the needle. In fact, it may backfire, causing individuals and their social circles to double down on their previously articulated beliefs.[83]

Social scientists have offered several suggestions for improving discourse and deliberation when polarization is at its height. Diversity of viewpoints can be helpful, at least before polarization has crystallized.[84] So too can the adverse statement of a person who previously identified as a member of a particular group.[85] Perhaps that is one of the reasons Judge Rakoff's *New York Review of Books* piece lamenting the dearth of post-Financial Crisis prosecutions attracted so much attention.[86] It wasn't just the persuasive writing, but the fact that a federal judge and former prosecutor was calling out the government for its lack of enforcement. An institutionalist was publicly questioning his current and former institutions.

The third antidote isn't really a cure so much as a process, which is the implementation of technocratic reforms. Technocracy, according to Sunstein, imposes a beneficial "cooling effect."[87] It helps people on both sides of a political spectrum reach agreement on depoliticized questions. It also invites into the conversation experts and (hopefully) those less prone to the pull of conformity norms and group

---

[80] Roth, *supra* note 64, at 537–45 (constructing framework for deciding when and how to announce declination decisions).

[81] Taub, *supra* note 46, at 213–14.

[82] *See generally* Sunstein et al., *supra* note 26. Glaeser & Sunstein, *supra* note 26, at 66.

[83] *See* Sunstein, *supra* note 26, at 1441–43.

[84] Glaeser & Sunstein, *supra* note 25, at 266–67 (setting forth argument for "intellectual diversity").

[85] Scholars refer to this as the "surprising validator." *See* Glaeser & Sunstein, *supra* note 26, at 91 (looking positively on the "the influence of the convert communicator, who once believed the opposite of his current position").

[86] Jed S. Rakoff, *The Financial Crisis: Why Have No High-Level Executives Been Prosecuted?* N.Y. REV. BOOKS (Jan. 2014), at 4–8.

[87] "Technocratic judgments can have a cooling function." Cass R. Sunstein, *The Regulatory Lookback*, 94 B.U. L. REV. 579, 579 (2014).

pressure.[88] It is with these benefits in mind that this book embarks on its final two chapters, which suggest a series of reforms to the federal criminal code that one could easily call "technocratic." I like to think of them as myth-busters as well.

---

[88] For evidence that professional training can reduce biased cognition, see Dan M. Kahan et al., *"Ideology" or "Situation Sense"? An Experimental Investigation of Motivated Reasoning and Professional Judgment*, 164 U. PA. L. REV. 349, 354 (2016) (reporting empirical study results that "strongly support the hypothesis that professional judgment can be expected to counteract 'identity-protective cognition'").

7

Breaking Down the Code

INTRODUCTION

One of this book's recurring themes is that white-collar crime's institutions have confused and misled us, tempting us with a series of counterproductive and unhelpful myths. A combination of poorly tracked offenses, ungraded laws, and underwritten codes obfuscates the federal government's enforcement activities and distorts our assessment of deception and its enforcement.[1] We lack a clear understanding of what our institutions are doing, and we lose faith in them as a result. Moreover, because so much of white-collar crime occupies a space limned by the technically *liable* offense and the strategically *viable* prosecution, gaps in enforcement remain misunderstood and undertheorized.[2]

Our blind spots, paired with our strongly held intuitions that elite executives repeatedly escape responsibility for even the most monstrous crimes, amplify and reinforce our negative attitudes toward government institutions.[3] When the question of prosecution is a black box and the wealthy and powerful always seem to "get away with it," we begin to wonder (or indeed, come to strongly believe) that government elites are colluding with corporate elites. This can either be a gauzy story of government actors too enamored of corporate celebrity or a more troubling narrative of graft among corporate and government actors. Either way, it spells disaster for enforcement institutions that rely heavily on public support.

To date, the Department of Justice (DOJ) has shown little ability (or, frankly, interest) in trying to dispel these narratives. As a result, our problem isn't simply one of overcriminalization or underenforcement, but also one of poor information flow, as well as the corrosive atmosphere that develops when the government pays too little attention to its obligation to inform and enlighten.

---

[1] *See generally* Chapters 2, 3, and 4.
[2] *See* Chapter 5.
[3] *See* Chapter 6.

Even if our institutions have done a better job enforcing and punishing white-collar offenses than many popular accounts presume, they have done a terrible job *informing* the public of relevant harms and risks, and of the decision-making underlying their enforcement decisions. One of the major reasons we lack useful knowledge is that our criminal statutes render the job of collecting, analyzing, and conveying information more difficult. If one were to deliberately design a criminal code to make information production shoddy, difficult, and incomplete, one couldn't do much better than the federal code we currently have.

Public law scholars have made a compelling case that democratic lawmaking means more than periodically electing a representative legislative body.[4] It also "requires government officials to render a justifiable account of what they are doing on behalf of the public."[5] That requirement – to explain, to document and to reliably tabulate one's activities – applies as much if not more to enforcement agencies as it does to our regulatory institutions.[6] If federal enforcers are as responsible for educating the public as they are for investigating and punishing white-collar offenses, they need laws to facilitate this objective. Laws that undermine the government's efforts to produce and disseminate information are laws that we should revise, rewrite, and retire. Laws that support this mission are the ones we should retain and build upon.

Accordingly, this book's remaining two chapters introduce a series of statutory reforms crafted to improve the overall design of the major white-collar provisions of the federal code. The proposals proceed from the assumption that white-collar crime will retain its basic sentencing structure (generated by the much-criticized Sentencing Guidelines[7]), its procedural tools, and its substantive prohibitions on fraud, bribery, and obstruction of justice. I assume as well that prosecutors will remain firmly in control of corporate and individual prosecutions, retaining the

---

[4] Michael Sant'Ambrogio & Glen Staszewski, *Democratizing Rule Development*, 98 WASH. U. L. REV. 793, 844 (2021).

[5] *Id.*

[6] Rory van Loo perceptively distinguishes agencies whose sole mission is the detection and punishment of crime and those responsible for regulating an area of business. *See generally* Rory van Loo, *The Missing Regulatory State: Monitoring Businesses in an Age of Surveillance*, 72 VAND. L. REV. 1563, 1607 (2019).

[7] There is plenty to find lacking in the United States Sentencing Guidelines' approach to fraud. For a helpful overview, see Frank O. Bowman III, *Damp Squib: The Disappointing Denouement of the Sentencing Commission's Economic Crime Project (and What They Should Do Now)*, 27 FED. SENT. R. 270, 270 (2015); Mark W. Bennett et al., *Judging Federal White-Collar Fraud Sentencing: An Empirical Study Revealing the Need for Further Reform*, 102 IOWA L. REV. 939, 946, 964 (2017); Stephen Ferro, *It's All About (Re)location: Interpreting the Federal Sentencing Enhancement for Relocating a Fraudulent Scheme*, 88 U. CHI. L. REV. 1465, 1510 (2021).

discretion and plea-bargaining power that commentators abjure but which the judiciary repeatedly affirms.[8]

With these ground rules in mind, the remainder of this book proposes a partial, phased redesign of parts of the federal criminal code. To lay the conceptual foundation for this work, the first half of this chapter revisits the question of criminal law's purpose and objectives, with a particular focus on the government's production of enforcement information, an essential mission I describe in greater detail in the following section.

7.1 INFORMATION AS SELF-DEFENSE

For those who subscribe to the "offense-based" theory of white-collar crime (see Chapter 2), white-collar crime is primarily a crime of deception.[9] It abuses our trust, undermines our business relationships, distorts our markets, and causes us to over-invest in self-help. Moreover, preexisting information asymmetries that arise across markets and industries create fertile ground for deceptive schemes.[10] Offenders benefit from complexity, sophistication, and expertise, granting them the ability to mask illicit behavior and agilely move from one mark to the next.

Information disarms offenders of many of their advantages, warning victims of new and harmful schemes, and counseling regulators and compliance professionals on unaddressed blind spots. Disarmament, in turn, leads to deterrence. If you realize you cannot deceive your target very easily and that you will be punished even for your *unsuccessful* efforts, you won't waste the requisite resources trying.[11] The scheme that is consigned to failure isn't worth the effort.

Thus, information benefits the public broadly. *Everyone* benefits from markets that are free of fraud and corruption. *Everyone* is more likely to transact under those circumstances and to do so at a lower cost. (That is, after all, one of the founding themes underlying the securities laws and the creation of the Securities Exchange Commission.) This is also why economists treat white-collar crime's

---

[8] Brady v. United States, 397 U.S. 742 (1970) (affirming constitutionality of plea bargaining). *See also*, United States v. HSBC Bank USA, N.A., 863 F.3d 125, 129 (2d Cir. 2017) (highlighting prosecutor's discretion to charge or decline cases); United States v. Fokker Servs. BV, 818 F.3d 733, 741–43 (D.C. Cir. 2016) (same).

[9] Susan P. Shapiro, *Collaring the Crime, not the Criminal: Reconsidering the Concept of White-Collar Crime*, 55 AMER. SOCIOL. REV. 346 (1990).

[10] On information asymmetries and their effect on fraud enforcement, see generally EDWARD BALLEISEN, FRAUD: AN AMERICAN HISTORY FROM BARNUM TO MADOFF (2017) at 108 (explaining how information asymmetries caused by industrialization fueled antifraud efforts).

[11] Such thinking partially explains the criminalization of inchoate behavior. Criminal liability for attempts (or simply perpetrating an unfinished "scheme") increases the probability of detection and punishment. Steven Shavell, *Criminal Law and the Optimal Use of Nonmonetary Sanctions as a Deterrent*, 85 COLUM. L. REV. 1232, 1250–53 (1985).

enforcement-information as the equivalent of a public good.[12] But to the extent information *is* a public good, we must rely on the government to produce it; private individuals are unlikely to engage in the costly and uncertain production of information that inherently benefits many people other than themselves.

There is plenty that the government *can* do in terms of information generation, but the government's capabilities are far weaker and more unpredictable than we would prefer them to be. Pertinent information – about crimes, about offenders, and about the government's enforcement activity – remains hidden and delayed in its release, as well as siloed and prone to misunderstanding.[13] Messages are either incomplete or completely garbled. Many critics recognize this problem and blame prosecutors and enforcement agents. *You guys hide the ball too much!* is an oft-heard criticism in academic and journalistic circles.[14]

This "black box" critique of prosecutorial decision-making reflects an oversimplified narrative. Factors outside the prosecutor's direct control are additionally responsible for white-collar crime's information problem. Our federal criminal code generates and exacerbates many of white-collar crime's information deficits; few of our statutes even *employ* the term "white-collar crime," rendering the collection of accurate information difficult, time-consuming, and prone to error.[15]

7.2 THE DEFINITIONAL DEBATE REDUX[16]

Before delving further into this information-based problem, it is necessary to briefly revisit the definitional debate that underlies much of white-collar crime's academic

---

[12] That is, the fact that one person uses it has no effect on whether it is available for others to use; and by the same token, there is no effective way to limit who can use it once it becomes known. On public goods generally, see Paul A. Samuelson, *The Pure Theory of Public Expenditure*, 36 Rev. Econ. & Stat. 387, 387–89 (1954). As Elizabeth Burch and Alexandra Lahav point out, litigation information is not exactly a public good, since its production can be limited through protection orders. Nevertheless, it does function as a "common good" and therefore displays many of the collective action problems that attach to public goods. Elizabeth Chamblee Burch & Alexandra D. Lahav, *Information for the Common Good in Mass Torts*, 70 DePaul L. Rev. 345, 349 (2021). For more on the ways in which adjudicative information functions as a public good, see Kevin E. Davis & Helen Hershkoff, *Contracting for Procedure*, 53 Wm. & Mary L. Rev. 507, 513 (2011) ("it is commonplace in law-and-economics literature to characterize adjudication as a source of public goods").

[13] Veronica Root, *Coordinating Compliance Incentives*, 102 Cornell L. Rev. 1003, 1029–31 (2017).

[14] For an excellent excavation into these issues and a partial refutation of this claim, see Samuel W. Buell, *Why Do Prosecutors Say Anything? The Case of Corporate Crime*, 96 N.C. L. Rev. 823 (2018).

[15] Stuart P. Green, *The Concept of White-Collar Crime in Law and Legal Theory*, 8 Buff. Crim. L. Rev. 1, 1 (2004) (observing that "[the] term appears in only a handful of relatively obscure criminal statutes").

[16] *See generally* Chapter 2 (describing the debate) and Gerald Cliff & Christian Desilets, *White Collar Crime: What It Is and Where It's Going*, 28 Notre Dame J.L. Ethics & Pub. Pol'y 481, 482–87 (2014) (detailing the various positions taken by criminologists).

discourse. For nearly a century, two competing schools of thought have debated white-collar crime's definition. Invoking Edwin Sutherland, the sociologist who coined the term in a 1939 address, many still use it to denote occupational, high social-status misconduct that is not necessarily illegal as a formal matter, but nevertheless exploitive and perpetrated by members of the socioeconomic elite (the "offender" approach). In contrast, for lawmakers and practitioners, white-collar crime denotes a certain type of legislatively proscribed offense (the "offense" approach). This narrower, positive law approach has in mind a nonviolent crime that involves the use of deception to obtain property, money or services.[17]

This book has consistently favored the offense-based definition. Criminal law itself is, in Judge Lynch's words, "transaction-bound."[18] It punishes actions (or omissions) that coincide with certain states of mind. It does not punish people or organizations for behaving greedily, hoarding wealth, or being "criminogenic." Unless we are inclined to upend many other institutions, it makes little sense to talk about white-collar crime unmoored from the substantive penal laws, prosecutorial charging policies, and sentencing rules that flow from criminal offenses. It may well be that every billionaire or "neoliberal" is, in some sense, a "criminal" under certain sociopolitical frameworks, but that is not the world in which we currently live.

Accordingly, if we want to properly judge the enforcement system we *currently* have, we ought to at least judge it according to its own internal goals and constraints. And here, the federal code runs into a serious problem: However successfully it delineates the difference between prohibited and innocent behavior, it utterly drops the ball on organizing and conveying useful information. Criminal law and its enforcement send terribly confusing signals when it comes to the prosecution of white-collar misconduct.

7.3 SIGNALS

Let us return to the question of enforcement. Why do we criminalize offenses of deceit? Why do we enforce and punish these offenses with such harsh sanctions, up to and including long terms of imprisonment?

Our society relies, in the first instance, on a hybrid system of private civil lawsuits and administrative and civil enforcement proceedings that impose fines,

---

[17] Some scholars have used the term more expansively to refer to any nonviolent crime, such as public urination. *See, e.g.*, Dan M. Kahan & Eric A. Posner, *Shaming White-Collar Criminals: A Proposal for Reform of the Federal Sentencing Guidelines*, 42 J. L. & ECON. 365 (1999). This expansive treatment, however, appears to be an outlier and is at odds with how experts and lawmakers use the term.

[18] *See* Gerard E. Lynch, *RICO: The Crime of Being a Criminal, Parts III & IV*, 87 COLUM. L. REV. 920, 932–33 (1987) ("Fundamental to our traditional law of crimes . . . is a conception of crime that is transaction-bound. Synthesizers of the common-law tradition tell us that the core of any definition of crime is a particular act or omission").

injunctions, and noncarceral remedies.[19] Civil lawsuits often ensure some degree of compensation for plaintiffs and deter at least some defendants insofar as punitive and collateral damages arise in litigation.[20] But civil liability on its own has proven insufficient to deter those who are adept at evading detection, those who refuse to pay penalties, and those who are "judgment proof," that is, they lack the funds to pay government penalties or compensate victims.[21] Moreover, civil liability cannot incapacitate repeat offenders.[22]

Private civil enforcement suffers along a different dimension. Because white-collar crime's victims are diffuse and often unaware of their victimization until long after the first contact with a perpetrator has occurred, it requires the coordinating force of a government agency (well, several) to take the reins in investigating and punishing deception and its noxious spillovers. Compared to private litigants, government actors are better positioned to collect, share, and communicate relevant information.[23] Moreover, unlike private litigants, government actors should have no qualms producing information that benefits society diffusely.[24] Public service is, after all, their job.

There is another reason we criminalize white-collar offenses, which is criminal liability's potent expressive signal. Criminal liability is unique among coercive legal institutions in that it permits the deprivation of someone's liberty. Imprisonment incapacitates the undeterred and *also* provokes shame. At the same time, it conveys to law enforcement officials that society takes a given offense seriously enough to

---

[19] *See, e.g.,* Daniel R. Fischel & Alan O. Sykes, *Corporate Crime*, 25 J. LEGAL STUD. 319 (1996); Anthony O'Rourke, *Parallel Enforcement and Agency Interdependence*, 77 MD. L. REV. 985 (2018).

[20] If the probability of detection were less than 1, a civil system of solely compensatory damages would underdeter wrongdoers, particularly in instances where benefits of wrongdoing were certain. That is the expected value of punishment would fail to wipe out the wrongdoer's expected gain. A. Mitchell Polinsky & Steven Shavell, *On the Disutility and Discounting of Imprisonment and Theory of Deterrence*, 28 J. LEGAL STUD. 1, 4 (1999) ("We assume that deterrence is determined by the *expected disutility* of sanctions: if the probability p of an imprisonment sentence, multiplied by its total disutility $d(s)$, exceeds the benefit a person would derive from a criminal act, he will be discouraged from committing it").

[21] "Imprisonment is more socially costly than monetary sanctions but is better able to deter judgment proof individuals." AMANDA ROSE, *Public Enforcement: Criminal versus Civil* in OXFORD HANDBOOK OF CORPORATE LAW AND GOVERNANCE (Jeffery N. Gordon & Wolf-Georg Ringe, eds., 2018) 946 (summarizing arguments in Gary Becker's seminal 1968 article, *Crime and Punishment: An Economic Approach*). *See also* A. Mitchell Polinsky & Steven Shavell, *The Economic Theory of Public Enforcement of Law*, 38 J. ECON. LIT. 45, 46 (2000) ("force may be needed to gather information, capture violators and prevent reprisal").

[22] *See, e.g., id.* at 68–70 (citing criminal law's incapacitation rationale).

[23] A. MITCHELL POLINSKY & STEVEN SHAVELL, *The Theory of Public Enforcement of Law*, in 1 HANDBOOK LAW & ECON. 406 (2007).

[24] This is admittedly an overstatement, as government officials can themselves be imperfect agents. *See* Matthew C. Stephenson, *Information Acquisition and Institutional Design*, 124 HARV. L. REV. 1422, 1430–31 (2011) (explaining how, for a given action, a government agent's tally of her private costs and benefits diverge from society's costs and benefits).

denominate it a crime and deprive its perpetrator of the right to live freely among others.

Criminal punishment invites tradeoffs. On the one hand, the criminal justice system promises the offender due process protections that raise the enforcer's costs of securing a conviction.[25] The "beyond a reasonable doubt" evidentiary standard, guaranteed counsel, and the privilege against self-incrimination all increase the government's costs of enforcement.[26] But criminal law is also a boon to the enforcer. If she can conduct much of her investigation under the aegis of the grand jury, she benefits from the grand jury's secrecy rules and its powers to compel the production of mountains of data and information.[27] The government enforcer who amasses "probable cause" of a crime may seek a search warrant to search a person's home, car, or office, often with little advance warning. She can use derivative and group-crime doctrines to pressure one party to snitch or gather evidence pertaining to another party.

Criminal punishment also communicates to offenders and victims alike the government's views about the dangers posed by conduct, as well as the wrongfulness of such conduct.[28] Richard McAdams succinctly summarizes this expressive effect:

> [Law] expresses normative principles and symbolizes societal values, and these moralizing features may affect behavior. Under this view, for example, criminal punishments do not merely state prices for prohibited behaviors. Rather, as sanctions, punishments express society's condemnation of the behavior.[29]

---

[25] This is most true of federal white-collar crimes. *See, e.g.*, ALEXANDRA NATAPOFF, *The Penal Pyramid*, in THE NEW CRIMINAL JUSTICE THINKING 71, 72 (Sharon Dolovich & Alexandra Natapoff, eds., 2017) (conceptualizing the criminal justice system as a pyramid and arguing that its top "is the world of federal offenses [and] serious cases ... [in which] rules dominate" and its bottom consists of state and local systems where "offenses are petty and caseloads number in the thousands").

[26] Procedural hoops such as these "constrain the costs associated with abuses of prosecutorial or punishment authority." Keith N. Hylton & Vikramaditya Khanna, *A Public Choice Theory of Criminal Procedure*, 15 SUP. CT. ECON. REV. 61, 63 (2007).

[27] Miriam H. Baer, *Law Enforcement's Lochner*, 105 MINN. L. REV. 1667, 1698–701 (2021) (cataloguing the various advantages that prosecutors and enforcement agents derive from the grand-jury's process).

[28] *See generally* Dan M. Kahan, *Social Influence, Social Meaning and Deterrence*, 83 VA. L. REV. 349 (1997); Jennifer Arlen & Lewis Kornhauser, *Does the Law Change Preferences?* 22 THEORETICAL INQ. L. 175, 187 (2021). *See also* Elizabeth S. Anderson & Richard H. Pildes, *Expressive Theories of Law: A General Restatement*, 148 U. PA. L. REV. 1503, 1504 (2000) ("At the most general level, expressive theories tell actors – whether individuals, associations, or the State – to act in ways that express appropriate attitudes toward various substantive values").

[29] Richard H. McAdams, *The Origin, Development, and Regulation of Norms*, 96 MICH. L. REV. 338, 398 (1997). On the difference between "pricing" undesirable behavior and outright prohibiting it through condemnation and punishment, see, e.g., John C. Coffee, Jr., *Does "Unlawful" Mean "Criminal"? Reflections on the Disappearing Tort/Crime Distinction in American Law*, 71 B.U. L. REV. 193, 194–200 (1991); Robert Cooter, *Prices and Sanctions*, 84 COLUM. L. REV. 1523, 1524–25 (1984) (explaining that "[a] sanction is a detriment

Some regulatory crimes are technical or rest solely upon strict liability; there's arguably not too much shame bound up in these crimes. But many white-collar crimes – certainly the core crimes of fraud, bribery, and obstruction – do in fact reflect commonly held notions of how people should conduct themselves. Fraudsters would prefer *not* to be thought of as cheaters and thieves. Public officials and employees chafe under labels such as "grifter" or "corrupt politician." And no one wants to be called a liar or obstructionist. In its best iteration, this aversion to shame improves deterrence. In its less valuable iteration, fear of shame becomes the impetus for detection avoidance or post hoc rationalizations.

7.4 CRIMINAL LAW'S DUTY TO INFORM

Criminal law is *expressive* in that it tells us something about society's view of the behavior the government has formally prohibited. But it is also independently *informative*, in that it categorizes, catalogues, and collects data regarding the incidence of certain behaviors (how many frauds, bribers, regulatory crimes per year), as well as their respective enforcement.

To some degree, private institutions can collect and monitor some of this information. But the government, because of its size, power, and resources, will always be in the best position to fulfill this function. Through press releases and public filings (e.g., the criminal complaint, the grand jury's indictment, or the filed information and plea agreement), the DOJ and its components inform the public of specific crimes undertaken by charged offenders. They tell us what went wrong, who was responsible for it, and who is about to be prosecuted and punished. They can also provide more general information about nascent trends and emerging threats.

This cache of information exists independently of criminal law's "expressive" value. Informing the public through enforcement is different from condemning behavior or actions. In the white-collar context, government-supplied information can:

- alert victims
- identify root causes of crime
- repair trust
- inform future regulatory efforts, and
- promote oversight of enforcers.

I offer a brief description of each of these benefits in the pages that follow, highlighting the ways in which contemporary enforcement practices often frustrate their implementation.

Alert victims. A healthy enforcement regime ought to alert actual and putative victims of maleficent schemes. Indeed, it should warn not only of those schemes that have already caused harms, but also those that are poised to inflict future harms.

imposed for doing what is forbidden" whereas "a price is payment of money which is required in order to do what is permitted" [emphasis omitted]).

For routine schemes and swindles, regulatory agencies issue warnings and periodically set up task forces to enable citizens to report harms and suspected scams.[30] Given how easily such schemes proliferate and how frequently Americans fall prey to them anyway (approximately 3 million people[31] in just the annual year of 2017 according to one survey), one might reasonably wonder just how effective the warnings have been. Often, it appears that the government falls into the familiar role of playing catch-up to more sophisticated networks of fraudsters.[32]

Moreover, as one graduates from low-level swindles to more publicly held firms and financial institutions, the information account takes a darker turn. The government clearly *collects* reams of information from corporations,[33] but it conveys only a fraction of its knowledge to the general public.

For example, as part of a corporate settlement (usually a deferred or nonprosecution agreement), prosecutors often develop with an offender an agreed upon narrative ("statement of facts") that provides, at best, a pared down version of the underlying wrongdoing that has occurred. The more the government values the settlement or plea agreement, the more information-disclosure it will be inclined to bargain away. As I have argued elsewhere, "For every criminal resolution it enters, the government agrees to keep certain information private. The less there is to prove, the less there is also to say in public charging documents."[34]

The extent of this problem remains undocumented. For celebrated cases such as the government's ill-fated Purdue Pharma prosecution in 2007, we know from subsequent journalistic accounts and later tort cases that the government's criminal settlements buried relevant facts.[35] Barring journalistic discoveries, however, we are often at a loss to know what we don't know.

---

[30] *See, e.g.,* Frauds Targeting Main Street Investors – Investor Alert, SECURITIES & EXCH. COMM'N (Apr. 10, 2020); Seena Gressin, *Scammers Reportedly Using Fake Unemployment Benefits Websites as Phishing Lures,* FED. TRADE COMM'N (Mar. 16, 2021) ; Digital Asset and "Crypto" Investment Scams – Investor Alert, SECURITIES & EXCH. COMM'N (Sept. 1, 2021); SEC Announces Enforcement Task Force Focused on Climate and ESG Issues, SECURITIES & EXCH. COMM'N (Mar. 4, 2021).

[31] https://bjs.ojp.gov/content/pub/pdf/ffus17.pdf.

[32] For a recent example of this dynamic, see Jay P. Kennedy, Melissa Rorie, & Michael L. Benson, *Covid 19 Frauds, An Exploratory Study of Victimization during a Global Crisis,* 20 CRIMINOLOGY & PUB. POL'Y 493 (2021).

[33] Dorothy S. Lund & Natasha Sarin, *Corporate Crime and Punishment: An Empirical Study,* 100 TEX L. REV. 285, 289 (2022) (tracking increases in suspicious activity reports filed with the Department of Treasury's Financial Crimes Network; whistleblower complaints filed with the SEC's whistleblower program for allegations relating to violations of the securities laws; and consumer complaints filed with the Consumer Financial Protection Bureau).

[34] Miriam H. Baer, *The Information Shortfalls of Prosecuting Irresponsible Executives,* 70 DEPAUL L. REV. 191, 222 (2021).

[35] The opioid crisis and Purdue Pharma's role in creating it serve as extreme examples. "Tort law played a crucial role as a backstop capable of generating information, public attention, and, eventually, credible risks of penalties and negative publicity that could reshape the incentives of large private organizations." Mariano-Florentino Cuéllar & Keith Humphreys, *The Political*

Identify root causes. Beyond warnings, white-collar enforcement can also play a theoretical role in unearthing the "root causes" of wrongdoing within firms, across industries, and within and between networks. Corporate and white-collar crimes arise in response to recurring set of motivations and circumstances. Some offenders are sociopathic opportunists. Many more are "good people" who act on impulse or under the belief they have no other choice but to violate the law.[36] To this day, Donald Cressey's famous fraud triangle – which explains fraud as the product of interwoven situational characteristics of opportunity, pressure, and rationalization – dominates discussions of fraud among fraud examiners, legal scholars, and practitioners.[37]

At its best, white-collar enforcement enables theorists and practitioners to operationalize theories such as Cressey's, or alternatively, construct alternate valid explanations of criminal behavior. When enforcement agencies depict complex schemes within businesses and industries, they facilitate the identification of the hypercompetitive influences (pressure), weak governance links (opportunity), and unhealthy norms and cultures (neutralizations) that promote wrongdoing within organizations and within networks of organizations. Case studies further enable researchers to study the impact of phenomena ranging from organizational culture and architectural governance to ethical reasoning and cognitive blindness.

Yet again, this is a story of enforcement in its *best* light. In a world characterized by declinations, settlements, and plea bargains, it is difficult to portray contemporary enforcement practices as optimally designed to reveal the root causes of any crime. To be sure, scholars and academics make good use of the materials that exist and of data voluntarily supplied to them. Moreover, some enforcers, sensitive to the public's need for information, may be more inclined to explore and discuss root causes. But the criminal justice system itself is not set up to determine and broadly disseminate such information. Criminal law is far too transactional and decentralized to meet that goal. Line prosecutors ordinarily finish one case and then move on to the next – and then move on to another unit or leave the government altogether.

Repair trust. The flip side of alerting potential victims is that government enforcement can also repair society's trust in markets and institutions. When the government announces a noisy "crackdown" on deceptive behaviors, it effectively tells the general public, "Don't worry, we've got you covered." Of course, the problem with this line of thinking is that sometimes the government induces "trust" where trust

---

Economy of the Opioid Epidemic, 38 Yale L. & Pol'y Rev. 1, 68 (2019) (explaining tort law's significance considering criminal enforcement's shortcomings in this area).

[36] Yuval Feldman, The Law of Good People: Challenging States' Ability to Regulate Human Behavior ix, 4 (2018).

[37] Donald Cressey, Other People's Money: Study in the Psychology of Embezzlement (1971); Todd Haugh, *The Power Few of Corporate Compliance*, 53 Ga. L. Rev. 129 (2018); Leandra Lederman, *The Fraud Triangle and Tax Evasion*, 106 Iowa L. Rev. 1153 (2020); Elizabeth Pollman, *Private Company Lies*, 109 Georgetown L.J. 353 (2020); Nathaniel Grow & Todd Haugh, *Assessing the NCAA as a Compliance Organization*, Wis. L. Rev. 787, 831–44 (2021).

does not belong. If the crackdown is more for symbolic than real, its efforts to reassure the public leave it vulnerable to future harms.[38] Moreover, when trust is undeserved, the government's assurances eventually come back to haunt it.

Inform future regulatory efforts. When a business has violated a law and the means and methods of that violation become clear, regulators can draft new regulations to either prevent or mitigate future violations. In addition, regulatory enforcers – who ordinarily traffic in administrative and civil liability – can learn from criminal prosecutors and investigators about newer schemes, enforcement-related blind spots, and other weak links.[39]

These are the potential feedback loops and pathways that exist both within the federal government and between the federal government and state and local agencies. But the government's investigative norms and settlement procedures jointly weaken and disable these loops. Turf wars and coordination problems undermine the sharing of information during jointly or sequentially conducted investigations.[40] Embattled regulators prefer *not* to highlight their previous lapses, if they can help it. And secrecy norms designed to protect the integrity of ongoing investigations delay, into infinite future periods, the moment it is safe to publicly disclose "bad facts."

Promote oversight of enforcers and their agencies. Finally, the system ought to produce enough information that the public can judge, efficiently and effectively, its enforcers and enforcement institutions. That is, sophisticated researchers ought to have the raw data available to assess: (1) how well, as of a certain date, enforcers have met their proclaimed enforcement goals; (2) how well they have positioned themselves to address future challenges; and (3) how well enforcers have fared in producing timely, relevant, and useable information.

7.5 INFORMATION FAILURES AND THE UNDERSTATED IMPORTANCE OF STATUTORY DESIGN

Enforcement information has the potential to protect society, improve regulation, and promote democratic participation and oversight. Enforcement *failures* come about when the criminal justice system's processes short-circuit information's collection and dissemination.

Qualitative failures arise when the government fails to provide sufficient information about a specific case or investigation. These are the mistakes we rightfully ascribe to prosecutors and enforcement agencies. *Quantitative* failures arise out of the government's collection, disclosure, and portrayal of its longitudinal,

---

[38] Mila Sohoni, *Crackdowns*, 103 VA. L. REV. 31 (2017).

[39] "Information feedback loops are conduits that allow information to flow within the compliance system among regulators, firms, executives, and inter-organizational structures." David Orozco, *Compliance by Fire Alarm: Regulatory Oversight through Information Feedback Loops*, 46 J. CORP. L. 97, 125 (2020).

[40] *See, e.g.*, Root, *supra* note 13, at 1028.

interagency data. These are the lapses whose origins lie not just with the DOJ, but also with our laws and our federal code. *Both* varieties of failures undermine the various benefits described in Section 7.4. When information fails to flow freely, we are less able to protect ourselves from those who might do us harm. We are also less able to improve future regulation, or to engage in the oversight activities that make government more responsive to our needs.

That takes us to the question of statutory design. How does a code's design impact qualitative and quantitative information failures?

A criminal code represents more than a pithy recitation of society's values and prohibitions. It is also – under the right circumstances – an important coordination device. Its own design enables (or subverts) the executive branch's efforts to collect, organize, and disseminate information to and from enforcers, as well as to the general public. *This* is the aspect of our criminal code that has been least discussed among scholars or practitioners, even though our code's information failures clearly feed the general public's disillusionment and restlessness where white-collar and corporate enforcement issues are concerned.

Many of the federal code's shortcomings are well known to white-collar crime's insiders.[41] The strongest of its criticisms have coalesced into the concern that prosecutors, and not legislators or judges, play far too large a role in deciding what constitutes crime and which punishments to dole out in response to those crimes. Thus, as the late William Stuntz memorably argued:

> [C]riminal law and the law of sentencing define prosecutors' options, not litigation outcomes. They are not rules in the shadow of which litigants must bargain. Rather, they are items on a menu from which the prosecutor may order as she wishes. She has no incentive to order the biggest meal possible. Instead, her incentive is to get whatever meal she wants, as long as the menu offers it.[42]

The criminal code-as-menu thesis has retained its dominance since Stuntz first articulated it in 2004.[43] As applied to federal law, it remains remarkably on point, although one can cite several of its limitations as a portrayal of white-collar enforcement practice.

For example, if the code operated like a true "menu," everyone would know what the prosecutor ordered.[44] When less and more serious crimes are clearly demarcated

---

[41] On the difference between insiders and outsiders in criminal law and the ways in which inside knowledge shapes one's understanding of criminal law's institutions, see Stephanos Bibas, *Transparency and Participation in Criminal Procedure*, 81 N.Y.U. L. REV. 911 (2006).

[42] William J. Stuntz, *Plea Bargaining and Criminal Law's Disappearing Shadow*, 117 HARV. L. REV. 2548, 2549 (2004) Stuntz's critique, it should be noted, was aimed at criminal law broadly, and not white-collar crime.

[43] Some have questioned the claim that prosecutors enjoy so much power. *See, e.g.,* Jeffrey Bellin, *The Power of Prosecutors*, 94 N.Y.U. L. REV. 171 (2019) (challenging Stuntz's portrait of prosecutorial predominance).

[44] The menu metaphor arguably works better with a more "orderly" code. *See, e.g.,* Paul H. Robinson, *The Rise and Fall and Resurrection of American Criminal Codes*, 53 LOUISVILLE L. REV. 173, 175 (2015) (defining an "orderly" code as one in which the "offenses are segregated

in degrees, the prosecutor's initial and later "orders" can be fairly transparent, even if the process of deciding which one of them to charge occurs outside the public's observation.[45] By contrast, the prosecutor's "movement" within the white-collar context remains hidden behind our federal code's statutory umbrellas, described at length in Chapter 3.[46] The prosecutor can charge a "serious" mail fraud case and plead it out as a nonserious fraud offense, all without changing a single charge. *That's* a very different type of menu.

Even worse, the "menu" that is the federal code contains a number of "orders" (i.e., statutes) that are affirmatively misleading as to their content and meaning. As anyone well acquainted with federal criminal law will attest, the code's umbrella statutes not only overlap and create redundancy[47] but also bundle a number of white-collar and *non*white-collar offenses under the same statutory provisions.[48]

Imagine Ernie, the local city employee who also happens to be a procurement officer and vested with the power to decide which trash bags to purchase for his department or agency. One day, Ernie violates the federal "honest services fraud" statute because he accepts a $5,000 payment in exchange for granting Acme Trash Bags Inc. a $50,000 contract to service the city. His *charge* will fall under the mail or wire fraud statutes, depending on how he accepts his bribe. But his behavior sounds far more like bribery than it does like fraud.

Although designating Acme the city's trash bag supplier in exchange for a personal payment sounds like a canonical case of bribery, it cannot be charged under the federal bribery statute (18 USC 201) because Ernie is a city employee. Happily for prosecutors, the local bribe can instead be charged under several other

into different chapters according to their interest at stake and ... organized in order of seriousness").

[45] On the ways in which a "thick" code with multiple "landing spots" facilitates plea bargaining between the prosecutor and defense attorney (a notably nontransparent process), see Ronald F. Wright & Rodney L. Engen, *Charge Movement and Theories of Prosecutors*, 91 MARQ. L. REV. 9, 9 (2007) ("[C]riminal charges move. The more serious charges filed at the start of the case often move down to less serious charges that form the basis for a guilty plea and conviction. Concurrent charges of less serious crimes are often dismissed outright as part of a plea agreement").

[46] For more on the umbrella metaphor, see Chapter 3.

[47] State statutes can also be umbrella-like and are apt to move in this direction as legislatures revise their laws and override Model Penal Code-era reforms. *See* Robinson, *supra* note 44, at 177–79 (describing degradation of state codes); Paul H. Robinson & Michael T. Cahill, *The Accelerating Degradation of American Criminal Codes*, 56 HASTINGS L. J. 633 (2005).

[48] One of the few commentators to reflect on this has been Judge Lynch, who writes:

Statutes like RICO encompass a huge range of different levels of crime, including under the same rubric violent and non-violent acts, criminal organizations and legitimate businesses gone wrong, relatively limited schemes and open-ended, decades-long criminal endeavors. Statutes prohibiting appallingly destructive conduct are jumbled together with others prohibiting relatively minor violations of social mores.

Gerard E. Lynch, *Our Administrative System of Criminal Justice*, 66 FORDHAM L. REV. 2117, 2137 (1998).

statutes, and not just "honest services fraud." If Ernie works for a program that receives in excess of $25,000 annually from the federal government, the illegal payment can be charged under 18 USC 666. If his scheme had any connection with interstate commerce (likely, if the trash bags were manufactured elsewhere), it may well qualify as extortion under color of official right, 18 USC 1961, one of the crimes defined by the Hobbs Act.

All of these are plausible charges for Ernie, as well as obstruction of justice and making false statements to federal investigators, 18 USC 1503 and 18 USC 1001, if Ernie endeavors to cover up the payoff during a subsequent federal investigation.

Now, for punishment purposes, the label and name of the statute are of less consequence. If a court treats the charged crime as a humdrum case of bribery, the case will be analyzed under Section 2C1.1 of the United States Sentencing Guidelines, and Ernie's resulting punishment will be fairly light because of the relatively small amounts of money involved. Whatever punishment Ernie receives, it won't be anything close to the statutory maxima prescribed by *any* of the honest services fraud, Hobbs Act, or program bribery statutes, much less an aggregate of their statutory maxima.

Notice the information implications of this setup. To a prosecutor eager to settle this case, there probably is very little difference, in terms of punishment, between an honest services, Hobbs Act, or program bribery charge. They will be treated as equivalents under the Sentencing Guidelines, the starting point for a sentencing judge's analysis. Even a charge bargain "down" to an obstruction or false statements conviction is unlikely to make much of a difference, given the low amount of money involved. If the prosecutor's reservation price is something in the realm of three to six months' imprisonment, she probably doesn't care which of the bribery, obstruction, or false statement statutes she uses to get there.[49]

Notwithstanding the foregoing, how the employee's crime is subsequently *coded* and described in filing documents hinges quite a bit on the charge the prosecutor selects. If Ernie's prosecutor is already inclined to downplay the *qualitative* information costs[50] that inhere in agreeing to a weaker set of charges (i.e., the reduced value of a filed Information that charges Ernie with the narrower crime of making false statements), so too is she likely to be ignorant of the *quantitative* information costs of her decision. In fact, I would feel quite comfortable speculating that prosecutors are far less knowledgeable of a settlement's eventual *coding*

---

[49] On the incentives that drive prosecutorial decision-making and plea-bargaining, see generally Richard Lorren Jolly & J. J. Prescott, *Beyond Plea Bargaining: A Theory of Criminal Settlement*, 62 B.C. L. Rev. 1047, 1049 (2021) ("criminal settlement behavior, just like civil settlement behavior, is at root driven by the goals of cost minimization, risk mitigation, and value maximization").

[50] On the ways in which plea-bargaining results in reduced flows of relevant information to the public, and not simply reduced punishment, see Baer, *supra* note 34, at 218–22 (pinpointing information costs that arise in criminal litigation and explaining why these costs are not likely to be salient to the typical prosecutor).

consequences than they are of its direct and collateral consequences on an individual defendant.

Thus, regardless of what the prosecutor decides to do, the federal code contributes to information failures across both the qualitative and quantitative dimensions. This problem flows from something deeper than plea-bargaining and its many ills. Its root cause is the federal code's tendency to bundle disparate offenses into one statute. Bundling dilutes the labeling effect of a given criminal offense: the official label is either a misnomer or so broadly phrased as to be meaningless. At the same time, bundling *also* increases the likelihood of coding error. Tabulating the number of fraud and bribery cases the government has prosecuted in a single year becomes more fraught and more prone to coding error. Consider the statutes, the crimes they punish, and their official titles as described in Table 7.1.

TABLE 7.1. *Bribery bundles*

Code section	Official title (i.e., the title one sees upon looking up the specific sections in the federal code)	Unofficial name of crime	Underlying behavior punished by statute
18 USC 1346	Definition of "scheme or artifice to defraud"	Honest services fraud	Bribery by local, state officials, and by private individuals
18 USC 666	Theft or bribery concerning programs receiving federal funds	Program bribery	Theft, misappropriation, fraud, bribery, or gratuities
18 USC 1951[51]	Interference with commerce by threats or violence	Extortion under color of official right (no threat of violence required) "Hobbs Act Bribery"	Bribery (offer or acceptance) by local/state employees
18 USC 201	Bribery of public officials and witnesses	Offer or acceptance of bribery OR offer or acceptance of gratuities (lesser offense)	Punish bribery schemes (by up to twenty years' imprisonment) Punish gratuities by up to two years' imprisonment

[51] The Hobbs Act punishes several distinct acts, including robbery, economic extortion, violent extortion, and bribery. Although many of the Hobbs Act's provisions require violence or the threat of violence, extortion under color of official right requires no such proof. *See generally* Evans v. United States, 504 U.S. 255 (1992).

TABLE 7.2. *Obstruction bundles*

Code section	Official title (i.e., the title one sees upon looking up the specific sections in the federal code)	Unofficial name of crime	Underlying behavior for which the statute is used
18 USC 1001	Statements or entries generally	Making "false statements" to a federal officer	Lying to/misleading/ concealing information from federal officials
18 USC 1503	Influencing or injuring officer or juror generally	Obstruction of justice	Obstructing or endeavoring to corruptly undermine or interfere with a government proceeding

If one were to add the various obstruction-related statutes, we might include the statutes described in Table 7.2.

As Tables 7.1 and 7.2 illustrate, an agency's enforcement staff, acting in good faith and under substantial pressure, could easily miscode or inconsistently code instances of fraud, bribery, and obstruction of justice. Misleading statutory labels that purportedly extend to a bundle of crimes all but ensure these types of errors. They may make prosecution easier (especially at the case level), but over the long term, they make accurate and complete data collection more difficult.

7.6 CODE REFORM IN FOUR NOT-SO-EASY STEPS

Our federal criminal code suffers a number of problems, but four in particular stand out: It is overly *bundled*, and therefore *mislabels* certain crimes.[52] Its core crimes of fraud, bribery, and obstruction are frustratingly *fractured* across multiple statutes, but those statutes are also flat and fail to include any rigorous form of *gradation*. Rather than adjust the entire federal code to make it "feel" more like the Model Penal Code (MPC), federal reformers would do well to adopt a different mission: to unbundle, relabel, consolidate, and grade the core white-collar offenses on which prosecutors and investigators most often depend. This four-part task is hardly easy, but it is doable and would vastly improve the government's ability to collect and relay enforcement information to the general public.

---

[52] Bundling is neither a new problem nor one unique to white-collar crime. Scholars have explored similar dynamics in legislative and administrative contexts. *See* Jennifer Nou & Edward H. Stiglitz, *Regulatory Bundling*, 128 YALE L. J. 1174 (2018). For a book-length treatment of the topic (and an excellent overview of the multiple ways "bundling" appears in private and public life), see LEE ANNE FENNELL, SLICES & LUMPS, DIVISION AND AGGREGATION IN LAW AND LIFE (2019).

7.7 THE FIRST TWO STEPS: UNBUNDLING AND RELABELING

Imagine we accepted the following ground rules of statutory design, with an eye toward facilitating the collection of information, the provision of information to the public, and the facilitation of oversight of government enforcers:

Proposition #1: A code should avoid bundling offenses that impose conceptually different types of harms

Proposition #2: A code provision's title should communicate the core behavior the perpetrator is accused of committing

Proposition #3: A code provision's title should be readily comprehended by a layperson

Each of these propositions, if followed, would result in a more transparent federal code, and in turn, a more transparent and accurately coded enforcement process. A new jurisdiction, drafting its criminal code for the first time, should harbor no interest in misleading the public it serves. Nor should it wish to saddle or inadvertently reward its offenders with statutory crimes whose labels suggest worse (or less harmful) behavior than is actually the case.[53] Moreover, we can pragmatically recognize the drawbacks associated with bundled offenses that confusingly entwine distinct harms.[54]

---

[53] On the normative implications of labeling for criminal defendants in different settings, see James Chalmers & Fiona Leverick, *Fair Labelling in Criminal Law*, 71 Mod. L. Rev. 217, 222 (2008) (contrasting the manslaughter label with murder); Hilmi Zawati, Fair Labelling and the Dilemma of Prosecuting Gender-Based Crimes at the International Criminal Tribunals 31–32 (2014) (explaining that fair labeling prevents undeserved stigmata), and Stuart P. Green, Thirteen Ways to Steal a Bicycle: Theft Law in the Information Age 18, 52–54 (2012) (explaining how the consolidation of theft crimes has undermined fair labeling). On fair labeling's interaction with offense differentiation (what I refer to as criminal law's bundling problem later in this chapter), see Andrew Cornford, *Beyond Fair Labelling: Offense Differentiation in Criminal Law*, 42 Oxford Legal Stud. 985 (2022).

Finally, regarding the code's accessibility to laypeople, consider the sensible proposition: "A new code should be written in plain English, so that it will be understandable by most or all judges, lawyers, witnesses, investigators, and defendants." Robert H. Joost, *Federal Criminal Code Reform: Is It Possible?* 1 Buff. Crim. L. Rev. 195, 196 (1997) (arguing for the enactment of a clearer, shorter federal criminal code).

[54] I am taking as a given the fact that a criminal offense comprises, as an irreducible minimum, an *actus reus* and a *mens rea* component. One might argue that this too is a "bundle." That may be the case, but unlike the law that knits multiple offenses together, the bundle of elements that comprises a *single* offense cannot be subdivided without undermining criminal law's longstanding principles of culpability and legality. By contrast, one could easily split up the statutes described in this chapter (e.g., the Hobbs Act, the Program Bribery statute) and abide by criminal law's norms. Indeed, one might argue that an *unbundled* criminal code more closely approximates the aspirations described in treatises and criminal law casebooks. *See generally* Miriam H. Baer, *Corporate Criminal Law Unbounded*, in Oxford Handbook of Prosecutors and Prosecution (Ronald F. Wright, Kay Levine, & Russell M. Gold, eds., 2021), 481–84 (citing Sanford H. Kadish et al., Criminal Law and Its Processes [10th ed. 2017]). For criticisms of the Kadish school's perspective on criminal law, see Alice

Antibundling and fair labeling rules improve criminal law's transparency at both the wholesale and retail levels. Most of us would want to know whether Ernie has been charged with bribery (extortion under color of official right) or classic extortion. (Ernie, too, should care about the label that applies to his offense.) And at a quantitative level, those of us who specialize in local corruption should also want to know how many crimes charged under 18 USC 666 were bribery cases, how many were embezzlement crimes, and how many were misappropriation cases. Employee embezzlement, after all, tells us something very different about an institution's weaknesses than employee bribery. The former suggests a lack of internal controls, while the latter implicates deeper concerns about political corruption and government decision-making.

Statutory unbundling is useful insofar as it eases the executive branch's duty in producing and disseminating such information. It serves as a useful building block to securing a more orderly code, and it also places in stark relief the number of overlapping, irrelevant, and inconsistent crimes a legislature has created over the years. For all of those reasons, unbundling is an information-generating activity that improves criminal law's democratic responsiveness. We cannot reform the mistakes we cannot see, and unbundling helps us see many things that otherwise remain hidden.

Were Congress to embrace these propositions, it would at a minimum find itself rewriting provisions such as 18 USC 1951 (the Hobbs Act), 18 USC 666 (program bribery, theft, and embezzlement), and 18 USC 1503 (obstruction of justice). Bribery (at least when it involves no threats of violence) would no longer be charged under the same statute that punishes violent extortion (18 USC 1951).[55] Obstruction of justice (18 USC 1503) would almost certainly be broken and up and rewritten to distinguish interference promulgated through threats and violence of court actors, and nonviolent acts such as the destruction of documents and data.

The crime known as honest services fraud would be rewritten, relabeled, and regrouped to reflect the fact that it is in fact a form of bribery and not another variant of intangible property fraud. Some might argue that this is a petty concern, or that all honest services fraud is a form of fraud insofar as it deceptively deprives a principal of his intangible right of honest services. That argument, however, overlooks the practical point that bribery is conceptualized by enforcers, scholars, and *victims* as a distinct form of wrongdoing, one that the federal government itself has elected to

---

Ristroph, *The Curriculum of the Carceral State*, 120 COLUM. L. REV. 1631, 1707 (2020) (arguing that Kadish casebook and similar texts have inadvertently promoted a "procarceral" view of criminal law).

[55] To be clear, I am advancing a disaggregation argument and not an interpretive one. Some jurists and scholars (e.g., Justice Thomas) strongly believe the Supreme Court misinterpreted the Hobbs Act's "extortion under color of official right" language when it held that even the passive acceptance of a bribe met its definition. *See* Kate Stith, *No Entrenchment: Thomas on the Hobbs Act, the Ocasio Mess, and the Vagueness Doctrine*, 127 YALE L. J. F. 233, 238–39 (2017). One can disagree with Justice Thomas and yet still believe that "extortion under color of official right" should be statutorily separate from the rest of the Hobbs Act.

describe and punish differently. Put simply: official corruption threatens our political and economic systems, as well as the public's trust in public institutions and public actors, all the while driving up the cost of certain goods and services.[56] Fraud, by contrast, deprives us of our property and money under deceptive circumstances. It makes us mistrust markets and engage in costly self-help measures. Neither is good, and both ills, left unchecked, undermine societal welfare. But most of us intuitively understand the distinction between these ills and would want our government to treat and document them separately.[57]

Notice, too, the interaction between bundled crimes and their labels. Were one to focus solely on Section 1503's title, one would reach the incorrect conclusion that it punishes efforts to "influence" or injure jurors or court officers. But the statute covers *far* more ground than this, and the ground that it does cover is quite *different* from the type of offense one imagines when one hears the words "injure" and "juror" within the same breath. Many (most) cases charged under Section 1503 have *nothing* to do with its title. They instead involve the rather mundane acts of destroying documents and wiping data. Bad behavior to be sure, but not the same thing as threatening a juror's well-being. Thus, a bundled law increases the likelihood of mislabeling an offender's crime. If we are serious about criminal law's expressive value, we ought to care more about the formal labels we attach to our crimes.

Bundling is hardly unique to criminal law, much less white-collar crime. Regulatory agencies bundle their rules for several reasons, and one of the primary ones is to reduce the political and economic costs of promulgating separate rules.[58] Professors Nou and Stiglitz also note that bundling imposes costs on the outside agency "monitors" (trade groups, regulated entities) who are most incentivized to scrutinize and challenge the regulations they dislike. If it's less costly for the *agency* to bundle a rule, and more costly for *an outsider* to monitor it, agencies are apt to

---

[56] "Studies show positive correlations between corruption and the stagnation of economic activity. Corruption imposes a cost on economic activity because contracts are made because of influence, as opposed to being made on criteria based on quality and price. Social and political costs are also associated with corruption in terms of reduced confidence in government and, typically, an undermining of civil societies in countries where bribery is prevalent." Timothy L. Fort & Todd Haugh, *Cultural Foundations of Peace: How Business, Law, Ethics, and Music Can Provide Infrastructure for Social Harmony*, 17 BERKELEY BUS. L.J. 194, 201 (2020). On the costs of bribery generally, Susan Rose-Ackerman, *The Law and Economics of Bribery and Extortion*, 6 ANN. REV. L. & SOC. SCI 217, 218–21 (2010).

[57] Moreover, there exists good reason to employ a different approach to punishing bribery from fraud. Whereas fraud's punishment is usually tied to losses, bribery may be best deterred by tying it to the bribing party's gains. See Rose-Ackerman, *supra* note 56, at 223–24.

[58] Nou & Stiglitz, *supra* note 52, at 1203 (explaining how decreasing marginal costs "offer economies of scale and thus encourage [the] bundling" of more than one subject into a single rule).

take advantage of the bundling mechanism.[59] That's not exactly a good story, but it casts some light on why political actors will be reluctant to *un*bundle statutes that have been in existence for decades.

Criminal law's bundling is particularly difficult to defend. Indeed, it may be worse than its regulatory counterpart. The bundling we see in the federal code is primarily the result of historical accident, not strategic political calculation. Moreover, criminal law not only deprives people of their liberty but also affixes a permanent label onto an offender's conduct.[60] At its best, that label educates victims, third parties, and the general public. Excessive bundling distorts labels and widens the knowledge gap between insiders and outsiders, leaving outsiders dependent on insiders to explain the implications of a given statutory charge. We might put up with this insider/outsider gap in other contexts, but criminal law is supposed to be both a product *of* the people and a body of laws that speak directly *to* the people.[61]

Reasonable people could disagree on how far Congress should go in splitting up certain criminal statutes. It might make little sense, for example, to split up the banking fraud statute, even though that statute technically punishes two distinct crimes.[62] But splitting a nonviolent crime from a violent one ought to be a no-brainer, as should be the unbundling of statutes that broadly criminalize distinctive activities (e.g., embezzlement, fraud, bribery) directed at the same victim.

7.8 AFTER UNBUNDLING

Federal criminal code reform has a regrettable history of starts and stops.[63] An advocate of unbundling, however, can highlight its distinction from other code-reform projects and predict some degree of success. Subdividing a statute into two, three, or four separate statutory offenses implies no inherent outcome for each component's specificity or breadth. At least in theory, it neither contracts nor

---

[59] *Id.* at 1205 ("Bundling makes it more expensive for monitors to review [regulation] because each additional subject in a rule is increasingly costly to evaluate, which may lead resource-constrained agencies to skim over some provisions").

[60] JAMES B. JACOBS, THE ETERNAL CRIMINAL RECORD (2015).

[61] For an excellent discussion of the interplay between the legality principle (which encapsulates the notion that criminal law should be the product of a democratic process) and criminal code drafting, see Michael Serota, *Proportional Mens Rea and the Future of Criminal Code Reform*, 52 WAKE FOREST L. REV. 29 (2017). On the insiders/outsiders distinction generally, see Bibas, *supra* note 41.

[62] 18 USC 1344 punishes the scheme to defraud a bank (clause 1) as well as the separate act of taking or attempting to take money or property controlled by the bank through means of false statements or representations (clause 2). Loughrin v. United States, 573 U.S. 351, 356–57 (2014).

[63] *See, e.g.,* Paul H. Robinson, *Reforming the Federal Criminal Code: A Top Ten List*, 1 BUFF. CRIM L. REV. 225 (1997); Joost, *supra* note 53, at 196.

expands federal law's scope or overlap with state laws.[64] The legislator who favors broad and open-textured laws could theoretically achieve the same result, regardless of how much aggregation a code featured. This point alone might persuade the DOJ to acquiesce in and even embrace unbundling, insofar as it eventually eases the DOJ's reporting efforts, improves the accuracy of the information it disseminates, and enhances its legitimacy.

If legislators can agree on which statutes need to be unbundled and relabeled, they can use that consensus as a foundation for tackling weightier problems. Unbundling is therefore a gateway to more comprehensive code reforms, which form the subject of the next and final chapter.

---

[64] "[T]he conduct constituting a breach of [the criminal code] commonly constitutes, simultaneously, a breach of the law of the state jurisdiction within which the conduct occurs." Ronald L. Gainer, *Federal Criminal Code Reform: Past and Future*, 2 BUFF. CRIM. L. REV. 45, 53 (1998).

8

Consolidation and Grading

Chapter 7 advocates two reforms: unbundling and relabeling relevant statutes of the federal criminal code. The goal that propels these reforms – the production of more and more accurate information – remains the driving force of this chapter's remaining two proposals; consolidation and grading of white-collar statutes.[1]

A system that fails to communicate the scope and frequency of its enforcement activities sets itself up for a crisis of confidence. The reforms set forth in Chapter 7 and this chapter aim to redress that crisis. We cannot tame our lawmaking pathologies, reconfigure our enforcement priorities, or improve our data collection until we gain a better understanding of what is actually happening on the ground. Far from facilitating the production of information, our present code subverts that effort.

Chapter 7 highlighted two aspects of the code that could be reformed with comparative ease: unbundling statutes that criminalize different types of misconduct and relabeling them to more precisely reflect the behaviors the criminal justice system seeks to prohibit and condemn. This chapter explains how our system would be further improved, first by consolidating federal statutes that purport to punish nearly identical conduct (consolidation), and then offering a brief recipe for statutorily subdividing fraud, bribery, and obstruction, so that worse and less bad variations of those offenses can be differentiated and signalled by statute (grading) .

8.1 THE PROBLEM OF REDUNDANT STATUTES

Consider two relatively uncontroversial statements: Like cases ought to be treated alike, and different cases ought to be treated differently. This simple sorting

---

[1] Portions of this chapter incorporate aspects of my 2018 article, *Sorting Out White-Collar Crime*. Miriam H. Baer, *Sorting Out White-Collar Crime*, 97 Tex. L. Rev. 225 (2018).

concept continues to animate much of modern-day criminal law's practice and scholarship.[2]

Unfortunately, it does not animate the federal criminal code's language or organization. Federal statutes that define crimes like fraud, bribery, and obstruction are numerous but lack moral distinction. No fewer than five statutes criminalize domestic and federal bribery.[3] The number of statutes that prohibit fraud run into double digits.[4] And over ten statutes criminalize variations of obstruction.[5] Many of these statutes feature different maximum terms of imprisonment (five, ten, or twenty years). Until 2006, those distinctions were largely meaningless, as the Sentencing Guidelines were mandatory and controlling.[6] Even today, statutory maxima rarely play a decisive role in white-collar cases, and the distinctions themselves reflect accidents of history and ad hoc judgments more than they suggest considered analyses of wrongfulness or risk of harm.[7]

Redundant statutes undermine the criminal justice system's core concepts of legality and proportionality.[8] The surfeit of statutes covering roughly the same problem endow the prosecutor with enormous discretion to pick and choose the combination of offenses most apt to force a defendant into a guilty plea. The availability of multiple counts, meanwhile, increases the potential for overpunishment. These problems have been well described by other scholars.

My own contribution to the redundancy critique focuses on information. Overlapping, ungraded statutes confuse the public, on both the case level and the aggregate level. Only the insider can understand what it means when someone is

---

[2] Stephen Breyer, *The Federal Sentencing Guidelines and the Key Compromises upon Which They Rest*, 17 HOFSTRA L. REV. 51 (1988); Richard A. Bierschbach & Stephanos Bibas, *What's Wrong with Sentencing Equality?* 102 VA. L. REV. 76 (2016).

[3] 18 U.S.C. § 202 (federal bribery); 15 U.S.C. § 78dd-2 (foreign bribery); 18 U.S.C. § 666 (program bribery); 18 U.S.C. § 1951 (Hobbs Act bribery); and 18 U.S.C. § 1341, 1343, 1347 (honest services fraud/bribery).

[4] For examples of federal fraud statutes, see 15 U.S.C. § 78j (2012) (securities fraud); 18 U.S.C. § 1341 (2012) (mail fraud); 18 U.S.C. § 1343 (2012) (wire fraud); 18 U.S.C. § 1344 (2012) (bank fraud); 18 U.S.C. § 1347 (2012) (health-care fraud); 18 U.S.C. § 1348 (2012) (securities fraud); and 17 C.F.R. § 240.10b-5 (2018) (securities fraud).

[5] 18 U.S.C. § 1503; 18 U.S.C. § 1505; 18 U.S.C. § 1512 and more. For criticism, see Julie R. O'Sullivan, *The Federal Criminal Code Is a Disgrace: Obstruction Statutes as a Case Study*, 96 J. CRIM. L. & CRIMINOLOGY 643, 648–50 (2006).

[6] *See* U.S. v. Booker, 543 U.S. 220 (2005). On Booker's effect on white-collar sentencing, see Peter J. Henning, *White Collar Crime Sentences after Booker: Was the Sentencing of Bernie Ebbers Too Harsh?* 37 MCGEORGE L. REV. 757, 757–58, 761–63 (2006); Robert J. Conrad & Katy L. Clements, *The Vanishing Criminal Jury Trial: From Trial Judges to Sentencing Judges*, 86 GEO. WASH. L. REV. 99, 128–36 (2018).

[7] Frank O. Bowman III, *Pour Encourager les Autres? The Curious History and Distressing Implications of the Criminal Provisions of the Sarbanes-Oxley Act and the Sentencing Guidelines Amendments That Followed*, 1 OHIO ST J. CRIM. L. 373, 375–76 (2004).

[8] "[F]ederal and state codes alike are filled with overlapping crimes, such that a single criminal incident typically violates a half dozen or more prohibitions." William J. Stuntz, *The Pathological Politics of Criminal Law*, 100 MICH. L. REV. 505, 507 (2001).

charged in four or five counts of similar sounding offenses, and not even the insider can determine the scope and frequency of the government's white-collar enforcement activities over a longer period of time. Redundancy thus harms the public by depriving it of valuable information. Over the long run, that information loss harms the government's enforcement institutions as well.

8.2 A HYPOTHETICAL EXAMPLE

Imagine three individuals, all of whom adopt the same scheme, with the same state of mind to commit a fraud on the same category of victims. Katya uses the mails to defraud someone of $50,000. Marley engages in an identical scheme but does so using emails and interstate wires. Rose executes the same scheme but uses *both* the mails and interstate wires to carry out her scheme.

Katya will be charged with mail fraud under 18 U.S.C. § 1341. Marley, with wire fraud, pursuant to 18 U.S.C. § 1343. Rose can be charged under both statutes. The statutory maximum term of imprisonment for either is usually twenty years' imprisonment. Thus, were Katya and Marley celebrities or well-known politicians, one might well expect to hear on the evening news that they are "facing" twenty years' imprisonment (more, if the government charges each mailing or use of the wires is charged as a separate count). Even though Rose will never receive a consecutive sentence, one might also say she nevertheless faces a maximum sentence of forty years' imprisonment.[9]

The good news is that for sentencing purposes, all three offenders will be punished under the same Sentencing Guideline, Section 2B1.1.[10] The Sentencing Guidelines (rightly) make no moral distinction between mail fraud and wire fraud. And they treat the scheme accomplished in five mailings no differently than the same scheme accomplished in one.[11] The Guidelines were in fact promulgated with an eye toward eliminating arbitrary decisions to charge one statute (mail) over the other (health care) or to charge a crime five counts (to reflect five mailings) or just one (to reflect the overall scheme).[12] And, in our modern world, knowing nothing else about the underlying scheme, no reasonable person

[9] For more on this, see Chapter 3. *See also* Bowman, *supra* note 7, at 384 ("[B]efore the advent of the Federal Sentencing Guidelines, the possible sentence faced by a federal economic crime offender ran from a minimum of probation to a maximum term of imprisonment calculated by adding up the statutory maximum sentences for all counts of conviction." Post-Booker, "The theoretical upper limit on a defendant's sentence remains the sum of the statutory maxima for all counts of conviction").

[10] The original Guidelines bifurcated economic crimes into a guideline for thefts and embezzlement (2B1.1) and a separate guideline for frauds (2F1.1). Eventually, the Sentencing Commission merged the two. *See* Bowman, *supra* note 7, at 386, 388–89.

[11] USSC §2B1.1.

[12] "[T]he true limit on a fraud defendant's sentence had virtually nothing to do with the ostensible five-year statutory maximum but was determined by the discretionary prosecutorial choice of how many counts to charge." Bowman, *supra* note 7, at 384.

can contend defend treating a mail fraud differently than a wire fraud, or either of those two differently from a securities or health care fraud. There *is* no inherent distinction in terms of moral culpability, risk, or harm. The use of the mails or wires is simply a jurisdictional trigger, something that allows the federal government to constitutionally prosecute a fraud because of its interaction with interstate commerce.[13]

Justice Thomas once remarked, "The Federal Criminal Code is replete with provisions that criminalize overlapping conduct."[14] That may be true, but it does not make for good public policy. It is a curious state of affairs that our sentencing system consolidates near-identical[15] offenses under a single, umbrella-like guideline such as section 2B1.1 while our statutory code assiduously preserves meaningless jurisdictional distinctions that have steadily multiplied since the nation's founding.[16] There is no good reason for this dichotomous treatment, except that the decades reformers spent trying to fix the federal criminal code failed, giving birth to a guidelines system instead.[17]

---

[13] To some, this pragmatic but expansive conception of fraud triggers federalism concerns. *See, e. g.*, United States v. Mikell, 163 F. Supp. 2d 720, 729 (E.D. Mich. 2001) ("the purpose of the mail fraud legislation is to protect the postal agency, not to prevent frauds in general, a task within the province of state law"); United States v. Turner, 573 F. Supp. 1104, 1106 (D.D.C. 1983) ("The manifest purpose of the mail fraud statute is to protect the post office from being used in the execution of frauds"). *But see* United States v. Louisiana Pac. Corp., 908 F. Supp. 835, 847 (D. Colo. 1995) ("the purpose of the mail fraud statute is *to protect the public* from being defrauded through scheme or artifice") (emphasis added).

[14] Pasquantino v. United States, 544 U.S. 349, 359 n.4 (2005).

[15] "The elements of mail fraud and wire fraud are essentially identical: the government must show (1) a scheme to defraud, (2) the use of either the mail or wire, radio, or television to further the scheme, and (3) the specific intent to defraud." United States v. Diamond, 851 F. App'x 14, 15 (9th Cir. 2021). "Mail and wire fraud are analytically identical save for the method of execution." United States v. Bradley, 644 F.3d 1213, 1238 (11th Cir. 2011). "[C]ourts typically interpret the mail and wire fraud statutes the same way, as their language is largely identical." United States v. Miller, 953 F.3d 1095, 1102 (9th Cir. 2020), *cert. denied*, 141 S. Ct. 1085 (2021).

[16] "[W]hile Congress had created a variety of fraud statutes, with miscellaneous sentencing provisions, the Commission imposed the same sentencing structure on all offenses involving fraud or deceit and applied its own calculus of aggravating factors to determine the specific sentence to be applied." Gerard Lynch, *Towards a Model Penal Code, Second (Federal?): The Challenge of the Special Part*, 2 BUFF. CRIM. L. REV. 297, 316 (1998) (describing the creation of Sentencing Guidelines). For a decade-old argument in favor of federal code consolidation (albeit a different framework from the one explored here), see Edwin Meese III, *Principles for Revising the Criminal Code*, HERITAGE FOUND. (Dec. 13, 2011), www.heritage.org/testi mony/principles-revising-the-criminal-code [https://perma.cc/VUN7-XWGU].

[17] For very helpful background regarding pre-guidelines sentencing and the guidelines' evolution, see Frank O. Bowman III, *The Failure of the Federal Sentencing Guidelines: A Structural Analysis*, 105 COLUM. L. REV. 1315, 1321–26 (2005). For a discussion of white-collar sentencing's evolution under the guidelines, see Mark W. Bennett, Justin D. Levinson, & Koichi Hioki, *Judging Federal White-Collar Fraud Sentencing: An Empirical Study Revealing the Need for Further Reform*, 102 IOWA L. REV. 939, 943 (2017).

To be fair, criminal defense organizations have far more to worry about than the fact that federal code contains too many fraud statutes. From the perspective of Katya, Marley, or Rose, a lack of consolidation in the federal criminal code is the least of their worries. Their core concerns revolve around the formal sanctions they can expect to receive at sentencing and any collateral effects those sanctions pose for them and their families.

Over the long run, however, the federal criminal code's redundancy generates real harms. It sows confusion – even among lawyers and professional pundits – and creates more than just a touch of unfair pressure.[18] In those instances where a prosecutor can charge multiple fraud statutes for the same scheme, she creates a well-known piling-on effect. The offender who can be charged in one or two counts may suddenly learn that she has been charged in six or seven. If she is a celebrity, politician, or well-known business executive, the multicount indictment's effect becomes amplified. We hear breathless claims on television and in social media that X has been charged in YY counts! And is facing ZZZ years in prison![19] Never mind the fact that the guidelines will collapse most of those counts into a single guideline provision if they all stem from the same scheme or event. Such a "charge stacking" phenomenon creates unwarranted notoriety, fear, and a desire to cave quickly to the government's demands.[20] It also induces an unhealthy degree of schadenfreude in those who hope for an offender's comeuppance.[21] Indeed, it bolsters expectations unreasonably and unrealistically, causing one set of critics to decry the government's *over*criminalization of a humdrum case (usually at the charging stage) and then just as lustily accuse the government of *under*enforcement when the offender is sentenced.

Imagine instead if we consolidated all of our various fraud statutes into a single statute with a large appendix[22] that catalogued the methods by which a fraud scheme triggered federal jurisdiction. Imagine as well if we included a rule that

---

[18] Moreover, it transfers power from the legislature to the prosecutor. "When a criminal code has many overlapping offenses, it creates discretion and power in prosecutors to decide which of the different offenses will be charged and punished, or whether they should all be." Paul Robinson, *The Rise and Fall and Resurrection of American Criminal Codes*, 53 U. LOUISVILLE L. REV. 173, 176 (2015).

[19] *See* discussion in Chapter 3.

[20] Michael L. Siegel & Christopher Slobogin, *Prosecuting Martha: Federal Prosecutorial Power and the Need for a Law of Counts*, 109 PENN. ST. L. REV. 1107 (2005).

[21] For a case study in such schadenfreude, readers should consider Colleen Eren's insightful account of Bernie Madoff's sentencing. According to Eren, much of what drove both the tabloid and mainstream media's reporting was a perceived desire, among consumers and the general public, for Madoff's social comeuppance. COLLEEN P. EREN, BERNIE MADOFF AND THE CRISIS: THE PUBLIC TRIAL OF CAPITALISM 90–101, 100 (2017) (including a remark of *London Times* reporter that the story was "emotionally satisfying for readers" because "the bad guy gets his comeuppance and has to go live in a cell with serial killers").

[22] To avoid several of the criticisms discussed in Chapter 4, I am assuming this appendix would be legislatively enacted and updated, as needed, by Congress.

forbade judges from sentencing defendants to consecutive terms under multiple charges if the charges merely represented different appendix provisions relating to an identical scheme. Under our hypothetical, Rose (who carried out her scheme by using the mails and wires) would face the same sentence as Katya and Marley, who engaged in near-identical conduct. That is *already* what occurs under the Sentencing Guidelines, but now the rest of the world, and not just insiders familiar with federal sentencing practices, would comprehend this fact as well. More importantly, Rose would be freed of both the psychological and reputational costs of facing multiple counts instead of just one.

8.3 CONSOLIDATION AND CODING

As we saw in Chapters 2 and 7, the proliferation of similar-conduct statutes increases the likelihood of coding error. Recall how difficult it is to figure out how many white-collar crime offenders are arrested, prosecuted, and convicted each year. Some of the difficulty is attributable to how the government's enforcement institutions collect and track information. When systems fail to speak to each other, their compatibility and interoperability suffer. But some of the information loss arises from the confusing overlap of so many similar offenses. The more offenses there are, the greater the possibility for error caused by miscoding or inconsistently coding one or more offenses.

Consolidation mitigates the potential for such error. If there is just *one* fraud statute, *one* bribery statute, and *one* obstruction statute, government agencies can better standardize the reporting process for white-collar crime. They can decide, for example, whether bribery fits within the government's accepted definition of a white-collar offense. (I would argue that it does.) They can decide whether all obstruction cases should be denominated white-collar offenses or only those obstruction cases whose underlying investigations pertain to white-collar crime. (I could be persuaded either way.) Finally, they can do this in a way that provides various stakeholders the opportunity for advance notice and comment.

Scholars have long recognized the importance of consolidation as a means of curbing excess prosecutorial discretion and reducing the risk of excessive punishment.[23] This chapter reveals an additional benefit of consolidation, which is its impact on the government's ability to collect and disseminate information.

8.4 CONSOLIDATION AND LAWMAKING

Because the federal code is already overrun with multiple fraud, bribery, and obstruction statutes, it currently places no constraint on symbolic and reactive

---

[23] *See* John F Stinneford, *Dividing Crime, Multiplying Punishments*, 48 UC Davis. L. Rev. 1955 (2015) (about punishment); Robinson, *supra* note 18 (with respect to prosecutorial power).

lawmaking.[24] The marginal political cost of throwing another fraud, bribery, or obstruction statute into the mix is negligible. Consolidation is therefore valuable insofar as it raises both the visibility and political costs of enacting redundant statutes.

Consider the "new" securities fraud statute, which Congress enacted in response to the Financial Crisis.[25] Commentators initially regarded it as Congress's largely symbolic effort to demonstrate a "get-tough" mindset in the wake of the crisis and the revelation that Bernard Madoff had perpetrated a billion-dollar Ponzi scheme. Soon, however, the statute took on an unexpected life of its own, as discussed in Chapter 4's account of insider trading.

Although the new statute, codified at 18 U.S.C. §1348, featured a higher statutory maximum than Section 10(B) of the 1934 Securities Exchange Act, crimes charged under *both* statutes fell within the same Sentencing Guideline.[18] So, if one was under the impression that charging a defendant under the new law would result in a longer sentence, that impression was inaccurate. Indeed, given that most securities fraud cases can simultaneously be charged as wire fraud cases, the "old" statute's statutory maximum (ten years' imprisonment) never posed much of a problem for the offenders who were guilty of promulgating massive schemes. Madoff, one of the worst fraudsters in history was duly sentenced to 150 years' imprisonment under the *old* securities fraud regime (in multiple counts, of course).[26] The government didn't need a more punitive statute to place Madoff in jail for the remainder of his life.

We shouldn't oversell the ease or benefits of consolidation. As Stuart Green and Judge Lynch have observed in disparate contexts, there are times when legislatures can overdo consolidation, erasing valid moral distinctions and effectively placing too much power back in the hands of either judges or prosecutors.[27] *Good* consolidation is a complex endeavor. By aggregating numerous related statutes into a single "family level" offense, Congress would have to determine, at a minimum:

- (1) which statutes fall within the designated family;
- (2) the elements of this new family statute;
- (3) the statutory punishment range for the new statute; and

---

[24] Paul Robinson observes the same dynamic for "degraded" state codes. *See* Robinson, *supra* note 18.

[25] *See* discussion in Chapter 4.

[26] *See* EREN, *supra* note 21, at 120 (explaining that Madoff's sentencing judge arrived at the 150-year sentence "through the summation of the statutory maximum sentence for all eleven counts" with which he was charged). *See also* Government's Sentencing Memorandum at 1, United States v. Madoff. 626 F. Supp. 2d 420 (S.D.N.Y. 2009) (No. 09 Cr. 213 (DC)), 2009 WL 1899501; Peter J. Henning, *The Limits of Bigger Penalties in Fighting Financial Crime*, N.Y. TIMES (Dec. 12, 2011), http://dealbook.nytimes.com/2011/12/12/the-limits-of-bigger-penalties-in-fighting-financial-crime.

[27] STUART GREEN, THIRTEEN WAYS TO STEAL A BICYCLE: THEFT LAW IN THE INFORMATION AGE (2012) 4 ("the theft law reformers threw out the baby with the bathwater") and 28–33 (citing problems caused by the excessive consolidation of theft laws).

- (4) the various activities (use of the mails, wires, etc.) that would trigger federal jurisdiction, which could be collected and publicized in an attached appendix.

This would present a difficult challenge in any environment. Most will agree, however, that it will be even more challenging in the highly polarized atmosphere that we presently live under. But Congress need not begin from scratch – indeed, we would want to preserve as much of our court-made law as possible. We could do this by taking either the mail or wire fraud statute's language as the basic template for the consolidated statute and replace all other fraud statutes with a comprehensive jurisdictional appendix. One could imagine a similar process for bribery, obstruction, and other crimes. The aim – at least in the beginning – would be to craft a punishment-neutral consolidation of the federal code's white-collar provisions. Individuals currently liable for mail, wire, or health fraud, for example, would be just as liable (or just as innocent) under the new, consolidated code.

Concededly, even a good faith effort might fall short of the mark and produce partial consolidation, because, for example, certain crimes are deemed so "different" that lawmakers decide they cannot lump them within the same family. Congress might also agree on fraud's consolidation but not bribery's or vice versa. And finally, it is also possible that even if Congress achieved full consolidation for all three offenses *now*, its members might eventually upend this progress in the future. These are all possibilities, but they hardly justify the status quo.

8.5 GRADATION: THE HEAVIER LIFT

Once we consolidate our white-collar statutes by removing the distinctions that are morally meaningless (i.e., mail versus wire fraud), we can then pivot to placing the dividing lines that *should* matter. That is, we can start considering the features of fraud, bribery, and obstruction that make some offenses invariably worse or less condemnable than other similar offenses. Those familiar with state codes are also familiar with the subject of *grading*, or as Herbert Packer described it, "the determination of the comparative severity of punishment for different but related offenses."[28] Within each family of white-collar offenses one can make principled distinctions between worse and less condemnable versions of wrongdoing. For those who are visually inclined, the aim here is to make the federal code less horizontal in its orientation and more vertical.

As Chapter 3 pointed out, our federal criminal justice system shies away from grading white-collar offenses. There is no rigorous statutory rubric for first, second, and third degree.[29] To the extent our federal system sorts or differentiates

---

[28] HERBERT L. PACKER, THE LIMITS OF THE CRIMINAL SANCTION 108 (1968).
[29] *See generally* Chapter 3. I have introduced these concerns previously in my article, *Sorting Out White-Collar Crime*, Baer, *supra* note 1, at 245–46.

wrongdoing, it reserves the bulk of this activity for the sentencing stage, at least where white-collar crimes are concerned. As a result, the sorting of offenses becomes hopelessly intertwined with the sorting of individual *offenders*. This flattened dynamic, in turn, causes us to miss out on several benefits. First, our code fails to convey the factors that our society considers most relevant in distinguishing similar offenses. If a legislative code is supposed to express a community's values, it ought to say something about the major factors that separate the worst frauds from the merely bad ones. And it can also tell us whether "worst" means "most dangerous" or something closer to "most condemnable."

Second, apart from what the finished product conveys to its audience, we also lost the benefits of engaging a process of constructing a code and its relevant subdivisions. When a legislature punts that hard work to an agency such as the Sentencing Commission, it relinquishes the opportunity to debate key questions of code design as they relate to white-collar crime.

Let's return to our three offenders, Katya, Marley, and Rose. Instead of committing an identical harm, imagine they commit quite different offenses, but are all charged under the same all-purpose fraud statute. (Assume as well that they all use interstate wires to carry out their schemes, thereby triggering federal jurisdiction.)

Katya defrauds her corporate employer, who has placed enormous pressure on its workplace of late, threatening to summarily fire all salespeople who fall within the bottom 10 percent in terms of producing new business. To preserve her job and place herself in line for a bonus and promotion, Katya overstates her sales figures for three years in a row, thereby causing her employer to pay her excess and unearned commissions of $225,000.

Marley, who holds a relatively safe job as an administrator at a nursing home, causes five of its elderly residents to pay her a total of $125,000, which they believe will be used for the nursing home's senior center but that Marley instead plans to use to pay for her new car and a fancy vacation.

Rose, who works for an auditing firm, forwards a fraudulent expense report to one of her colleagues, which ultimately plays a role in covering up a major accounting fraud at one of their client companies. Although Rose is technically unaware of the document's falsehoods, there is evidence she purposely avoided scrutinizing it and checking its figures, even though she was aware of her obligation to check its accuracy. The client company's aggregate accounting fraud amounts to $30,000,000.

And let's add a fourth offender to the mix: Natalie devises a scheme to sell equity investments in a nonexistent Siberian pipeline. She offers a $5,000,000 investment to Carl, who, unbeknownst to her, is an undercover FBI agent.

How should the law treat these offenses and offenders? At the lawmaking stage, the question boils down to an abstract debate over the appropriate criterion one should use for ordering and punishing a range of behaviors. It reflects a search for the appropriate feature (or, as we shall see, features) that makes one variation of an offense more dangerous or deserving of punishment than the others.[30] For the lawmakers attempting to grade a crime like fraud or bribery, the operative question is, which factors should predominate?[31]

We could grade offenses according to a culpable offender's *state of mind*, or *mens rea*; according to the *actual harm* she has caused; or according to the *risks* she has created and unjustifiably imposed on others. This choice matters quite a bit. It makes certain aspects of the crime far more important – and arguably, salient – than others, and it results in substantially different ordinal outcomes. Grading brings moves these issues to the foreground. Legislative grading, in turn, paves the way for a fruitful conversation about which of these factors should take precedence.[32]

8.6 GRADING ACCORDING TO *MENS REA*: A GENERAL PRIMER

For the first-year law student, statutory gradation and *mens rea* are tightly inter-twined.[33] The introductory criminal law course's focus on homicide introduces the student to a veritable statutory ladder of hierarchical offenses.[34] The highest degreed offense, first-degree murder, is often defined by a particular state of mind. In some states, it is the willful, deliberate, and premeditated murder that elevates its wrong-fulness from the merely purposeful murder. In others, the "purposeful" killing does the trick. Although courts have disagreed on what the willful-premeditated-deliber-ate formula means, most commentators agree that it reflects something more than an instantaneous intention to kill. Instead, it suggests "time for reflection," and perhaps planning.[35]

For those who subscribe to a deontological, retributivist theory of punishment, the state of mind is enormously important.[36] Dying at the hands of an evil sociopath who enjoys torturing and strangling his victims is morally different (and more

---

[30] Concededly, "dangerousness" and "desert" are distinct concepts.

[31] As Judge Lynch has observed, "the grading of offenses within a penal code depends on the sentencing philosophy of its drafters." Lynch, *supra* note 16, at 308.

[32] "Where the consequences are less severe, but where grading considerations are nevertheless made part of the definitions of offenses, we have traditionally given them less intense scrutiny, but the issues remain visible for statutory drafting choices. But where the grading issues have been relegated to the black hole of broad and unreviewable judicial sentencing discretion, we have chosen not to think about the underlying issues of principle very much at all." Lynch, *supra* note 16, at 306.

[33] PACKER, *supra* note 28, at 108 (describing statutory distinctions that "turn entirely upon the ascription of some sort of *mens rea* to the actor"). As Packer points out, *mens rea* issues fall into two categories: those that arise in regard to whether conduct or a result should be criminalized at all, those that arise in regard to grading. *Id. See also* Michael Serota, *Proportional* Mens Rea *and the Future of Criminal Code Reform*, 52 WAKE FOREST L. REV. 1201 (2017).

[34] Victor Tadros, *The Homicide Ladder*, 69 MOD. L. REV. 601 (2006).

[35] Baer, *supra* note 1 (citing authorities).

[36] "To a deontologist, the way in which a loss is inflicted is hugely important." Leo Katz, *Incommensurable Choices and the Problem of Moral Ignorance*, 146 U. PA. L. REV. 1465, 1474 (1998). *See also* Serota, *supra* note 33.

deserving of punishment) than dying at the hands of a negligent driver in a traffic accident. The outcome may be the same, but the normative valence is quite different.

Fortuitously, gradation by *mens rea also* meets the interests of deterrence theorists.[37] Deterrence hinges on three variables: the likelihood of punishment, the government's sanction (and the speed with which it is levied), and the offender's expected gain. People who intentionally harm others arguably derive greater gain from their behavior and often take greater pains to cover it up.[38] Thus, deterrence theory easily justifies the higher sanction for the purposeful offender. If the offender is inclined to cover her tracks (and therefore reduce the probabilities of detection and punishment), the government can respond by increasing the corresponding sanction. It can also correspond by increasing the probability of detection through enhanced enforcement, but that enhancement may be insufficient or excessively costly. Moreover, the higher sanction also cues enforcement personnel to devote their scarce resources to the particular offense.

Thus, regardless of the theory of punishment, be it based in deterrence or retributive theory, it justifies the adoption of a framework that punishes intentional acts more harshly than unintentional ones.[39] And if those intentional acts are particularly well-thought-out and "premeditated," the state may take the extra step of singling out that category for special treatment. It can do this on the front end, through statutory grading, or on the back end, through sentencing enhancements. The point is that if enough of us think "premeditation" should matter, there is an argument for finding the language that will capture that concept and duly distinguish premeditated acts from merely intentional acts.

The curious thing about premeditation is that it remains embedded in homicide law. Most would agree with the proposition that, in most instances, a meticulously planned murder is more chilling and therefore deserving of greater punishment than the purely impulsive one.[40] This intuition has never been formally carried over, however, to crimes outside the homicide context, even though premeditation

---

[37] On the different theories and justifications for punishment, see Jack Boeglin & Zachary Shapiro, A *Theory of Differential Punishment*, 70 VAND. L. REV. 1499, 1505–21 (2017) (describing the retributive, deterrence-based, rehabilitative, and – expressive theories of punishment).

[38] "Because it is a planned activity, often planned by people who went to the very best schools and have extensive resources at their disposal, it can be highly complex in its design, and thus difficult to detect and demonstrate." Edward Rubin, *The Citizen Lawyer and the Administrative State*, 50 WM. & MARY L. REV. 1335, 1355 (2009) (explaining need for specialized agencies to police crimes such as securities fraud).

[39] This distinction does not address the problem that arises when two equally "intentional" acts produce widely differing degrees of harm and therefore divergent sentences.

[40] A scholar writes of a notable Canadian fraud offender, "It was not a crime of passion or one committed on impulse. Instead, it was the result of careful planning and premeditation which allowed Coffin to receive money from the government from 1997 to 2002 for an advertising campaign he never executed." Zvi D. Gabbay, *Exploring the Limits of the Restorative Justice*

potentially could play a useful role in subdividing white-collar offenses of fraud, bribery, or obstruction.[41] Some might conclude that this reluctance to employ a premeditation (or impulse) concept reflects the limits of its usage. After all, if nearly all fraud cases involve "impulse" (or nearly all fraud cases involve "premeditation"), the term isn't doing too much in terms of sorting.

On the other hand, the lack of premeditation as a statutory sorting concept may instead reflect Congress's unwillingness to employ *any* real sorting devices in its fraud statutes, other than the jurisdictional triggers that are conceptually meaningless. Partially supporting this point is the fact that the Sentencing Guidelines do, in some way, analyze the fraudster's level of planning. The "sophisticated means" enhancement, although not particularly exacting, adds two levels to an offender's overall offense level whenever his participation in the scheme involves particularly "sophisticated means."[42] To the extent premeditated frauds are more likely to be "sophisticated" while impulsive ones are not, one can take comfort in this guidelines provision, even though a sentencing provision functions far differently from a statutory grade. We also know judges take these considerations into account when they impose sentences shorter and less punitive than called for by the guidelines. If the distinction between premeditation and impulse is a concept that silently affects *some* or *many* sentencings, it ought to be enshrined in statutory law so that it is maximally and openly available to *all* offenders.

The same could be said of the "provocation" concept. Many states further subdivide the intentional killing by reducing punishment for the intentional killing upon "provocation," such as under the heat of passion (the older formulation) or an extreme mental or emotional disturbance (the Model Penal Code's [MPC's] variant). Each of these implies a sudden break with convention, and often an impulsive killing. The killing might be "purposeful," as that term is legally defined, but the term further implies an outcome that would not have occurred had the offender had the time to cool off or emerge from her disturbance.

As the foregoing discussion demonstrates, *mens rea* can effectively divide and subdivide offenses in a manner that forces prosecutors to prove certain facts to a jury.[43] Notice, in this graded world of homicide, courts still exercise the power to

---

Paradigm: Restorative Justice and White-Collar Crime, 8 Cardozo J. Conflict Resol. 421 (2007).

[41] For an interesting proposal for a "general mitigation" defense that would expand provocation's framework to crimes generally, see Paul H. Robinson, *Mitigations: The Forgotten Side of the Proportionality Principle,* 57 Harv. J. Legis. 219, 263–65 (2020) (setting forth framework).

[42] U.S. Sent'g Guidelines Manual § 2B1.1(b)(10)(C) (U.S. Sent'g Comm'n 2018); Miriam H. Baer, *Unsophisticated Sentencing,* 61 Wayne L. Rev. 61, 65–67 (2015).

[43] Kenneth W. Simons, *The Willful Blindness Doctrine: Justifiable in Principle, Problematic in Practice,* 53 Ariz. St. L.J. 655, 676 (2021) ("for some crimes, perhaps the legislature should grade degrees of the offense according to mens rea, creating an aggravated degree of the crime when a defendant acts with knowledge and a lesser degree when he or she acts only with recklessness").

examine *additional* factors at sentencing, including the defendant's character and criminal history. But when *mens rea* is written into the statute itself, it must be proven beyond a reasonable doubt. And for the most part, mental states that occupy the upper rungs of the hierarchy are more difficult to prove than mental states on the lower rungs.

Finally, statutory grading is salutary because it enables the efficient collection and communication of relevant information. If I want to know how many murders were charged, convicted, and punished each year relative to unintentional killings, it is relatively easy to figure that out under the graded system. I just compare the number of crimes charged under Category A with Category B. (To be sure, there are numerous ways the government can manipulate this figure, but manipulation only goes so far.) Because grading produces blunter and thicker categories, it's categories become easier to track and easier to comprehend.[44] The graded system also performs an important service insofar as it compels the legislature (and later, the judiciary) to debate the relevance and meaning of the various graded factors. There is something healthy and valuable to be gained from asking – and answering – why it is so many of us judge an unintentional killing differently from the purposeful one.

8.7 GRADING FRAUD BY *MENS REA*

Now let's return to our four offenders. Recall, Marley stole $125,000 from the residents of a nursing home; Katya defrauded her employer of $125,000 in commissions; Rose forwarded and vouched for a fraudulent document that helped cover a portion of a client's $30,000,000 fraud; and hapless Natalie unsuccessfully attempted to perpetrate a $5,000,000 swindle on an undercover FBI agent. How helpful would it be to use *mens rea* as a device for "grading" their fraud offenses? Would a graduated fraud rubric based solely on *mens rea* appropriately distinguish Marley, Katya, Rose, and Natalie's offenses? Would it deliver a ranking that reflects (1) their respective dangerousness, or (2) the moral wrongfulness of their conduct?

From the outset, one might reflexively answer that *mens rea* is an unhelpful marker in this instance because fraud, by definition, is always intentional. After all, that's what we mean when we say fraud is a specific intent crime. Thus, although it is entirely reasonable to use *mens rea* to separate intentional and unintentional killings, it offers no utility as a grading device in the fraud context.

Let me offer two reasons why this might not be the case. *First*, even in regard to homicide, we still subdivide intentional killings. As noted earlier, some state codes elevate the more reflective or wanton killings from the merely purposeful ones. At

---

[44] On the limits of categorization and mental comprehension and memory, see generally George A. Miller, *The Magical Number Seven, Plus or Minus Two: Some Limits on Our Capacity for Processing Information*, 63 PSYCH. REV. 81 (1956).

the other end of the spectrum, many states mitigate the impulsive (and usually provoked or emotionally disturbed) killings from the more deliberative ones. Not all intentional killings are the same.

Second, thanks to the courts' increasingly expansive interpretations of fraud offenses, criminal fraud no longer functions as a single *mens rea* offense. Courts originally interpreted the mail and wire fraud statutes (and later, the securities fraud statute that was patterned off of them) to require a "specific intent to defraud."[45] Over time, however, the federal courts loosened this element. Some held that prosecutors could demonstrate the specific intent to defraud by relying on a defendant's reckless indifference as to the accuracy of her statements. Others took the analysis a step further by concluding that the recklessly false statement was sufficient to prove criminal fraud.

Some might say that "reckless fraud" is just a misnomer. Those that subscribe to this view might argue that courts should rectify this mistake by instructing juries to find a specific intent to defraud, through direct or indirect evidence, and leave the words "reckless" and "deliberate indifference" out of the jury charge altogether. That's fine if we are willing to rely on a single fraud statute. But we might want to create a criminal statute that embraces and punishes certain "reckless frauds." Just because we think a "reckless fraud" is different from an intentional one doesn't mean we should ignore it.

If we wanted to grade fraud by *mens rea*, we might implement an aggravated offense for those whose frauds that exhibited significant degree of planning (since advance planning tells us something about someone's state of mind). We might treat impulsive frauds with a bit less opprobrium. And finally, we might want to treat "reckless" frauds differently from intentional ones. Thus, the rubric might look like:

First-degree fraud – A purposeful and premeditated scheme

Second-degree fraud – An impulsive and nonpremeditated scheme

Third-degree fraud – Knowing facilitation of another's scheme; reckless indifference to the truth

Assume we stick with this very streamlined rubric. For three of our four offenders, the sorting is straightforward. Marley, who took money from elderly residents of a nursing home probably receives first-degree treatment, as she devised a purposeful and premeditated scheme. Katya, whose offense against her employer unfolded over a period of years, might also be lumped in the same category as Marley, although it might be interesting if we could imagine a partial "provocation" for employees who act upon their employers' pressure. (I admit such a defense is unlikely to ever be embraced.) Rose, who apparently acted impulsively and was arguably reckless in her handling of information (although some may disagree on that characterization)

---

[45] For an overview of cases and their inconsistent treatment, see Samuel Buell, *What Is Securities Fraud?* 61 DUKE L.J. 511 (2011).

might enjoy the benefit of a third-degree or perhaps second-degree charge, notwithstanding her position and the amount of money involved.

Notice, however, that the rubric doesn't help us with Natalie's case. Recall, Natalie ineptly devised a scheme to defraud investors of $5,000,000 in a nonexistent pipeline. The scheme was outlandish and bound to fail; the first person Natalie approached happened to be an undercover FBI agent. Some might say implausible schemes like these should simply be decriminalized. I am not so sure. For now, I can accept the argument that an implausible fraud is problematic enough to warrant the criminal justice system's intervention.

I am, however, interested in a different question: Does the implausible fraud's features differentiate it enough to warrant different statutory treatment under a criminal code? Should we signal to enforcers and putative criminals that we care about this type of crime *less* than we care about its more plausible version? Wouldn't we be better off if we designed our code in such a way that we would be able to quickly identify how many of a given year's arrests and convictions stemmed from wholly "implausible" fraud schemes and how many were of the more serious crime?

If our grading rubric relies solely on *mens rea*, Natalie's scheme will be treated no differently from Marley's (at least as a charging matter; a judge still might sentence Natalie to a lesser punishment). If Natalie expended sufficient time considering and planning her Siberian pipeline scheme, she meets the rubric's definition of first-degree fraud since her plan clearly was "premeditated." And even though it was impossible for her to complete her transaction with her "victim," her mental state and "substantial step" more than established that she would have moved forward with this scheme, but for the fortuity of being apprehended by a federal officer. Accordingly, we might double down on Natalie's classification as a first-degree fraudster. Indeed, this is how the MPC treats Natalie's case; it explicitly disregards impossibility and declares attempt to be the equivalent of completed offenses in all but the most serious capital offenses.

At the end of the day, it is difficult to deny the fact that Natalie created no real risk of harm to anyone. Our intuitions tell us that Natalie falls in a different category than Marley and is probably less dangerous than Katya or Rose. That seems to be the problem with grading solely by *mens rea*: it places the hapless but intentional fraudster in a category to which she does not belong.

8.8 GRADING FRAUD BY HARM AND RISK

Instead of focusing on the offender's *mens rea*, we could instead grade fraud offenses according to the actual harm they cause, the risk of harm they impose, or some combination of the two. These are the factors that several state codes employ to grade various property crimes.

Gradation adjudged by degree of harm is defensible for two reasons. First, the "harm" factor may reflect a more dangerous crime. If it does, then it's one for which we wish to expend greater resources to prevent and deter. A first-degree label is valuable because it speaks to *two* audiences at the same time: the putative wrong-doers we wish to deter, and the law enforcement community tasked with allocating limited resources. At the same time, the degree of harm may also tell us which crimes are more morally condemnable and therefore deserving of the opprobrium and additional time in prison that accompany the first-degree category.

Thus, it is not surprising that many state larceny and fraud statutes are demarcated by the amounts of money involved. It's easy enough to declare a $5,000 or $10,000 fraud a "petty" or low-degree fraud, and a $5,000,000 fraud a more serious offense. However, actual loss amounts can generate incongruous results. Moreover, potential loss amounts can add fuel to the fire when those loss amounts represent very little risk. And finally, a grading rubric that features little more than mechanical dollar amounts (e.g., first-degree fraud for anything over $10,000,000; second-degree fraud for anything between $1,000,000 and $9,999,999, and so forth) exemplifies the problems that arise when a legislature resorts to using arbitrary and easily manipu-lated distinctions to grade crimes. Just like the "sentencing cliffs" that plague the Sentencing Commission's fraud loss table, a state code's loss-dominated code can create bumpy distortions in liability and punishment.[46]

But let's return to our hypothetical. If we were to judge the four offenders solely by the aggregate loss they have caused, Rose comes out on top. She may not have intended her accounting firm's client to defraud investors of $30,000,000, but she knowingly participated in its fraud. Moreover, even though she was "technically unaware" of the expense report's falsity, she apparently took pains *not* to learn of those falsehoods. Thus, one might say she exhibited willful blindness as to the document's falsehoods. Were Rose to take her case to court, a judge would likely instruct a jury that Rose's "specific intent to defraud" could be proven by her reckless indifference to the truth of the document she forwarded to her supervisor.[47]

Natalie might be next in line if we adjudge crimes from the perspective of "intended loss," but her scheme was so ridiculous and ineptly executed that it caused zero harm. Thus, if we consider "risk" in a serious manner, we might decide her case should land somewhere toward the bottom of the pack.[48]

Marley and Katya pose an interesting dilemma. From a loss perspective, Katya's crime is clearly the more serious one. She overstated her company's earnings and caused it to pay her $225,000 that did not belong to her.[49] But her company was also

---

[46] On sentencing cliffs, see Stephanos Bibas, *Plea Bargaining Outside the Shadow of Trial*, 117 HARV. L. REV. 2463, 2487 (2004).

[47] Willful blindness is usually treated as the equivalent of knowledge, even though such know-ledge is a constructed fiction. *See, e.g.*, Global Tech Appliances v. SEB SA, 563 U.S. 754 (2011).

[48] The plausibility of the risk is obviously doing a lot of work here.

[49] The loss amount may be greater than the unearned commission, but I am purposely using the $225,000 to demonstrate problems with relying on "loss" as a metric.

placing enormous pressure on her to deliver results. Indeed, she might even argue that her company was effectively aware of her falsehoods because the company's cutthroat culture encouraged all of its employees to cut corners and inflate their sales reports. The argument seems unlikely to help Katya much at trial. At most, it might place her company in the government's crosshairs, but it won't absolve her of her guilt. Still, I imagine many readers – particularly those who have worked within highly pressured settings – can reserve some small reservoir of sympathy for Katya. If her situation is truly idiosyncratic, we might conclude that her company's pressure is a factor that a judge can consider at sentencing. If it is the type of situation that arises frequently, however, and we want to be in a better position to document it, then we derive greater social value from baking it directly into our criminal code. Statutory hierarchies are useful when we want to know how often the government encounters (or charges) crimes on lower and higher rungs of the statutory ladder.

Of the four schemes, Marley's is easily the most repugnant. She exploits her access and position of power to take advantage of the residents of a nursing home. In some ways, she is the paradigmatic villain, the modern-day thief we envision stealing from our loved ones and depleting us of our college and retirement accounts.[50] And yet, because the "loss amount" of $125,000 is relatively modest, Marley's crime falls toward the bottom of the pack if we sort our cases solely according to actual or potential harm.

If the law is supposed to match and communicate society's intuitive attitudes toward crime, Marley's case strongly demonstrates the problem with a gradation scheme premised solely on loss. A rubric based solely on money understates the wrongfulness of certain frauds. A diffuse million-dollar fraud such as the one Rose facilitated may have caused far less harm than Marley's diabolic nursing home scheme.

When a crime reflects premeditation and planning, when it benefits from a person's position or special skill, and when it exploits those who are particularly vulnerable, it ought to serve as the apotheosis of that crime family. Reasonable people will disagree what to do about people like Rose and Katya, but a grading rubric that consistently places Marley at the bottom and Natalie at the top is likely one we should reject.

Thus, the answer might be to mix and match the different factors – that is, to develop a rubric that draws freely, as needed, on theories of *mens rea*, actual harm, and plausible risk. That effort, however, runs into a different problem: incommensurability.

---

[50] For a helpful account of how the modern fraud scheme undermines feelings of safety and security in one's investments, Christine Hurt, *Evil Has a New Name (and a New Narrative): Bernard Madoff*, 2009 MICH. ST. L. REV. 947, 985 ("corporate fraudsters incited the ire of the general public, and names like Bernard Ebbers and Jeffrey Skilling took the places of Jeffrey Dahmer and Ted Bundy as shorthand references to evil").

First degree fraud	Purposeful and premeditated scheme
Second degree fraud	Impulsive, non-premeditated scheme
Third degree fraud	Knowing facilitation of another's scheme; reckless indifference to the truth

FIGURE 8.1. Gradation by different factors

8.9 GRADATION'S INCOMMENSURABILITY PROBLEM

As the foregoing discussion demonstrates, neither *mens rea* nor harm and risk serve as perfect metrics for grading fraud. Were we to perform the same function for bribery or obstruction, we would encounter similar results. When we adopt a single metric to grade offenses, we wind up with counterintuitive results. "Harm" elevates the impulsive, large-ticket offense to the top of the heap, notwithstanding the offender's backstory. Culpable *mens rea* ignores the risk and dangerousness an offender poses to others. More troubling, the metrics themselves deliver widely different results, as demonstrated in Figure 8.1.

Should we give up? Some readers might conclude that this chapter has inadvertently constructed a strong argument *against* gradation: that it is too difficult, too complex, and far too likely to fail. If so, it is a curious phenomenon that gradation, for all its shortcomings, is still the norm for state codes.[51] Indeed, many state codes jump from one kind of a metric (*mens rea*) to another (harm and risk) with barely an acknowledgment. Homicide, for example, is divided by *mens rea*. Robbery and theft gradations are grounded in notions of harm and risk. Crimes such as rape and sexual assault rely on both concepts.

Accordingly, one might conclude that the answer is to devise a grading system that incorporates more than one metric. After all, our sentencing system explicitly directs judges to account for different punishment goals and factors.[52] Why shouldn't our statutory grading system resist doing the same?

The conceptual challenge is that gradation forces policymakers to make ordinal determinations based on incomparable values. Criminal theorists refer to this problem as one of incommensurability.[53] Incommensurability arises "when we try to compare plural, irreducible, and conflicting values, or choose between options

---

[51] "[T]oday, nearly every state uses degrees of murder as the first slice at determining which murderers should live and which should die." Sam Kamin & Justin Marceau, *Vicarious Aggravators*, 65 FLA. L. REV. 769, 776 (2013).

[52] *See generally* Paul H. Robinson, *Hybrid Principles for the Distribution of Criminal Sanctions*, 82 NW. L. REV. 19 (1988).

[53] On the incommensurability of culpability and harm, see Tadros, *supra* note 34, at 602, (rhetorically asking, "[i]s it as bad to rape another as it is to risk the death of another?" and a series of similar questions). *See also* Kenneth W. Simons, *When Is Strict Criminal Liability Just?* 87 J. CRIM. L. & CRIMINOLOGY 1075, 1093–94 (1997) (describing incommensurability problem as "pervasive" in criminal law).

that exhibit or will result in the realization of plural, irreducible, and conflicting values."[54]

One way to address this problem is to convert different metrics into a single currency.[55] This is the approach of the Sentencing Guidelines' criminal history analysis. To derive an offender's criminal history category score on the Guidelines' sentencing grid, one examines the number of criminal convictions the offender has had and assigns points to each conviction in relation to how much time in prison each offense occasioned. To be sure, the metric hinges on an arbitrary distinction. Nevertheless the "time in prison" proxy converts into a useable scale what would otherwise be an impossible comparison of previous crimes reflecting different degrees of harm, risk, and culpability.

Another way to address incommensurability is to assign different metrics to successive stages of the criminal justice process. For example, one could rely solely on *mens rea* (a proxy for blameworthiness) to statutorily grade offenses, and then additionally measure harm and risk at the sentencing stage (or vice versa) to come up with a final punishment.[56] If we do this, it will matter quite a bit which metric we assign to the guilt stage and which ones we save for later stages.

Finally, we could rely primarily on one metric, but permit the defendant to cite a competing consideration as a partial defense.[57] This might be the best way to deal with Natalie. A grading rubric premised on *mens rea* would place Natalie's crime at the top of the heap because she planned her implausible pipeline scheme. A framework that *also* reflected her scheme inherent likelihood of failure would appropriately downgrade her offense, provided she could raise a partial "implausibility" defense. We could create this downgrade for *all* incomplete offenses (by, for example, treating all attempts as second-degree offenses), or we could require of defendants an affirmative showing that their fraud schemes were substantially less likely to occur than some hypothetical paradigmatic offense. Again, reasonable people could disagree on who should bear the burden of demonstrating risk (or lack of risk), but the creation of various fraud defenses would be another way to subdivide the crime at the statutory level. Thus, we might, at the end of the day, end up with a graded fraud statute that looks something like:

First-degree fraud – A purposeful perpetration of a scheme (completed)

---

[54] Brett G. Scharffs, *Adjudication and the Problems of Incommensurability*, 42 WM. & MARY L. REV. 1367, 1372 (2001); Jennifer K. Robbennolt, John M. Darley, & Robert J. MacCoun, *Symbolism and Incommensurability in Civil Sanctioning: Decision Makers as Goal Managers*, 68 BROOK. L. REV. 1121, 1136 (2003) (citing "the cognitive difficulty that individuals have with comparing and making trade-offs between incommensurable entities").

[55] Robinson, *supra* note 18, at 31.

[56] Robinson alludes to this a bit when he writes that liability rules and sentencing practices collectively "govern the quantitative distribution of sanction." Robinson, *supra* note 18, at 34.

[57] Cf. Robinson, *supra* note 18, at 29–30 (contrasting "priority" purposes of punishment and "limiting" purposes that mitigate punishment).

Second-degree fraud (Attempt) – A purposeful planning of a scheme to defraud (inchoate)

Second-degree fraud (Impulsive perpetration [affirmative defense]) – An impulsive and provoked perpetration of a scheme (affirmative defense)

Third-degree fraud (Facilitation) – Knowing facilitation of another's scheme; reckless indifference to the truth

Affirmative defense (reduce by one degree) – Implausible scheme

Sharp readers will note that this rubric makes several deliberate moves. First, it treats the purposeful *and* completed scheme as the worst of all frauds, combining intuitions about *mens rea* and harm into a single category. Second, it grants all purposeful attempts the grace of a second-degree designation, even though many (or nearly all) of those attempts signify risky and potentially harmful misconduct.[58] This treatment of attempt – of recognizing its wrongfulness while assigning it a lesser degree of statutory punishment – reflects a broad and deep empirical literature on social attitudes. In contravention with the MPC, our society agrees that attempt should be a crime but generally views it as a lesser crime.[59]

Next, the rubric accords second-degree status to the "impulsive and provoked" scheme, akin to Katya's ill-advised lies to her employer about her commissions. Because this is an affirmative defense, she only enjoys this downgrade if she offers evidence showing that her activity was impulsive and the result of illegal or unethical pressure. And yes, I fully realize that courts will have a field day figuring out what "provocation" means in this context, much less "unethical" pressure. But courts have managed to differentiate offenses in other contexts, and they will have the benefit of a large cache of research that demonstrates the difference between offensive and defensive frauds.[60]

One more step down and we get to the type of behavior typified by Rose's scheme: facilitation of someone else's scheme or fraud signified by one's "reckless indifference to the truth." The concept of facilitation is not exactly new. State codes employ it as a less culpable version of aiding and abetting. Given its ubiquity in corporate fraud cases, it could go a long way toward statutorily dividing the ringleaders of

---

[58] An attempt, by definition, is purposeful. Accordingly, a "reckless" attempted fraud should theoretically be a noncognizable offense. *See* Michael T. Cahill, *Attempt, Reckless Homicide and the Design of the Criminal Law*, 78 U. Colo. L. Rev., 900–1 (describing near universal rejection of an "attempted reckless murder" offense because the concept of "attempt" is incompatible with an unintended result, including a reckless homicide).

[59] Although the MPC envisioned attempt as the same grade as a completed offense, many states have rejected this equivalence and continue to recognize the difference between incomplete and complete schemes. *See, e.g.*, Paul H. Robinson et al., *Realism, Punishment, and Reform*, 77 U. Chi. L. Rev. 1611, 1614 n.16 (2010) ("[M]ost states, even those following the Model Penal Code, reject this approach and grade completed offenses higher than attempt.")

[60] *See, e.g.*, Julia Y. Lee, *Prosocial Fraud*, 52 Seton Hall L. Rev. 199 (2021) (examining different motivations for fraud); Miriam H. Baer, *Confronting the Two Faces of Corporate Fraud*, 66 Fla. L. Rev. 87 (2014) (contrasting opportunistic schemes with impulsive, spur of the moment frauds).

various schemes from the various backbenchers and hangers-on. The latter would still get in trouble, but they would be subject to a far less serious offense than their compatriots. Again, *some* judges already recognize these conceptual distinctions at sentencing.[61] A codification project would move those decisions from the discretionary realm of judicial sentencing to the more transparent domain of formal lawmaking. As I have argued in the past, "Rather than relying on the occasional well-argued judicial sentencing opinion, we might benefit more from an explicit debate over these scenarios, such as whether they reflect diluted culpability and reduced danger and whether they are distinct enough to merit their own statutory designation."[62]

Sentencing judges already possess the power to impose punishments that reflect much of this section's reasoning. Power, however, is not the same thing as legal obligation.[63]

8.10 GRADING OTHER CRIMES

Subdivision by *mens rea* or by harm and risk could theoretically transfer to the bribery and obstruction contexts. A multiyear reform project might also pave the way for more ambitious reforms, such as the subdivision of conspiracy and aiding and abetting to reflect different degrees of participation and assistance.[64] Reasonable people could disagree on the language one might employ to denote certain terms (provocation, implausibility). Reasonable people might also disagree on whether certain factors merit heightened or mitigated status. And finally, any rubric would need statutory ranges of punishment to function as a true sorting mechanism. That is all fine, because a grading exercise, *by definition*, should facilitate hearings, testimony, research, and feedback.

8.11 LIMITATIONS AND BUGS

This section briefly anticipates several of the objections that readers –especially, those familiar with state criminal codes – are likely to raise in response to proposals for consolidation and grading. I address several of them here.

---

[61] *See, e.g.,* United States v. Adelson, 441 F.Supp.2d 506, 512 (S.D.N.Y. 2006) (Rakoff, J.) (commenting on the distinction between a "belated entrant" into a fraud conspiracy and an "active leader").

[62] Baer, *supra* note 1, at 277.

[63] *See, e.g.,* United States v. Corsey, 723 F.3d 366, 377 (2d Cir. 2013) (Underhill. J, concurring and arguing that guidelines' analysis premised on intended loss amount is "valueless" because the fraud scheme at issue "was more farcical than dangerous"). The district court judge in Corsey showed no inclination to take the scheme's underlying implausibility into account – and the scheme in Corsey (inducing strangers to invest in a "billion-dollar" trans-Siberian pipeline) was far more fantastical than the hypothetical scheme described in this chapter.

[64] Joshua Dressler, *Reassessing the Theoretical Underpinnings of Accomplice Liability: New Solutions to an Old Problem*, 37 HASTINGS L.J. 91, 93, 120 (1985).

Count-stacking. One of gradation's benefits is that it is effectively imposes a statutory ceiling on prison sentences for defendants charged with low-level (i.e., "low-grade") crimes. That cap, however, becomes meaningless if prosecutors can file multiple counts corresponding to a single offense, and judges can impose consecutive sentence terms. For example, even if we capped a low-level fraud at two years' imprisonment, a prosecutor could threaten the recalcitrant offender with a robust sentence (a maximum of ten years' imprisonment) by charging a fraud scheme in five counts.

To some degree, consolidation-style reforms alleviate this problem. If there exists only one "fraud" statute, the prosecutor can no longer rely on overlapping statutes to pile on redundant counts; consolidation reduces the threat of count-stacking because it streamlines the code.[65] By the same token, Congress could also enact a law prohibiting consecutive sentences for multiple fraud counts pertaining to the same scheme.[66] Such a rule would constrain judges *and* simultaneously influence prosecutors. Gone would be any incentive to charge fourteen redundant counts for a single, straightforward scheme.

Conspiracy and other workarounds. Even if we put in place limitations on count-stacking, prosecutors can undermine a graded code in other ways. For example, the prosecutor might file, in addition to a substantive fraud charge, an additional conspiracy charge in cases involving two or more wrongdoers working in concert.[67] A statutory ceiling of five years' imprisonment might suddenly double to ten.

Indeed, the crime of conspiracy itself raises questions of gradation that courts and legislators have never fully answered. It is the relatively rare case where society will perceive each member of a group as equally harmful, equally dangerous, or equally deserving of moral condemnation. And yet our federal law adheres to a harsh "all for one, one for all" rule that not only treats all conspirators as equals, but also holds them responsible for each other's foreseeable substantive acts taken in "furtherance" of the conspiracy.[68] The instrumental defense of such severity is that it enables prosecutors to cut cooperation deals with criminal defendants and possibly deters a

---

[65] *See also* Robinson, *supra* note 18, at 182 ("Identify the harm or evil, and capture it in one offense").

[66] In previous work, I have argued that we can redress count-stacking pathologies by having "legislatures ... select from a menu of options: they could place direct restraints on a prosecutor's charging of multiple related counts, redefine the unit of crime to make count-stacking more difficult, or severely limit the availability of consecutive sentences." Baer, *supra* note 1, at 270.

[67] *See* 18 U.S.C. § 371 (quote language). "Conspiracy [effectively] 'collapses the distinction between accessories and perpetrators' [in that it treats] conspirators as principals in any substantive offense committed in furtherance of the conspiracy, whether or not they directly participated in that offense." United States v. Alvarez, 610 F.2d 1250, 1253 (5th Cir. 1980) (citing GEORGE P. FLETCHER, RETHINKING CRIMINAL LAW 674 [1978]).

[68] United States v. Pinkerton, 328 U.S. 640 (1946).

few individuals from joining conspiracies in the first place.[69] But cooperation is far from a failsafe, and deterrence can fall by the wayside when individuals underestimate their likelihood of detection. Thus, even under a reformed and partially graded code, crimes such as conspiracy undermine our statutory sorting project.

Imperviousness to bad policing. Gradation is useful statutory reform, but it is no panacea for the many problems that ail the criminal justice system. Grading cannot cure a criminal justice system of its implicit bias, policing abuses, structural racism, or dependence on incarceration.[70] Nor can it eliminate or even reduce the ills of mass incarceration (especially if all the "grades" receive high sentence ranges)[71] or the various blind spots and lack of transparency that have characterized white-collar and corporate prosecutions. Combined with the other proposals set forth in this book, grading is but one tool we can use to alleviate white-collar crime's pathologies and produce a better understanding of what our enforcement institutions are doing.

Too many grades. Moreover, we know from our experience with state codes and with other parts of the federal code that grading itself can become pathological. For example, if the legislature engages in too much subdivision, the numerosity of categories undermines their expressive and informational value.[72] Being charged with seventh-degree theft in a system that features twelve degrees of similar property crimes doesn't convey much information, much less an appropriate expressive signal, to anyone.[73]

Bad grading. There is no value in a code that grades mechanistically or arbitrarily.[74] We already have experience with this type of problem; the Sentencing Guideline that controls roughly 10 percent of the federal system's criminal docket, Section 2B1.1, is increasingly – if politely – discounted by federal sentencing

---

[69] Neal Kumar Katyal, *Conspiracy Theory*, 112 YALE L. J. 1307 (2003) (describing strategic benefits of conspiracy laws).

[70] "[A] graded system can easily fall short of its ideals – its actors can violate procedural rules, twist the meaning of criminal statutes, or attach crude sentencing triggers that all but destroy the legislature's formal gradations." Baer, *Sorting, supra* note 1, at 261.

[71] "American sentencing practices remain the harshest in the world." Jane Bambauer & Andrea Roth, *From Damage Caps to Decarceration: Extending Tort Law Safeguards to Criminal Sentencing*, 101 B.U. L. REV. 1667, 1670 (2021).

[72] Lynch, *supra* note 16, at 308 (explaining how New York's code grew to eventually feature at least ten grades for certain crimes).

[73] Under current state laws, a seven-degree or even ten-degree rubric would not be out of the question. *See* Michael T. Cahill, *Grading Arson*, 3 CRIM & PHIL. 79, 83 (2009) (observing that "a scheme recognizing seven offense levels – say, four or five degrees of felony, and two or three degrees of misdemeanor – would be in the mainstream of current American offense-grading systems").

[74] The federal identity fraud statutes, 18 U.S.C. §§ 1029 *et seq.* exemplify the confusion that can result from poorly devised grading. The statutes' penalty provisions are so numerous and confusing that the Department of Justice has created a table to assist its prosecutors in understanding the statutory scheme. DEPARTMENT OF JUSTICE, PROSECUTING COMPUTER CRIMES 2–3 (2010).

judges.[75] There are many reasons for this, but one of them is that Section 2B1.1 is so poorly constructed.[76] It is highly technical, larded with overlapping add-on provisions that heighten a person's recommended sentence range, and embedded with numerous sentencing "cliffs." The fraudster who obtains $155,000 receives two more offense levels (and therefore at least a year longer in prison) than the person who defrauds someone of $145,000. Ten thousand dollars places a person over a Maginot line that results in a substantially longer sentence.

The limitations and problems described above are real and should be taken seriously by any government reformer. But they fail to offer any principled reason for abandoning the twin projects of grading and consolidation.

8.12 THE MECHANICS OF GRADATION AND CONSOLIDATION

More than twenty years ago, a number of scholars convened to discuss the federal code's potential reform, resulting in a publication of insightful articles in the (then) newly created *Buffalo Criminal Law Review*.[77] All agreed that the federal criminal code was a mess, that it featured too many poorly written and overlapping statutes, and that it was in dire need of a reorganization. There was additional consensus that code reform could not be undertaken in a piecemeal fashion, and that it would likely require the expertise of a standalone commission.[78] Just like earlier attempts at reform, the authors' ideas failed to become law.

We can either view these failures as evidence of code reform's impossibility or as a helpful source of "lessons learned." For example, the intuition to reform the federal code in its entirety[79] is just that: an intuition that has ultimately served as roadblock

---

[75] "[J]udges resist the harsh sentencing guidelines for today's economic crimes, and do so in interesting ways." Bennett, Levinson, & Hioki, *supra* note 17, at 943. Jillian Hewitt, *Note, Fifty Shades of Gray: Sentencing Trends in Major White-Collar Cases*, 125 YALE L.J. 1018, 1025 (2016) (revealing findings that a "significant majority of defendants in major white-collar cases today receive sentences shorter than the Guidelines range").

[76] Daniel S. Guarnera, *A Fatally Flawed Proxy: The Role of "Intended Loss" in the U.S. Sentencing Guidelines for Fraud*, 81 MO. L. REV. 715, 739 (2016) ("Actual and intended loss often point in the same direction, but they do not always do so"). For broader criticisms of the guidelines, see Kate Stith & José A. Cabranes, *Judging under the Federal Sentencing Guidelines*, 91 NW. U. L. REV. 1247, 1266 (1997) (criticizing the guidelines' complexity and hypertechnicality).

[77] Robert H. Joost, *Federal Criminal Code Reform: Is It Possible?* 1 BUFF. CRIM. L. REV. 195, 201–03 (1997). Kathleen F. Brickey, *Federal Criminal Code Reform: Hidden Costs, Illusory Benefits*, 2 BUFF. CRIM. L. REV. 161, 188 (1998); Ronald L. Gainer, *Federal Criminal Code Reform: Past and Future*, 2 BUFF. CRIM. L. REV. 45, 79–83 (1998).

[78] Joost, *supra* note 77, at 219 ("The President and Congress should submit and pass legislation to establish a federal criminal code commission. The commission's task would be to hold hearings, collect evidence, and develop and recommend the text of a federal criminal code bill").

[79] "Title 18, the criminal code title of the United States Code, should be completely rewritten. That was the recommendation by the National Commission on Reform of Federal Criminal

to success. I don't disagree with the concern that piecemeal lawmaking can be meaningless, but given the federal code's enormous size and scope,[80] its different conceptual approaches to white-collar and street crime, and the powerful pull of political inertia, I see no reason to saddle a commission with the task of codifying and reforming the *entire* code, especially when that code covers crimes that raise radically different political and social concerns.

Accordingly, this book envisions a targeted set of reforms focused solely on the federal code's most "popular" (i.e., most utilized) white-collar crimes. It is better to start with three or four major crime groups and aim to unbundle, relabel, consolidate, and grade those groups – all within a doable thirty-six to forty-eight months. If this "pilot" reform program works supremely well, it can always be expanded to additional portions of the code. Moreover, it makes sense as well to begin in phases. Bundling and relabeling (the basis of Chapter 7) are valuable activities in their own right. They allow us to see just how badly the code has fissioned, and just how redundant and overlapping its statutes have become. Gradation and consolidation are the follow-up reforms that place white-collar offenses on the track to becoming, in Professor Robinson's words, more orderly and more principled.[81] First, we eliminate the meaningless horizontal distinctions (between wire and mail fraud), and then, we devise the meaningful vertical distinctions (between first- and second-degree fraud and so forth).

Moreover, although these statutory reforms would necessarily inform and the Sentencing Commission's work, they would not require the Guidelines' abandonment. As is the case with many state systems, federal judges would still turn to the Guidelines to tease out further distinctions in offenses, and to tailor sentences to reflect an offender's specific circumstance. As Judge Lynch observed over two decades ago, "[W]hatever the degree of precision our penal codes were to attain, there would always be some morally relevant factual variation within the offenses defined."[82] In other words, we will always need guidelines but we should not make them a substitute for well-written laws.

As for the question of *who* should make these changes, Congress would almost certainly rely on committees and perhaps a standalone commission to spearhead this effort. The specific body Congress chooses to do this work, however, is less important than its makeup, its transparency, and its responsiveness to the general public. The group that eventually advises Congress in the revision of its white-collar crimes

---

Laws in 1971 and by the Office of Legal Policy to the United States Attorney General in 1989, and that is my recommendation now." Joost, *supra* note 777, at 195.

[80] "In the last forty years, Congress has passed more than a thousand federal criminal laws, many of which are unclear on their face." Shon Hopwood, *Two Sides of the Same Interpretive Coin: The Presumption of Mens Rea and the Historical Rule of Lenity*, 53 ARIZ. ST. L.J. 507, 507 (2021).

[81] Robinson, *supra* note 18, at 175 (describing what an "orderly" code is and why it is preferable).

[82] Lynch, *supra* note 16, at 321.

should reflect the views of insiders and outsiders, of the general public, and of the various stakeholders affected by government enforcement. It should hear the viewpoints of regulators, investigators, judges, and the Sentencing Commission's staff. It should also listen to prosecutors and investigators, who are indeed on-the-ground experts in this area, but it should not favor prosecutors to the detriment of everyone else. It should be responsive, deliberative, informed, and principled, and it should act with the goal not simply of formulating a coherent or just set of laws, but also one that will facilitate the collection and dissemination of relevant enforcement information. It should be cognizant of white-collar crime's numerous pathologies and create a code that can partially mitigate these pathologies. Mitigation may sound modest to some, but for a public that has grown so disenchanted with its enforcement institutions, it represents an important first step.

Conclusion

INTRODUCTION

The proposals described in Chapters 7 and 8 are components of a reform agenda best described as "code-design." Code-design invests the legislature not only with the responsibility to write criminal laws, but also to focus on how those laws are arranged and intersect within a broader code.

The study of code-design directs its adherents to questions other than the content of a specific statute. It asks, in a rigorous way, how we can best subdivide, compile, and order offenses that fall within the same "family." Code-design also helps us decide what those families are, and just how broadly or narrowly they should be defined. It recognizes that the compilation of a series of criminal statutes can impact strategic decisions by prosecutors; amplify expressive signals; and facilitate the subsequent collection of information. It also assumes that the actors responsible for drafting and maintaining the code will continuously update and improve its design, and not simply tack on new statutes in a scattershot fashion.

Code-design is not new, although scholars have often referred to it with other labels. In the heady years leading up to the American Law Institute's publication of the Model Penal Code, criminal law professors conducted extensive debates over what shape criminal statutes should take, as well as the overall code they occupied. That discussion continued well into the twenty-first century. The academy's interest in statutory codes was eventually eclipsed, however, by concerns with mass incarceration and the realist recognition that prosecutors – and mainly prosecutors – defined the law, set the "price" of punishment, and meted out a twisted version of justice as they saw it. As the late William Stuntz, author of *The Pathological Politics of Criminal Law*, wrote: "Anyone who reads criminal codes in search of a picture of what conduct leads to a prison term, or who reads sentencing rules in order to discover how severely different sorts of crimes are punished, will be seriously misled."[1] Although not everyone agreed with Stuntz's conclusion that prosecutors were the sole authors of criminal law, most agreed with the overall thrust of his argument.[2] Over the next two decades, scholars increasingly turned away from analyzing codes and instead focused more intently on criminal law "on the ground."

But whatever the story of street crime may be, its narrative has never adequately described white-collar crime. Federal white-collar statutes have always required more work of the prosecutor – certainly more work than suggested by the standard critique mass incarceration. And white-collar defendants, although far from uniformly wealthy or powerful, have frequently possessed greater means to employ competent counsel in their favor.[3] For those reasons, the white-collar law-on-the-books still *matters*, and in some cases, predominates. Even the most aggressive, freewheeling prosecutor is constrained by law and evidence; she cannot choose her targets at will. That is, quite frankly, one of white-collar crime's most positive features: it requires the government to actually prove something – and usually something relatively important – prior to depriving someone of their liberty.

Federal criminal code-design has never dominated academic scholarship, but it all but disappeared a few decades after the enactment of the 1984 Sentencing Reform Act, which ushered in a highly complex determinate sentencing system and effectively enabled Congress to punt the most vexatious questions of gradation and sorting to the newly created Sentencing Commission.[4] Although the Supreme Court would eventually declare the Guidelines advisory, the damage was done. Just as video killed the radio star, the study of sentencing and prosecutorial power eclipsed the study of federal code reform.[5]

---

[1] William J. Stuntz, *The Pathological Politics of Criminal Law*, 100 MICH. L. REV. 505, 506–7 (2001).

[2] For a very measured assessment of just how close we are (or were) to reaching the point where law did not matter at all, see RICHARD H. MCADAMS, *The Political Economy of Criminal Law and Procedure* in CRIMINAL LAW CONVERSATIONS (Paul H. Robinson, Stephen Garvey, & Kimberley Kessler Ferzan, eds., 2011) (expressing skepticism that our system has reached the law-on-the-books irrelevance forecast by Stuntz).

[3] "No one could dispute that a defendant who has millions to spend on an attorney is better off, on average and all else equal, than one who has to rely on a minimalist, state-funded defense." Samuel W. Buell, *Is the White Collar Offender Privileged?*, 63 DUKE LAW JOURNAL 823, 878 (2014).

[4] Numerous pieces on federal code reform were published in the late 1990s, primarily in the *Buffalo Criminal Law Review's* first two volumes: Robert H. Joost, *Federal Criminal Code Reform: Is It Possible?*, 1 BUFF. CRIM. L. REV. 195, 201–03 (1997); Paul H. Robinson, *Reforming the Federal Criminal Code: A Top Ten List*, 1 BUFF. CRIM. L. REV. 225 (1997); Kathleen F. Brickey, *Federal Criminal Code Reform: Hidden Costs, Illusory Benefits*, 2 BUFF. CRIM. L. REV. 161, 188 (1998); Ronald L. Gainer, *Federal Criminal Code Reform: Past and Future*, 2 BUFF. CRIM. L. REV. 45, 79–83 (1998). Later discussions of code reform focused on specific families of statutes. *See, e.g.*, Julie R. O'Sullivan, *The Federal Criminal Code Is a Disgrace: Obstruction Statutes as a Case Study*, 96 J. CRIM. L. & CRIMINOLOGY 643, 648–50 (2006) (obstruction statutes).

[5] *Video Killed the Radio Star* (MTV television broadcast Aug. 1, 1981).

One of the aims of this book has been to demonstrate code-design's essential role in reducing white-collar crime's pathologies. Scholars have long recognized how a criminal code's overall design affects plea-bargaining,[6] trial practice,[7] and the community's condemnation of wrongdoing.[8] Numerous scholars have capably demonstrated the federal code's flaws and expressive failures.[9] The final two chapters of this book build on this literature by theorizing code-design's information-producing effects, as well as its potential for improving public discourse. Recognizing these connections is crucial. Absent the production of relevant and accurate information, we are bound to misunderstand and misstate white-collar crime's depth, degree of harm, and corresponding enforcement gaps.

The pathologies described throughout this book are deep-seated. They pervade questions of statutory construction and enforcement. Some might argue the book's proposals sidestep these pathologies. We can unbundle as many statutes as we like, but that isn't likely to fix the various enforcement errors and overly narrow prototypes discussed in Chapter 5. Nor will it cure our society of the discourse pathologies discussed in Chapter 6. Nevertheless, the four-part regimen of unbundling, relabeling, consolidation, and grading promotes deliberative lawmaking and informational benefits that are absent from our present framework.

Imagine a highway filled with potholes and cracks, but also filled with distracting neon flashing signs, stalled cars, and small trucks that appear to be on fire. Clearing the signs, the stalled cars, and the burning trucks doesn't *directly* fill the potholes or repair the cracks, but it does help us see that they are there and that they need to be fixed. That is the aim of the latter third of this book: to clear white-collar crime of its latent distractions so that we can implement longer-term repairs that enable us to better redress the endemic behaviors of opportunism and deception that weaken our economic and social institutions. If we perceive white-collar crime as a chronic problem, then we ought to conceptualize white-collar crime's reform as an incremental, long-term project.

---

[6] *See generally* Andrew Manuel Crespo, *The Hidden Law of Plea Bargaining*, 118 COLUMBIA LAW REV. 1303 (2018); Ronald F. Wright & Rodney L. Engen, *Charge Movement and Theories of Prosecutors*, 91 MARQ. L. REV. 9, 10 (2007) (explaining connection between a criminal code's "depth" and plea-bargaining).

[7] *See, e.g.*, Miriam Baer, *Sorting Out White-Collar Crime*, 97 TEX. L. REV. 225, 274–75, 276 n.253 (2019); Crespo, *supra* note 6, at 1364–66; Michael H. Hoffheimer, *The Rise and Fall of Lesser Included Offenses*, 36 RUTGERS L.J. 351, 437 (2005) (tracking the "significant decline" in the applicability of the "lesser included offense" doctrine). *See also* Allison Orr Larsen, *Bargaining inside the Black Box*, 99 GEO. L.J. 1567, 1602 (2011) (examining compromise jury verdicts in criminal cases).

[8] James Chalmers & Fiona Leverick, *Fair Labelling in Criminal Law*, 71 MOD. L. REV. 217, 222 (2008); STUART P. GREEN, THIRTEEN WAYS TO STEAL A BICYCLE: THEFT LAW IN THE INFORMATION AGE 52–54 (2012); Michael Serota, *Proportional* Mens Rea *and the Future of Criminal Code Reform*, 52 WAKE FOREST L. REV. 1201, 1206-07 (2017).

[9] *See* various authorities, *supra* note 4.

THE BENEFITS OF A CODE-DESIGN APPROACH

This book began with an overview of the various beliefs that pervade white-collar crime's discourse. We are *positive* that white-collar crime is underenforced, just as we are equally sure that it is also *overcriminalized*. In truth, we lack decent information about white-collar crime's frequency and scope, except we know that "it" happens often and costs us upward of billions of dollars a year. We possess all sorts of information about white-collar crime's federal enforcement, except much of it is inconsistent and unusable. We suffer several sustained pathologies in lawmaking and enforcement. Our laws are flat; convey inaccurate signals as to the amount of punishment a person actually "faces"; are often "underwritten" and therefore rely on the interpretations of nondemocratic branches; and become further twisted by enforcement institutions who adhere to certain prototypes.

Code-design cannot cure all of these pathologies, but it can go a long way toward exposing and eventually redressing many of them. The four-part regimen urged here most directly confronts the federal code's problem of flat and redundant statutes (Chapter 3) by directly eliminating redundancies and building in morally and conceptually meaningful statutory degrees.[10] To the extent it spurs Congress to acquire the important habit of revising and drafting criminal codes (as opposed to symbolically articulating or increasing the maximum punishment attached to established crimes), it shows promise as a means of eventually confronting the "underwritten" crime phenomenon discussed in Chapter 4. Indeed, the irony here is that it may be more feasible for Congress to enact a series of *graded* statutes that address insider trading and corporate criminal liability, rather than attempt to write a *single* statute that covers the entire ocean of wrongdoing for a given type of crime.

Finally, the creation of graded statutes, paired with other reforms such as the provision of enhanced resources, might enable prosecutors and the general public to better understand the distinction between policy-driven nonenforcement, practical attention to legislative gaps, and fear-driven adherence to prototypes. These latter concepts form the basis of Chapter 5's discussion of white-collar crime's poorly understood viability line. Statutory code-design can play some role in influencing where prosecutors draw this line, and an even greater role in helping prosecutors and the general public debate where prosecutors *should* draw that line.

In sum, code-design promises a more coherent code, a drafting process that is potentially more responsive to the public, and a less myth-driven discourse of white-collar crime and its enforcement. It won't displace the urge to deceive others any more than our current framework, but it may place enforcers, defense attorneys, and

---

[10] The argument in favor of statutory grading is hardly new. Several criminal law scholars have insightfully mined the risks of streamlining a series of crimes into just a handful of unhelpful categories. *See, e.g.,* GREEN, *supra* note 8, at 46.

public critics in a far better position to assess our enforcement institutions and work on making them more effective.

THEORIES OF CRIMINAL JUSTICE REFORM AND WHITE-COLLAR CRIME

It may seem odd to address this toward the end of a book, but for a project like this, it seems fitting to admit at the *end* of this discussion that my book rests upon my transparent belief that a punishment-oriented criminal justice system remains a legitimate pillar of a democratic society and therefore should continue to exist. An anti-abolition defense of criminal enforcement is beyond the scope of this book, but I do offer a thumbnail sketch of the beliefs that drive this project.

First, it should be noted that there is no movement in support of purely white-collar abolitionism. I am aware of no serious scholar who argues for the abolition of *only* white-collar criminal punishment. Some scholars have argued for the abolition of *corporate* criminal liability, in part because the corporation itself is not a natural person, and because the system that has evolved isn't really a form of criminal law at all.[11] My work in this area has been largely sympathetic to this latter view, although my own preference is for a legislatively enacted definition of corporate criminal liability, and not the *respondeat superior* doctrine and its shadow law that persist today.[12]

Beyond corporate liability, I am aware of no scholar who has argued that white-collar criminals should benefit specially from the demise of the criminal justice system. Nor am I aware of any movement, analogous to developments in the local and state context, to engage in the open and deliberate nonenforcment of certain categories of white-collar crimes. What one does find, however, are numerous arguments favoring a world with no prisons or police.[13] Some of these arguments have been paired with calls for radically different systems of economic, political, and social organization.[14] That, for me, is a bridge too far. As Maximo Langer argues, the

---

[11] For the former approach, see John Hasnas, *The Centenary of a Mistake: One Hundred Years of Corporate Criminal Liability*, 46 AM. CRIM. L. REV. 1329, 1329 (2009) (arguing that "there is no theoretical justification for corporate criminal liability"). For the latter, see Steven Smith, *Corporate Criminal Liability: End It, Don't Mend It*, 47 J. CORP. L. 1089 (2022).

[12] Miriam H. Baer, *Too Vast to Succeed*, 114 MICH. L. REV. 1109, 1133 (2016); Miriam H. Baer, *Three Conceptions of Corporate Crime (and One Avenue for Reform)*, 83 LAW & CONTEMP. PROBS. 1, 21–23 (2020); Miriam H. Baer, *Corporate Criminal Law Unbounded* in OXFORD HANDBOOK OF PROSECUTORS AND PROSECUTION (Ronald F. Wright, Kay Levine, & Russell M. Gold, eds., 2022).

[13] *See generally* Anna Roberts, *Victims, Right?* 42 CARDOZO L. REV. 1449, 1454 (2021) (citing Amna Akbar, *Teaching Penal Abolition*, L. & POL. ECON. PROJECT (July 15, 2019), https://lpeblog.org/2019/07/15/teaching-abolition [https://perma.cc/29L8-9TD2]) (describing calls for abolition that have "enter[ed] the mainstream").

[14] "Justice for abolitionists is an integrated endeavor to prevent harm, intervene in harm, obtain reparations, and transform the conditions in which we live." Allegra M. McLeod, *Envisioning*

outcomes under an abolitionist regime could just as easily propagate harms as bad, if not far worse, than those that have been produced by our current systems of political, economic, and social organization.[15]

The abolitionist argument often imagines a very local approach to antisocial behavior, whereby some predefined community is invested with the responsibility of responding to and facilitating the restoration of various victims.[16] Whatever the merits of this approach elsewhere, it does not map well onto white-collar crime. For many white-collar offenses, there is no such thing as a "local" community, much less a specifically identifiable victim. Crimes like fraud and bribery thrive in large, interconnected cities and global networks. Its victims are often diffuse, unaware of the schemes that have robbed them of money and property, and unable to investigate their source and scope. Accordingly, offenses such as these require a sophisticated, national, and bureaucratically supported approach to enforcement. We need local efforts, as well, but local enforcement agencies cannot do the job on their own.

The argument in favor of a strong system of white-collar criminal enforcement is admittedly also an argument for a strong, capitalist state. If we intend to host a strong federal government that encourages the development of an economy that relies on overlapping markets and that facilitates tens of millions of private and public transactions, then we will also need laws and institutions that regulate, monitor, and punish transgressions within those markets.

That brings us to abolitionism's opposite pole, what one might call *white-collar maximalism*. Whereas the abolitionist imagines a world with no criminal law or prisons, the maximalist focuses most intently on eliminating the disparity one sees between the treatment of street crime and white-collar crime. Jennifer Taub's recent book fits this bill, as does the work of several other scholars.[17]

Abolition Democracy, 132 HARV. L. REV. 1613, 1615 (2019). Some abolitionist accounts ironically hold up the civil treatment of white-collar crimes as an example of the ways in which civil adjudication can bypass criminal law and its punitive outcomes. Matthew Clair & Amanda Woog, *Courts and the Abolition Movement*, 110 CAL. L. REV. 1, 41 (2022) (observing that "among the wealthy and corporations, criminalizable behavior has historically been adjudicated in civil proceedings").

[15] "It is not clear to me that any of the many possible variations of societies without any prisons – including the ones suggested by various penal abolitionists – would necessarily be more just than a set of societies that would still give to law enforcement, prisons, or other forms of punishment a role in addressing harmful behavior." Maximo Langer, *Penal Abolitionism and Criminal Law Minimalism: Here and There, Now and Then*, 134 HARV. L. REV. F. 42, 45 (2020). *See also* Rachel Barkow, *Promise or Peril? The Political Path of Prison Abolition in America*, 58 WAKE FOREST L. REV. (forthcoming 2023) (predicting political backlash if "prison downsizing gets associated with broader abolitionist goals of ending capitalism and replacing it with communism or some other kind of communal governance structure"), available at https://papers.ssrn.com/sol3/papers.cfm?abstract_id=4232267.

[16] Jocelyn Simonson, *Police Reform through a Power Lens*, 130 YALE L.J. 778, 813 (2021) (articulating "community control" concepts regarding police reform).

[17] JENNIFER TAUB, BIG DIRTY MONEY: THE SHOCKING INJUSTICE AND UNSEEN COST OF WHITE COLLAR CRIME (2020); RENA STEINZOR, WHY NOT JAIL? INDUSTRIAL

My issue with white-collar maximalism mirrors concerns others have raised in response to maximalism generally. It imposes enormous collateral costs on the offender, the offender's family, and their social and economic networks; it (often) reflects rage and panic instead of informed policymaking; it displaces more effective *ex ante* approaches; and in the wrong hands, it can be used for malevolent purposes.[18] And of course, once in place, maximalism's tools are awfully difficult to constrain or pare back. As criminologist Michael Benson and others have demonstrated, white-collar crime is no longer carried out solely by the wealthy and the uber-privileged. (Query if it ever was). It has visibly "democratized" to women, people of color, and many who occupy the middle class.[19] Benson's work thus demonstrates the challenges of a maximalist approach. If we choose to define white-collar statutes broadly, apply them frequently, and seek harsh punishments, it won't be just the CEOs who spend more time in prison.

If we discount abolition and discard maximalism, where does that leave us? Some might pursue *criminal minimalism*, an approach that hews closely to predefined harms and detectable risks, which is constrained by intelligible law and processes, and administered by experts insulated from political pressure. Rachel Barkow's work fits this definition, as does Langer's response to abolitionism.[20] Both scholars embrace a much smaller, leaner criminal justice system, informed by data and more responsive to community concerns.[21] But minimalism's prototypical crime is the kind of offense that dominates state and local court dockets, such as interpersonal violence, simple property crime, and narcotics. Minimalism does not have much of an answer for the policymaker confronted with cartels and foreign bribery, with insider trading and securities fraud, and with complex schemes of wrongdoing that implicate multiple regulatory agencies, a raft of administrative rules, and a constrained enforcement budget.

Minimalism appears to be the safest, most morally responsible course we can take in guiding the criminal justice system's future. And yet, for white-collar crimes, minimalism's conception of criminal law as strictly a "last resort" poses an array of

---

CATASTROPHES, CORPORATE MALFEASANCE, AND GOVERNMENT INACTION 7–9 (2015). Politicians also tend to embrace maximalist goals and rhetoric, naming entire industries "criminals" when it is rhetorically expedient to do so. *See* Baer, *Three Conceptions of Corporate Crime, supra* note 12, at 1, 19 (explaining that it is not surprising that "the public has come to view the word 'criminal' as an appropriate status term to apply to selected corporations and entire industries").

[18] *See* Miriam H. Baer, *Choosing Punishment*, 92 B.U. L. REV. 577, 631–39 (2012).

[19] Michael L. Benson et al., *Race, Ethnicity, and Social Change: The Democratization of Middle-Class Crime*, 59 CRIMINOLOGY 10 (2021).

[20] "For criminal law minimalism, the penal system still has a role to play in society, but a radically reduced, reimagined and redesigned role relative to the one it has played in the United States." Langer, *supra* note 155, at 44. *See also* RACHEL ELISE BARKOW, PRISONERS OF POLITICS: BREAKING THE CYCLE OF MASS INCARCERATION (2019).

[21] *See* Langer, *supra* note 155, at 75–76 (describing a framework in which criminal law truly is a "last resort").

concerns. In the world we currently live in, criminal law plays a far greater role in preventing and redressing corporate and white-collar crime than it would under a minimalist framework.

Moreover, corporate interests have already done quite a bit to impose their version of "minimalism" on federal agencies' regulatory and enforcement units. Consider Samuel Buell's description of how corporate liability (civil and criminal) is supposed to work:

> The prosecutor's decision whether and how to charge a corporate case criminally depends in important part on the operation of civil liability regimes that run alongside the criminal enforcement apparatus. Ian Ayers and John Braithwaite famously argued that the effective scheme for regulating organizations should be pyramidal, with escalating layers of increasingly sharp measures of control, starting at the bottom with self-regulation and capping off at the top with harsh forms of punishment. In such a pyramidal scheme, each more serious form of control ought to be used more sparingly than the less intrusive measure below it. The most powerful sanctions should be used least. But some form of very damaging sanction is essential because, without a sharp point on the pyramid, lower tiers of control lose influence.[22]

Notice Buell's final sentence: "some form of very damaging sanction is *essential*" (emphasis added). Although his discussion of criminal law's sparing use echoes minimalism's "last resort" concept, Buell adds an additional insight, which is that tinkering with the top layer (criminal law) necessarily disturbs the lower layers, causing them to "lose influence." Accordingly, we can embrace minimalism's desire for proportion and restraint, but we should also realize that dangers of an decontextualized approach to minimalism, especially one that fails to take account of the political fights that have, in the past, defanged civil and administrative enforcement. The fact is, white-collar actors *already* enjoy the benefits of "regulatory minimalism," and they have enjoyed it for an awfully long time. To add on another layer of minimalism is to risk a world in which enforcement appears more chimerical than minimal.

Accordingly, the path this book adopts might best be described as a variant of legal pragmatism. Pragmatism, according to Richard Boldt, "contemplates those guiding generalizations or principles [that] can be derived from the data of experience, and insists that these principles should be employed to shape and direct future practice."[23] Rewriting the federal code may not *sound* pragmatic, but to my mind it is exactly the kind of Dewey-esque problem-solving approach that meets

---

[22] SAMUEL W. BUELL, *Potentially Perverse Effects of Corporate Civil Liability* in PROSECUTORS IN THE BOARDROOM 87, 88 (Anthony S. Barkow & Rachel E. Barkow, eds., 2011).

[23] "Pragmatism thus is committed to the proposition that theory necessarily is embedded in practice and becomes most meaningful when it is directed systematically to the solving of problems." Richard C. Boldt, *Problem-Solving Courts and Pragmatism*, 73 MD. L. REV. 1120, 1131 (2014).

white-collar crime's institutions where they are and tries to improve them. Moreover, because pragmatism places great stock in actual practice on the ground, it values the collection and dissemination of accurate information. If there is a problem with white-collar crime's discourse, a pragmatic approach seems far more likely to ameliorate it, compared to the absolute, ideological stances that have grown in popularity over the past decade or so.

TAKING THE PLUNGE

It goes without saying that a proposal of this magnitude invites difficult tradeoffs. That is a universal characteristic of serious code-design and reform. Well-designed statutes do not simply write themselves.[24] Several years ago, I predicted that reforms of this magnitude were impossible and unlikely to occur, barring the emergence of a new bipartisan coalition in Congress.[25] That was in 2018; today, I am more optimistic that Congress might embark on and successfully complete this project. It will take years to accomplish, and the finished project will look profoundly different from the rough sketch I have laid out in Chapters 7 and 8. Still, I cannot help but believe that the process of writing such a code would be well worth the trouble.[26] We won't know until we try. For all of these reasons, I'm ready to take the plunge. I hope you are as well.

---

[24] Ronald L. Gainer, *Remarks on the Introduction of Criminal Law Reform Initiatives*, 7 J.L. ECON. & POL'Y 587, 589–90 (2011). Erin Murphy, *Writing on an Unclean Slate: Challenges in Substantive Reform of a Penal Code*, 76 N.Y.U. ANN. SURV. AM. L. 473, 474 (2021) (drawing upon her experience as Associate Reporter in American Law Institute's project to reform the Model Penal Code's sexual offense provisions).

[25] Baer, *supra* note 7, at 271. In lieu of a fully revised code, I argued in *Sorting Out White-Collar Crime* for the adoption of misdemeanor provisions. *See id.* at 272–73.

[26] For arguments that penal legislation moves in an absolutist direction, see William J. Stuntz, *The Political Constitution of Criminal Justice*, 119 HARV. L. REV. 780, 804 (2006). Stuntz expressed concern that criminal law legislation, "is one-dimensional, zero-sum. Criminal liability either expands or contracts; sentences rise or fall. Policy choices that help both sides are hard to find. Compromise seems morally obtuse. Moderation is rare." *Id.*

Index

9 781009 279796